BEST SERMONS

EDITED BY GEORGE PAUL BUTLER

BEST
SERMONS

1949-1950 EDITION

Essay Index Reprint Series

 BOOKS FOR LIBRARIES PRESS
FREEPORT, NEW YORK

INTERNATIONAL STANDARD BOOK NUMBER:
0-8369-2488-6

LIBRARY OF CONGRESS CATALOG CARD NUMBER:
74-134065

PRINTED IN THE UNITED STATES OF AMERICA
BY
NEW WORLD BOOK MANUFACTURING CO., INC.
HALLANDALE, FLORIDA 33009

To
CHARLES B. McCABE
whose Youth Program
could prevent
juvenile delinquency
in every
community in
America

THE EDITOR'S APOLOGIA

The 52 sermons in this volume have been selected from 6,585 submitted to the editor for consideration.

A sincere attempt has been made to choose the sermons that represent the best sermonic efforts of the great preachers of our day, as well as to discover and recognize unusual excellence in the sermons submitted by younger men who may be the great preachers of tomorrow.

All sermons have been selected for their homiletic value and their spiritual message for our time.

THE INCLUSION OF ANY SERMON IN THE VOLUME DOES NOT MEAN THAT THE AUTHOR OF THAT SERMON APPROVES OR AGREES WITH THE CONTENTS OF THE OTHER SERMONS OR WITH ANY SERMONS IN THE VOLUME. Each preacher has been allowed to speak his own words in accordance with the faith of his own church or denomination. No sermon criticizing any other religion by word or inference has been included.

Best Sermons is intended as an anthology, not a book of theology.

It is the editor's hope that clergymen of all faiths may find inspiration for finer preaching through reading these sermons, and that students in our theological seminaries and professors of homiletics will find the sermons a basis for inspiring and informative reading and discussion of current preaching by men of various faiths.

CONTENTS

[viii]

FOREWORD

THE AGE OF PREACHING
by
Reverend Joseph R. Sizoo, D.D.
*President of The New Brunswick Theological
Seminary, New Brunswick, New Jersey*

THIS IS the age of preaching. The greatest single need of our time is for men who can interpret the nature and purpose of God to our blundering age, who can preach the gospel of redemption unashamed, to bring hope to a frustrated, cynical world. Mankind wants to be redeemed from secularism which places having before being, from racialism which denies our oneness in God, from scientism which is more concerned with motion than direction, from intellectualism which smugly disavows the invisible and from existentialism which sees nothing beyond desolation.

What, then, must be the qualities of these prophets of God? First, the worthy prophet must be a man with conviction. He must think clearly. His feet must be planted upon a rock which no storm can beat down; he must carry a light which no darkness can dim. He must be able to take his stand, saying, "This one thing I know." This is no time for the minister to give ground to every whim and wind, or to accommodate himself to all manner of pressure groups. There has been too much indifference to and uncertainty about the truth once for all delivered to the saints. Perhaps that has become our greatest peril. One finds too frequently a considerable incomprehension of the meaning of the transcendence of God, the nature of man, the fact of sin and the ultimate goal of life. The minister cannot stand with his tongue in his cheek, leaning first on one foot, then on the other, apologizing for everything that is omnipotent in God, divine in Christ and miraculous in His kingdom.

The true preacher may well heed the last admonition of Peter, "Always be able to give to every man that asketh a reason of the hope that is in you."

The preacher who has no deep, underlying convictions to which he conditions all he says and does; who adjusts his message to every whim, never sure of his footing, yielding here and giving ground somewhere else, is like a man, who, having dug a hole, is forced to dig another in order to get rid of the earth which he has taken out of the first hole, and then must dig a third hole to get rid of the earth which he has taken out of the second hole and so, ad infinitum. Vagueness often ends in vacancy. The glib and fashionable skepticism with which education has veneered us has no place in preaching.

There is a second quality which must characterize the true prophet. If conviction comes first, then compassion must come second. Thinking clearly must be followed by feeling deeply. The preacher lives in a world which is tired—tired of struggling and tired of trying. It wants to be made secure from hunger, disease, hate, cold and aggression—these elemental urges which are reappearing in society. The prophet must come down out of the stratosphere of abstraction and do something about them. It is a significant fact that all the great prophets of the past from Isaiah and Amos through Wesley and Gladden have been moved by this sense of understanding. It was written of Moses, "He went out unto his brethren and looked on their burden." That was a fine self-revealing of the prophet who wrote, "I sat where they sat."

We shall have little to say to the dilemmas and disillusionments of our age unless we approach them with compassion. It is so easy for the minister to live a comfortable life, wrap himself up in the dry ice of calloused unconcern. He is so prone to climb into his ivory tower, look at the hurt of the world, say "what a mess," and then pull the curtain down after him. Believe me, this blundering world is waiting for the sunrise of those men of God who see the sordid shambles, the pitiful disillusionments, the devastating injustice and the dreadful cynicism of the hour, not with callousness, but with compassion; not with indifference, but with concern. We need today a ministry which shall once again see the travail and tears, the dreadful intolerances and prejudices, the shocking indignities, the muddled living and the appalling suffering in terms of compassion.

These qualities one soon discovers in the sermons of this volume. They represent a type of preaching which must warm and gladden the heart. Through prophets such as these the world will find the open road to reconciliation and peace and victorious living. Let us say it in all humility and pride that there are in the Church today many who have that prophetic voice. These men will kindle anew the fire of faith. They seem to call across the ages, "This is the way, walk ye in it."

INTRODUCTION

PREACHING IN THE MODERN WORLD

Whereunto I am ordained a preacher.   I TIMOTHY 2:7

THE Church in all the centuries since Christ has been the most creative and unifying force in man's long journey on the road from barbarism to civilization. In education, charity, medicine, humane public relations, peace, justice for labor, fair play for capital, right treatment for women—and hundreds of other situations the Christian Church has led the way. Preaching has blazed the trail of faith on every frontier.

There is no time for pettifoggery in the church of God. There is far too much to be done to waste time on useless things, when there are seventy million in America who never give their allegiance to any church. When men or institutions get lost in the maze of red tape that churches and religious organizations, as well as governments, sometimes allow to grow up, when reports become more important than saving souls or the spiritual growth of a child or when there is no time to help a young man or woman to find the right place in life—then there is need for a reformation in the Church.

The finest preaching in any age is being done in our own time; there is a renewed emphasis on the grand philosophy of personalism, so ably expounded by Borden P. Bowne, emphasis on the dignity and worth of every human being as a personality endowed with a divine spark. Preaching must catch the attention and hold the interest of men from banks, farms, garages, the men who work or think or do, of women who are busy with homes and women who have nothing to do. It must offer a daring challenge to the youth of our day. Yet in all the preacher's efforts to catch the wandering attention of people he must be sure that he, like Paul, feeds both milk and meat to his hearers, leading them to the Gospel week by week, for his job is saving and cultivating souls. In this he is utterly different from the actor or lecturer who merely entertains his audience. Every minister should make up his mind that he is going to preach sermons that will fill his church! Men spend forty hours a week in an office or sixty hours on a farm; we send our children to school for twenty-five hours a week, and we have great trouble in getting millions of people to spend one hour a week in church. In some way we must make the church attractive enough to those seventy million who never go so they will want to attend.

Some sermons may be helpful without being inspired or inspiring. A message on self-help or the combination of psychology and religion may solve health problems for thousands of mildly ailing people who think about themselves too much and who need to think of the world, other people, themselves and life objectively. It is good to forget oneself most of the time, to lose self in accomplishment, duties, faith and love.

Preaching needs all of the talents a man possesses, brilliance of style, penetrating thinking, deep analysis, emotional insight, knowledge of men and women, spiritual depth—it demands everything the novelist or playwright can bring to his craft.

Yet preaching needs more than all these: it must have faith and love and God; while the novelist or playwright may create out of pure imagination, the preacher must speak the truth of God to men in their Hour of Truth. It is this that makes preaching great, enduring, important, for it brings God to man and man to God in the midst of the problems and joys and recreations of life and the world.

In preparing this volume, 21,385 personal or printed invitations were sent to clergymen in every state in the United States, most of the Provinces of Canada, Mexico, Central and South America, the West Indies, Europe, Australia, China, Japan and several countries of South Africa. The 52 sermons chosen for inclusion were selected from 6,585 received in response to these invitations and from others gratuitously submitted.

I have tried not to include men whose sermons have been in previous volumes in this series, but some men preach so excellently all the time that it is impossible not to repeat. I do so with great pleasure and with sincere appreciation to them for their consent to be in this book again.

As much as possible I will continue to search for the world's greatest preaching, as well as to seek new men who have not been recognized before. To this end I solicit all the help I can get.

Several clergymen have written to ask why there were not more ministers of their own denomination included in these volumes. In choosing the sermons an honest effort was made to give representation to as many different denominations as possible, but with 252 denominations in the United States, it is manifestly impossible to give all a place in this series, although ministers of every denomination were asked to submit sermons for consideration and all sermons received were carefully read. The major standard rigidly applied in deciding upon the inclusion of any sermon has been its spiritual message. As the editor I welcome criticism so that I may improve future volumes, asking only that the critics read the sermons with care.

"Best is a large word." Some critics have attacked my use of the word "Best" in the title of these volumes. Perhaps my critics may agree with my use of the title more if they know that I have sent out over 81,000 printed or personal invitations between January 1, 1943, and January 31, 1949, a search on such a scale has likely never before been made; 21,211 sermons have been received during those six years. Several hundred of these sermons have come from abroad, approximately 21,000 from the clergy in the United States. Since there are 231,000 clergy in our country, this averages about one sermon to every eleven ministers, priests or rabbis. This is a figure much greater than that for most other pieces of scholarly or scientific research. There are many clergy who seldom or never preach, but are teachers, visitors, administrators and such. I have carefully considered giving up the title "Best Sermons." But each time I have supplied denominational or critical leaders with the above figures, they have urged me to retain the title and give recognition to the best of our contemporary preaching by including representative "best" sermons in my volumes. Most men will realize that no one book could contain all the "best" preaching done in the world in any single year, and I know that I have missed thousands of sermons—but 6,585 sermons for this one volume is a big sampling of the preaching done in something over a year.

It is my hope to find the great preaching of our time for these annual volumes, now biennial because of the immense amount of reading required in preparation. The search is among the outstanding preachers known for their preaching ability, among others whose names are sent to me and among the younger, unknown or rising preachers. To recognize their work may be to encourage them to do still better.

I am attempting to secure and include the best in all the different types of preaching. Suggestions, criticisms, nominations and typed manuscripts of sermons are welcomed at any time and are requested from clergymen everywhere in the hope that real gems of spiritual power will be discovered. The four volumes of *Best Sermons* are only a small cross section of the preaching being done in the world. Yet I believe some of the sermons included in the 208 published to date have true greatness and deserve the name "best" in all that it means.

G. Paul Butler

New York and Fairlee Haven
September 1, 1949

ACKNOWLEDGMENTS

M Y VERY first thanks are to the 6,585 ministers, priests and rabbis who so graciously and generously sent me their sermons for reading and consideration. I have read every one of the sermons received and have hunted for the sermons that could be included to make the best collection of useful and inspiring sermons.

To the publishers who have kindly granted permission to quote from their copyrighted volumes, I am happy to express my sincere appreciation, including:

American Tract Society for permission to quote the first verse of John Oxenham's poem, "In Christ There Is No East nor West," from his volume, *Bees in Amber*. This poem is used in Dr. Cavert's and Dr. Ellison's sermons.

Brandt & Brandt for permission to include five lines from Edna St. Vincent Millay's poem, "Wine from These Grapes."

Dodd, Mead and Company for permission to quote seven lines of the last stanza of the poem "The House of Christmas" by G. K. Chesterton.

Henry Holt and Company, Inc. for permission to quote the last stanza of "The Road Not Taken" from the *Complete Poems of Robert Frost*.

Houghton Mifflin Company for permission to use Jessie B. Rittenhouse's poem "My Wage."

Georgia Douglas Johnson for permission to quote from the poem "Tomorrow's World."

Mr. Virgil Markham for the use of a quatrain by Edwin Markham.

Miss Juanita Miller for permission to use eight lines from "Beyond Jordan," from *The Poetical Works of Joaquin Miller*.

The New Yorker Magazine, Inc. for the lines from the October, 1948, issue.

The Pilgrim Press for permission to use the poem "Ultima Veritas," from *Ultima Veritas and Other Poems* by Washington Gladden.

Charles Scribner's Sons for permission to use Dr. Paul Tillich's sermon, "The Escape from God," from *The Shaking of the Foundations*; for a selection from Henry Van Dyke's "The Gospel of Labor" from *The Toiling of Felix and Other Poems*; for the lines from Mary Britton Miller's *The Crucifixion*.

William L. Stidger for permission to use his poem "I Am the Cross."

I want to express again my sincere appreciation to the members of my Advisory Committee, Dr. Joseph R. Sizoo, Dr. Ralph W. Sockman, Dr. Paul E. Scherer, Dr. Adolph Keller, the Very Reverend Ignatius Smith, O.P., the Reverend Gerald G. Walsh, S.J., Dr. Israel Bettan, Dr. David de Sola Pool.

Dr. Israel Goldstein, who has been one of my Jewish advisers for each of the other three volumes, was absent in Israel at the time the selections were being made, so that he is not responsible for the Jewish sermons included, although it is my sincere hope that he will find time in spite of his added duties to continue as a member of my Advisory Committee.

Dr. Clayton Williams of the American Church in Paris rendered valuable service to the volume in his recommendations concerning European preaching. Without the help of these men and their careful judgment in assisting with the selection of the sermons to be included the volume would not have the ecumenical character and broad and representative scope which I believe it does possess.

It is a pleasure to express my continued appreciation to the National Council of Catholic Men for the assistance William Smith and other members of the Council rendered in advising the editor concerning outstanding Catholic preaching and preachers.

It is a further pleasure to express my appreciation to Camille A. Chazeaud for his excellent translation of the brilliant sermon by Pere Michel Riquet and to Father Richard F. Grady for his careful checking of this translation for American usage.

Dr. Sizoo's Foreword is so fine that I can only express my happiness that he wrote it for my book.

To the bishops, archbishops, denominational heads, officers of councils of churches, presidents of ministerial associations and hundreds of others I am deeply grateful for suggestions and direct assistance in reaching men who preached sermons I needed to secure for reading and consideration for possible inclusion in my volumes. So many others helped with encouragement, correction of errors, typing, reading the manuscript and many other courtesies that I cannot list all of their names for lack of space, but I do thank them all.

G.P.B.

BEST SERMONS

A Religion That Sings

REVEREND JAMES T. CLELAND

Preacher to the University and Professor of Preaching in the Divinity School of Duke University, Durham, North Carolina; a minister of the Presbyterian Church.

James T. Cleland has a glow in his preaching that captures the imagination and the heart. Born in Glasgow, Scotland, in 1903, he attended school in Glasgow, graduated from Glasgow University, and served as assistant in three parishes in the Church of Scotland, at Bridgeton (Glasgow), Old Kilpatrick, and at Dunblane Cathedral. He graduated from Glasgow University Divinity Hall with his divinity degree in 1927, with distinction in ecclesiastical history, after which he came to America.

He was appointed to the Jarvie Fellowship at Union Theological Seminary in New York and took an advanced divinity degree there in 1928, then returned to Scotland on the Black Fellowship at Divinity Hall, Glasgow University, where he assisted the professors of theology and of New Testament criticism; in 1929 to 1931 he was Faulds Teaching Fellow at the University. In 1931 Amherst College called him to the chair of religion.

On May 23, 1938 he was ordained a minister of the Presbyterian Church (U.S.A.), and spent 1938-39 on leave of absence in Europe and the Near East. He spent 1944-45 in graduate work at Union, and in 1945 was appointed to Duke University, Durham, North Carolina, as Preacher to the University and Professor of Preaching in the Divinity School. In the summer of 1948 he was guest Professor of Homiletics at Union. During the winter months Professor Cleland preaches in many of the preparatory schools, colleges, and universities on the eastern seaboard. One of Professor Cleland's interests, in addition to an acquired enthusiasm for Robert Burns, is the collecting of religious poetry. In Scotland he played soccer, and at Amherst and Duke has had a hand, as assistant coach, in turning out consistently successful soccer teams. His preaching has a fine understanding of the problems of man, a kindly sense of humor, and an ability to say the exact, right word in the right place. So far he has tried not to break into print; this sermon is one of the first he has permitted to be published. The editor believes it will be a definite contribution to those who discover it.

Sermon One

Text: Thy statutes are my songs, as I wander through the world.
Psalm 119:54 (Moffatt).

FOR many years I have had an aversion to the 119th Psalm, and that for two reasons. In the first place, it recalls an incident from my boyhood. On one of my birthdays my mother presented me with a Bible and a few well-chosen words: "When the King was a small boy he promised his mother that he would read one chapter of the Bible every night; he has kept that promise. If the King could do that for his mother it is surely not too much to expect that one of his subjects will do as much for his mother." So I began to read the Bible, one chapter a night, as requested. Now, the Bible starts interestingly enough. Genesis One describes a kind of celestial Boulder Dam project with God as a super engineer. Genesis Two is a more delightful story of the same cosmic undertaking. The third chapter tells how a snake deceived a woman, and how a woman deceived a man; I did not gather the full import of that then. In chapter four there is a good murder, and then in five begin the "begats." However, the book rallies quickly and through the rest of Genesis and Exodus the narrative is plain and interesting sailing. But the Laws of the Priests in Leviticus, the census of the tribes in Numbers, and the second account of the Law in Deuteronomy were an uninteresting grind. "But the King had promised his mother . . ."; perhaps then were sown the deeds of a republicanism that blossomed when I came to the United States. But I persevered, one dose each night as prescribed, and months later I was rewarded. The chapter for the night was Psalm 117, only two verses! It was unbelievable. Only two verses! Without a doubt God was good. Two nights later the reading was Psalm 119, one hundred and seventy-six verses, at one sitting! It was a symbol of the fact that man could not win. It was a devastating experience, and I heartily rebelled against the 119th Psalm.

The other reason for my aversion to this Psalm is chronologically a much later one, and was caused by the realization that it was written in praise of the Law. Being a follower of Paul, albeit at times a very distant one, I was not overenthusiastic about a rhapsody on the Law that gave vent to such observations as: It is good for me that I have been afflicted; that I might learn thy statutes. These were not my sentiments.

So for many years the Psalm was more or less anathema to me. Then recently a verse from it was quoted in a letter from Scotland: "Thy statutes have been my songs in the house of my pilgrimage" (54). The verse intrigued me, and I turned to the Moffatt translation for further light: "Thy statutes are my songs as I wander through the world." The verse took possession of me; and when such a thing happens there is but one way to exercise it: preach on it. And this is how it developed, as I began to cast it out.

Religion as statutes. First my mind turned to the idea of religion as statutes, commands, regulations, decrees; that is, to what God lays down as binding on man if he is to be considered righteous. Any faith that is sensitive to the need for ethical living, personal and social, is almost bound to view religion as statutes: "Do this," "Do not do that." Right relations with God are created and maintained by meticulous obedience to the will of God as revealed in His Law. The man who keeps the ordinances is the good man. The 1st Psalm corroborates that viewpoint. "Blessed is the man that walketh not in the counsel of the ungodly, nor standeth in the way of sinners, nor sitteth in the seat of the scornful. But his delight is in the Law of the Lord; and in his Law doth he meditate day and night" (1-2). You don't have to be a Presbyterian to grasp that—though it helps. I can recall as a boy of seven in a Glasgow school having to buy the Shorter Catechism. It is a series of questions and answers on Presbyterian doctrine and was bound in a brown pamphlet, which cost four cents, and which had the multiplication table on the back cover. Scottish thrift and foresight had decided that if we learned nothing from within the book, we might from without. Here are three questions and answers:

Q 39. What is the duty which God requires of man?
A.   The duty which God requires of man is obedience to His revealed will.
Q 40. What did God at first reveal to man for the rule of His obedience?
A.   The rule which God at first revealed to man for His obedience was the moral law.
Q 41. Wherein is the moral law summarily comprehended?
A.   The moral law is summarily comprehended in the Ten Commandments.

Then follow forty questions on the Ten Commandments, forty out of a total of one hundred and seven. Almost two-fifths of the digest of Presbyterian doctrine is on the Summary of the Law! That and oatmeal were staple diet for Scotland. How firm a foundation for Saints of the Lord! And that type of religion did create saints, but very dour saints. They were distinguished by probity and severity, by chastity and censoriousness, by uprightness and rigidity. Robert Burns describes the women in kirk as even "tied up in godly laces." These men and women had grit rather than grace, and stability rather than charity. They were easily distinguished in their "Sabbath blacks," which covered both their bodies and their spirits. One of our theological professors in Scotland was a tall spare man, a Calvinistic Cassius, whose face normally looked like the edge of a hatchet dipped in

[3]

vinegar. He stood one day on the edge of an open-air meeting, and when asked by a Salvation Army girl, "Are you a Christian?" replied, "Of course I'm a Christian." She looked at him and smiled a little ruefully, then gasped, "What a face for a Christian." Maybe, but it was a sound face for a Scots Presbyterian.

. There was strength there, an earnest, sincere effort to fulfill the requirements of their faith. They worked at it, labored at it. But in that strength lay the fundamental weakness. Too often they carried their religion, instead of letting it carry them. Read "The Transformation of Lachlan Campbell" in Ian Maclaren's *Beside the Bonnie Brier Bush* and you will see that strength and that weakness side by side. It is not the highest compliment we can pay a man to say that he keeps the law: it is not the highest compliment we can pay a religion to say that it requires us to keep the Law. "Religion as statutes" is good, but it is not the best.

Religion as statutes and songs. So my mind moved to a second idea; religion as statutes and songs. There are times and occasions when a religious man, even one who obeys the revealed decrees of God, has to shout "Hallelujah" or stand the risk of an inner explosion. Song is present as well as statutes in any vital faith. Then the worshiper raises his hosannas, his paeans of adoration, his psalms of praise. Even Judaism with all its legalism knew this. Alongside the Law was the Psalter, which some Old Testament scholars have regarded as the hymnbook of the Second Temple. Do you remember how it describes the music of the Temple? The 150th Psalm tells us:

> Praise ye the Lord. Praise God in his sanctuary: praise him in the firmament of his power.
> Praise him for his mighty acts: praise him according to his excellent greatness.
> Praise him with the sound of the trumpet: praise him with the psaltery and harp.
> Praise him with the timbrel and dance: praise him with stringed instruments and organs.
> Praise him upon the loud cymbals: praise him upon the high sounding cymbals.
> Let everything that hath breath praise the Lord. Praise ye the Lord.

There is nothing quiet about that, no soft overtones in a dim religious light. That is as obvious as a Salvation Army band, and as enthusiastic. Praise of God goes hand in hand with obedience to God. Yes, there is a type of religion which is statutes and songs.

When one of the authors of the Bible thought of God at work on the creation of the world he pictured the cornerstone being laid to music: "Where wast thou when I laid the foundations of the earth? . . . When the morning stars sang together, and all the Sons of God shouted for joy" (Job 38:4, 7).

When another author sought to recapture the glory of the deliverance from Pharaoh at the Red Sea, he began: "Sing ye to the Lord, for he hath triumphed gloriously; the horse and his rider hath he thrown into the sea" (Exod. 15:21).

The chapters in Luke telling of the birth of Jesus are filled with hymns: the *Magnificat* of Mary, the *Benedictus* of Zacharias, the *Gloria* of the angels, and the *Nunc Dimittis* of Simeon. The Last Supper ended with a hymn. And in his picture of the climax of the age in the New Jerusalem, John wrote about those who had won the victory for God against the beast standing "having the harps of God. And they sing the song of Moses the servant of God, and the song of the Lamb, saying, Great and marvelous are thy words, Lord God Almighty; just and true are thy ways, thou King of saints. Who shall not fear thee, O Lord, and glorify thy name? for thou only art holy: for all nations shall come and worship before thee; for thy judgments are made manifest" (Rev. 15:2-4).

In the Bible religion in its high moments breaks into song. And that experience is repeated with a quiet regularity down the years. Fighting against inward doubt and outer foes Martin Luther sang the praise of the God who stood by him in *Ein feste Burg*. Newman, groping his way from a religion which he could not entirely accept to one which entirely accepted him, wrote in faith, "Lead kindly light amid the encircling gloom."

Do you begin to grasp why a choir is so important in our church service? And why it is for the good of your souls that you sing too, including the "Amen"? Recall the serenely wise and gently chiding words of Epictetus:

> Why, if we had sense, ought we to be doing anything else, publicly and privately, than hymning and praising the Deity, and rehearsing His benefits? Ought we not, as we dig and plough and eat, to sing the hymn of praise to God? "Great is God, that He hath furnished us these instruments wherewith we shall till the earth. Great is God, that He hath given us hands, and power to swallow, and a belly, and power to grow unconsciously, and to breathe while asleep." This is what we ought to sing on every occasion, and above all to sing the greatest and divinest hymn, that God has given us the faculty to comprehend these things and to follow the path of reason. What then? Since most of you have become blind, ought there not to be someone to fulfill this office for you, and in behalf of all sing the hymn of praise to God? Why, what else can I, a lame old man, do but sing hymns to God? If, indeed, I were a nightingale, I should be singing as a nightingale; if a swan, as a swan. But as it is, I am a rational being, therefore I must be singing hymns of praise to God. This is my task; I do it, and will not desert this post, as long as it may be given me to fill it; and I exhort you to join me in this same song.

Beware of a religion that does not sing; steer clear of a congregation that does not sing. The Law *and* the Psalms; the Psalms *and* the Law; neither without the other is typical of the average religion of the more than average worshiper. He combines statute and song: he unites obedience and praise. Most of us are content with that; it is a good balance.

[5]

Religion as statutes that are songs. But my mind had to move one step further, because the solution of statutes *and* songs was not satisfactory to our Psalmist. Turn back to our text: "Thy statutes *are* my songs, as I journey through the world." The two are identified: stern, relentless duty has become a "Hallelujah." His obedience to the will of God is as spontaneous as a song of praise. For him religion is law set to music, the transformation of legalism into melody.

What has happened to the Law? Nothing. It still stands inflexible. What has become of the statutes? They are still binding, personally and socially. Well, what has come over the Psalmist? Now we are asking the right question. He has changed his attitude to the Law. He no longer says what is required of him in reluctant, legal phraseology. He is singing the Law; it has become a chant, a canticle, a carol. But why? Why? What has happened to him? I am not sure, but I am willing to hazard a guess. He has grasped what God is trying to do by means of the Law. Think of that. He has sought to know God, to understand Him, to fathom the reason for the Law. And the answer has come to him: God cares for man. That is the reason for the Law, with its religious requirements and its ethical obligations. It is not a sign of the anger of God, nor is it merely the seal of His justice; it is a revelation of His mercy. He breathes that thought in two other verses: "The earth, O Lord, is full of thy mercy: teach me thy statutes" (64). "Thou are good, and doest good; teach me thy statutes" (68). Notice the juxtaposition of words in these verses; mercy, statutes; good, statutes. God loves man; that is the reason for the Law.

The Law is still there, but the Psalmist's understanding of it has changed. He no longer keeps it from a lowly obedience motivated by fear; he goes out to fulfill it from an enthusiastic devotion inspired by love. That love still includes fear, as awe and wonder. Of course it does. It must, because he is a creature over against the Creator. But he is also the willing servant of a beloved master, the recipient of the tender mercies and loving kindness of his Lord. His duty is the same; he must abide by the Law. But his motives are so different that the very Law becomes a song of praise. It is no longer dread but understanding, no longer apprehension but admiration, no longer fear but loving devotion that marks his attitude to the statutes. He no longer forces himself to obey because he feels he must. His obedience is the spontaneous overflow of one who knows what is good for God and for himself. There is a lilt in his submission, and a buoyancy in his loyalty. God and he are in harmony, therefore duties become privileges. Jesus would have said "Amen."

Does that make sense to us? Take a modern example. Let us suppose the food crop fails in Europe and Asia this year and we must be rationed to relieve the famine overseas. How shall we behave? Assuming that we avoid the black market there are two ways we may act. We may observe every jot and tittle of the law, with scowling face and bitter comment, making life a hell on earth for every grocer and baker in our vicinity. We may be legalists who obey and grumble. Or we may be like the Psalmist, understanding the "why" of the Law. Then we shall see on the front of our ration books the invisible words, "To the glory of God through the relief of man's estate." And the ration book will become a hymnbook, and every stamp a *Te Deum Laudamus*. That is law set to music, statutes which are songs. The Psalmist would understand it; so would Jesus.

"Thy statutes are my songs, as I wander through the world." How are you going to travel? I ask you to consider going like the Psalmist, "a wandering minstrel" with the law singing in your heart.

It has been said of St. Francis of Assisi that "of all the medieval Saints he was probably the one who would seem least out of place in the twentieth century." I commend him to you as our text become flesh. He was both God's man and man's man. He is described as possessing "an original and well-balanced mind, extraordinary common sense, an iron will and indomitable courage. He insisted that the statutes of his Order be obeyed unswervingly. But he was so gay, even playful, that he described God's good children as the Lord's players, acrobats, jugglers. He was what I think the Psalmist wanted the man of God to be, a troubadour.

The behavior I commend to you, as to myself, in the hope that one day we too may say with lyric spontaneity: "Thy statutes are my songs, as I wander through the world."

THE BIBLE

The Place of the Bible in a Time of Calamity

REVEREND EARL HUBERT FURGESON, PH.D.

Professor of Preaching and Pastoral Theology, Westminster Theological Seminary, Westminster, Maryland

Dr. Furgeson has a deep conviction of the importance of the Church and is giving himself to train and develop other consecrated and well-trained young men for the ministry of the contemporary Church.

Earl H. Furgeson was born in Terre Haute, Indiana, March 27, 1906, graduated from De Pauw University with honors in 1928, and entered Boston University School of Theology from which he received a bachelor's degree in theology in 1932. His Ph.D. was earned in the Graduate School of Boston University, with a year of special study at Harvard. Social philosophy was his major field of concentration.

From 1931 to 1948 Dr. Furgeson served as a minister of the Methodist Church with full-time work in parishes in Connecticut and Massachusetts. For three and a half years he was minister of the Harvard-Epworth Church in Cambridge, Massachusetts, and director of the Wesley Foundation at Harvard University. He served as chairman of the Committee on Mixed Marriages of the Massachusetts Council of Churches and as a member of the Board of Governors of the Institute of Pastoral Care in Boston. His ministry to students in Harvard, Radcliffe, and M.I.T. brought him into the chairmanship of the Inter-Conference Commission on Student Work of the Methodist Church in the New England Area.

In 1948 Dr. Furgeson was invited to become Professor of Preaching and Pastoral Theology in the Westminster Theological Seminary, Westminster, Maryland, having completed three years as Special Lecturer in Homiletics at Boston University. Articles on social and religious questions from his pen have appeared in The Christian Century, Zions Herald, Religion in Life and The Journal of Pastoral Care.

His sermon on the Bible in troubled times has a message for thousands of people in all walks of life.

Sermon Two

TEXT: All scripture is inspired by God and profitable for teaching . . . and for moral discipline, to make the man of God proficient and equip him for good work of every kind.
II TIMOTHY 3:16-17 (Moffatt).

THE twentieth century will be remembered as a time of revolutions and upheavals. Before half its years are spent it will have recorded violent convulsions in most of the civilized world and left for posterity the picture of a humanity blinded and bewildered by the passing of ancient landmarks and stricken with the fears of earth-shaking changes yet to come. Even now the ancient words of Isaiah seem to have once more a tragic relevance: "We grope like a blind man along the wall . . . we live in darkness like the dead." Our ears have caught the cries of more people suffering from tyranny, violence, starvation and disease than any generation of the sons of men have ever before heard, and our eyes have seen destruction and devastation on a scale unprecedented in history. Professor Kenneth Latourette calls ours a "fluid and urgent" world—"fluid" because it contains unimaginable possibilities of prosperity and plenty, "urgent" because it contains almost equal possibilities of death and destruction.

[8]

The question which concerns us today as students and teachers of religion is the problem of the place of the Bible in a world of disorder. What has it to contribute to a chaotic time? How can the literature of a pastoral people developed two or three thousand years ago have any relevance to the complex problems of a lost civilization in its time of calamity?

The first fact which confronts any apologist for the Bible is the widespread indifference on the part of the people toward the Book itself. Dr. Ralph Sockman, writing with an intimate knowledge of the religious practices of the American people, has pointed out that our contemporary situation illustrates what the prophet Amos predicted, namely, "A famine . . . of hearing the words of the Lord." The Bible continues to be the world's best seller, surpassing, even in the Germany of 1939, the sale of *Mein Kampf;* but the volume of the Bible's sales is no certain proof of its regular use in the homes of the nation or by the majority of our people. The widespread sale of the Book is no sure ground for optimism or confidence in view of its widespread neglect. Anyone interested in a better life for our world and richer lives for our people will agree with Dr. Sockman that "to correct this condition is imperative," and a correction will depend in part at least upon an understanding of the causes and reasons for the widespread neglect. The fault is not with the Book. It would be unusual indeed if this Book of Life, which has been the source of strength and guidance for needy men throughout the ages, were suddenly to prove itself useless in the lives of people today. The fault is with the people; but even so the faulty notions of people have their explanations.

Why have our people become estranged? What misunderstandings or abuses underlie the prevailing cult of condescension toward the Bible? Some no doubt pass the Bible by because of its inadequate scientific conceptions, an understandable reaction on the part of people who are accustomed to taking all their texts for living from the scientists. What, for example, does the man of scientific temper encounter in the pages of Holy Writ? He finds there stories of axheads which float on the surface of the water, stories of donkeys endowed with the power of human speech, sober suppositions that diseases like palsy and epilepsy are caused by the presence of demons in the soul; he encounters a cosmology which became obsolete with Copernicus and an anthropogeny which was rebuked by Darwin nearly a hundred years ago with the publication in 1859 of *The Origin of Species.* Finding these things, the scientific man, unless he has been wise enough to cultivate a religion along with his science, lays the Book aside as an interesting but irrelevant collection of fable and folklore.

Would it not be strange, however, if God who is the God of all truth should have given one revelation of His laws to the scientist, and another but contradictory revelation to the writers of the Bible? The conflict at this point arises from a double fault: Lovers of the Bible are at fault in supposing that the Bible is a textbook of science, and scientists are at fault in supposing that there are no questions which are not scientific.

With respect to the first of these errors it is helpful to recall that since the corpus of Holy Writ was completed many centuries before the scientific method was discovered the Bible could hardly have been intended as a textbook of science. If one is curious about the natural properties of axheads and other metals he ought to turn to physics or metallurgy; if one is curious about the powers and limitations of such quadrupeds as donkeys he ought to turn to zoology, for the Scriptures are not primarily concerned with the natural properties of axheads and asses. The Scriptures are concerned with spiritual matters. Their grandeur is revealed in the fidelity with which they record the story of man's long search for God and the good life and the assurance with which they proclaim God's highest revelations for man in the life of his Son. The Bible is a guidebook in religion; it is not a textbook of science.

On the other hand, our generation needs to be disabused of the widespread prejudice, formulated so concisely by Sigmund Freud, that "it would be an illusion to suppose that we could get anywhere else what it [science] cannot give us." The fact is that the pressing questions of our day are not scientific, but moral and religious, questions which have to do with the good life for the individual as a person and for persons in their communal relations.

Scientific questions have received in our day answers to a degree once unimaginable. The frontiers of knowledge have been pushed out beyond the power of any one mind to comprehend their vast extent. The specialist, that inevitable by-product of an abundance of knowledge, is a man who knows more and more, about less and less. Knowledge has come, but wisdom lingers. For what purpose shall this vast expanse of information be used? What are the ends or aims which our vastly extended technology shall be called upon to serve? These are the burning questions of the hour, and they arise out of the areas of our greatest confusion. If we do not find better answers to them than those which have emerged thus far, we shall surely perish; for, as one discerning critic has put it, the best answer we have been able to devise is "improved means to an unimproved end." The most ironic and pitable situation of our time is the plight in which the scientists, especially the physicists and the biochemists, have been placed. By the circumstance of what is called a military necessity these peace-loving men of intelligence and good will have been compelled to turn their talents to the production of more and more frightful methods of destruction. Instead of creating an international community of knowledge they must learn how to destroy nations. Instead of lifting the burdens of disease and toil from the backs of men they must now learn how to spread disease more efficiently. "Improved means to an unimproved end"!

Now, if the main problem is the ends of life and not the means of living, if the basic need is for wisdom that is righteous, then what body of writing is more relevant to our predicement than the Bible? To whom shall we go? "For there is none other name under heaven given among men, whereby we must be saved" than the name of Him whose life and teaching are the supreme revelation of Holy Scripture.

A second problem confronting the apologist is the variety of interpretation on the basic question of the nature of the Bible's authority. Professor Walter Horton reports that the Study Department of the World Council of Churches found, in the deliberations which preceded the calling of the first Assembly, that the most fundamental point of difference among those participating in the World Council was in respect to convictions about the authority of the Bible. It is possible to imagine on this question a panorama of opinion extending from the Fundamentalists on the extreme right to the Humanists on the extreme left with many gradations in between representing differences of fundamental importance. What a difference between the Fundamentalists who believe that "Scriputre is from God; it is everywhere from God, and everywhere it is entirely from God," and the Humanists who, if they use the Bible at all, reduce it to poetry and symbolism! What a difference between Karl Barth, on the one hand, who, although he rejects the "peripheral biblicism" of the Fundamentalists, says he prefers that to the historical-critical methods of Bible study, and the liberal rationalists, on the other hand, who base their interpretations upon the methods of historical criticism, believing with John Locke that "he who destroys reason to make room for revelation puts out the light of both"! Such a variety of scholarly opinion does indeed create a problem for the student of the Bible.

No one ought to feel, however, that this state of affairs condemns us to hopeless division and squalid bickering. The obvious fact that all minds are finite ought to inspire us with a decent regard for the opinions of those with whom we differ especially when finite minds are wrestling with truths of infinite depth. This condition of diversity rightly construed is a challenge to seek the positive grounds of reconciliation and to build a Christian fellowship among those who know how to differ without being divided. It is a challenge to bring into being that charity of which the Bible speaks and to cultivate an understanding which, in the open competition of free inquiry, permits the God of all truth to select for survival those truths most suitable to His purpose. Diversity of opinion with respect to the Bible, instead of canceling its usefulness is itself a reflection of the richness of Biblical inspiration and we ought to receive it as God's invitation to cultivate a wider charity among those who love the Bible in the name of Him who is our peace and who breaks down the walls of separation between us.

Aside from the difficulties attending a defense of the Bible as a useful book for our day, there are certain positive contributions which the Bible is prepared to make to the confusions of our time. The first of these is the teaching that optimism is possible even in a time of crisis.

With the exception of the book of Ecclesiastes, it may be said that the prevailing temper of the Bible is optimistic, reflecting the conviction that existence is basically good, not evil, and proclaiming the truth that a time of adversity may be also a time of opportunity. Within the Bible these crucial teachings find expression in literary forms as sublime as any poetry. Consider, for example, the words of Jesus on anxiety: "Consider the lilies of the field, how they grow; they toil not, neither do they spin: And yet I say unto you. That even Solomon in all his glory was not arrayed like one of these. Wherefore, if God so clothe the grass of the field, which today is and tomorrow is cast into the oven, shall he not much more clothe you, O ye of little faith?" The Bible not only "has been a greater influence on the course of English literature than all other forces put together," as Professor William Lyon Phelps has said, but it also contains some of the world's finest literature. Much of this, like the passage above, is a literature of encouragement in the face of difficulty. The book of First Peter, written when the Christians of Asia were suffering under the persecutions of a pagan emperor, is one of the world's great expressions of the value of fortitude. Like it, is the great apostrophe to faithfulness penned by the Apostle Paul in his letter to the Romans: "If God be for us who can be against us? Who shall separate us from the love of God. . . . I am persuaded that neither death nor life, nor angels nor principalities nor powers, nor things present, nor things to come, nor height, nor depth, nor any other creature shall be able to separate us from the love of God which is in Christ Jesus our Lord."

The important thing to remember about these sublime expressions of optimism is that they are not expressions of fantasy published for literary effect. They are the basic convictions of men who had met calamity in the personal dimension and distilled from its hardships these philosophic insights. The faith which sustained them, and which will sustain us, was the basic conviction that behind tribulation there is an Everlasting Mercy; behind chaos there is a principle of order. The "Ultimate Truth" which they discovered was the one envisaged by the poet:

> In the darkest night of the year
>   When the stars have all gone out,
> That courage is better than fear,
>   That faith is truer than doubt;
>
> And fierce though the fiends may fight,
>   And long though the angels hide
> I know that Truth and Right
>   Have the universe on their side.[1]

The optimism of the Bible arises like a sweet fragrance out of adversity, and like the perfume of roses it becomes more fragrant when crushed.

Unless an age of calamity can recover the confidence that behind the confusion there is a principle of Order, there is no ground whereon to stand while fighting the battle. Without the conviction that there is at work in the universe a power which is capable of overcoming evil, there is no point

[1] "Ultima Veritas," from *Ultima Veritas and Other Poems* by Washington Gladden (Pilgrim Press, 1912).

[12]

in sacrificing even the shallow material comforts of life in a warfare against evil. Perseverance becomes pointless, and the drama of human history becomes a play without a plot. Because the people of the Bible had sound insights about ultimate truth they were not overcome by evil; they overcame evil with good.

This is the basic consideration which makes optimism rational and realistic and cynicism short-sighted and foolhardy. Professor G. H. Sabine has noted that the final problem of an emancipated intelligence is the development of an idealism without illusions and a realism without cynicism. This is the kind of idealism, and the kind of realism, we have in the Bible. No preacher was ever more realistic in estimating the results of his work than Jesus. Seventy-five per cent of the seed sown would not come to fruition; tares would be found growing among the wheat; and many would find it as hard to come into his kingdom as for a camel to go through the eye of a needle. His way of life was idealistic, but his idealism was under no illusions about the presence and the power of evil. A first principle in his thinking, and a general presupposition of the entire Bible, is the acknowledgment that evil exists. But the final principle is the conviction that evil is not omnipotent. Anyone holding such a philosophy will find his way through a time of calamity without despair, as the Christians in all ages have done. In a time of tribulation God's man will remain optimistic, for an optimist is one who finds the opportunities in every difficulty while a pessimist is one who is overcome by the difficulties in any opportunity.

The second contribution which the Bible is prepared to make to a time of calamity is the crowning insight of Scripture that love is the supreme law of life because it is the highest attribute of God. This is a conclusion to which the Bible does not come all at once. In the beginning the people were more impressed with the power of God than they were with the love of God. Yahweh, the Mountain God of Sinai, was a jealous god of power associated with the violent exhibitions of nature and of war. The Psalmist observed that he "thundered in the heavens" and "hurled his hailstones and coals of fire." The writer of I Samuel reports David meeting Goliath with the challenge, "I come to thee in the name of Yahweh of hosts, the God of the armies of Israel," and the same writer observes that "they that strive with Yahweh shall be broken in pieces." It was in the name of this same Yahweh that the gentle Samuel "hewed the priests of Agag to pieces before the Lord in Gilgal"—which is probably the most repulsive piece of writing in all literature.

It is a long way from these primitive notions about the nature of God to the crowning insight of the New Testament that God is love. "Love is of God. He that loveth is begotten of God and knoweth God. He that loveth not knoweth not God for God is love." The implication of this insight is no less significant than the insight itself: "Herein is love, not that we loved God, but he loved us, and sent his Son to be the propitiation for our sins.

Beloved, if God so loved us, we ought also to love one another." Here we have what may be safely called the high-water mark of Biblical revelation, the insight that love is the supreme law of life because it is the fundamental attribute of God; and here we have also the message which our time of calamity most needs. This quality of love, which the Apostle called the most lasting of all the values, and which Henry Drumond called "the greatest thing in the world," must somehow be made the basic law of our lives, individual and social.

If one may use the jargon of psychology, the prime difficulty in our predicament is the fact that we have become "fixated" at the power level. Like the primitive people of the Old Testament, we are most impressed with the potentialities of power; our age is characteristically referred to as the "power age." Our generation, through the labors of one of the great geniuses of all time, Albert Einstein, has given to civilization the most powerful formula ever discovered by the mind of man, the formula for atomic energy, $E=MC^2$. The Atomic Energy Commission has pointed out that from 1940, the year when the first basic discovery in atomic energy was made, to 1945, the date of Hiroshima, mankind traveled as far as it had traveled from the date of the discovery of fire to the building of the first locomotive—five thousand years of progress telescoped into five. An English report on the subject has added the information that those who understood the implications best were terrified most. The reasons are easy to find. The only tangible evidence we have thus far of the manner in which we will use these vastly augmented sources of power lies in the ashes of two wasted Japanese cities and in the broken bodies of those who lived there. By persistent pushing and probing mankind has at last pried open the great door behind which for centuries the innermost secrets of the universe were hidden, and, as a reward for his persistent labors, he has released a force which, unless it is brought into subservience under the moral and ethical laws of love, will wipe him forever from the face of the earth. One of our poets, Edna St. Vincent Millay, has already written an "Epitaph for the Race of Man." and the unredeemed selfishness of the human soul conjoined with the unlimited powers released by natural science seem to make this writing altogether timely and appropriate.

We do not stand in terror of the power of God, although it is the greatest power in the universe, because we believe God's power is joined with a supreme love. We should not need to stand in terror of our lives before the power controlled by man if that power were likewise brought into subservience under the principles of righteous love.

The incontrovertible teaching of the Bible with which our age in its crisis is brought face to face is this basic law of the universe that power must become the servant of love, for in the absence of that control power destroys those who use it. The areas of application for this principle in our time are many; they are as manifold as the organizations of power in our time.

President Charles P. Taft of the Federal Council of Churches said recently that the Church has done its job well in serving human beings who face the problem of sickness and sorrow, but, he added, "in meeting the problems laymen face in responsible leadership of their communities in business and politics and labor and agriculture the Church has missed the boat entirely." Why? A clear answer would seem to be that we have failed because we have not shown the people of a power age *why* and *how* all organizations of power, economic, political, international, must and can be brought under the control of the moral law of love. Since the moral laws of love have not been made to rule, the immoral principle of selfishness has been permitted to rule. Contests between nations become naked manifestations of power politics. Contests between the classes within nations become tactical or violent struggles characterized by private smartness or collective pressure in the interest of selfish ends. Sometime—and that before long—this pagan behavior must yield to the laws of love and brotherhood embodied in the principle of the general welfare, or a time of calamity will bring forth a day of destruction.

Bishop Hans Lilje of Hanover, Germany, writing on *The Spiritual Problem of Europe* observes that "a sense of crisis has accompanied modern man on his spiritual journey in the past century as shadow trails light." It is our belief that these shadows which trail the light will be banished only when the basic truths of the Bible are made once more to shine. Into the dark depths of our despair must come the realistic rational optimism of the Bible, the belief that every crisis produces its opportunities as well as its difficulties because there is behind every chaos a Principle of Order and a Power for Good which is greater than the forces of evil. Into the suicidal selfishness of our individual and collective life must come the Bible's law of benevolent love, which is the supreme law of life because it is the most fundamental attribute of God. The servant of the present age whose life and thought have been nourished upon the great Biblical truths will find that he has a gospel for the time. His loins will be girt about with relevant truth and his feet will be shod with the preparation of the gospel of peace.

The encouragement of an optimistic hope, and the inspiration of God's eternal law of love—these are the contributions of the Bible to a time of calamity.

Wanted: A New Moral Sense

REVEREND ROBERT JAMES McCRACKEN, D.D.

Minister, The Riverside Church, New York

Dr. McCracken has had a very busy life. Born on March 28, 1904, in Mother-well, Scotland, in a home that had inherited the great traditions of Scotch Presbyterianism, he attended school in Motherwell, and having been spiritu-ally awakened in the Motherwell Baptist Church, became a member of it in 1918. He attended Glasgow University, from which he graduated in arts with an M.A. degree in 1925 and with a B.D. in theology in 1928. Soon after he became minister of the Marshall Street Baptist Church in Edinburgh.

After four years in Edinburgh, Dr. McCracken was called to be minister of the Dennistoun Baptist Church in Glasgow, and in 1933 was appointed lecturer in systematic theology in the Baptist Theological College of Scotland. For the next four years he carried responsibilities both as preacher and teacher. In 1937 McMaster University at Hamilton, Ontario, invited him to become associate professor of Christian theology and philosophy of religion. Then followed a year of special study at Cambridge University, after which Dr. McCracken returned to Canada. From the outset he associated himself with ecumenical interests and activities. All the Protestant communions in Canada have sought his spiritual leadership. During the last three years he was in Canada he was on one occasion or another daily preacher at the Toronto Conference of the United Church, daily preacher at the General Council of the United Church of Canada, lecturer on the Pitcairn-Crabbe Foundation at Western Theological Seminary in Pittsburgh, lecturer before the McGill Theological Alumni in Montreal and before the Knox College Alumni in Toronto. For five years he was the guest preacher during the sum-mer at Yorkminster Church in Toronto. He had a term of notable service as president of the Baptist Convention of Ontario and Quebec.

As preacher, pastor, teacher and administrator, he has had a wide and useful experience before becoming the successor to Dr. Harry Emerson Fosdick. In May, 1946, McMaster University awarded the honorary doctorate to Dr. McCracken and on October 2, 1946, he was installed as minister of the River-side Church, New York City. He has proven himself a worthy successor to Dr. Fosdick in this important pulpit. In June, 1949, he received the honorary D.D. from Glasgow University.

Dr. McCracken urges a new moral sense for Christian men and women and for the people of the world if peace, faith, and the right kind of life and civilization are to be brought to mankind. This sermon had a tremendous *effect when delivered in the Riverside Church. As a preacher, he is clear in his thinking, persuasive in his presentation and modest and sincere in his manner. He is deeply concerned to communicate the message which he has felt called to give. He does not lose sight of the individual, but speaks to his needs with an insight that makes his words challenging, and with a personal interest that makes them acceptable. At the same time, he has a strong concern for the state of society in which individuals must live and recognizes and stresses the implications of the Christian Gospel for the world in which men are required to live.*

Sermon Three

A SENTENCE in John Buchan's *Memory, Hold the Door* has power to haunt the mind. "The pillars of civilization," he wrote, "are cracking and tilting." That is not just a vivid phrase. In the judgment of careful observers of the human situation—and Buchan was a careful observer—it is uncomfortably close to literal fact. The newspapers make sorry reading these days. Things are going steadily from bad to worse in the world. In vast areas of it decency is a legend and civilization no more than a name. There were people sanguine enough to believe that once Hitler, Mussolini and the Japanese war lords were disposed of all would be well. They know better now. They have discovered that the war was not so much the source of our maladies as it was a symptom of them; that the evil things against which we fought—the contempt for truth, the flouting of conscience, the glorification of aggression—all had their rise in a civilization in which spiritual forces had become weak. They have discovered that war can smash moral standards as viciously as it levels cities. It is a disillusioning discovery. Despite all our efforts, though for years great regions of the world were like a shambles and blood flowed like water, things have not worked out as it was hoped they would. The war between dictatorship and democracy has not been settled. Forces of unreason and evil are still in the ascendant and so stubborn and unyielding that men are beginning to speak of them as demonic. To cope with them, to subdue and control them is proving a superhuman undertaking. Baffled in the attempt multitudes are suffering a deep, spiritual frustration. They look out on the chaotic condition of the world and say to themselves: If these are times of peace, what is peace but a kind of political purgatory in which humanity lives while awaiting the next Armageddon? And on every side the next Armageddon is discussed as inevitable and imminent.

That there is something radically wrong with civilization is a point that

[17]

need not be labored. What is wrong? Of the answers given to that question, there is simply no end. Economists say one thing, politicians say another, churchmen say yet another. There is one answer, however, of which more should be made than generally is. The historians tell us that every age has a blind spot. It fails to see weaknesses in practices and institutions which to later generations are clear as the noonday. The drowning of witches in the seventeenth century, penal laws in the eighteenth, slavery in the nineteenth! What will our successors say about the twentieth century? Will it not surprise them that we were so strangely blind to our chief problem—the disparity between scientific development on the one hand and moral development on the other? Sir Richard Livingstone predicts that our grandchildren will say of us:

> They boasted that science had unified the world. They never saw that the only real unity is spiritual, and that however great the advantage of being able to cross the Atlantic in eight hours, cooperation depends not on rapid transport but on common ideals. They were conscious of the defects in their commercial and industrial systems, but though their standards and values were far more chaotic, they did nothing to remedy the chaos. So their peacetime civilization was both impressive and depressing; the unlimited means at their disposal were largely misused. Their education did little to help them. It was like a half-assembled motor car; most of the parts were there but they were not put together. Reformers wished to base it on science and technology, or on sociology and economics, whose importance they saw; if they had had their way, they would have produced a good chassis, but overlooked the need of an engine—not to speak of a driver who knew where to go. Their real problem lay deeper than science or sociology or politics; it was spiritual.[1]

It is to be hoped that our grandchildren will speak in such fashion, for if they do they will be much wiser than their grandparents. Why can we not learn to think and speak so now? We cannot praise too highly the scientific achievements of our time. Man's control over nature, his subordination of it to his purpose, his manipulation of its infinite resources, approaches the miraculous. Every day science puts into his hands greater and still greater powers. And every day with growing concern we find ourselves asking: Can he be trusted with them? Does his wisdom about "ends" match his ingenuity about "means"? Is his moral sense as well developed as his technical skill? His attitude to the atomic bomb provides and crystallizes the answer. In international circles what matters most is the mastery of its secrets, not the principles to be observed in its use. Technique is erected into a kind of absolute. Ends are subordinated to means. Everywhere it is the "know-how" that counts. To have that is to be in the driver's seat. It is the thing that compels respect and clinches argument. By comparison questions of principle are deemed of secondary importance. Do you see how immoral

[1] From *Education for a World Adrift* by Sir Richard Livingstone (Cambridge University Press, 1943), preface.

[18]

such a temper is, how essentially and inherently immoral? If persisted in, its consequences cannot be other than disastrous.

An English Bishop, preaching before the British Association, a society made up of the country's top-ranking scientists, facetiously threw out the suggestion that it might not be a bad thing if all science lecture rooms and laboratories were closed for twenty years so that man's moral and spiritual development might have a chance to catch up with his scientific knowledge. By the very suggestion he brought down on himself an avalanche of ridicule and abuse. He must have known in advance what would happen. I suppose he said what he did not with any expectation that his proposal would be acted upon but to secure publicity for a perfectly sound contention, namely that ingenuity about means must be matched by wisdom about ends, that moral sense should not lag behind technical skill, that for every advance in man's scientific knowledge there ought to be a corresponding advance in his moral character.

There ought to be but there is not. Man has made nature his servant, has bound the continents together, has created for himself numberless comforts and luxuries, but he has not rooted out of his soul the instincts of greed, pugnacity and cruelty. He has conquered nature but he has not conquered himself. He has multiplied his powers but his designs are sometimes as mean and narrow as when his forbears dwelt in ignorance and squalor. Will Durant is very emphatic about this. "We are spiritual pygmies," he says, "in gigantic frames. Utopia has come everywhere except in the soul of man. Human nature has ruined every Utopia." Elton Trueblood is equally emphatic. "Man has been more successful in making machines than achieving the will and wisdom to use his engines for humane purposes. This is the predicament of Western man. He has built up a complex civilization, but he may lose it because in his proud hour of achievement, he has so largely lost or never developed the inner resources that are needed to keep a possible boon from becoming a calamity."

Have you read about the achievements of the Boeing stratocruiser? It can hold seven jeeps, four ambulances, two ton-and-a-half trucks, or two baby tanks. It can carry 120 passengers, and it has a cocktail lounge. It has a cruising speed of 340 miles an hour. As a matter of fact, it covered the 2,323 miles between Seattle and Washington in 6 hours 3 minutes and 50 seconds. It flew at a height of 30,000 feet, and to land at Washington it had to start letting down at Pittsburgh. Incidentally, it covered the distance between Pittsburgh and Washington in twenty minutes. There you have it—man's mastery of nature and of the forces of nature. It chanced that on the same evening that I came across the story of the Boeing stratocruiser I read about a stormy session at the General Assembly of the United Nations. Tempers had flared, passions had been roused, charges had been met with counter-charges. Rivalry, suspicion, animosity, hostility were too near the surface to be concealed. Day after day it is the same pitiful story, and not

[19]

only at Flushing Meadows. "Advanced, united, international in our material civilization; when we pass beyond it Babel begins." Nationalists and Communists in China, Moslems and Hindus in India, Arabs and Zionists in Palestine, employers and employees in this country—there is a woeful abundance of dissension, bitterness and bad feeling in the world, and it all goes to illustrate the disparity between material and moral achievement.

This, I suggest, is our generation's blind spot. We merit in the twentieth century the rebuke which Plato administered to the Greeks in the fourth century before Christ. "They have filled the city with docks and arsenals and trash of that kind; they have not tried to put temperance and righteousness into the people's souls." We have taken endless pains in exploring external conditions and physical functions and all the elements which compose the environment of man but have been peculiarly indifferent to the study of man himself, his nature, his character, what he should be and how he should live. We are spending billions on the perfecting of the technique whereby we may establish and extend our control of atomic energy. How much by comparison are we spending on the moral education and development of the men and women in whose hands the power released by atomic energy will mean life or death, a blessing or a curse? If we were to devote the same time, the same determination, the same ingenuity, the same intelligence, to the study of man's moral nature that we do to the manufacture of machines and the control of the elements, a new and brighter day might soon dawn for all mankind. We are far from doing any such thing. Our universities are crowded as never before. For one student however, studying ethics or theology there are hundreds studying physics or chemistry or engineering. There could be no quicker, no surer way of inviting trouble. We are not employing our best men for our highest work. We are not schooling our best men for our highest work. Engineering sense is one thing and moral sense is another, but God help us if we go on cultivating the one and turning a blind eye on the other. Let me quote Plato again. "It is not the life of knowledge, not even if it included all the sciences, that creates happiness and well being, but a single branch of knowledge—the science of good and evil. If you exclude this from the other branches, medicine will be equally able to give us health, and shoemaking shoes and weaving clothes. Seamanship will still save lives at sea and strategy will win battles. But without the knowledge of good and evil, the use and excellence of these sciences will be found to have failed us."

Exactly! Do ponder that last phrase. "The use and excellence of these sciences will be found to have failed us." The prediction is true in general; it is uncannily true in one particular. The power released by atomic energy which could make our life on earth paradise constitutes instead a permanent threat to the very continuance of civilization. And why? Because twentieth century man is neither wise enough nor good enough to handle such power. He is too self-centered, too greedy for power, too self-righteous. Absorbed by his science, economics, industry, commerce, he is neglectful of standards and values. One hopeful sign however is that here and there, and not least among the scientists, there are men and women who see that the moral element in civilization must be cultivated equally with the material, and that at the moment it is the moral element that needs attention most if the life of twentieth century man is not to become, in the words of John Hobbes, "nasty, brutish and short." It is significant that the people who are most deeply concerned about the arousing and quickening of a new moral sense are the atomic physicists, and well might they be concerned. Aside altogether from the burden of personal responsibility bound up with their world-shaking invention, and on a sensitive man that burden must lie heavily, they appreciate, as lay folk do not, the extent to which it hangs like the sword of Damocles over our heads, and they know that unless men are wise enough and good enough to turn its energies to beneficent use and only to beneficent use, it will prove the most disastrous and destructive discovery ever made by man. J. R. Oppenheimer, who helped to develop the bomb, did not hesitate to tell the American public that atomic weapons might conceivably wipe out forty million Americans in a single night. The man who believes that is bound to be a frightened man. He is bound to be a seeking man. He needs no one to tell him that man's moral sense has lagged lamentably behind his scientific sense. It goes without saying that he is out to do what he can, and to get others to do what they can, to make up the leeway.

What, in terms of everyday life, does all this amount to? It means, of course, that international machinery for the prevention of war is more than ever necessary now. But in his heart every man knows that something more than machinery is needed. The plain fact of the matter is that only one thing can save us now and that is a new moral sense, a spiritual conversion, a deliberate turning to God and Christ and goodness with the resolve that first things will be put first and not last. If you reply that preachers have been saying that until you are weary of hearing it and put it down as pious and conventional verbiage, my concern is whether you can have noticed that columnists, educators, statesmen and scientists are now saying the same thing. David Lilienthal is saying it. Anne O'Hare McCormick is saying it. A physicist in a state university recently put it in this way: "I have come to three conclusions. The first is that salvation is not to be found in science. Secondly, we must have a moral revival. Thirdly, we can have no moral revival without a living religion."

The question is not whether man's political skill can catch up with his technical skill. It runs deeper than that. Primarily it is not a question of politics but of ethics. The problem lies not in the devising of charters—the foreign offices of the nations are littered with them—but in finding men who will act in accordance with the principles, the just and sound principles, enunciated in the charters. The new order we need is a moral order. Primarily the question is this: Can we get people to do justly, and love mercy, and walk humbly with God? Never have self-interest and self-righteousness in the national and international spheres been so naked and unashamed. What prospect is there of persuading men and nations to have done with both? Said a Frenchman who knows France from end to end, "France's trouble is a matter of morals and morale." Everywhere that is the trouble. It is at the root of the inner disintegrations going on in country after country. After a war as devastating as that from which we have just emerged a reconstruction of the outer framework of society is imperative. Granted. But what will it avail if men lack the character, the wisdom, the rectitude, the moral quality to turn it to account?

The history of the last thirty years demonstrates that humanity is not going to be saved by treaties and conferences. Things have come to such a pass that nothing in the world can save us now but a change of direction in the spiritual trek of mankind. The crisis in which we find ourselves in its essential nature is neither political nor economic but spiritual. Listen to what was virtually the last will and testament of the internationally known French scientist Lecomte du Noüy. "At present everybody is preoccupied by the organization of peace. All are agreed that this is the crucial problem which dominates every other. But we hear only of 'external' solutions—of treaties, signatures, understandings, conventions, international police, courts of arbitration. We never hear anything about the *respect* of these treaties and signatures, the *integrity* of the commissions, the *impartiality* of the judges, the *good faith* of all, without which these instruments lose all their value. Yet we should know by this time that their effectiveness depends entirely on the character of the men who have drafted them or participated in them." That needed to be said. And what is this plea for respect, integrity, impartiality, good faith but the plea for a new moral sense?

It would never do to stop there—with a plea for a new moral sense. The practical question is where it is to be got. How are men and nations to be saved from self-seeking and self-righteousness? How are they to acquire integrity, impartiality, respect, good faith? I know no other answer than that of the physicist with his three conclusions—"Salvation is not to be found in science; we must have a moral revival; we can have no moral revival without a living religion." If a nation has a living religion, it acquires a habit of mind, a sense of values, a respect for standards which gives it stability and coherence. If an individual has a living religion, he has a definite ideal to guide, discipline, dominate and elevate his life. He is like salt, light and leaven in the world.

Life's Saving Tension

REVEREND HALFORD EDWARD LUCCOCK, D.D., LITT.D.

A Methodist Minister and Professor of Homiletics,
Yale University, Divinity School, New Haven, Connecticut

In his preaching Dr. Luccock has a flair for using just the right word, a touch of humor, and an insight into the life people live today. When he speaks people always listen with enjoyment and with spiritual profit. There is faith and joy in his religion!

Born in Pittsburgh in 1885, he took his college degree at Northwestern University, his divinity degree at Union Theological Seminary, New York, in 1909, and did graduate work at Columbia University. Syracuse University, Wesleyan University, and the University of Vermont recognized the value of his work with the D.D.; Allegheny College with the Litt.D.

He was ordained in the Methodist ministry in 1910, was pastor at Windsor, Connecticut, 1910-12; instructor at Hartford Theological Seminary, 1912-14; pastor of St. Andrews Church, New Haven, Connecticut, 1914-16; was appointed registrar and instructor in New Testament at Drew Theological Seminary, 1916-18. He became editorial secretary of the Methodist Board of Foreign Missions, 1918-24, contributing editor of the Christian Advocate, 1924-28. He has been professor of homiletics at Yale since 1928.

He is the author of many excellent books, including Fares, Please, Studies in the Parables of Jesus, The Christian Crusade for World Democracy, The Haunted House and Other Sermons, The Story of Methodism, Jesus and the American Mind, The Acts of the Apostles in Present Day Preaching, American Mirror, *and co-editor (with Frances Brentano) of* The Questing Spirit.

There is a fine combination of psychology and religion in this sermon, emphasis on the right kind of tension, and good material to suggest still other sermons and ideas to the busy minister in other communities.

Sermon Four

TEXTS: I must work the work of Him that sent me while it is yet day, for the night cometh when no man can work.   JOHN 9:14.
Now is my soul troubled.   JOHN 12:27.
When he saw the multitude he was moved with compassion because they were harassed and helpless.   MATTHEW 9:36.

THESE are all pictures of a man in a state of disturbance. The first was the pressure of a deadline—"while it is yet day." The second was an inward strain—"Now is my soul troubled." The third was a deeply upsetting sympathy.

These portray an aspect of Jesus necessary to a rounded picture of a complex personality. They also furnish a remembrance of Jesus greatly needed in our day. They all reflect a state of tension which fits most of the dictionary definitions of that word—"the act of stretching," "suppressed emotional excitement," "strong intellectual effort."

There is another side of Jesus, of course, which must never be forgotten. It was etched deep into the minds of men—his confidence, serenity and trust. But without the complementary picture of the disturbed Jesus, we get only a fractional, distorted view. Swinburne once wrote of a preacher, "For tender souls he served up half a Christ." There have been a good many servings of half a Christ.

What we have called tension is a very different thing from two common marks of our time—anxiety and confusion. It is hard for us to escape either one of them. This saving tension of life is not anxiety, where the spirit is frayed with apprehension and goes into a permanent state of fidgets. It is not confusion, where the mind sees all things through a fog darkly. There is no salvation in a nervous breakdown; it is a poor tool for meeting life. Yet we never really meet life without mental and spiritual tension, stretching, disturbance, and effort.

There is real danger of taking this tension out of life and leaving it limp. We may look at the mainspring of a watch, see it bound and tense, and say, "Loose it, and let it go." But if we take away the tension, we take away the watch and all we have left is an ingenious collection of junk. People who have lost the tension out of their lives, the *qui vive* alertness, the desperate caring and sense of a dead line, have become in real ways useless collections of junk.

A best selling non-fiction book in the United States is a volume entitled *How to Stop Worrying and Start Living*. What we really need is a good book on "How to Stop Living and Start Worrying." We have too much routine living and too little dedicated worrying; too much existence fenced in with immediate preoccupations, too little deep concern for the hazards of our time. So much living goes on beyond a very opaque iron curtain.

Recently in a dentist's office, I had a rather terrible choice to make—whether to read a *National Geographic Magazine* for May, 1935, or a more recent *Harper's Bazaar*. Doubtfully, I put my money on the *Bazaar*. My eye caught a two-page spread with the heading over it, "The Big News from Paris." I was alert—Paris has been the center of the world, with the assembly of the United Nations. Here was the big news. I cannot remember it all, but this is some of it: necklines will be lower; skirts somewhat longer and considerably fuller; three new perfumes have been created, all apparently guaranteed to kill at twenty yards. That is the big news to many people.

In another magazine I read this in a full page advertisement: "At last you can get the best of life with television." This thesis was documented with three pictures; two men trying to hit each other on the jaw; another getting a base on balls; and a girl doing a tap dance. The best of life! Best is a large word.

In this day of psychology of all brands, good, almost good, and charlatan, the business of not worrying has been elevated into a national cult. The magic word is "Relax," more magical than "Open Sesame!" We have it in a score of books every season: *You Must Relax; Overcoming Nervous Tension; How Never to Be Tired*—all of them aimed at a real and growing need; yet all of them contributing to the elevation of semi-consciousness to a panacea for human ills. Many ministers have discovered the blessed word "relaxed," and have compressed the whole Gospel into it, like abbreviating an eighty-eight note piano into one note. One man I know seems to have been preaching for years on "Peace, Poise, and Power in Perpetual Possession." They are almost on the verge of rewriting the Scriptures to read, "If any man will come after me, let him relax," or "Go into all the world and keep down your blood pressure." Something is missing. It is the tension of Jesus. I saw a sermon topic announced not long ago, "How to Live a Serene and Successful Life." Very attractive; but we have to remember that Jesus lived a very disturbed and unsuccessful life. He died on a cross.

We have had moving examples recently of two men who stopped living in a fool's paradise and started worrying. I do not mean that they are dead. They are both living, and may the Lord bless and keep them. One is Fairfield Osborne, who wrote *Our Plundered Planet*. The other is William Vogt, who wrote *Road to Survival*. They started worrying over the depletion of the world's resources, the pressure of the increasing population of the globe against the decreasing fertility of an earth already inadequate for the existence of two billions. They have given us a vision of S-Day—Starvation Day—around the corner, unless we develop a new sense of stewardship. That is a saving tension—a scream, if you will, to save ourselves while it is yet day. Perhaps others will begin to do some redeeming worrying.

[25]

In order to bring this home to ourselves, may we stress three areas where this fruitful tension is needed:

First, we need a tension between our actual and our potential world. One of the meanings of tension is a dissatisfied restlessness, a "strong intellectual effort." We get that in the hymn, "Turn Back, O Man, Foreswear Thy Foolish Ways":

> Earth might be fair . . .
> Would man but wake from out his haunted sleep.

The need for this restlessness is increased by the changed conditions of our world. A picture of what has happened to us is, I think, found in Harold Lamb's *Life of Alexander the Great.* He describes graphically the great consternation which struck Alexander's army when they found that they had marched clear off the map. All the maps they had were Greek maps of Asia Minor. They had passed those and were marching into the Himalayas. Our world has marched off old maps in every realm. We have done it in medicine. The old map was plainly marked, "Take out blood." Our new map says, "Put in blood"—in other words, transfusion instead of bleeding. Here is an old medical map used in the last days of Charles II of England: "A pint of blood was extracted from his right arm and half a pint from his left shoulder, followed by an emetic. The royal head was then shaved and blisters raised. Then sneezing powder, more emetics, and plaster of pitch on his foot. Finally forty drops of extract of human skull. After which His Majesty gave up the ghost." It sounds reasonable.

There is no need to elaborate the obvious. We have marched off the map of scientific certainties, of Francis Bacon's dictum that the application of science to invention tends to perfect man's estate. Lewis Mumford has lately pointed out that science has been largely occupied in creating Seven League Boots and Magic Carpets. We now know that boots and carpets are not enough.

Every day makes clearer that our world has marched off the map of competing national sovereignties. Any nation that insists on its right of individual decision on issues affecting the peace of the world is using a language that is out of date when nations are triggering an earthquake. We have marched off the map of fixed economic sovereignties. Every day it becomes more impossible to build a fence around anything—peace, war, wealth, poverty, welfare, liberty. Every day calls for dedicated worry and concern, instead of casual living. The War Department issued a striking document with the arresting title, "What to Do If an Atomic Bomb Falls." It had ten points. The first was a masterpiece. It said, "Keep calm." An ordinary man would not have thought of that. It took at least a three-star general. If an atom bomb falls, we will all keep calm—permanently. But if we all get disturbed and excited enough about it beforehand, it may not need to fall. One of the most moving stories of the war is one by Irving Shaw entitled

Preach on Dusty Roads. There is no battle in it. No blood is shed. It simply describes a constrained luncheon at which a father says good-bye to his son going off to Europe. On his way back to the office, the father remembers how he had given all his efforts to making profits for his company, while all the time this gathering calamity had been growing. He says that during that time he should have been out and preaching on dusty roads against war. That call has come to us.

In the economic field we have mastered the mechanical arts of addition and multiplication; we have failed in the ethical art of division. We have done something in short division, dividing the resources of the earth among small groups; we must also learn the art of long division.

Second, we must keep the tension between our achieved and our possible self. The worst thing we can say of anyone is, "He has arrived." That is something to put on a tombstone. There is always a little tombstone standing erect over any arrival, if that is taken as final. The common phrase, "a finished artist" often has a sting to it. It may mean just that. He is finished. There is nothing more. The tragedy is greatest in that greatest of all creative arts, the creation of a person, of a character. To lose the tension, the restless dissatisfaction with what I am, to lose the vision of what I might be, to cease to be a belligerent in the moral battle and run up the white flag of capitulation—that is to lose life.

In the parable of the rich fool there are arresting words. When the man possessed of many barns said, "Soul, take thine ease, thou hast goods laid up for many years," the words came to him, "Thou fool, this night thy soul shall be required of thee." Whenever anyone says, in any way, "Take thine ease, don't worry about any improvement," the words come up from the center of the earth, "Thou fool!" It is true of the teacher when he says, "Soul, take thine ease, thou hast lectures laid up for many semesters." Then something with authority says, "Thou fool! This night thy soul shall be required of thee,"—for all that makes a real teacher, the continuing search for truth, the communication of life and enthusiasm, has gone, and another scratchy phonograph record is added to the word's overstock. With this, contrast Paul's great word, "I press on." To shorten the gap between what is and what might be is an unfailing source of zest. Recently on a trip up Madison Avenue, New York, from 42nd Street north, I read the signs all along the way, and every block had a "lounge" of some sort: the Onyx Lounge, the Ritz Lounge, the Orchid Lounge; here a lounge, there a lounge, everywhere a lounge. It is a disturbing word. There is too much lounging. The tension too often is gone, and moral effort ceases in favor of some kind of a sprawl.

Third, keep the tension between the visible and the invisible world. If we allow the sense of wonder to atrophy, if we lose the feeling of what Professor Hocking calls "the mysterious altitudes of ourselves," we become

[27]

the prisoners of time and space. We can shut out the message which come from "the beyond which is within" and "the beyond which is akin" to us. Not long ago a friend of mine described an incident of a voyage on the Red Sea which gives a picture of this. He was greatly interested to learn that during the morning the ship would come within sight of Mount Sinai. He let his imagination picture all that that mountain had meant in the history and culture of the race. He was deeply stirred. When the mountain became visible, he ran through the ship calling out to people that Mount Sinai was visible. In the game room he came across a company to whom he said "Mount Sinai over on the left!" One man looked up and said, "So what? I bid three spades." So all that Mount Sinai represents means little to those who go on living routine and enclosed lives. And tomorrow and tomorrow and tomorrow there is this little house and this little street. That is all.

We often hear the phrase, "Get off the earth!" In these days it has a new meaning, for it is true that unless we get off the earth spiritually, we may have to get off it physically. But beyond that, it is a saving word. "Get off the earth!" is your response to the evidences of the spiritual world that come in upon you. For only by getting off the earth in our awareness of the eternal world can we have fullness of life in this one.

THE CHRISTIAN LIFE

The Psychology of a Frustrated Soul

THE RIGHT REVERVEND MONSIGNOR FULTON J. SHEEN, PH.D., D.D.

Associate Professor of Philosophy, The Catholic University of America, Washington, D. C.

Monsignor Sheen's is one of the important living voices of our day. His forceful and convincing preaching makes every listener eager to catch each word. To hear him is to realize that here is a man who believes what he says and who has thought out his message calmly and prayerfully. Year by year his following increases and the sphere of his influence becomes larger.

After graduate work at the Catholic University of America, the University of Louvain, Belgium, and Angelico University, Rome, he was ordained in Peoria, Illinois, in 1919. Step by step he has risen from very modest places in the Church to be one of the most honored Catholic preachers. He taught at St. Edmund's College, Ware, and the Westminster (London) Diocesan Seminary in 1925-26; in 1926 the University of Louvain, recognizing his genius, awarded him the Cardinal Mercier prize for International Philosophy, the first time this honor was ever given an American.

Before the war, he was called to preach in Europe nearly every summer from 1925 to 1939, speaking in London at Westminster Cathedral and St. Patrick's Church, Soho Square; at the University of Cambridge Summer School, at Glasgow; in Rome, and elsewhere on the continent. In 1934 he was named a Papal Chamberlain of the late Pontiff, Pope Pius XI, with the title of Very Reverend Monsignor, and the following year, Pius XI made him a Domestic Prelate with the title of Right Reverend Monsignor.

During most of the year, he is busy teaching philosophy at the Catholic University of America, but is in such demand as a speaker, that he gives more than one hundred sermons and addresses each year, speaking in almost every major city in the United States to secular and religious groups who throng to hear him. For years he has been the regular Lenten preacher at St. Patrick's Cathedral, New York, and is the special Advent preacher at the Church of the Blessed Sacrament, New York, where his Advent messages are enthusiastically received.

He has written some twenty books on philosophy, religion, morals and socio-economic questions, including Freedom Under God, Whence Come Wars, Philosophies at War, and Peace of Soul.

"The Psychology of a Frustrated Soul" was given as one of thirteen messages on the nationwide Catholic Hour between January 4, 1948, through March 28, 1948. The Catholic Hour is sponsored by the National Council of Catholic Men in co-operation with the National Broadcasting Company. His combination of psychology and faith is excellent. This sermon was preached January 4, 1948.

Sermon Five

TEXT: What have I to do with thee, Jesus, the Son of the most high God? I adjure thee by God that thou torment me not.

MARK 5:7.

Friends:

TO REVISIT you on the airways is a privilege; to bring you a message is a responsibility; to hope that you and I will love God more in the coming year is the bond that makes "Friends."

As you know, our mission on the air is to save souls—nothing else matters—for unless souls are saved, nothing is saved. There is no such thing as world peace unless there is soul peace. World wars are nothing but projections of the conflicts waged inside our own souls, for nothing happens in the world that does not first happen inside a soul.

During the war the Holy Father said that the postwar man would be more changed than the map of postwar Europe. It is this postwar, frustrated man or what we will call the modern soul, which interests us in these broadcasts. This interest is heightened by the fact that the modern soul presents a new problem in technique to the Christian theologian for two reasons: (1) It no longer is interested in going to God through nature, and (2) It is imprisoned inside itself with its anxieties, fears and worries. Let me explain. In other generations, man went to God through nature. Looking out on the vastness of creation, the beauty of the skies and the order of the planets, man concluded to the power, the beauty and wisdom of God who created and sustained the world. The modern man is unfortunately not using the approach for several reasons; (1) He is impressed less with the order of nature than he is with the disorder of his own mind; (2) the atomic bomb has made him realize that man can use nature to destroy man and even to commit cosmic suicide; (3) finally, science of nature is too impersonal. Not only does it make man a spectator of reality instead of its creator; it also demands that the personality never intrude itself in investigation. But it is now personality, not nature which is the problem.

This does not mean that the modern soul has given up God but only that it has abandoned the more rational and even more normal way of finding Him. Not the order in the cosmos, but the disorder in himself, not the visible things of the world, but the invisible frustrations, complexes and anxieties of his own personality, is the modern man's starting point of religion. In more happy days philosophers discussed the problem of man; now they discuss man as a problem. Formerly, man lived in a three-dimensional universe, where from earth he looked to heaven above and to hell below. With the modern forgetfulness of God this vision has been corrupted to a single dimension; man now thinks of himself as limited to the surface of the earth—a plane whereon he moves not up to God nor down to Satan, but only to the right and left. The theological division of men into those who are in the state of grace and those who are not, has given way to the political one of whether man is a rightist or a leftist. The modern soul has definitely limited its horizons; having negated the eternal destinies, it has even lost its trust in nature, for nature without God is traitorous. Where can modern man go now that a road block has been thrown up against every external outlet? Obviously, like a city in war which has had all its outer ramparts seized, man must retreat inside himself. As a body of water that is blocked turns back upon itself, collecting scum, refuse and silt, so the modern soul which has none of the outside securities of the Christian man, backs up upon itself, and in that choked condition collects all subrational, instinctive, dark, unconscious forces which would never have existed had there been the normal exits of more normal times. Man finds he is locked up within himself as his own prisoner, and he himself is the jailer. Imprisoned within himself, he now attempts to compensate for the loss of the three dimensional universe of faith by finding three new dimensions with his own mind. Above his conscious level, in place of heaven he substitutes his own ideals, totems and taboos which he calls a superego. Below his consciousness, in place of hell he substitutes unconscious biological sexual instincts which he calls the id, although there are some who would call this hell their heaven.

Given this subjective world where man is a captive with his own mind, you have the reason for the popularity of the science of psychology.

Through its study of the unconscious realm, unhappy modern man seeks to find a relief which the conscious realm could not give. Using psychology as a kind of file, he hopes to escape out of his mental prison where he has locked himself as his own turnkey.

The complexes, anxieties, and fears of the modern soul did not exist for previous generations because they were shaken off and integrated in a great social-spiritual organism of Christian civilization. They are, however, so much a part of modern man that one would think they were tatooed on him. But, whatever be his condition, the modern soul must be brought back to happiness and to God. But how? Should the Christian, with his eternal verities, insist that modern man go back to the traditional approach, which started with nature, and approach God by the five arguments of St. Thomas? It would be a saner world if he did. But it is the point of these broadcasts that we ought to start with modern man as he is, not as we would like to find him, nor as we find man in our books. Our apologetic literature for that reason is about fifty years behind the times. It leaves the modern soul cold, not because its arguments are unconvincing, but because the modern soul is confused. We who are heirs of twenty centuries of sound thinking must not be with the supernatural as a dog with a bone. If the modern soul wants to begin its quest for peace with its psychology instead of with our own metaphysics, we will begin where it wants to begin. God's truth would have but few facets if it could not start with human nature in any degree of perfection or even degradation. Even if the modern man wants to go to God through the devil, we will start with the devil. That is where our dear Lord began with Magdalen and He told His followers that with prayer and fasting, they, too, could start their evangelical work there. The psychological approach constitutes no difficulty for us, for Christianity's theology is, in a certain sense, a psychology, for its primary interest is the soul. Our Lord balances a universe and a soul and found a soul worth more than gaining the world.

But it may be asked, is not the modern soul so different that no previous age had any experience of such a phenomenon and, therefore, cannot offer a cure? No! There is nothing really new in the world; there are only the same old problems happening to new people. As a proof, take the three characteristic notes of the modern soul and I will prove that such a soul appeared in the Gospel and that our Lord cured him. These three characteristics of the modern soul are: it is divided from itself, from its fellow man, and from God.

(1) Self-estrangement: The modern man is no longer a unit, but a confused bundle of complexes and nerves. He is less a personality than a battlefield whereon a civil war rages between his thousand and one conflicting loyalties. There is no single overall purpose in his life. He projects his own mental confusion to the outside world and concludes that since he knows no truth, nobody can know it.

(2) Isolation from fellow men: The man who cannot live with himself cannot live with his fellow men. This is evident from his living in the two world wars in twenty-one years and a constant threat of a third. It is clear also not only from the growth of class conflict and selfishness wherein each man seeks his own, but also by man's break with tradition and the accumulated heritage of the centuries. Nothing is more tragic to man or civilization than the loss of memory.

(3) Estrangement from God: Alienation from self and from fellow men has its roots in separation from God. For once the hub of the wheel, which is God, is lost, the spokes, which are men, fall apart. God seems very far away from the modern man, which is due, to a great extent, to his own behavior. Goodness always appears as a reproach to those who are not living right, and this reproach on the part of the sinner expresses itself in hatred and persecution. There is not a single disrupted, frustrated soul in the world who is critical and envious of his neighbor, who is not at the same time an antireligious man. The organized atheism of the present hour is a projection of self-hatred. No man hates God without first hating himself.

Does such a confused soul exist in the Gospel? Is modern psychology studying the different type of man than the one our Lord came to redeem? If we turn to St. Mark, we find that a young man in the land of the Gerasenes is described as suffering from the same three identical frustrations as the modern soul:

(1) He was self-estranged, for we find that when our Lord asked: "What is thy name?" (Mark 5:9), the young man answered, "My name is legion, for we are many." Notice the personality conflict and the confusion between "my" and "we," between "my name" and "we are many." It is obvious that he is a problem to himself, a bewildered backwash of a thousand conflicting anxieties. For that reason, he called himself "legion," multiple, confused.

(2) He was separated from his fellow men for the Gospel describes him: "living in the monuments and in the mountains" (Mark 5:5), because he was a menace to men. Isolation is a peculiar quality of godlessness. Its natural habitat is away from fellow men, among the tombs in the region of death. There is no cement in sin; its nature is divisive and disruptive and discordant.

(3) He was separated from God, for when he saw the Divine Saviour, he shouted: "What have I to do with thee, Jesus the Son of the most high God? I adjure thee by God that thou torment me not" (Mark 5:7). In other words, what have we in common? Your presence is my destruction. It is an interesting psychological fact that the frustrated soul hates goodness and wants to be separated from it.

You see the modern soul is not so modern after all. Like the Gerasene youth he is estranged from himself, his fellow man and his God. How deal with him?

One thing is certain, the modern soul is not going to find peace so long as he is locked up inside himself, mulling around the scum and sediment of his unconscious mind. It is interesting that the very individual who thought such a solution the right one, took as the motto of one of his books: "If I cannot bend the gods on high I will set all hell in an uproar." This is not the answer? Because in dethroning the concious values of the world, one does indeed set hell in an uproar and ends in neuroses worse confounded.

The true answer is, man must be released from his inner prison. He will go mad if he must chase the tail of his own mind, being both seeker and sought, rabbit and hound. Peace of soul cannot come from himself, any more than he can lift himself by his own ears. Help must come from without; it must be not merely human, but divine. Nothing short of a divine invasion Who restores man to ethical reality can make man happy when he is alone and in the dark.

Thus was the frustrated youth of the Gerasenes cured, for when our Lord had finished with him, he was restored to himself, his fellow man and God. He recovered the purpose of life. Instead of calling himself "legion," the Gospel describes him ". . . sitting, clothed and well in his wits" (Mark 5:15). In our language, he was feeling like his own self. Instead of being isolated from community life, we, find him restored to fellowship by our Lord, Who told him: "Go into thy house to thy friends . . ." (Mark 5:19). Finally, instead of hating God we find that he became an apostle, and begins to ". . . publish in Decapolis how great things Jesus had done for him, and all men wondered" (Mark 5:20).

What our Lord did for him, He can do for you. If your soul is too harassed with fears and anxieties to come to God through the loveliness of a star, then come to Him through the loneliness of a heart. If you cannot find God through the argument of motion, you can come by way of your own disgusts —aye, even through the handle of your sins. Though you have locked yourself in this prison of your mind, remember that only God can let you out as He let Peter out of his dungeon. But you must desire to get out. God will not fail: it is only our desire that is weak.

Be not discouraged. It was the bleating lamb in the thickets more than the flock in the peaceful pastures which attracted the Saviour's heart and helping hand. To be worthy of that help resolve to spend an hour a day in

[33]

meditation, and if you be Catholic, spend it in the presence of our dear Lord in the tabernacle. During this meditation ask yourselves these two questions: If you are only for yourself—then what good are you? If you are not for yourself—then who are you for?

THE CHRISTIAN LIFE

Faith to Build the House and the City

REVEREND C. C. MARTINDALE, S.J.
Farm Street Church (Roman Catholic), London, England

Father Martindale is one of the great voices of the Catholic Church in the contemporary English-speaking world. His sermons, books and personal conferences have influenced thousands of people in England and America, yet he is still just as much interested in one individual as in a great crowd, for he realizes that even in a group the speaker must reach individual hearts and minds or his message fails of its personal and collective purpose. In 1946 he made a plea for prayer for all men, Japanese, Jews, Russians, in the love of God.

Born in 1879, he entered the Jesuit novitiate, took highest classical honours at Oxford, and was ordained in 1911. He worked among soldiers during and after World War I, and has written almost without ceasing. Probably the most influential of his numerous books are Does God Matter to Me? *Essay on the Passion,* Our Blessed Lady (Sermons), *Poplar Leaves and Seaweed* (Poems), *and* Sweet Singer of Israel. *He is one of the people Monsignor Knox consulted when doing his translation of the Bible. For five and one-half years he was interned in Denmark, where the events of the war had caught him, and he was kept in custody by the Danish authorities who refused to deliver him to the Germans.*

Father Martindale speaks in various sermons of peace and justice, spirit and will, morals and motives, right and wrong, greed and guilt, of expediency and "interests," of heroism and sacrifice, of power and politics. He pleads for a peace that is a true peace, for men of conscience to live by faith. His sermons are widely accepted for their deeply spiritual messages. This sermon on faith to build the house and the city will come close to the hearts and minds of all who read it.

Sermon Six

Text: Unless the Lord build the house, they labour in vain who build it: Unless the Lord watch over the city, the watchman waketh but in vain. Psalm 127:1 (A.V.).

BY "CITY" I mean the whole human society within which men live: and by "house" I mean those special departments within which they live—larger, or smaller, from each man's country to each man's home, and the various organizations into which men group themselves, such as unions or parties of whatever sort. We want a happy life to be lived within each of these, and among all of them; and for that, we need peace; and peace is not just not-fighting, but freedom for orderly action; but we want more than the mere chance of such activity: we want the will to work, to work co-operatively, as hard as possible and on the widest possible scale.

Fifty years ago we were still being told that this happy sort of future lay before us: more and more wealth; better and better health; stability together with progress; the end of fear and the unthinkability of war. Science had triumphed over superstition. Then somehow we rushed down a steep place into the first World War. After it, optimism revived. Grandiose systems were evolved. The League of Nations built its palaces by the Lake of Geneva and filled them with innumerable clerks. There were countless committees, cataracts of talk, an avalanche of print. Yet in less than ten years a novelist was writing: "I suppose that people believe in something nowadays, but I don't know what it is." And another critic saw: "veneration killed, self-denial written-off, sentiment derided, the future in the air, and modern life a dance of gnats." And a philosopher wrote his famous sentence: "Only on the firm foundations of unyielding despair can the soul's habitation be safely built." Strange indeed to start building a house, when you have ceased to hope in anything: paradoxical the city, whose very foundations are disbelief! Inexorably the second war arrived. I remember how we entered on it in a mood of stunned bewilderment; and even more clearly—I was then in another country—how the radio abruptly announced: "Unconditional surrender." The words were negative, no doubt. They told us that fighting had stopped, but not what sort of peace had begun. The more optimistic trusted that surely the mistakes made after the previous war would not be repeated; that plans for reconstruction must exist and would be put into immediate effect; that bitter words would die upon men's lips; that party would no more degenerate into partisanship; that men would abandon the ignoble aim of getting as much as each of them could, for the

[35]

sake of working together so as to give their maximum contribution. And, that they would tell the truth.

I could not quite expect all that. Still, I remembered how in the early days of the war the world "spiritual" kept cropping up: "civilization," people said, "must be based on spiritual principles"; "we must not lose sight of spiritual values." Cardinal Hinsley's broadcast on "The Sword of the Spirit" had an immense reverberation. Yet the word soon was used so glibly! What did it mean, exactly? That God was somehow at the back of human affairs and must be attended to . . . but? How, in the reconstruction of our national life? How, in our treatment of ex-enemies? Doubtless it also meant that men were not mere machines but living souls—not to be pawns in the hands of politicians or financiers. They must be treated "morally." But what was "morality," when prominent persons declared they could attach no meaning to the expression "The Law of Nature"—still less, therefore, to "The Law of God"? When the followers of Karl Marx reminded you that he indignantly rejected "morality" as a factor in the upbuilding of society?

By the happiest chance, I heard, during the war, the King's appeal for prayer, among the most sober yet stirring words ever addressed to the nation and beginning at the only true beginning. Prayer is a first consequence of belief in God, and the first difference among men is between those who pray and those who never do. Prayer is a simple thing. It is the "lifting up of the mind and the heart to God," and this can be done at any time, in any place, in any attitude, in any form of words or quite wordlessly. Yet associated prayer is certainly important, simply because men do associate themselves with others for every imaginable purpose. There is the first group of all—the family; and may parents join in teaching their small child to pray, and pray with it: it was good to hear, recently, of a new town dedicating itself to God by special united prayer; any collectivity of men might well unite in prayer when embarking on any joint enterprise, such as a sea-voyage, or a parliamentary session when God's help is most certainly needed for the whole nation's sake. Nor need set forms of words be out of place. They crystallize one's thought: one can see deeper and deeper into them. Happy are we if we even begin to say the Lord's Prayer with something of the meaning which was our Lord's when He taught it to us.

But if it is our first duty thus to lift our heart up to God in adoration, gratitude, repentance and petition, our second duty is "like to it"; to descend, as it were, from God, and take stock of our fellow men, but always from God's point of view. Men, not seen from the point of view of their Creator and Preserver, not seen as spiritual and immortal, have no personal value at all. They are far too numerous, too short-lived, too insignificant for any one of them to matter. They become at once the victim of the man, or group of men, in power. That is why those who *wish* the citizen to be the possession of the State, who hold—falsely—that the citizen exists *for* the State, always try to get rid of the doctrine of God, of the soul, and of conscience. This cannot be done equally everywhere, nor all of a sudden. But by imposing a materialist doctrine in the schools, by muzzling press, platform and pulpit, by establishing, in a word, the Police State, it can be managed until the human spirit, created for liberty, smashes its way out of that imprisonment.

A recent book, *Religion and Culture*, has displayed the tragic intellectual disintegration, the corruption of the social mind, which are the consequence of this secularizing of human life. Science can provide us with all sorts of machinery—to use one name for so many new inventions—but not with the moral principles needed if it is not to be used destructively. Science cannot provide any common spiritual aim. Its products are ready for anyone who can buy them; and short of moral principles and spiritual aims, only opportunism will dictate how the purchaser will use them. All such things, without God and the moral law, become idols: neither diplomacy nor economics nor the most solemn treaties can ever replace God. I recall the terrible words of the prophet (Hosea 5:7): "Ephraim is wedded to idols—let him alone."

Idols, in old days, were called "false gods"; and the very fact that men are so suspicious of one another proves that they cannot trust what is said. Now God is the absolute Truth; and our Lord defines the Adversary (which is what "Satan" means) as "a liar and the father of lies," and St. John sees that nothing which "loves or makes a lie" can have any part in the heavenly city. And St. Paul tells every man to speak truth with his neighbor, "for, you are members of one another." Lies tear into shreds the whole human fabric. We must, as always, begin by examining our own personal behavior; but also, extend the ideal of truthfulness into all our business dealings, difficult as this may be, and likely to leave us poorer than if we indulged in what are all too accurately called the "tricks of the trade." But I am really thinking on the widest scale—that of national and international relations. It is sinister that the very word "propaganda" has sunk to meaning almost the same as lying. It is disgraceful if a public speech is itself untruthful, and a scandal if it is reported untruthfully to delude the helpless public. The whole of society is ruined at the very base if the word of honor no more can be relied upon —is derided, as I have heard it, as "Victorian"; if no bond can be trusted, from the troth plighted in marriage, up to the treaties signed and sealed between whole nations through their representatives.

But that we should even want to lie proves a lack of unity and good will. All of us, let us hope, have vigorous opinions about many things. Apathy is a symptom of interior decay and holds out hope for nothing. And we shall express our opinions. But any word of rancor, any sneer, any clever but wounding epigram is a positive attack upon someone or something that simply does harm all round. It poisons him who uses it quite as much as him who suffers from it. Hatred breeds hatred and makes union ever less possible. Here is what will sound to you quixotic. If there are two parties, political or other, which are honest and not lying when they say that they have the good of all at heart, their only chance of ever getting anywhere is to seek, each of them, what is good in the other, to bring it to light, applaud it and foster it, and to develop it, by co-operation, into something better still. Thus and thus only can you rinse out of parties the ignoble taint of partisanship. Satan, said our Lord, is not only the liar and father of lies, but a murderer from the beginning. He attacks life when he injures love: his aim is chaos; whereas God creates: to God's "Let there *be!*" he retorts his never-ceasing No.

We pray, then, not only for peace, but what alone makes peace possible, and what alone makes it fruitful and no mere vacuum. Truthfulness, there-fore, and the maximum of co-operation with as many as possible—not that minimum of work which enables *me* to *get*; not that greedy grabbing which gets for *me* as *much* as possible; not that destructive energy devoted to the advantage of my side, my union, my party however much it be to the dis-advantage of others; but first that self-surrender which is the only "uncon-ditional surrender" worth talking about, then, that maximum of hard work along with others which alone can build the walls of any city.

And even as God is the sole foundation of any lasting edifice, so Christ must be its cornerstone, or, if you like, the keystone of its every arch. And in a moment it is the blessing of Christ, truly present amongst us in His Blessed Sacrament, that we shall be asking: that Blessed Sacrament which is the very symbol and the cause of charity, unity and peace. In the ancient hymn "O Salutaris" we acknowledge that a stern fight awaits us, and we beg for hardihood never to play the coward; and in that other hymn, the "Tantum Ergo," we confess that there has been a past which must yield place to a future infinitely better—but one which can be insured only if the Lord of Truth and Love and Life is building it by our hands, here upon our earth, though its towers shall reach high as heaven. Amen.

Tell the Vision to No Man

THE REVEREND FREDERICK EPPLING REINARTZ, D.D.

*A Minister of the United Lutheran Church and Secretary
of the United Lutheran Church in America, New York City*

*Dr. Reinartz is a warm-hearted individual who can look very stern at times
but there is no coldness in him. In fact, there is a good deal of the poet in
him and he is a sharp observer of life, sometimes a vice as well as a virtue.
He is much beloved as a preacher throughout the United Lutheran Church.*

*He is the great-nephew of the first Lutheran missionary to Borneo, the
martyred Johannes Huppertz, and great-nephew of the leader (Sister Elizabeth Huppertz) of the first four Protestant deaconesses to come to America
(1849), and who founded with Dr. V. A. Passavant that same year, America's
first general Protestant hospital, i.e., Passavant Hospital, Pittsburgh, Pennsylvania. Born in 1901 in East Liverpool, Ohio, he attended school there,
then went to Gettysburg College, was composer of the Gettysburg College
Alma Mater Song, and captain of the college track team. At Harvard University he held a graduate fellowship, 1924-25, and was graduated from
Lutheran Theological Seminary, Philadelphia, Pennsylvania. Gettysburg
and Wagner Memorial colleges have conferred the honorary D.D. upon him
in recognition of his work.*

*He was ordained by the Evangelical Lutheran Ministerium of Penn-
sylvania and Adjacent States, June 5, 1929, in St. John's Church, Scranton,
Pennsylvania, and was Graduate Fellow and Instructor in New Testament
Greek at Lutheran Theological Seminary, Philadelphia. In 1930 he suc-
ceeded his father as pastor of St. John's Evangelical Lutheran Church, East
Liverpool, Ohio, until 1938. Jointly, father and son served the congregation
for fifty-two years. 1938-45, he was First Secretary for Promotion in the
United Lutheran Church in America with headquarters in Philadelphia,
Pennsylvania. 1945-46, pastor, The Evangelical Lutheran Church of the
Holy Trinity, New York City, succeeding Dr. Paul E. Scherer. In 1947 he
was elected Secretary of the United Lutheran Church in America, helping,
with Dr. Fry, to direct the work of 4144 churches. His general church activities include being a Member, 1936-42, Board of Foreign Missions of the
Lutheran Church in America, member, 1935-45 Board of Directors, Lutheran
Theological Seminary, Philadelphia, Secretary, ULCA Committee of Executive Secretaries, 1939-45, Staff, The Lutheran, 1939-45, Chairman, ULCA
commission to Federal Council of Churches, 1942-. Member, Advisory and
Executive Committees, Federal Council of Churches, 1944-, Member, Church*

World Service, Promotion Division, 1946-, Member, Board of Directors, Wagner Memorial College, 1946-.

His love of children and his interest in ecumenical matters is very real. His most absorbing hobby is music. He has done a little composing.

This sermon is typical of his preaching, showing a penetrating analysis, excellent word choice, spiritual insight and vision.

Sermon Seven

OPENING PRAYER: O God, Whose Word is a light making bright our path to Thee: Open our minds to understand, our hearts to love, our memories to cherish, and our lives to show forth, Thy blessed Word borne to us this day; through Jesus Christ, our Lord.

TEXT: And after six days Jesus taketh Peter, James, and John his brother, and bringeth them up into an high mountain apart, And was transfigured before them: and his face did shine as the sun, and his raiment was white as the light. . . . And as they came down from the mountain, Jesus charged them, saying, Tell the vision to no man. . . .   MATTHEW 17:1,2,9.

THAT was high drama on the holy mount. The white light of God broke into man's abysmal darkness. That heightened the power of the divine action for the choice little executive committee of Jesus' apostolic band, Peter, James and John. Their eyes had seen and their ears had heard what no other human senses had ever received. At midnight they had seen the dawn of deity. Into the dead vast and middle of the silent night had come the voice of God. Roll into one sum the blinding brightness of all other visions which have been given to our human kind and their total will pale utterly by comparison with the vision of the Sun of Righteousness seen in unclouded glory that fateful night.

But even that matchless light faded. Soon the vision incomparable was nowhere to be found but on the sensitive photographic plates of the memories of three men. The light of God had deeply etched it there.

Now what to do with this vision? Peter was not asking himself that question. He knew what to do with it. He was probably framing tart, racy sentences with which he would make covetous those who had not shared his vision. The poetry of it all was doubtless singing itself into majestic verse within the soul of John. Bold, blasting descriptions were being marshaled in the mind of James, that other son of thunder. Each was readying himself to do the natural thing with this vision; tell of it to everyman. Tell it! Tell it quickly! Tell it all! These were demands of their unrestrained human nature.

With one crisp and direct mandate Jesus threw a dam across the onrushing torrent of their eagerness. One command suddenly stopped the headlong drive of their desire to make eyes out of the ears of their listeners so that they too might see the transfigured Jesus. Lips atremble with awe and wonder were suddenly sealed. With authority absolute and final Jesus commanded, *"Tell the vision to no man.* Lock it into the deepest depths of your soul. Treasure it. Hoard it in your hearts. Hide it where none can see or hear it. Surround it with sacred and sublime silence. *Tell the vision to no man."*

This was not an isolated instance of Jesus' making such a demand. Repeatedly, when he let the power of his deity shine through in a work of wonder, he insisted, "See thou tell no man!" But the walky-talky human spirit could not bear it. Ever and again the Gospel writers go on to comment, "And the more he charged them, so much the more, a great deal they published it."

It is fair to ask, "Why were such restrictions spoken by Jesus? Why would he who advocated so constantly the free and loving exchange and sharing of life insist concerning some of its most glowing experiences that they should be kept a solemn secret?"

Well, there were obvious historical reasons for his insisting that the vision of the Mount of Transfiguration should not be told. He did not want his hand forced more rapidly. The march toward Calvary was already at double time. For his disciples openly to declare his deity would have caused the fashioning of a cross straightway. The scribes who were never so happy as when they found a fresh incitement to vain disputation would have seized upon the vision. Confounding it would have given them fierce delight. "Was not Elias to come before the Messiah appeared?" they would contend. Then, too, Jesus understood that the vision would be more generally credible, and could be presented with more confirming power after his resurrection. He also knew that the encouragement and energizing light of this vision would be needed in the dark and demanding hours which lay in the tomorrows of these choice friends of his.

But there were subtler, less obvious reasons for his breaking the circuit. "Tell the vision to no man." How right that is! Visions are precious. Like angel visits, they are few and far between. Visions are not to be cheaply trafficked in or bartered. In another setting the Master put this stabbingly when he said, "Give not that which is holy unto the dogs, neither cast your pearls before swine, lest they trample them under their feet, and turn again and rend you."

And of course visions are for those who are prepared for them. Any talk of them to the unprepared is hocus-pocus. Nothing is accomplished but the lessening of the power of the vision for him who tries to tell it. Robert Browning makes Saul Paul say concerning his vision:

Oh, could I tell, you surely would believe it.
Oh, could I show what I myself have seen.
How can I tell, and how can you receive it,
How till he bringeth you where I myself have been?

But mainly, visions are dissipated by overmuch talk about them. Like rose bushes, they cannot stand much exposing of their roots. And visions, like electrical energy, must be passed through insulated wires, so that when they are called upon to deliver light and power they will not have been dissipated in sputtery, flashy short circuits. These sometimes blow fuses and cut off all power.

A Chinese religious leader was once asked to make an appraisal of Christianity in North America. His ready answer was, "Well, it's a talky religion." Our Lord knew that when high emotion is under sure control it is never wordy.

Something of Jesus' meaning is suggested by an experience most of us have had. You have come under the spell of a commanding inspiration. It has been soulful music, overawing scenery, or an inspiring address which has taken you, as you say, "out of this world." You rush home from a symphony concert, your winged feet spurning the earth beneath them. You dash into the living room. There sits friend husband sunk into the deepest comforts of his favorite chair. His slippered feet are supported by the yielding upholstery of a hassock. His favorite sports page is before him, and the light from the reading lamp falls on it from exactly the right angle. Your vision bursts from you in excited words. "Oh, John, John, John!, the music tonight! It was heavenly! Beethoven's Fifth. I'm in a cloud! I just can't come down to earth."

The man of the house reluctantly bends down the top half of his paper, looks at you with mild amazement, the sort that has no understanding in it, and says, "Yeah, yeah, dear, glad you liked it. Careful you don't trip over the golf bag I left on the first landing as you go upstairs."

"Well!" you say to yourself as, completely deflated, you let yourself down into the nearest chair. "If I can't pass on my inspiration any better than that, maybe it wasn't so impressive after all." You begin to hate the words that failed you so painfully when you wanted to sing out the music of your soul.

My own mother learned the truth of this text the hard way. She was a Lutheran pastor's wife who, with glad abandon, gave gifts from the storehouse of her richly furnished soul. She gave them to her seven children, to her husband, her intimate friends, and to large circles of Christian associates in the organizations of our home congregation and community. For her to live was to give. In middle life she gradually began to sense that her spiritual energies were diminishing. In little talks that she made, in her letter writing (which was one of her most beloved employs) and in her private counseling, she felt that checks she was drawing on the bank of her soul were bouncing back too frequently marked "Insufficient funds." She was quietly searching for the reason for the reduction of her spiritual effectiveness, when, by the happiest providence, she came across a sentence which led her to understand what Jesus meant when he said, "Tell the vision to no man." The sentence ran, "Secrecy, personal conspiracy, and intense desire used to create conscious energy—when these three combine they form a subtle principle of spiritual success." Look at those words again. "Secrecy." Keep the visions dark. Put the jewel in a precious casket, there treasure it. Standing alone with God there will come "a mystic sense of sudden quickening." "Personal conspiracy." Conspire against that talkative self who wants to speak about all of God's goodness as quickly as it is experienced. Battle against that person in you who is so fatally fluent. To accomplish this, our desire for success in imparting spiritual power must be *intense*. It must be life's overmastering passion, its magnificent obsession.

"Tell the vision to no man." As she began to understand the practical applications of that divine command she proceeded to deepen her prayer life, to concentrate afresh on devotional reading and to seek human contacts which would enrich her soul. The new potential of all this was caught in the reservoir far back in the hinterland of her spirit. She began to release the refreshment and power of God's disclosures with ever-increasing delicacy and care. Soon she found herself knowing afresh the blessing of those who walking through the valley of Baca make it a well. All who met her, quickly perceived that "Far off in [her] fountains God had been raining."

It is not betraying professional secrets to say that right at this point the Christian preacher experiences one of his greatest difficulties. Sunday after Sunday at a sharply appointed hour his congregation sits before him as he mounts to his pulpit. The old, the middle-aged, youth and the children look up with hungry eyes that say, "Come now, seer. Tell us what bright visions God has shown you since last we met." But the straight truth is that many a week, and many a month pass by without *any* great unearthly visions of the goodness, grace and glory of God falling into his eyes. Does a miner pan a nugget of gold daily? Does an artist paint a masterpiece every fortnight? Does a Handel write more than one Hallelujah Chorus in a lifetime? Small wonder that it must occasionally be said after sermons, "The hungry sheep looked up and were not fed"—at least not on vision. The sign celestial cannot often be on the preacher's forehead. Do not expect it.

The father of President Woodrow Wilson was a clergyman whose spiritual gifts and discernment were widely known. God made of him one of His choicest vessels. One day Dr. Wilson was in the company of some fellow pastors who were talking to one another somewhat glibly about their visions. He sat in troubled silence through it all. Finally, one of his colleagues made bold to ask him, "Dr. Wilson, haven't you had some great word from God? Haven't you experienced some ecstatic vision of God in Christ?" The widely beloved pastor let his eyes wander slowly round the circle from face to face, and then, settling his serene gaze on the countenance of the questioner, said, "No, none to speak of—none to speak of."

In a parish I served for a short period there was a girl who had gone to a summer assembly for the first time in her life. In that week her soul had come alive. She had had transfiguring experiences. God had broken through with light and beauty to her. His agents had been a deeply consecrated missionary, an inspiring teacher of teachers, and a vesper hour preacher who had made life with God equal in beauty to the sunsets which kissed into gold the lake across which she had looked as she worshipped. Reaching home after that week of intoxicating visions she came at once to the parsonage porch. The stimulation of her soul was symbolized by the rapidity and vigor with which she agitated the porch glider. All the while she was telling out her vision. She had caught new sight of herself as a Church-school teacher. She had discovered new channels to the heart of God. She was desperately determined, "Starting tomorrow!" to release the power of her vision. Her outrushing words reminded one of a huge coil spring which had been wound and wound until it was perfectly tight, then, when suddenly released, loses all its energy. I was within earshot of all this, and took occasion next morning to check up. I looked for a dedicated, disciplined, determined teacher. Instead I found her unprepared, carelessly attired, impatient—the irritations of her spirit clearly evident in a rasping voice and harsh manner. In place of sleep, quiet resolve, careful preparation and prayerful commitment she had substituted an extravagant three-hour-long throwing away of the gold of God which was in her vision. Her capacity had been lost in loquacity.

But the climax of illustration is in the biography of St. Paul. You remember how in that intimate correspondence with the church in Corinth he says, "I will come to visions and revelations of the Lord." Note how he at once hides away the connection of his own heart with those visions and revelations. Catch the anonymity in which he couches his narrative. "I knew a man in Christ," he continues, "about fourteen years ago (whether in the body I cannot tell; or whether out of the body, I cannot tell; God knoweth;) such as one caught up into the third heaven. And I know such a man (whether in the body or out of the body, I cannot tell; God knoweth;) how that he was caught up into Paradise, and heard unspeakable words, which it is not lawful for a man to utter."

So, for fourteen years, as he testified to Festus and Agrippa, he was not disobedient to that heavenly vision which he had had on the road to Damascus. With this testimony in mind, look again at his biography. How are these for chapter headings? Imprisonments, Stonings, Shipwrecks, Defections, Scourgings. Yet all these crosses lifted up his head because his mind was vision-led, and his heart love-anointed.

Now let me press the point of this truth straight home to your heart.

Has God broken through to you in some glorious, some new vision? Has He shown you more clearly than ever before His purpose for you? Has He given you a vision of your life in the light of His loving grace and favor. Then share that vision with Him only.

He may have given you a vision of yourself with that besetting sin conquered. Then silence! He may show you the vision of a cross of sorrow or pain which you must bear. Hide it in your pondering heart. He may plant in your mind the purpose to give your whole life to a Christian vocation. Put it in the secret place of the most high. He may give you a vision of some truly worthy generosity which should come from you. Keep the brightly burning beauty of it in your own soul. Don't reveal it to others. Not even your left hand should know what the vision is luring your right hand to do.

But I would be untrue to this text and to you if I did not mention that this command is followed by a little preposition. It is the word "until." The full text that reads, "Tell the vision to no man, until the Son of man be risen again from the dead."

Truly there comes a time when visions are to be shared. In the economy of God, heaven's visions are wasted on those who do not one day rise and testify of them. The hour does arrive when it is clearly our duty and joy to say, "I love the Lord because. . . ." Each of us must finish that sentence out of the memory of the mountains of transfiguration where our dust has seen His deity.

Until that day comes, I plead with you on the authority of Him who knows the power and purpose of these trysts with God, *"Tell the vision to no man."*

PRAYER:
O Christ, Who dost transfigure life for those who climb to the heights with Thee, help us to be obedient to the visions Thou dost give us, letting them infuse energy and kindle fervor within us, and lest their power be exhausted through vain and wanton words, set Thou a seal upon our lips.—Amen.

The Value of the Individual

REVEREND WILLARD L. SPERRY, D.D., D.LITT.

*Congregational Minister, and Dean of the Chapel, Harvard Divinity School,
Cambridge, Massachusetts*

Dean Sperry is respected for his insight into the problems of men of our day, for his spiritual guidance of Harvard students, and for the excellence of his preaching. As dean of Harvard Divinity School and professor of practical theology he has exercised a profound influence on the theological training of hundreds of ministers in important churches all over the country. As chairman of the board of preachers to the University (college chaplain) he has drawn to Harvard many of the world's outstanding ministers for special sermons and courses of religious lectures for the last seventeen years.

The distinguished theologian was born in Peabody, Massachusetts, in 1882, was a Rhodes scholar at Oxford (first class honors in theology), studied at Yale, and has received the doctorate from Yale, Amherst, Brown, Williams, Harvard, and Boston. He served in the pastorate in Fall River and Boston, joined the faculty of Andover Theological Seminary, and has been dean of Harvard Divinity School since 1922. For four years he was also dean of the National Council on Religion in Higher Education (1927-31), has given many famous lecture series, including the Upton Lectures at Manchester College, Oxford, the Hibbert Lectures, Essex Hall Lectures, London, and the Lyman Beecher Lectures at Yale. He is a Fellow of the American Academy of Arts and Sciences and is known for several significant books, The Discipline of Liberty, Reality in Worship. The Paradox of Religion, What You Owe Your Child, Wordsworth's Anti-Climax, What We Mean by Religion, Summer Yesterdays in Maine, Rebuilding our World and Jesus Then and Now.

Dean Sperry is accustomed to distinguish between words written to be read and written to be spoken. His sermons deny themselves the leisure and literary elaboration which is found in his books. They reveal a certain bluntness and brevity in sentence style, which he thinks suited to the spoken word, and to the school and college groups to which he habitually speaks. This sermon was preached at Harvard April 11, 1948, and shows his understanding of people, of life and faith.

Sermon Eight

TEXT: Are not two sparrows sold for a farthing? and one of them shall not fall on the ground without your Father? Fear ye not therefore, ye are of more value than many sparrows.

MATTHEW 10:29, 31

SOME years ago at the end of a northeast storm, I was walking along the seashore with a friend. A sullen surf was still breaking on the beach. The waves piled up a drumlike roll of kelp and seaweed the whole length of the beach. Just ahead of us the pile of weed stirred, as it were on its own account. We looked down and found a bedraggled sea gull with a broken wing, a victim of the storm, washed ashore and tangled in the seaweed. In response to its piteous gaze, we disentangled the bird, took it home, tried to nurse it back to life, but to no purpose. It died in the little nest we made for it by the kitchen stove. My friend, who was by no means a conventional Christian, turned and said, "You, you who are a Christian minister and are supposed to be able to explain these matters, read me the riddle of that verse in the Gospels, 'one of them shall not fall on the ground without your Father.' "

He then went on to say that of all the statements in the Gospels this verse about the fallen sparrow was for him the hardest to believe. If he could believe that, he could believe everything else, even the most improbable miracles, without the least difficulty. In so saying he was a normal representative of the temper of our times. He had classical warrant for his doubts and difficulties in a famous letter which Thomas Huxley once wrote to Charles Kingsley. "I cannot see one shadow or tittle of evidence that the great unknown underlying the phenomena of the universe stands to us in the relation of a Father—loves us and cares for us as Christianity asserts." Those words were written more than seventy-five years ago, but the intervening years, so far from easing them, have only given them added weight. Two world wars have added the testimony of history to the evidence of biology.

I am not going to be so bold as to profess to solve this problem in half an hour. I merely venture one or two preliminary considerations. Some of our difficulty in believing that God cares for the individual arises from the fact that most of our thinking today is done in the terms of science rather than of art. For science, individual facts are of service mainly as they provide material for the deduction of general laws. Once the individual fact has served this purpose it has little further worth. The artist, on the other hand, looks at a single concrete fact and sees in it a universal meaning. Wordsworth's gaze, for instance, was always fixed upon a single tree, a single flower,

[47]

a single sheep, a single shepherd seen against the skyline of the hills of Cumberland or Westmoreland. And he said of these single facts that they could give thoughts that do often lie too deep for tears. He had not the slightest interest in general laws or abstract universals.

Furthermore, we live in a world in which the organization of life involves more and more persons in a given process. The day has passed when the owner of a little intimate New England cotton mill knew every one of his employees. The president of the modern industrial corporation sits in an office in New York and is wholly unaware of the men and women who work in his mills.

Our thought of God always has been, and presumably always must be, conditioned in part by our own mental habits. Therefore, today, we think of God as a being concerned with the general laws of his creation, and as the business manager of the universe. If we were even once to try to think of God as an artist, we might not find it so difficult to believe that he cares above all else for the concrete individual. Indeed, one great thinker of our time has gone so far as to say that individuals are probably the only thing that God does care for; that there is not the slightest proof that some single all-over process is going on for which he uses individuals and to which he sacrifices them. What other possible end than itself, he asks, does a rose serve? It is beautiful in and for itself and so far as we can see serves no end other than being what it is during its brief life. If it means that to us, it may mean that to God. He may well have made it to be just what it is, and for itself alone.

But I would point out, however, that the truths proposed by the Christian religion have never been regarded as self-explanatory or self-vindicating. We are supposed to learn their truth by putting them into operation. "He that doeth the will shall know the doctrine." That is supremely true in this instance. If we do not care for individual human beings, it will be just that much more difficult for us to understand how God can care for them.

At this point Christianity and democracy, of which after all our culture is compounded, share a common hereditary faith. Both are traditionally committed to a belief in the worth of the single individual. The one says the Sabbath was made for man, not man for the Sabbath. The other says, the state was made for man, not man for the state. It is here that we part company with all totalitarian evaluations of life. Yet the heresy of the party-of-the-other-part creeps into our thinking and affects our way of life. When we fight him, the adversary compels us to choose his weapons, and to this extent defeats us even in our victory over him.

Two words have been cropping up lately in contemporary writings concerned with modern society, even in a land like our own. The first is the word "depersonalization." It is said to represent what has been happening to each one of us. The second is the term "mass man," which is said to describe the actual structure of society. The human fact today is said to be that of the depersonalized mass man at the disposal of vast industries and great states. There is too much truth in this account of the matter for us to dismiss it as an idle or malicious charge. All of us have felt the warrant for this statement in the terms of our own experience. A man today is expendable; it sometimes seems as though he were more so than his tools or his weapons. So we all drift listlessly and helplessly into this attitude toward our own lives and the lives of others—concluding that probably no life matters very much. Should this temper prevail, that would be the end of both democracy and Christianity, no matter how long we might go on repeating the ancient hollow words of our joint hereditary faith. A godless totalitarian account of things would have conquered us.

Some years ago Georges Clemenceau, as a young man, went to visit England. After he got back to France, he said that he had met two great men in England. One of them was an English parson, Samuel Barnett, who had become the warden of Toynbee Hall, the first settlement house in the East End of London. In her biography of her husband his wife said of Barnett that all kinds of persons used to come down to the East End from London's West End, with large blueprint plans for the redemption of those dreary slums, but they never really accomplished anything. She said that her husband concluded that the only permanent good ever done in East London was done by those who were "willing to take time and trouble with individuals," and that this conviction was his own rule of life.

If one hopes to do good in the world, this is a strategic time in history to remember those words and to try to live by them. Taking time and trouble with individuals is the most costly vocation that is open to any one of us. In so far as any of us meet persons who border on greatness, they have this quality. No one knows better than they what this quality costs in time, patience, sympathy and imagination; but they are willing to pay the price for it. They are willing to pay the price because they are persuaded that the case for either democracy or Christianity, or of both together, cannot be made at any cheaper price. Let me assert again, if you are concerned to vindicate democracy and Christianity in our time you must make up your mind that you will have to "take time and trouble with individuals."

There is a theory abroad today that this kind of rugged individualism, whether given or received, is today an old-fashioned and outmoded survival of a nineteenth century culture which may have served an earlier day but now has been superseded by a more modern and a more mature interpretation of human life.

Nothing could be farther from the fact. We think that the modern pattern of mass man committed to mass production in the interest of abstract totalitarian interests is the latest and the logical conclusion of the ongoing processes of history. Whereas, in actual fact, the theory of mass man committed to mass concerns was the most primitive of all the conceptions of organized human life. It is a matter of common knowledge among anthropologists that among savage peoples the tribe was all-important. Their religious ideas and ceremonies centered about initiation into the tribe, and identification with the tribe thereafter. That was true of the religion of the Old Testament during all its earlier years. The indiv:dual, in and for himself, counted for nothing apart from the people of Israel in its totality. The Wise Man said, "The days of man are numbered, but the days of Israel are innumberable."

You heard, as a first lesson, a classic passage from the prophecy of Ezekiel. It was only after Israel had gone into captivity, had suffered in captivity, and had returned from captivity with its sober second thoughts upon this experience that a prophet ventured to say that morally and spiritually what mattered was the single individual. This was a mature rather than a primitive reflection upon long experience with human life.

Nothing is more characteristic of the life and teaching of Jesus than his aesthetic concern for single human beings, a handful of disciples, Mary and Martha in the home of Bethany, the woman by the well of Samaria, Nicodemus, his solitary visitor by night. And nothing is more characteristic of the Early Church than its instinctive concern for every single Christian who belonged to it as a member.

Think of the last chapter of Paul's epistle to the Romans. The epistle as a whole is a rather abstruse discussion of the relation of the Law to the Gospel. But at its close Paul sends not less than thirty personal greetings to members of the Church of Rome, each of whom he names by name and identifies in a brief characterization. Perhaps the loveliest reference is that to a disciple with him as he writes, who also sends greetings to his Roman fellow Christians, "Quartus a brother." We know no more of him than those three words, but those three words lift him from "the dark backward and abysm of time" and give him his immortality in history. The Gospels and the Epistles are transcripts of a very mature religious society, and mature precisely for this reason, that the dogma of mass man had been outgrown and had been superseded by a community which was prepared to vindicate in human terms the picturesque statement of Jesus about the sparrow fallen to the ground.

The leading religious journal in this country carried not long ago a statement by an American Army officer that if our bombing of Japan, with the resultant loss of thousands upon thousands of lives, saved the life of one American soldier it was fully warranted. If this statement implies that the lives of those Japanese meant nothing to God and were worth nothing in his sight, the statement may be good military strategy, but it is nevertheless religiously immature and imperfect. If one American soldier matters to God, and we stand by that affirmation, so does the life of one Japanese. If you believe that there is one God and father of us all and that because of that fact we are all brethren, you cannot have it otherwise. In want of this conviction you must go back of the seventh century B.C. to the doctrine of some tribal deity who is on your side only.

I would point out to you, therefore, that the doctrines of mass man, engaged in mass industry, and serving abstract mass causes are not the final expression of a mature religion. They are merely reversions to a primitive religion, which after centuries of costly trial and error, thoughtful men finally outgrew.

The joint causes of democracy and Christianity have not yet been lost in countries like England and America, but that cause is still far from being proved beyond all contradiction. If you really wish to give your life to proving those causes, in fact as well as in theory, you have got to be willing to pay the personal and costly price of "taking time and trouble with individuals." That is the point at which you may be a co-worker with God. Let me end with a paragraph from a letter which has just come from a friend in Europe, where the skies are overcast, "the clouds returning after the rain." The letter, though untheological, seems to me to breathe the spirit of a mature Christianity:

In these days it is good to have a fund of private and personal happiness, for there has never been a more depressing time in the history of the world. Czechoslovakia today, Finland tomorrow, and the subsequent steps clearly outlined. If it isn't as wearing as the stages before the last war, it is simply because at that time we knew what ought to be done, and the feeling of strain that came from knowing what ought to be done against a cowardly reluctance to do it. The fantastic thing is that all this is happening just a few short years after everyone was saying that it could never happen again. All this makes one cling all the more firmly to stable and worth-while personal relationships.

THE CHRISTIAN LIFE

Hope and Disenchantment

THE VERY REVEREND JOHN BAILLIE, D.D., D.LITT., S.T.D.
*Professor of Divinity, New College, Edinburgh, Scotland
and a Minister of the Church of Scotland*

The Very Reverend Professor John Baillie is one of the great theologians and preachers of our world today. His teaching and his preaching in Scotland, England, Canada and the United States have a profound influence because he has something important to say and his forthrightness and excellence of thought make his words burn their way into men's souls by their logic and by their sheer truth.

He was educated at Inverness Royal Academy, Edinburgh University, M.A., 1908; D.Litt., 1928 honorary D.D., 1930, New College, Edinburgh; Jena; and Marburg. In 1909-10 he was appointed assistant to the professor of moral philosophy at Edinburgh University; assistant to the professor of logic and metaphysics, Edinburgh; examiner in philosophy, Edinburgh University, 1917-19; assistant minister, Broughton Place Church, Edinburgh, 1912-14; served under Y.M.C.A. with British armies in France, 1915-19; professor of Christian theology, Auburn Theological Seminary, Auburn, New York; professor of systematic theology, Emmanuel College, University of Toronto, 1927-30; professor of systematic theology in Union Theological Seminary, New York, 1930-34.

His work has been recognized with the honorary doctorate from Victoria University, Toronto; Dickinson College, and Yale University. He was Ely Lecturer, Union Theological Seminary, New York, 1929; Dudleian Lecturer, Harvard University, 1931; Deems Philosophical Lecturer, New York University, 1931-32; Taylor Lecturer at Yale, 1936; and has held many other special lectureships. He has been professor of divinity at New College, Edinburgh, since 1934.

His books have depth and penetration and include The Roots of Religion in the Human Soul, 1926; The Interpretation of Religion, 1929; The Place of Jesus Christ in Modern Christianity, 1929; Our Knowledge of God, 1939; Invitation to Pilgrimage, 1942. He works hard, thinks deeply, writes constructively, rests by fishing and travel.

Hope and Disenchantment is representative of the penetrating power of his preaching.

Sermon Nine

TEXT: When they therefore were come together, they asked of him, saying, Lord, wilt thou at this time restore again the kingdom to Israel? And he said unto them, It is not for you to know the times or the seasons, which the Father hath put in his own power. But ye shall receive power after that the Holy Ghost is come upon you: and ye shall be witnesses unto me both in Jerusalem and in all Judaea, and in Samaria, and unto the uttermost parts of the earth.   ACTS 1:6-8

THE outlook of our Western nations is at present wavering in the most uncertain way between hope and despair. In the time of my youth we were all cheerful optimists who believed that everything was getting better and better all the time. Eagerly we

dipt into the future, far as human eye could see,
Saw the vision of the world, and all the wonders that would be. . . .
Till the war-drum throbb'd no longer, and the battle-flags were furled
In the Parliament of man, the Federation of the world.

And passionately we believed that

Better fifty years of Europe than a cycle of Cathay.

We regarded human history as a tale of continuous progress, and we believed that in our own twentieth century the tempo of this progress was going to be marvelously stepped up, so that the brave new world of our dreams was now very near at hand.

Today there are still many among us who cling to this belief. They are impressed by the vast increase of power which advancing science is putting into the hands of mankind, and they feel assured that mankind has sufficient good sense and sufficient good will to employ this power in the service of the highest ends. Yet there are as many or even more who now feel quite differently. It may be that our remaining Utopians are only the rear guard of the nineteenth century, representing the last flickerings of the fire that still burned so brightly in my youth. This seems to be evidenced by the fact that there are more of them among my own gray-haired contemporaries than there are in the younger generation, and more also among the intellectually second-rate than among the leaders of thought. But among the youth of our Western nations, and in the books of many of our most penetrating writers, optimism has largely given way to disenchantment. The gloomiest forebodings are now in fashion, and in many quarters a spirit of hopelessness has begun to take possession of men's minds.

In these circumstances it is well that Christians should consider what guidance their Christian religion has to give them in this whole matter of hope and despair. And this guidance is nowhere more clearly indicated than in the words I have chosen for my text. We are here told by St. Luke that when Jesus appeared to his apostles after his death, they put this question to him: "Lord, will you at this time restore the kingdom to Israel?" That was the form which hope had long taken among the Jews. They looked forward to the establishment of an independent Israelite monarchy after being delivered from the foreign yoke. The restoration of the kingdom was understood by many in a political sense, as it is among the Zionist Jews to this day. But it was always understood in a spiritual sense also; and in the teaching of the great Prophets the political aspiration had largely given way to a spiritual one. The promised king was to be no mere earthly ruler, but the Messiah sent by God for the final salvation of His people and through them of the whole world. The apostles were convinced that Jesus Christ was this promised Messiah. Their hopes had been indeed severely shaken by his cruel death on the cross, but when after three days he appeared to them again, hope rose once more so high as to prompt the question whether the Kingdom of God was not now to appear in its full glory without further delay, whether Christ was not at this time to restore the kingdom to Israel.

John Calvin writes in his commentary that this question has as many errors in it as words—*totidem errores quot verba*. He thinks the apostles were still conceiving the Kingdom of God in a political sense, and the phrasing of their question certainly gives us this impression. But even if the restoration they had in mind was no merely nationalistic one but the dawning of the era of final blessedness for all mankind, their question still showed how little they had taken to heart what their Lord had been at pains to teach them during the years of his ministry. So in the answer he now gives to them, he reminds them what that teaching was.

His answer is as follows: "It is not for you to know the times or the seasons, which the Father has kept within his own authority. But you shall receive power . . . and you shall be my witnesses. . . ." You will notice that this answer is in two parts. In the first part it is a warning against false hopes, in the second against an equally false despondency.

Let us take the two parts separately.

Jesus had again and again warned his disciples that they must not attempt to assign any date for the appearance of the promised Kingdom of God. He said he did not know the date himself. "But of that day and that hour knoweth no man, no, not the angels which are in heaven, neither the Son, but the Father only." And this he now repeats when he tells them that it is not for them to know the times and the appointed seasons, which the Father has kept within His own authority. That was the answer the first Christians got when they wanted to forecast the course of future history, and that answer is as valid for us today as it was for them long ago. It is not given to you and me to know the long-term strategy of God. He has kept that within His own authority. The final end of history is indeed assured to us. Its end is in a glorious consummation such as eye has not seen nor ear heard neither has it entered into the heart of man to conceive. The end of history will be the glory of God. But when it will come about, or in what manner, or by what stages, or if indeed at all by stages, we are not informed. Any forecasts we make are made at our own risk and peril, and the exigency in which the mind of our Western nations now finds itself is largely due to the fact that for many generations past it has been fond of taking this risk, which has now turned out to be a bad one. It has made belief in the almost automatic progress of mankind into a central article of its faith. It has been full of Utopian illusions about the promise of the future. Frequently it has been lured by promises that the Golden Age was very close at hand, just round the next turning as it were, and capable of being established, some said by swift and sudden revolution, others by a somewhat more slowly evolving legislative reform.

In one of his books Jacques Maritain expresses his amazement at discovering how much the nineteenth century, which at first sight seems to be an age of positive knowledge, was really an age of prophesying. And some-where else I recently read the remark that our own age puts the palmiest days of Ahab quite in the shade for the number of false prophets it has produced. We have for long been accustomed to laugh at those who from time to time have claimed foreknowledge of the date of the end of the world and of Christ's Second Coming. We have rightly judged them to be the victims of superstitious ignorance. Yet we ourselves have often been super-stitious in another way, putting an equally superstitious trust in the gradual evolution of human nature, in the omnipotence of science, and in the salva-tion of mankind by the advance of scientific knowledge. Therefore no less than the quaint folk who watched the skies for Christ's Second Coming, we need to be reminded that it is not for us to know the times and the seasons. We too need to be told that the time is not yet, that we are living in an evil world in which we are nevertheless called upon to do our daily duty in obedience to our Lord's command, while we wait in hope for that which is to come.

But now let us attend to the second part of Christ's answer to the apostles' question: "But ye shall receive power when the Holy Ghost has come upon you, and ye shall be witnesses unto me . . . unto the uttermost parts of the earth." I have said that the intemperate optimism in which we had so long indulged is now taking its revenge upon us. The tide of events in our own lifetimes has expelled these false hopes from the minds of large numbers of our contemporaries, and especially from the minds of the rising generation, and often leaves literally nothing in their place. The belief in inevitable progress was an ill-founded one, yet we are sad to see it disappear when it leaves men without any spiritual anchorage at all. How many young men and women in how many countries in Europe today are literally without hope? I have spoken to many of them during my visits to Germany since the end of the war. Hitler promised them his *tausend jähriges Reich,* his grand "New Order" that was to last for a thousand years. They know now how absolutely without substance that promise was, and they are left with nothing to live for, with no belief in the future, with nothing before them but dull despair. Among ourselves things are not as bad as that, but they are bad enough. There is a growing uncertainty of direction, a growing fear of the future, a growing lack of confidence and trustfulness as we face the business of living.

What we need then is to listen to the second part of Christ's answer, the part introduced by the word "But." "It is not for you to know the times and the seasons, *but* ye shall receive power . . . and ye shall be my wit-nesses. . . ." This promise of power was the promise of the descent of the Holy Spirit at Pentecost, and the rest of the chapter shows us that the promise was redeemed without delay. The disciples found that after their Lord's disappearance from their midst, they still had to go on living in the same old evil world, and today we are still living in it. They had still to

[55]

wait, and to wait indefinitely, for the glory that was to be. But they were not left in despondency. They were not left in despair. They were not left to let their hands hang idly and listlessly by their sides. On the contrary, they were filled with zest. They were filled with hope. They were filled with joy—and with faith and love. Are there any books in the world so full of hope, so full of joy, so full of faith and love as the books of the New Testament, which were written by these same men and their immediate associates? And the reason was that they had received power—the power of the Pentecostal Spirit—and that they proceeded at once to rely upon this power and to use it to the glory of God.

Now what I so often find wrong with our mind and mood today, what I find wrong with many of the books now being written by those who are influencing the mind of youth, is that they lack this New Testament sense of the power of the Spirit. It is as if, being disenchanted of our Utopian illusions, we were now ready enough to accept the first half of our Lord's sentence, but had not yet stayed to listen to the second half of it. Yet if that should be true to us, then our last state is worse than our first.

When I turn from such books as these to the New Testament, two things impress themselves upon my mind. On the one hand, the New Testament writers have their eyes wide open to the limitations of our human situation in the present evil world. They know the desperate corruption of the human heart. They know that the powers of evil are still rampant in the world about them. They cherish no illusions about human perfectibility or inevitable progress. They never confuse Christ's eternal Kingdom with the kingdoms of this world. But on the other hand, they all declare that the advent of Jesus Christ and the gift of the Spirit at Pentecost have marked the dawn of a new age, a glorious age, an age in which all sorts of things are going to be possible that were not possible before; and they enter into this new age with eagerness and confidence and with a wonderful sense of the power now at their disposal. This, they felt, was a time at which it was good to be alive. "Blessed are the eyes which see the things which ye see," Jesus had said; "For I tell you that many prophets and kings have desired to see those things which ye see, and have not seen them; and to hear those things which ye hear, and have not heard them." "The darkness is passing," writes St. John, "and the true light is already shining." "We are being transfigured from glory to glory," writes St. Paul, "therefore, if any man be in Christ, it is a new creation; old things are passed away; behold, all things are become new."

That was the temper of St. Paul as he set about to cover the whole known world on his missionary journeys. None understood better than he how corrupt was the heart of man, and how powerful the forces of evil in the world in which he had to live. None was ever further from cherishing any illusions about the forward march of mankind. But he had been given a work to do, and power to do it. And such a work too! Christ had said here: "Ye shall be my witnesses . . . unto the uttermost parts of the earth." St. Paul took that command quite literally, and believed that the power of Christ was sufficient for its accomplishment. He even seems to have believed that the whole known world might be evangelized within his own generation, the leaven of the Spirit of Christ penetrating even to the pillars of Hercules and the gates of the Western seas.

The condition of the world today is indeed not such as to justify any light-hearted Utopian expectations, yet in many respects it is a far better world than that in which the first disciples found themselves, when their Lord was taken out of their sight. The doors of Christian opportunity are far more widely open to us than they were to them. Christ had then only a few score of possible witnesses in the world, but now, apparently, he has nearly seven hundred million—for that, according to Whitaker's Almanack, is the number of people who now profess and call themselves Christians. How bright a prospect would then be ours, if we Christians of today were as ready to use the resources at our disposal as was that first brave little band, realizing as they did the power that had been given them, and showing a like eagerness in our witness! Then indeed we might be able to sing with truth:

> Uplifted are the gates of brass;
>   The bars of iron yield;
> Behold the King of Glory pass!
>   The Cross hath won the field!

The difficulties and hazards of these present postwar years are indeed great, but if they are faced with Christian faith and Christian courage, there is about them also an exhilarating quality. And it may be that those who are now young may one day look back upon them as upon a time when great things were in the making; and they may say, as Wordsworth said about another period of storm and stress:

> Bliss was it in that dawn to be alive,
>   But to be young was very heaven.

A Mighty Rock in a Weary Land

REVEREND WARNER LEANDER HALL, PH.D.

Minister, Covenant Presbyterian Church, Charlotte, North Carolina

Dr. Hall captures the thinking of busy people with his preaching, a real tribute to any minister. Born November 9, 1907, in Covington, Tennessee, he studied at Southwestern University, Memphis, Tennessee, took his B.D. at Louisville Presbyterian Seminary, and his Ph.D. at the University of Edinburgh in 1934.

He has held the pastorate of four churches: the Presbyterian Church at Leland, Mississippi, from 1934-36; Maxwell Street Presbyterian Church, Lexington, Kentucky, 1936-40; First Presbyterian Church, Tuscaloosa, Alabama, 1940-46. In 1946 he became the minister of Second Presbyterian Church (now Covenant), in Charlotte, North Carolina, one of the largest Presbyterian churches, ranking fourth in size.

He was religious emphasis speaker in about twenty southern colleges and universities, a member of the Board of Home Missions, carries other denominational responsibilities, and is president of the Charlotte Christian Council.

"A Mighty Rock in a Weary Land" is an example of Southern preaching at its best, with a fine discussion of war, peace, the parable of the Lost Son, and man's need for faith, love, and God.

Sermon Ten

TEXT: And a man shall be as an hiding place from the wind, and a covert from the tempest; as rivers of water in a dry place, as the shadow of a great rock in a weary land.   ISAIAH 32:2

THE majestic poetry of Isaiah has spoken to the hearts of men and women for twenty-six centuries with a language which captivates the imagination and clings to the memory. Few sayings of the great poet-prophet stir the imagination more than this figure of a mighty rock casting its healing shadow across a weary land.

We may not know much about the mighty rock, but we are familiar with the weary land. We should be. We live there. Ours is a weary land because of frustrated purposes and broken hopes. At fifteen minutes before eleven on November 11, an elder was speaking to his pastor. "Do you know what time it is?" he inquired. Answering himself, he said, "It is a quarter till eleven. Thirty years ago today at this very moment I was seated at a command post near the front lines in France. My commanding officer had just finished briefing us for an attack that was to take place at one o'clock that day. My assignment was a dangerous scouting mission from which I might not return. At exactly a quarter till eleven the news came to that post that the Armistice was to be signed at eleven o'clock and all fighting should cease and the war would be over. "This," he said, "was the most welcomed news I had ever received." And so it was for untold millions in the Western world. November 11 became a holy day, for it marked the end of the war to end war. The forces of righteousness had triumphed. The millenium was waiting timidly in the wings to make its triumphal entry upon the stage of history. But for one reason or another, the millennium, whose other name was Utopia, never came out on the stage. The hopes which men had nourished became increasingly anemic until they died a horrible death in the second edition of the war which was fought grimly and cynically, unblessed by any hope that things would be much better because of it. It ended not with a sound of triumph, and hope held high, but with a sigh of relief that the bloody business was done. The frustration has increased. Hopes lie even more shattered than before.

The disappointment of Wordsworth, as he watched the machinations of statesmen in his day,

> Earth is sick
> And Heaven is weary, of the hollow words
> Which States and Kingdoms utter where they talk
> Of truth and justice.

evokes from us an "Amen." MacArthur's judgment that America's leadership is jeopardized and its usefulness for peace severely limited because there is among us "an evil spirit of avarice and greed and a lust for power" would find more acceptance outside the United States than in it. The judgment of others, however, may be less biased than ours.

The land has grown weary by reason of the steady encroachment of communism upon the world. Most eyes have been fastened upon the contest in Western Europe. Two years ago one of the wisest of our observers said the danger spot was not Europe but Asia. We poured our billions into Europe and forgot our friends in Asia. Our policy toward China changed with every veering of the wind. Today we are witnessing the beginning of the end for China and are confronted with the probability that China's five hundred million people will shortly be engulfed in the Communist orbit. Who has the temerity to say that if China goes, the rest of Eastern Asia will not also? A philosophy which denies man so many of his essential freedoms and despoils him of his dignity grows despite our efforts to contain it.

Take the world as a whole and its characteristics seem to be hunger, want, fear and jealousy. Age-old-hatreds still maintain their bitterness. Its people have but one hope—a hope that the future will not be as bad as they believe it will be.

Let us now turn from the weariness of the land to the mighty rock which casts its healing shadow. What did the prophet have in mind? A permissible reading might be that Isaiah's rock was the providential love of God, the truth of God become incarnate. For those of us who are Christians, God's truth and love became incarnate in Jesus.

Let us draw near unto this rock. We discern upon its sides ancient inscriptions. On the side nearest us we read, "The earth is the Lord's and the fullness thereof." It is the words of the Christian hymn, "This is My Father's World." The world belongs to God, not to any of its inhabitants. The world was not Alexander's or Caesar's. It did not belong to Napoleon, to Mussolini or to Hitler. It does not belong to Joseph Stalin or Harry Truman. It does not belong to the Communist party, or to the National Association of Manufacturers. It belongs to God. Furthermore, God cannot be frustrated or defeated. In such a world neither evil nor the designs of evil men can ultimately triumph. To bring to us quietness and confidence, nothing can equal that fact. One hundred four years ago a traveler in one of the far places of the earth, Alexander Kinglake, told of an incident: A little while before dawn he and his men were busy saddling and loading their horses. While they were so occupied, a band of about fifty savages from adjacent caves gathered themselves together and rushed toward the party with bloodcurdling shouts. Kinglake and his men kept on with the business of saddling and loading the horses and did not so much as turn around. The quietness of the party created an undefined terror in the minds of the savages. These quiet men must be relying upon some unseen power for their defense. The cave men stopped behind a thicket. Several times they tried to lash themselves into a battle fury with their unearthly cries but when they saw their fearsome screams and shouts did not halt the deliberate tying and strapping of even one box, their shouts lost their spirit. At last the travelers rode off without hindrance. There are many things in the world today which make faces at us and which scream in our ears and would frighten us, but quietness and confidence will remove much of the terror. The Christian who knows that this is his Father's world, can face the terrors that stalk abroad at noonday and haunt us by night with a stout heart and good courage.

On the second side of the rock is another inscription, which reads, "The Lord is holy." Ours is a holy God who has built this world in keeping with His holy purpose. At the base of all life and government is God's impregnable moral law. This moral law can neither be evaded nor outwitted. Whoever or whatever violates this moral law sows the seed of its own destruction. It is difficult for us to believe that. It was difficult for the people of Isaiah's time. They believed that since they were God's chosen people, God would not only temper justice with mercy, but would tamper with justice for their sakes. He

[60]

would close His eyes to every iniquity of His chosen people. No matter how far they might wander from His righteous law, God would protect them. They believed that—until Jerusalem stood desolate with not one stone upon another. We believe that America is God's chosen nation and that no evil which we commit will cause God to turn His back upon us or send judgment upon us as He did upon Israel and Judah. We believe that no matter what we do or how we live, God will still support us. We believe the fate of this nation depends far more upon bank balances, carloadings, the fate of this or that political party than upon the moral character of its people. We seek security in planes and plans rather than in righteousness and justice. Yet God is far more concerned for the purity of His people than for their prosperity.

Not only do we think God will tamper with justice for our sakes, even as the Jews of Isaiah's time believed, we do not think there is anything seriously wrong with us. Lincoln Barnwell in an article in the *Ladies' Home Journal* entitled "God and the American People" wrote:

> America's ethical position appears far from secure today. . . . The weakness of America's position stems from the self-satisfaction of its people, who assume that they are quite as virtuous as anyone can be and love their fellowmen as much as anyone should and thus mistake their partial and incomplete achievements for absolute and unconditional success and this, in the perspective of the Bible, is sin. Religion is not a private, purely personal and painless pathway to Heaven. It is "Merely the final battle ground between God and man's self esteem." Only by acknowledging his dependence on God, therefore, can the individual American avoid the sin of regarding himself as more important than anyone else and acquire the contrition through which all enlargement of brotherhood and justice are attained.

If one side of this word is judgment for us, its other side is hope. It means that the evil designs of evil men cannot ultimately prevail. Those who would enslave the world will be frustrated. If America is ever under the judgment of God, so is Russia. Hitler proposed to reshape the world for a thousand years to come. He missed his guess by nine hundred and ninety years. If the deeds of communism be evil, they too shall pass away. This faith was perfectly expressed by a German Christian recently when she wrote, "Bolshevism is terrible. But when God has had enough, even as with the Nazis, He will lift His hand and will destroy it."

Not only do the inscriptions upon the rock proclaim that this is God's world and is a holy world, a third side bears the inscription "Love never faileth." This is even more difficult for us to believe. The power of a tank or a battleship or an atomic bomb is so obvious. It is easy for us to believe that ultimate power resides in them. Jesus' whole life and death and resurrection were a testimony to his faith in the absolute supremacy of the power of love and goodness. This to most of our hard-headed generation seems to be the depth of maudlin sentimentality. We seek security by other means. We add bomber to bomber and aircraft carrier to aircraft carrier. We multiply rifles and increase regiments. Give us, we say, the biggest stick in the world and we will have peace and security. But, if Jesus was right, we, who so proudly wave our big stick, have hold of the wrong end of it. Arnold Toynbee, who certainly knows as much history as any man in our time and who has diligently scrutinized the story of ancient civilization in the hope that some light might be shed upon our darkened way, comes forth from his monumental study with certain conclusions. One of them is that "history warns modern man that nothing fails like worldly success." In the hour when a nation grows great, extends its borders, multiplies its wealth and enhances its military position, in that same hour its doom is sealed. A second conclusion which he has drawn is that "history shows that civilizations which have depended upon military prowess to survive have fallen." A soldier's skill will not solve the problems which victory brings. What further evidence of this truth do we require than that which our daily newspapers supply us? The cause which we are now pursuing is the broad way worn smooth by the feet of other nations and societies hastening to destruction. The Marshall Plan, which is a magnificent example of intelligent good will and compassion, is in danger of being quietly dropped in favor of a gigantic rearmament program for the Western world. If this should happen, it is but another example of paranoiac predilection for suicide. We might do well to remember that the Roman Empire which crucified the man of Nazareth, whose sole defense was the power of love, faded from the scene fifteen hundred years ago. Also the kingdom of our Lord has endured twice as long as Rome and will be strong when the United States and Russia "are one with Nineveh and Tyre." To our unbelieving heart, history joins with the New Testament in whispering "Love never faileth."

Not only is this God's world based upon moral law, not only is it a world in which the only enduring creative force is love, the fourth side of this great rock bears the inscription "Except your brother be with you, ye shall not see my face." Since God did create the world, all men, white, yellow, brown and black, are His creatures. We know through Jesus that God is supremely a loving God, that no sparrow falls to the ground without His notice. We can be sure, therefore, that God cares infinitely for each of His creatures. If this be the character of the world, then those causes and efforts which make the human betterment, human emancipation and brotherliness will, under the providence of God, succeed. All efforts in a contrary direction will, at last, fail. The only bases on which an enduring society can be built are the brotherliness of men, sacrificial service to others, the bearing of one another's burdens individually, nationally and internationally.

Such an attitude, such a pattern of brotherly love is not the most noticeable characteristic of contemporary society. To be sure, there has been kindness and the bearing of one another's burdens. Perhaps it is so in larger measure than ever before. There have also been cruelty and enmity in what would appear to be an unprecedented degree. Another amazing paradox of our time.

We fail at exactly the same point that all previous generations before us have failed—there is small sense of community among us. The difference between our time and earlier ages is that this which was a costly luxury in other years is now an intolerable liability. It has already brought us to the edge of the abyss. And it is the hand of God which has brought us to so perilous a position. If this world belongs to a holy God whose nature and method is love, we ought also to love the brethren. No other method of dealing with one another will support the fabric of life, since it has been ordered by a loving Father. God spoke once through Jonah, who declared to the men of Judah who looked with hate-filled eyes at their neighbors that God loved the cruelest of the ancients, the Assyrians, and was concerned for its capital Nineveh, that great city wherein dwelt more than six score thousand people who knew not their right hand from their left. God, who so loved the unlovely, also loved their despised cousins among the surrounding tribes. God spoke again through Jesus who revealed that the judgment of God was upon those who killed the souls of men with contempt. He stretched out wide arms in his death to embrace all men with redemption. We heeded neither the word of Jonah, nor the word of Jesus. God has spoken a third time, no longer in words but in deeds. This time, even he who runs may read, "Except your brother be with you, ye shall not see my face."

Within the weariness of our land this mighty rock of the providential purpose of God, His love, His mercy, His judgment revealed in Jesus Christ our Lord, casts its healing shadow across our days. It is the responsibility of those of us who are Christians to meet the despair, the frustration, the hopelessness, the blind wandering of our generation with God's revealed truth that we and all men may find relief from our distress, purpose in our being, confidence and hope with which to face the future.

The story is told that on the southeast coast of England, high upon the bluffs, was a church whose slim spire reached almost to the clouds. A hurricane destroyed the church. The congregation, being poor, felt they could not rebuild the church, and so made arrangements to worship elsewhere. One day a representative of the British Admiralty came and inquired of the congregation when they planned to rebuild the church. When he was informed the congregation could not rebuild it, he said, "Then the British Admiralty will rebuild it for you. That spire was on all our charts. Every one of His Britannic Majesty's ships set its course by that spire." If the ships of our concern are to reach the harbor, it will be because Christians have lifted high the truth of God which has been committed into our hands. For that truth is not only the shadow of a mighty rock, it is the beacon light which guides men to the only future which is worth the striving.

Man the Enigma

THE VERY REVEREND STUART BARTON BABBAGE, PH.D.

*Dean of the Cathedral Church of St. Andrew, Sydney, Australia, and
Examining Chaplain to the Most Reverend the Archbishop of Sydney
(Church of England)*

Dr. Babbage took his studies at St. John's College and Auckland University College (March Foundation Scholar), and the University of New Zealand (First Class Honors History); King's College, London and the University of London, Ph.D., 1942; B.C.M. and Theological College, Clifton, 1937.

He was ordained deacon in 1939; ordained priest in 1940 by the Bishop of Chelmsford. He was resident tutor, Oak Hill Theological College, London 1938-39; Lecturer in Old Testament 1940-42, became curate of Haveringatte-bower, Romford, 1939-41; assistant chaplain, Trinity College, Glenalmond, 1941; chaplain R.A.F., 1942-43; R.N.Z.A.F., 1944-46. He became diocesan missioner, 1946 (Diocese of Sydney); lecturer, Moore Theological College, 1946; dean of the Cathedral Church of St. Andrew, 1947; Rural Dean Cook's River Deanery; Examining Chaplain to the Most Reverend the Archbishop of Sydney, 1947. He is joint editor of the Reformed Theological Review, 1947; president, Council of Churches, 1948; author: Hauhauism, or the Religion of Pai Marire, 1937; contributor New Bible Handbook, 1947.

This short, pithy sermon from the dean of the Cathedral Church of St. Andrew in Sydney, Australia, has a pleasant English touch, combining brevity with clarity and firm conviction, saying what it has to say, then stopping quickly.

Sermon Eleven

Text: What is man, that thou are mindful of him? or the son of man, that thou visitest him? thou madest him a little lower than the angels; thou crownedst him with glory and honour.
Hebrews 2:6-7

D URING the past decade, all of us have been horrified by the authentic accounts of sadism and brutality that have come from Europe and Asia. The systematic extermination of whole populations; the sterilization of the young; the expulsion of the aged and infirm; the murder of the innocent —all these things are a sickening revelation of human depravity and sin. After reading of such things one exclaims, "What is man, that thou art mindful of him? or the son of man, that thou visitest him?"

On the other hand, there are times when one is reminded of the inherent nobility of human nature and its capacity for heroism. One thinks of a young man like Alexander Russell, an old boy of Trinity College, Glenalmond, in Scotland, who was commissioned to a regiment in India. His ship was torpedoed in tropical waters. The lifeboats were grossly overcrowded, and there were many struggling figures in the shark-infested waters. Russell found himself in charge of a small boat crowded to the utmost capacity. Suddenly a woman in the boat saw her husband struggling in the water, and desperately she cried out to someone to save him. Without a moment's hesitation Russell dived over the side, rescued the man, and then swam away to meet certain death himself. Or again, one thinks of an immortal episode like that associated with the name of Captain Oates. On that fateful Antarctic expedition, Captain Oakes, suffering from fearful frostbite, disappeared into the blizzard to die, so that his companions, instead of being delayed by his incapacity, might have a chance of reaching safety. It is in the light of such deeds that one exclaims: "Thou madest man a little lower than the angels; thou crownest him with glory and honour."

Now, which is the true picture of human nature? Is man really a creature of sadism, lust and brutality; or is he more truly a creature of nobility and heroism? An impartial diagnosis will suggest that he is both: a strange and disconcerting compound of beast and angel; of devil and saint; of egoism and altruism; of time and eternity; of finitude and infinitude. It is a fact of experience that, on the one hand, man can, in creative activity, transcend his temporal limitations, and create a thing of beauty which is a joy forever; and, on the other hand, it is a fact of common knowledge that man can also sink to levels of perversion and depravity completely unknown in the animal world.

[65]

It is altogether too simple and superficial a diagnosis to say that man is either bad or good: the truth is that within every man, even the best, there are tragic schisms and latent contradictions. It was Dostoevski, that strange, prophetic Russian genius of the last century, who said that man was neither good nor bad, moral nor immoral, but a whirling vortex of powers and passions and possibilities, both angelic and diabolic. Isn't it true? Isn't it a fact that within all of us there are confusions and contradictions; that we know both good and evil? Dostoevski expressed it in a vivid and epigrammatic phrase when he said that in the heart of every man there is both lust and beauty, depravity and goodness, the image of Sodom and the Madonna.

But within contemporary life there are few who reckon seriously with this fatal dualism in the life of man. There are very few who think of human nature in such terms of tragic realism. For instance, there are two popular views today which compete for the allegiance of men. On the one hand, there is the optimistic view of man. The advocates of this view believe, with pathetic tenacity, in the dogma of inevitable progress and the perfectability of human nature. They blithely sing with John Addington Symonds:

> These things shall be, a loftier race
> Than ere the world hath known shall rise,
> With flame of freedom in their souls
> And light of knowledge in their eyes.

Or, again they confidently affirm: "I am master of my fate and captain of my soul." This is the Renaissance or humanist view of human nature. But it is altogether too naïve. It ignores the dark, irrational and demonic forces which dwell in the heart of every man. As T. E. Hulme said, with mordant wit, it is as if you pointed out to an old lady at a garden party that there was an escaped lion twenty yards off, and she was to reply, "Oh yes," and then quietly take another cucumber sandwich. This optimistic view is both superficial and sentimental: it affirms, with Coué, that day by day in every way we are getting better and better. Needless to say, this dogma of inevitable progress has received some severe shocks in the course of two world wars. We are reminded, in this connection, of Niebuhr's profound statement that today we live in "an ever increasing cosmos creating ever increasing possibilities of chaos."

On the other hand, there are some who surrender themselves to cynical pessimism. They regard human nature as totally corrupt and irredeemable. In the classic words of Hobbes, they believe that human nature is "solitary, poor, nasty, brutish and short," and their only hope is in the totalitarian state, Leviathan. For others, this attitude of cynical pessimism is expressed in Nihilism, that is, in blasphemous, atheistic despair.

In contrast to these doctrines of evolutionary optimism and of dyspeptic pessimism, there is the Christian doctrine with its sober realism. The Christian faith takes seriously two fundamental facts: that man is created in the image of God, and that man is a sinner. Consequently, there is a dualism, a

[66]

contradiction: on the one hand, man is a spiritual being, made for fellowship with God; but, on the other hand, man has gone astray; his nature is corrupted, his will is enfeebled, his mind warped, and he is estranged and alienated from God.

How then can man the sinner, be healed and made whole? How can he be delivered from this fatal conflict at the centre of his personality, from inner schism and contradiction, from sin and self-centeredness? Modern man is a divided and confused being: he suffers from a kind of spiritual schizophrenia. It is only too apparent in widespread neurosis and suicide. Jung has written in this connection, in *Modern Man in Search of a Soul*: that he has never been able to effect a lasting cure until his patient has rediscovered a living and creative faith in God. He admits that the problem is ultimately a spiritual one. Augustine saw this long ago, when he cried to God: "Thou hast made us for Thyself, and our hearts are restless till they find their rest in Thee." Man's true center is in God, and apart from God man is lost and lonely, a divided, frustrated being. The interesting thing is that psychologists today are echoing what prophets and theologians have long affirmed—in the words of Jeremiah: that "the heart of man is deceitful above all things, and desperately sick."

How can man attain spiritual wholeness? How can the rent in his personality be healed? Since man is a sinner he cannot save himself: salvation must come from outside himself: it must come from God. Spiritual wholeness, therefore, cannot be achieved or attained by human effort: it is a gift of God. It is dependent upon the re-creation and renewal of the heart of man by God Himself. It is dependent upon a new birth through the spirit of God. But how is a man born again? The answer is that a man is only born again as he repents of his selfishness and sin, and as he experiences God's spirit remaking and renewing him within. Repentance means a drastic change of heart and change of mind; it means a conversion, a turning around. Of course, it is not a light or easy thing to be born again. It is radical, revolutionary. It means dethroning self at the center of our being and enthroning Christ; it means becoming Christocentric instead of egocentric. It means a transformation, a regeneration, a new life, a new order of existence, lived in the power of God. C. S. Lewis has some pointed and pertinent things to say in this connection: "It may be hard for an egg to turn into a bird: it would be a jolly sight harder for it to learn to fly while remaining an egg. We're like eggs at present. And you can't go on indefinitely being just an ordinary, decent egg. We must be hatched or go bad."

Are we willing to undergo this radical experience? Are we willing to be hatched? Are we earnest in our desire to begin a new life, to experience spiritual wholeness and integration? It is a personal question. Birth is always a personal and individual thing. We are born into this world as solitary individuals, and we are also born again into the spiritual world as solitary individuals.

[67]

There is no expeditious road
To pack and label souls for God
And save them by the barrel load.

While the process of birth is an individual thing, at the same time we are born into a community. Similarly, when we are born again, we are born into the community of the Church, the family of God's children. But it begins, in the first place, as a personal individual response to God's approach to us in Christ. "Verily, verily, I say unto you," Jesus said, "except a man be born again he cannot enter into the kingdom of God." This process of being born again necessitates a radical change in our innermost being: a new center for our existence. The Chinese philosopher Lao-tse used to point out how the spokes of a cart wheel all run together toward the center, but yet do not actually converge. If they were to converge it would be impossible to have an axle running through them. It is only when there is a hole at the center of the wheel through which an axle at a different angle can be thrust, that the wheel can be utilized to any purpose. So it is with us. It is only as a gaping hole is knocked in the fast-bound circularity of our human existence that we can experience God's grace fitting us for a new order of being. It is only as God impinges on our earthbound, circumscribed and temporal existence that we can be lifted into the sphere of God's love. Otherwise, we remain self-centered and sensual.

Man, as Brunner has well said, is created by love, in love and for love. Man can only realize his true destiny when the barrier of sin is removed, and when he returns to his true center and origin which is God. The Christian faith affirms that the barrier of sin is overcome by the cross of Christ: that the blood of Jesus Christ, God's Son, cleanses us from all sin. We realize our true destiny, we find our true center, we become new men, when we repent for our sin, and believe in Christ, crucified and risen. Will we repent and believe?

The Church as a World Community

REVEREND SAMUEL McCREA CAVERT, D.D., LL.D., D.THEOL.

*A Minister of the Presbyterian Church and General Secretary of the
Federal Council of the Churches of Christ in America, New York City*

Dr. Samuel McCrea Cavert, since 1921 general secretary of the Federal Council of the Churches of Christ in America, has found his chief work in the
field of interchurch co-operation and Christian unity. Ordained as a Presbyterian minister in 1915, he served as a chaplain in World War I, 1918-19.

He joined the Federal Council's staff in 1919 as secretary of the Committee
on the War and the Religious Outlook, which carried on a series of studies
dealing with major religious problems following World War I. In 1920 he
was elected associate secretary of the Council and in 1921 became one of the
two general secretaries. Since 1930 he has been the chief executive officer.

Dr. Cavert has been a delegate to most of the great church conferences
and has made frequent trips to Europe before and after the recent World
War. In 1933 and 1935 he visited Germany to study the problems confronting the churches after the rise of Hitler. In 1942 he was the first representative of American churches to go on a mission to the Continent of Europe,
after the entrance of the United States into World War II, to initiate the
program of reconstruction and relief under the auspices of the World Council
of Churches.

He was a member of the committee which prepared the plan for the organization of the World Council in 1937 and of the Utrecht, Holland, conference
in 1938, at which its constitution was drafted. From 1938 to 1948 he served
on the Provisional Committee of the World Council. After the war he spent
nearly a year in Europe helping to complete the organization of the World
Council and was chairman of the Committee on Arrangements for its first
Assembly in 1948.

In 1946 he was appointed by the Secretary of War of the United States to
serve as Protestant liaison officer between the American Military Government
in Germany and the German Church. He was appointed by President Roosevelt as a member of the Advisory Committee on Political Refugees and also
served as a member of the governing board of the United States Committee
for the Care of European Children.

He graduated from Union College, Schenectady, did graduate work at
Columbia University, took his B.D. at Union Theological Seminary, New
York, in 1915, then spent a year in the Orient, mainly in India. Five univer-
sities have conferred the honorary doctorate on him, the Doctor of Divinity by

Lawrence College, Union College, and Yale University; the Doctor of Laws by Ohio Wesleyan University and Doctor of Theology by the University of Göttingen, Germany. He is the author of Securing Christian Leaders for Tomorrow, The Adventure of the Church, and co-editor of The Church through Half a Century; he is a member of the editorial board of Religion in Life.

This message was given to help people to grasp the significance of the World Council and the Amsterdam meeting.

Sermon Twelve

TEXT: People will come from the east and west and the north and south, and take their places in the Kingdom of God.

LUKE 13:29 (Goodspeed)

A T THE time when our Lord spoke these prophetic words the Christian community consisted of the merest handful of his followers in an obscure corner of the earth. Today the community that acknowledges Him as Lord is world-wide. It has become literally true, as a result of the missionary movement, that men come from the east and the west and from the north and the south to take their place in the Kingdom which He inaugurated. Of this world-wide Christian community the first Assembly of the World Council of Churches, held in Amsterdam, Holland, in the summer of 1948, was the most vivid symbol that has yet been seen.

It would be presumptuous to attempt any full appraisal of this recent Amsterdam Assembly of the World Council of Churches at this time. It takes time for the significance of a new development to become clear. When, for example, Orville and Wilbur Wright in 1903 kept their homemade airplane in the air for a little less than a minute, who would have guessed that within a single generation we would be flying across the oceans as calmly as we then drove by horse-and-buggy to a neighboring village? On December 17, 1903, they sent this telegram from Kitty Hawk, North Carolina, where they had gone to carry on their experiments, to their sister in Dayton, Ohio: FIRST SUSTAINED FLIGHT TODAY FIFTY-NINE SECONDS. HOME FOR CHRISTMAS. The sister took the message to a Dayton newspaper office, and the next morning a brief news item appeared under the headline, POPULAR LOCAL BICYCLE MERCHANTS WILL BE HOME FOR THE HOLIDAYS!

One thing, however, which can be said of the Amsterdam Assembly with confidence is that it was the most widely representative Christian gathering ever held in nineteen centuries of history. So far as our life on earth is concerned, it was the nearest approximation to our Lord's prophecy that men shall

[70]

come from east and west, from north and south, and take their places in the kingdom of God. Amsterdam brought together the official delegates of one hundred and fifty different denominations, from forty-four different countries —almost a cross section of the great families of Christendom, except the Roman Catholic.

The procession of delegates into the opening service on August 22, 1948, at the Nieuw Kerke, the same church in which a fortnight later Queen Juliana came to the throne of the Netherlands, was a scene of amazing diversity. This was immediately evident in the colorful variety of raiment. In a single panoramic picture, you saw the gorgeous vestments of the Eastern Orthodox of the Near East, the quaint sixteenth century ruffs of the Scandinavian Lutherans, the severe Geneva gowns of the Reformed Churches of Europe, the gaiters and aprons of the Anglican bishops, the work-a-day uniforms of the Salvation Army, the beautiful saris of the Indian women, the red fez of the Egyptians, the striking costumes of African Negroes, the academic hoods of scores of American universities, the plain sack suits of Baptists and Methodists, and many, many other types of ecclesiastical garb.

The diversity of outward appearance was matched by a multiplicity of tongues. The languages on the Day of Pentecost, as recorded in the second chapter of Acts, were nothing in comparison with Amsterdam. When the Assembly joined in one of the great universal hymns, like "A Mighty Fortress Is Our God," you could hear it in English, in German, in French, in Swedish, in Dutch and in numerous other languages. When I prayed "Our Father," my neighbor on one side began "Unser Vater," and on the other side "Notre Père," with Chinese and Indians and Greeks and Brazilians and hosts of others in various tongues joining in a common adoration. When a speaker addressed us in any one of the three official languages (English, French or German), we heard each in his own tongue, thanks to the marvelous system of simultaneous translation and radio earphones which could be tuned in to any one of the interpreters.

On a deeper level, there was a baffling variety of ecclesiastical history and tradition. There were delegates from Greek Catholic churches that could trace an unbroken continuity back to the earliest Christian centuries, and other delegates from a church as young as that in South India, formed only two years ago. At one extreme there were churches with a complicated organization and a hierarchical structure like that of the Old Catholics. At the other extreme there were the Quakers, with almost no organization at all, some of them without even a ministry. And between the two there was almost every conceivable variety of order: Episcopal, Lutheran, Presbyterian, Congregational and various modifications of the more classic types.

There were also serious differences of a cultural and psychological character. The established or state churches, like the Church of England and the Church of Sweden, were of course represented, and also those which pride themselves on being "free," like the Baptists, the Disciples and the Methodists. There was likewise a great gulf of experience due to economic backgrounds. Delegates came from capitalistic America, from socialist England and from communist-controlled Hungary and Czecho-Slovakia. The political divergencies were equally marked. Some came from countries which have been called "imperialist," like Great Britain and Holland; others from countries which not long ago were colonies, like India and Indonesia. Still others represented countries which less than four years ago were on opposite sides of the battle line, like our own nation on one side and Germany, Italy and Japan on the other. And, of course, there were representatives of all the racial strains of mankind, white, black, yellow and brown.

Yet beneath all these differences—racial, political, economic, cultural, linguistic, ecclesiastical—there was an underlying unity. This is the thing about the Assembly which all were conscious of beyond everything else. It was the profound unity that came from knowing themselves bound to each other by a common faith in Jesus Christ as Lord and Saviour and by a common devotion to him.

In addition to all the obvious diversities, there was the difference in theological outlook. It goes without saying that all of the historic doctrinal positions had their spokesmen, but there was also something more subtle and elusive which cut across them all—the difference between what, in a rough-and-ready way, you may call the European and the American perspective. Most European Christians, especially under the influence of Karl Barth, put all their emphasis on God's action in history and beyond history, while Americans put most of their emphasis on man's responsibility under God. Professor Barth even went so far as to say at Amsterdam that "the final root and ground of all our human disorder" is just the "dreadful, godless, ridiculous opinion that man is the Atlas who is destined to bear the dome of heaven on his shoulders." Although Dr. Barth did not mention the Americans as particularly susceptible to this error, he doubtless had them in mind!

It was a good thing for Europeans and Americans to be mutually exposed to each other in Amsterdam. Americans came to understand that what they had patronizingly regarded as the "otherworldliness" of Europeans is a modern counterpart of the experience of Isaiah, who, when political hopes were shattered, still "saw the Lord, high and lifted up." Some of the Europeans, on the other hand, discovered that what they had thought of as the shallow "activism" of Americans represents that other side of Isaiah's experience, when his vision of the transcendent God awakened him to a social responsibility that made him say, "Here am I, send me."

The most significant thing about the Amsterdam Assembly is that it showed, through these very differences, that the Christian Church is today actually a world-wide community. It is no longer a national or a Western institution. It is rooted in the soil of all the great countries of the globe. In such a world-wide movement countless differences are to be expected. They testify to a rich fecundity of life. The unexpected and the unforgettable thing is that there is a unity in the midst of all this diversity. The miracle is that there is a single fellowship in Christ that encircles the earth and binds separated people together at the deepest level of their lives. Amsterdam was visible evidence that

> In Christ there is no east nor west,
> In Him no south or north,
> But one great fellowship of love
> Throughout the whole wide earth.[1]

A second thing which one can surely say about Amsterdam is that it did something unprecedented in Christian history. It completed a permanent association of the churches of the world on a world-wide scale. For the first time the churches are related to one another, around the world, not merely in the form of an occasional conference, but in a continuing fellowship in an organized form for united witness and united action. We have been familiar for nearly forty years with local councils of churches and with councils for co-operation on a national scale; but now for the first time there is a world council of churches. It becomes manifest, in a way that the individual church member could hardly realize before, that the church he belongs to is more than local, and more than national—that it is a world community, not only as a vague ideal but as an organized movement. Slight though the organizational structure is, it is an existent reality. One hundred and fifty denominations have a common headquarters—located at Geneva, with branch offices in London and New York—through which to keep in touch with each other, to co-ordinate their activities and to work together along many lines.

Already the Council is carrying on a program of postwar reconstruction and relief, in which the churches of countries less hurt by the war, like America and Sweden and Switzerland, are assisting their fellow Christians in those countries which have suffered most. The Church, in spite of all its divisions, is thus showing that there is truth in St. Paul's description of it as sufficiently one body so that "if one member suffer, all suffer with it."

When at Amsterdam the resolution was adopted officially declaring that "the World Council of Churches is hereby constituted," a hush fell over the assembly. The people realized that this might prove to be an historic hour, to which they would look back as marking the time when the churches began to function more truly as one body of Christ throughout the world. Another high point at Amsterdam was the closing session, when those who had thus come together for the first time at Amsterdam sent a message to the member churches saying, "We intend to stay together."

What has taken place is not church union; the denominations do not lose their identity in a single over-all structure. But it is co-operation, not fitful and sporadic, but co-operation as a deliberate and consistent policy. Our differences all remain but we face them in a new way. We face them together.

[1] From "In Christ There Is No East nor West," *Bees in Amber* by John Oxenham. Used by permission of American Tract Society.

We face them as groups of Christians who see in other groups of Christians not rivals but allies.

In this better ecclesiastical climate a still greater unity may emerge. The late Lord Tweedsmuir used to tell about a motorist in France who, uncertain of the way, asked a peasant, "How far is it to Carcassonne?" The peasant replied "How far it is to Carcassonne I cannot say, but I do know that this is the road to Carcassonne." We do not know how far it is to the full unity of the Church for which our Lord prayed, but we may be sure that if we keep on in that direction we shall arrive at the goal.

To be realistic, one must point out that two great branches of Christendom were not included in the family circle at Amsterdam. One was the Roman Catholic, which holds tenaciously to the view that it is the only true church and that the only possibility of unity is within its fold. Another great church whose chair was not filled was the Orthodox Church of Russia. The time may come when it will decide to take its place. At present it is too supine in its relation to the state to exercise such freedom.

The great test of what the World Council means will not be in Geneva or in any other national or international headquarters, but in your parish and mine in Main Street and Middletown. In one of his pithy sentences, Gilbert Chesterton remarked: "Nothing is real until it is local." That is notably true of the Church. The crucial question is, "To what extent does the congregation of which I am a part, to what extent do I as a member of it, live and act as a part of a truly world-wide fellowship?"

A third encouraging thing about Amsterdam is that the churches of the world faced together some of the great issues which confront them all and came to as much of a common mind as is now possible. For two years prior to the Assembly, Christian scholars around the world had been carrying on a process of study centering on the general theme, "Man's disorder and God's design." The delegates at Amsterdam brought these studies to a conclusion in the reports of four sections.

The first dealt with the nature of the Church itself in God's design, analyzing the points at which different bodies of Christians agree and disagree, and indicating the points at which much further study is necessary if we are ever to have a more united Church.

The second section dealt with the evangelistic and missionary spirit and program of the Church. It was in this area that there was the largest measure of unanimity. All agreed that the basic work of the Church is its witness to the gospel of Christ in all the world.

The third section dealt with the economic and social disorder of the world: the fourth, with the political and international disorder. Here the Assembly faced the most complicated issues which are before the Church as a world community.

If one is to understand the significance of what the Amsterdam Assembly said on these subjects, he must bear in mind that it was not a group of Americans. It represented all the widely separated points of view throughout the world. It was impossible for the economic and political differences to be glossed over, if the delegates were to speak with one another frankly as Christian brethren. So John Foster Dulles, for example, spoke with great candor of the points at which the philosophy and practice of Soviet communism seems to Western Christians to be in radical conflict with Christianity. On the other hand, Professor Joseph Hromadka, of Prague, diagnosed what he felt to be the failure of the West to establish social and racial justice acceptable to a Christian conscience. At first, one wondered whether the Assembly could do anything more than repeat the futile debates of the United Nations. But there was one difference between Lake Success and Amsterdam. For at Amsterdam all had a common frame-of-reference and a common standard of judgment. They all believed the Christian gospel. However much they might differ in their appraisal of what is happening, they could agree as to the kind of society, combining both freedom and justice, which all Christians should seek.

The report of this section, drafted by men of contrasting backgrounds of experience, is in some respects different from what any group of American Christians would have written. We would have been far more appreciative of the advantages of the economic order under which we live. But Americans were a small minority at Amsterdam, about one-fourth of the delegates, so you could hardly expect an American point of view to dominate the report.

There were, of course, only a handful of delegates from communist-controlled areas. There was a substantial group of representatives of the "younger churches" of Asia and Africa. Their feeling that their countries have in the past been exploited by Western nations makes them inclined to accept a considerable part of the communist criticism of the West, even though they are unsympathetic with communism. The largest body of delegates came from countries which are now practicing a moderate degree of socialism—like Great Britain, the Scandinavian countries, France, Holland—in combination with private enterprise.

The report which emerged from this section, representing Christians of such a mixture of experience, makes a clear-cut indictment of communism on five points: its materialistic philosophy, its assumption that private property is the root of all social evils, its views of morality as only a class concept, its totalitarian control over all of man's life, even his conscience, its terroristic methods of suppressing dissent.

The report also says that the church should reject "the ideology of laissez faire capitalism." Unfortunately, this statement lends itself to easy misunderstanding. It does not repudiate capitalism as we know it, subject to many restraints through labor unions, responsible management and legislation in the interest of the common good. It is the classical *ideology* of capitalism—the theory that if everybody seeks his own self-interest, this will automatically result in the social welfare—that is rejected. There is also a warning to socialism that concentrating both economic and political power in the same center may tend toward a totalitarian state and the loss of precious personal freedoms. The main conclusion is that Christianity is not to be identified with any system of man's devising, but that Christians in every country, under whatever order they live, must hold economic and social arrangements up to the light of the Christian gospel and strive to bring them into fuller conformity with the will of God.

In dealing with international affairs the duty was laid upon the Church to teach that every national sovereignty is under the sovereignty of God and His moral law. Christians in all lands were urged to support all efforts which looked toward the development of international law and the furtherance of international co-operation.

But the ultimate hope which Amsterdam saw for world unity and peace lies in the Church itself as a world community. If it can go on becoming, more truly and more deeply, a world-wide fellowship in Christ, it can make the most basic contribution—the spirit without which no world peace is possible. For no political or economic organization can itself produce peace. There must be a great increase of mutual understanding, of caring for one another, of the sense of togetherness, among all the peoples of the earth. For lack of that spirit, the United Nations, in spite of all our hopes for it and in it, is now hardly more than a skeleton. Can these bones live? Only if the spirit of Christ can permeate them. But that spirit, as Amsterdam shows, is at work in the churches. If that spirit can go on from strength to strength the Church can, under God, become the greatest of all forces for the unity of mankind.

THE CHURCH

United Nations and Divided Churches

REVEREND EDWARD HUGHES PRUDEN, PH.D., D.D.
Minister, First Baptist Church, Washington, D. C.

Edward Hughes Pruden was born in Chase City, Virginia, was educated at the University of Richmond, the Southern Baptist Theological Seminary at Louisville, Kentucky, Yale Divinity School, and the University of Edinburgh, Scotland, from which he received his Ph.D. The University of Richmond has also conferred on him the honorary degree of Doctor of Divinity.

Dr. Pruden was pastor of First Baptist Church, Petersburg, Virginia, for five years. Then he and Mrs. Pruden went to China for a year as guest teachers in the University of Shanghai. In December, 1936, he was called to this great church in Washington.

First Baptist Church, Washington, D. C., was founded in 1802 and is the mother or grandmother of over two hundred other churches in this area. It was organized in the Treasury Building, and the Reverend William Parkinson, who was one of the four ministers present when it was constituted a church, served for two years as its minister and also as a chaplain of the House of Representatives. The first regular pastor of the church was the Reverend Obadiah Brown of Newark, New Jersey, who was called in 1807. It was through the efforts of Luther Rice, the missionary statesman, that the first Sunday school in Washington was started in this church in 1819.

During Dr. Pruden's pastorate, the membership of the church has grown from 775 to more than 2,000; the church budget from $17,000 to $110,000; and the attendance Sunday mornings from a small congregation to the necessity of having two morning services each Sunday. Plans are under way for a large new church in the near future. He has served as president of the Washington Federation of Churches; president of the District of Columbia Baptist Convention; chairman of the Board of Managers of the Chinese Community Church of Washington; member of the Board of Managers of the American Baptist Foreign Mission Society, the Board of Founders of the University of Shanghai and the University of Nanking; speaker in the National Christian Mission sponsored by the Federal Council of Churches; Washington correspondent for The Christian Century; and Sunday-school lesson writer for both the Northern and the Southern Baptist Conventions.

President Truman frequently attends this church and sets a fine example of democracy and faith by doing his churchgoing like any other American.

Dr. Pruden's sermons for children are one of his fine contributions to the faith of boys and girls as the men and women of tomorrow.

Sermon Thirteen

TEXT: I pray . . . that they may all be one. JOHN 17:20, 21

IT WILL be readily recognized that the title of this message does not set one absolute idea over against another, since the United Nations are not absolutely united and the churches are not absolutely divided. However, the churches are sufficiently divided to cause us grave concern at a time like this, and the United Nations are sufficiently united to provide a pattern of cooperative action that is worthy of serious consideration.

When it became increasingly clear that the old League of Nations could no longer inspire the imaginations of men nor provide an adequate vehicle for combining the energies of peace-loving people, the United Nations organization came into being. It was recognized from the beginning that this new title signified an even closer unity than the League had suggested, but it was never thought for a moment that any one of the nations making up the United Nations would lose its identity nor compromise its individual convictions. For instance, when the Chinese subscribed to the ideals of international co-operation, it never occurred to them that they would ever be expected to become English; nor did the Russians ever intend to become French. Each recognized that certain rights and privileges of a minor nature might have to be sacrificed in the interest of world security, but no nation was requested or required to turn its back upon its honored traditions or to soft-pedal its present ideals. To go even further, it can be honestly said that no nation which became a part of the United Nations was even expected to endorse the national ideals or form of government of any other nation, and it is certain that not one of them would have been prepared to assume responsibility for the impact of any other nation's way of life upon the future destiny of mankind. The organization simply recognized in a realistic fashion that all of the nations subscribing to the purposes outlined in the United Nations Charter possessed one very important thing in common; namely, a desire to establish the kind of peace in the earth that would commend itself to the greatest number of human beings and, therefore, would have some chance for survival. Today we are witnessing some of the problems and difficulties involved in the efforts of nations to co-operate for peace, but few persons have dared suggest that the effort is not worth while. It was to have been expected that a group of nations possessing such a diversified background would have encountered obstacles to their united program for peace, but every new organization must pass through the period of "growing pains," and any ideal worth realizing deserves the sympathetic support of all thoughtful persons.

It must be granted, too, that genuine progress has been made in Christian unity during the last one hundred years. We know from our study of American church history that in other days there were heated debates and violent controversies between men of differing theological opinions. In the state of Kentucky the followers of Alexander Campbell were in constant conflict with the Baptists over divergent religious views; and Peter Cartwright, the Methodist, argued vigorously with the Presbyterians, whose Calvinistic doctrines were horrifying to him. These controversies, however, led to no pooling of spiritual resources, nor was either side to the controversy won over by the other's arguments. In the course of time the antagonisms of various communions were replaced by a growing sense of understanding, until today there is a degree of co-operation which encourages us to hope for a more united front in the not far distant future. Today the Federal Council of the Churches of Christ in America and the World Council of Churches are doing a magnificent piece of work in giving direction and expression to the influences generated by most of the major denominations in America and throughout the world, and in many local communities the Federation of Churches is providing a united voice for a wide variety of Protestant denominations.

It is worthy of note that the unity in diversity which characterizes several of the denominations which follow a democratic form of church government might provide an admirable pattern by which all denominations could work together in closer unity. There are few indeed who would plead for a super-church, and most Christians would certainly be opposed to any authoritarian centralization of power which would deprive local congregations of that freedom of action which they now enjoy. Christians generally are interested, however, in a closer co-operation among all the disciples of Christ, and are confident that this can be accomplished without endangering either the individual liberties of men or the autonomous actions of congregations. Such a procedure would simply result in carrying to its logical conclusion in the larger fellowship of Christians the spiritual ideal which has found such fine expression within the confines of several existing denominational fellowships. In such a communion there is a definite unity of purpose acknowledged among practically all of those who make up its membership, even though there may be a wide diversity of approach and method in the administration of the program. In such a communion there is usually also a wide variety of theological interpretation, but the very nature of the denomination requires a recognition of the right of individual interpretation, as well as a refusal to require individual persons or congregations to subscribe to a fixed pattern. Such an expression of co-operation recognizes not only the fact that individuals differ as persons, but that each individual's experience with God may be unique.

Instead of looking upon this diversity of outlook and expression with embarrassment and regret, there are certain denominations which rather rejoice in such a state of affairs. It is the opinion of these communions that the fellowship is enriched by the contribution which each person and church can make to the whole of which they are simply a part. It is felt, too, that a diversity of opinion and approach maintains interest and gives color to a fellowship that otherwise might become almost hopelessly monotonous and distressingly dull. If all the children in a given family looked alike, thought alike and reacted to life's situations alike, it would be an uninteresting family. The fact that each personality can be counted upon to be distinct is in itself a guarantee of the richness of the fellowship which makes up the family group.

Someone has said that if one could get religion like a Baptist, experience it like a Methodist, pay for it like a Presbyterian, be proud of it like an Episcopalian, propagate it like an Adventist, and enjoy it like a Negro, that would be *some* religion. Such an assertion simply underscores the fact that each communion does have some specific contribution to make to the larger fellowship of which each should be a part. Any effort to submerge the distinctiveness of the various communions now making up the Body of Christ would only tend to lessen the effectiveness of the contribution which each communion could make respectively to a united Christendom. When a man and woman are united in marriage, it never occurs to either of them that he should lose the peculiar gifts which have come to him from his own family, but rather do they feel that their new relationship is going to be enriched immeasurably by that which each can contribute out of his own background and family tradition. It can also be said with equal confidence that the children of such a union will be far better prepared to make some significant contribution to the world if they are the inheritors of two rich traditions rather than being merely the recipients of what one family might have to offer.

Most of our sectarian prejudices are inherited and are inseparably related to our historical background. This is evident from the fact that there is so little sectarianism among the younger churches on the foreign mission fields, where the Christians know little of our American church history, and where they have not inherited from past generations denominational prejudices. The average Christian in China does not care whether he is a Northern or a Southern Baptist, a Dutch Reformed or a Protestant Episcopalian. Being in a country, however, where so large a portion of the population is still in bondage to the fears and superstitions of their ancestors, they *are* deeply concerned over whether or not they are sincere disciples of Christ. Most of the major denominations that work in China have devised a plan of co-operative action, and have adopted the name, The Church of Christ in China. This has been accomplished without the sacrifice of principles or the compromise of convictions, and it has resulted in giving to the scattered Christian churches a sense of strength and unity they have not known before.

It now appears entirely possible that the younger churches in the lands where our missionaries have been sent may provide for the older churches a pattern for co-operation which will constitute a vital missionary contribution to our own spiritual welfare. Just prior to the outbreak of the conflict between our nation and Japan, a Japanese government order made it obligatory that the various Christian denominations in that country, with a few rare exceptions, should come together and form the Church of Christ in Japan. This government order was looked upon with some anxiety by most of the churches affected, and some of them were utterly opposed to it; however, there were many who felt that out of this enforced co-operation there might come certain discoveries which would be of inestimable value in formulating a policy of voluntary co-operation among the Christians of other countries. It is altogether possible that this government encroachment upon Christian liberties might be another example of how God can cause the wrath of men to serve him.

To say that Christians must agree in all things before they can work together in co-operative enterprises is to presuppose an intolerance which is hardly worthy of the followers of Christ. It has already been pointed out that the various nations making up the United Nations organization work together in spite of individual differences, and also that the churches of the same denomination have learned how to pool their resources even though they differ on a great many things among themselves; so it is only natural to suppose that this same spirit of understanding, forbearance and appreciation could be exercised in the larger area of one's relationship to all the followers of Christ everywhere. It would have been practically impossible for those first disciples gathered in the Upper Room to have agreed upon a common creed. Each disciple possessed a distinct personality, and one is rather inclined to believe that Jesus selected them as a sort of cross section of humanity in general. Some of them were brothers, but they were by no means alike. Could any two men have been more unlike than Andrew and Peter? The thing that bound these dissimilar disciples together in a remarkable unity was not a common creed, but a common loyalty to the great Personality to whom they had given their allegiance. If the Christians of the world wait until they can find absolute agreement on theological dogma and church polity, they will never experience that spirit of unity for which Jesus prayed. They do have, however, at this very moment a basis for Christian unity which should be sufficient for all their needs, and that is their common devotion and loyalty to him whose name they bear.

In the tragic war through which the world has so recently passed, it was the intent of our enemies from the very beginning to divide and conquer. In the early stages of the conflict this program was rather effective, and nation after nation was isolated and smashed. Later, however, when the nations opposing the Nazis and the Fascists took a united stand and pooled their resources in the interest of justice and freedom for all mankind, the tide was turned and the threat of totalitarianism was at least temporarily overcome. If Christians wonder why they have been so ineffective in their warfare against their spiritual foes, they will undoubtedly find the answer in the fate of isolated countries during the early days of the recent great war; and if they are to achieve those triumphs for which they constantly pray, they must emulate the wisdom of those nations which united against a common foe. If the major interest of Christians is the method by which a man shall be baptized, or how congregational programs are to be administered, then our present arrangement is unquestionably correct; but if the major interest of Christians is to make the spirit of Christ operative in the hearts of men and in the councils of nations, then it would seem that we are hardly organized for that purpose.

The tragic nature of our divided Christendom was revealed at the opening session of the San Francisco Conference on world peace. Someone has explained the reason for the absence of an opening prayer at this significant meeting as follows: Since there were so many different religions represented by the delegates to the conference, the risk would have been run of showing partiality to some group if the representative of any one of them had been selected as the person to offer the prayer. However, if one should argue that since most of the nations represented had some relationship to Christianity the embarrassment could have been avoided by recognizing this fact and selecting a Christian, a further difficulty would have arisen in the fact that there

[81]

are two separate groups in the world representing the Christian faith, and a problem would have been involved if either a Catholic or a Protestant had been selected as the representatives of Christianity. Then someone suggested that this latter dilemma might have been avoided by recognizing that the conference was being held in a country where Protestant numerical strength was far superior to that possessed by the Catholics; but here again a difficulty was involved over the fact that there are so many different Protestant denominations and each would have felt neglected if a representative from that particular group had not been chosen. Finally, it was proposed that since the largest group of Protestants in the United States was the Baptist denomination, it was only natural that one of their number should be chosen for this spiritual service. To this suggestion, however, objection was made on the grounds that the Baptists are also disunited and that one would be at a loss to know whether to select a Northern or a Southern Baptist. Whether this supposed reasoning actually took place or not, one can readily discern the tragic consequences to a world Christian witness that result from our present divided nature.

It would have been rather amusing if it had not been so tragic, that while certain denominations were passing vigorous resolutions on behalf of the co-operation of nations in the interest of world peace, they were at the same time seeking to rationalize their own refusal to become more closely associated with their fellow Christians in the promotion of Christ's cause. In a certain southern state the annual Baptist Convention unanimously adopted a resolution calling upon the nations of the earth to unite in preventing future wars, and within the next hour voted down a resolution to associate itself with the State Council of Churches. Such inconsistency neither promotes the welfare of Christ's kingdom nor lends much weight to international co-operative efforts.

A prominent college president declared sometime ago that psychologists now believe that it is better for a child to be reared in a second-rate home where the parents live and work together in harmony than it is for the same child to be reared in a home with every social and material advantage in which there is disagreement and dissension. In view of this fact, one wonders how a divided Christian household can ever expect to make its supreme contribution to the countless multitudes for whom it is spiritually responsible. When Jesus offered his prayer for the unity of Christians which is recorded in the seventeenth chapter of John's Gospel, he indicated that the whole triumph of his cause depended upon the answer to that prayer, for having prayed, "that they may all be one," he added, "that the world may believe that Thou didst send me." If we honestly desire that Christ shall be taken seriously throughout the world, we must acquire the grace and wisdom sufficient for the task of recognizing and translating into action the unity we already possess.

The Next Generation Is Ours

BISHOP GERALD KENNEDY, PH.D.

Resident Bishop of the Portland Area of the Methodist
Church, Portland, Oregon

Beginning his preaching as minister of First Congregational Church, Collins-ville, Connecticut, 1932-36, Dr. Kennedy was called to become minister of Calvary Methodist Church in San Jose, California, in 1936, and went to First Methodist Church, Palo Alto, in 1940, at the same time becoming director of the Wesley Foundation at Stanford University. During 1938 to 1942 he was acting professor of homiletics at the Pacific School of Religion, and was called to be minister of St. Paul Methodist Church, Lincoln, Nebraska, in 1942. The same year he was made lecturer in religion at Nebraska Wesleyan University.

In 1948 he was elected Bishop of the Portland Area of the Methodist Church, which includes Oregon, Washington, Idaho and Alaska. His election was the first to reach across jurisdictional boundaries since the unification of the three main branches of the Methodist Church and he is the youngest bishop in this denomination. His great success as a pastor, preacher and administrator drew such favorable attention to his work that it was inevitable that he would be selected for this high office in his church.

While he was pastor of St. Paul Methodist Church, he became known as the radio preacher on The Methodist Hour in that section and as the speaker every Sunday on the voice of St. Paul's. On Wednesday evenings he gave the popular radio program, Adventures Along the Book-Shelf. He was educated at the College of the Pacific, the Pacific School of Religion, and took his Ph.D. at Hartford Theological Seminary in 1934.

He is a contributor to national religious journals and is the author of The Pause for Reflection (sermons), His Word Through Preaching (a fine handbook about preaching), The Lion and the Lamb (a study of the paradoxes of the Gospel given on the Peyton Lectureship at Southern Methodist University in 1949). He is the editor of The Best of John Henry Jowett (sermons). He has written the first of a series of books for the church to be called the "Know Your Faith" series; his volume is entitled I Believe.

Sermon Fourteen

Text: Jesus said unto . . . the young man . . . come and follow me. Matthew 19:21, 22 (arranged)

THE work of the churches with the young people of our colleges and universities is one of the great chapters in the history of the Church. Protestants and Catholics have special foundations ministering to the spiritual and social needs of students, many of them living away from home for the first time. Parents can thank God that when their young people go to college, the Church will be there.

Like any organization that works with the growing edge, the Student Movement is often under fire. We wish it would do the impossible. We would like it to succeed where other agencies have failed. We want it to make all college students as conservative as their fathers and as pious as their grandfathers. We expect it to inspire students to spend their Sundays in church. But when we look at things realistically, we see that the Christian Student Movement is doing the best that can be expected. I have always been proud to be associated with it, and I have a deep admiration for the men who lead it.

We are to think about holding students for the Church in our own day. Let us begin by trying to discover the reasons we sometimes fail.

Some students have seen the Church as a denial of the gospel. As minister of a church in a college community, I tried to hold up the greatness of the Christian Church in my preaching. It seems to me that students must believe in the Church if they are to become churchmen. Every now and again a student would ask for an interview and would say something like this: "Some churches may fit your description, but most of them do not." Then I would hear a story about the Church at its worst. Perhaps there was a small town where there should have been one Protestant church, and there were five. I heard of official boards ruled by the same little group of people for the past thirty years. There was a tale of bickering between people with Nero complexes who would rule or ruin. They told of preachers underpaid and treated with contempt. The Church to them was reactionary and they would have agreed that

> All our fathers have been Churchmen,
> Nineteen hundred years or so,
> And to every new suggestion
> They have always answered No.[1]

The Church to these students was not a leader, but a follower. It did not ask what the will of God was, but what was the will of the most influential

[1] Riverside Church Monthly, Summer, 1946.

[84]

citizens of the community. Public opinion was the climate in which it worked, and it would never think of attempting to change that climate. It seemed to have no idea of pointing the way. It was not a voice, but an echo.

The Church, in the experience of these young people, had never challenged an injustice. It sat side by side with discrimination, immorality and hatred, and raised no voice of protest. It witnessed a daily denial of the gospel of Jesus, and made excuses for it, silencing the first whisper of revolt. The Church, to these students, seemed utterly irrelevant.

An old washer woman was one of the most faithful attendants at her church, and the minister asked her the reason for her faithfulness. Was it the music? No. Was it the sermon? No. Finally, she answered that, because she had to work hard all week, it was nice to have a comfortable place to sit for an hour with nothing to think about. To our shame, we must confess that sometimes the Church is little more than that.

Another reason we fail is the preaching of an inadequate religion. It manifests itself in a kind of piosity instead of in ennobled lives. As Raymond Calkins put it, some people seem to have been starched before they were washed. There is an artificiality about their religion, as if they had been perfumed but not cleansed.

Some religion is always on the defensive and is negative. It seems to make men fearful lest some new discovery topple the whole thing over. It carries a chip on its shoulder as if the main purpose of Christianity were to pick a fight. It seems to assume that there is a body of truth which has been established and the religious man is commissioned to stand in its defense. The old Sunday-school song, "Hold the Fort," expresses its spirit. It is so busy defending that it has no energy for attack. An offensive against anything but dogma would seem indelicate to the defenders of this kind of religion.

Such Christianity expresses itself in negations. Religion seems to consist in not doing this and in not doing that. The Christian is regarded as a man who shuns some of the more obvious bad habits. Young people, especially, come to regard this religion as a conspiracy to prevent their being alive, and a brake on spontaneous joy.

Negative Christianity is a burden to be carried and an extra weight handicap in the race of life. Besides carrying a heavy bag of our sins on one shoulder, as John Bunyan's Christian did as he started his journey in *Pilgrim's Progress*, this kind of religion hoists another heavy bag of painful virtues on the other shoulder. Such faith does not carry a man, but rather he has to carry his faith. Lives become like the bulletin board of the church, reading, SUNDAY AT 11.00 A.M., FORWARD WITH CHRIST; WEDNESDAY AT 7:30, THE MIDWEEK RETREAT. Backsliding is easy when it is a matter of getting rid of a burden.

Also, this inadequate religion prefers dogmas over adventure. It looks with suspicion on any Christian experimenting, and prefers the safe, dull, dead way of established procedure. It is no wonder that this brand of Christianity has no appeal for college students. They live in a world that is new and exciting. They are having their minds stretched and their eyes are opened to vistas beyond their imaginings. They are in that period described by Wordsworth as a time when

> Bliss was it in that dawn to be alive,
> But to be young was very heaven!

That which in their experience has been nothing but a stodgy adherence to gray precepts, has no power to hold them to itself.

This is not to suggest that the Church ought to divorce itself from the past and become a part of the silly spirit which assumes that all wisdom was born with us. But if it has lost the sense of the pioneer spirit of its Lord, it has lost its power to attract youth. A layman asked a friend how the members were liking the new minister in his church. He replied: "Our new minister, sir, can answer more questions that nobody is asking than any minister we ever had." You could hardly find a better definition of an inadequate religion. It answers questions nobody is asking.

But all of this is negative. To some, it will appear entirely unfair. It used to seem so to me and I had great difficulty in being sympathetic with those who insisted that this is a description of the Church. Whether we think this is overdrawn or not, at least we need to face the truth that many people think it is a fairly accurate picture of the Church. By looking at this caricature, we may learn what we must guard against. We will also have some guidance in our search for the way to succeed, for our heritage is rich beyond compare.

The modern Christian's ignorance of the Christian heritage is appalling. He becomes so entangled in the petty things of the Church that he is unaware of its greatness. He hears one little instrument, sometimes out of tune, but he has never heard the thrilling symphony of the whole orchestra. There are laymen proud of their service clubs and their lodges, with no real appreciation for their Church. Yet the truth is that none of these other organizations would exist, nor could they continue, if it were not for the Church. By any standard of measurement, it is head and shoulders above every other institution.

This lack of understanding is not the fault of the laymen so much as the fault of preachers. We have neglected to make enough of the Christian heritage. We have assumed that people know about it. Well, they don't. Nor will our young people hear about it in school. Even scholarly historians have such a secular blindness that they hardly mention the fundamental institution of Western civilization. One of the best ways to hold our young people for the Church is to acquaint them with the epic grandeur of the Church's history. Many a young person would be saved for the Church if he knew its heroic history.

Any fair-minded person who makes a study of the relationship between our religion and our society will discover that most of the great contributions came to us directly through the Church. Nothing has made such a difference in human life as the Church. No institution has affected the lives of so many people for good, as has the Church. Let it be made clear that education is the child of the Church, and the spirit of free inquiry is the gift of Christ. Our respect for persons has been a Christian product. Children and women won justice and dignity, because the Church fought for them. After we have pointed out all the weaknesses and piled up all the failings, still we have a picture of such wonderful goodness and greatness that one cannot but feel small and mean for all the high-handed attitudes we have taken toward this fellowship.

Individuals going their own way have not made the contributions they thought they would make. Too many have been like the passenger on the Toonerville Trolley who asked the skipper if he could not go faster. "Sure I can," he answered, "but I have to stay with the car." Too many have discovered too late that, when they left the car, they were forgotten and their speed was an illusion. You might as well talk about being an American without any America, as talk about being a Christian without the Church.

Henry Ward Beecher was on a walk with his dog when a woodchuck ran across the road and down a hole. The dog dashed over to the hole and barked madly. Every time they went down the road afterwards, the dog ran to the hole and barked. He did not realize it was now a dead issue. But when we talk about the Christian heritage, we are not barking down an empty hole. We are speaking of a living issue. For the Christian tradition is an agreement between the generations to keep central in the minds of men the creative spirit of Christ. Let us know that an awareness of the Christian heritage will hold students for the Church.

We are here to proclaim the Christian message, which, if truly announced, has the power to attract youth. It is a word of judgment on the sins of men and their societies. It is realistic and utterly devastating in its insights. It does not believe that war is merely a hang-over from the jungle. It regards it as man-made and inevitable when men worship their pride instead of God. It is aware that as long as men have war in their hearts, they will have it between nations. The gospel does not cry "peace" when unrepentant selfishness leads us on the road to war.

Our message is one of criticism. Long before most men seem to know what is happening to them, Christianity pierces the camouflage of high-sounding talk and sees the threat of tyranny. When the Methodist bishops spoke out against the fascist methods of the un-American Committee, a religious periodical (not Methodist) began an editorial with these words: "The Methodists, with their usual courage, have spoken." Youth is that period when sham and pretense are especially discernible. A church that lacks the courage to warn against the dangers of militarism and witch-hunting, will, as it deserves, be regarded with contempt. A church which remembers it has been commanded to pronounce God's judgment on sin, will prove to be an inescapable magnet for the idealism of youth.

[87]

But the Christian message is also one of healing. To every person it says,

> There is a balm in Gilead,
> A balm for sin-sick souls.

And we all, young and old alike, are sin-sick souls. Long before psychoanalysis made the amazing discovery that men are full of complexes, fears and neuroses, the Christian gospel proclaimed the reality of sin. But unlike the psychoanalyst, the Christian preacher has an answer that goes to the root of the disease. We know One who can heal all our diseases, control our discontents, and make our lives a pageant of victory. Let us stop our cautious whisperings and sound the trumpets of advance. The Christian invitation is not to enter a hospital, but to enlist in an army. What we all need, but especially youth, is to become a part of Christ's cavalcade.

Stanley Jones tells about an artist watching a sunset from a little mission station in India. As the light flamed on the monsoon clouds, she exclaimed, "What a wonderful sunset, especially for such a little place." The vision of Christ does not always come from the cathedral, and the sound of his voice is not always heard in the big church. From the small place there has come to many a young man and woman the message which opened the vistas of heaven.

There is no substitute for this. All the futile attempts to make the Church a pale copy of secular entertainment is doomed to failure. All the well-meaning attempts to substitute activity for spiritual power is worse than useless. All the pale preaching that makes our message fit the secularist pattern is profitless. Let the Church proclaim God's judgment on sin, and God's healing in Christ.

Our task is before us. Americans are supposed to be activists, but a European satire says that no Americans get to heaven because they prefer to follow the sign which reads, LECTURES ABOUT HEAVEN, rather than take the road marked, TO HEAVEN. There is something of that tendency in all of us. We spend so much time arriving at definitions that we are too exhausted to act. We stay on the periphery instead of getting into the center of things.

The Church often assumes that it is placed here to pick up the broken lives of men smashed by a ruthless society. It assumes that its task is to marry, bury and baptize, but never to get its hands soiled by attacking the forces which make a profit out of human lives. The Church which does not act does not live. The Church unaware of its power to change things is a mere shadow of what it ought to be.

The early Church Fathers referred to the Church as "an extension of the Incarnation." That is a great phrase, for it assumes that what Jesus did in the first century, the Church is to do in every century. This is to say, the Church must be an action—a demonstration. It ought to exert a constant pressure on evil, and every local church should be engaged in one or more specific projects to make the community better. May we be redeemed from the belief that our first goal is to stand as a symbol of tolerance. We need to remember that life gets better when somebody says, "I won't put up with this any longer."

In 1906, the Kaiser of Germany and the Emperor of Russia held a secret meeting on a yacht off the coast of Finland. Germany was the most powerful country in Europe, with a mighty army and a science harnessed for military purposes. Russia had unlimited resources and a great land mass which could not be invaded. She had a tremendous population of docile peasants. Among the notes of that historic meeting, there was found this statement: "The next generation is ours." But the time came when Kaiser Wilhelm was an exile from his own country. On one terrible day the Russian Emperor and his family died in bloody slaughter. The next generation was not theirs.

The Church is that institution which believes that the next generation, and every generation, is God's. We must tell the story of our heritage; we must proclaim our message; we must demonstrate a way of life, based on that mighty faith. Thus shall the Church hold young people for itself, and lead them and the world into the kingdom of our God.

EVANGELISTIC PREACHING

Perpetual Progress

REVEREND CLOVIS GILLHAM CHAPPELL, D.D., LITT.D.

Minister, First Methodist Church, Charlotte, North Carolina

Clovis Chappell is a popular preacher all through the South. His sermons, articles and speeches are in great demand. He is himself a Southerner, was born in Flatwood, Tennessee, in 1882, attended the Webb School at Bell Buckle, Tennessee, Duke University and Harvard University.

Ordained in the Methodist Church in 1908, he was pastor at Polytechnic and Gatesville, Texas, then went to Epworth Methodist Church, Oklahoma City, Oklahoma; Highland Park Church, Dallas, Texas, Mount Vernon Place Church, Washington, D. C.; First Methodist Church, Memphis, Tennessee, First Methodist Church, Houston, Texas, First Methodist Church, Birmingham, Alabama, 1932-36; St. Luke's Church, Oklahoma City in 1936, and is at present minister of First Methodist Church, Charlotte, North Carolina. He has built his churches and church attendance by faithful parish visiting and by preaching that attracts full congregations Sunday after Sunday all through the year.

He has written twenty or thirty books, among which are The Village Tragedy, Sermons on Bible Characters, Sermons on New Testament Char-

acters, Home Folks, Familiar Failures, Christ and the New Woman, The Sermon on the Mount, Sermons from the Miracles, The Road to Certainty, Faces about the Cross. *His sermons are popular with the readers of* The Pulpit Digest *and other publications where they appear from time to time. Duke University and Centenary College conferred the honorary D.D. upon him in 1920; Birmingham-Southern College the Litt.D. in 1936.*

This sermon illustrates his homely, simple, conversational style so well liked by Southern people.

Sermon Fifteen

TEXT: This one thing I do, forgetting those things which are behind, and reaching forth unto those things which are before, I press toward the mark for the prize. PHILIPPIANS 3:13, 14

THIS text is autobiographical. It flashes a flood of light upon the face of one of the greatest men that ever set foot upon this planet. He was a man who lived so richly and so beautifully, so joyously and helpfully that to come into his presence to this day is to be made at once glad and wistful. His life was a thrilling spiritual progress. He knew the joy of going on; the gladness of constantly climbing toward his goal.

What is his secret?

He was a man of one purpose. "This one thing I do." However weak you may be by nature if your life becomes unified, it becomes strong. There is enough heat in an acre of sunshine when focused to blast a stone as if it were powder. The strong men are the men who can say, "This one thing I do." That gives strength even to weakness.

On the other hand, even great strength becomes weakness if it has no fixed goal. Coleridge had a genius almost equal to that of Shakespeare. He planned enough books to have filled a library, yet all he left was a few glittering fragments. He could never say, "This one thing I do." However fast your car, if you do not know where you are going, you can never get anywhere. But any sort of jalopy may help if you know your goal.

Years ago this advertisement appeared in a sportsman's magazine: "Send us one dollar and we will tell you how to keep any gun from scattering shot." A certain farmer who had a gun that would put a shot in every plank on the side of his barn, sent in his dollar. In due time he received his answer. It was this: "Put one shot in your gun." This man may have felt himself cheated but he was not. The first step in living at once powerfully and joyfully is to load life with one purpose.

Not only did Paul have one purpose, but it was a worthy purpose. That is of supreme importance. You are selling your life day by day for something. What are you seeking to buy with it? You remember the young man in *Santa Claus' Partner* who determined to be worth a million dollars. When a friend asked him why, he did not say that he was bent on this wealth in order the better to serve his generation. He said rather, "I want a million so I can tell the other fellow to go to hell." What a shabby purpose!

Years ago a group of boys stood on the banks of the Tennessee river when it was at flood. They watched a spent rabbit that had been forced out of its burrow, swim and take refuge on a lumber stack several hundred feet from shore. One of the boys said to his companions, "I am going out there and catch that rabbit." So he got into his canoe, made his way to the lumber stack, caught the rabbit, struck its head against a plank and put his prize in the pocket of his overalls. On the way back he struck a crosscurrent, his boat capsized, and he was drowned. When they found his body three days later, one of the boys who had witnessed the tragedy drew the dead rabbit from his pocket, held it up and said, "This is what he gave his life for." Well, whether you sell out for a million or for a dead rabbit, both are too cheap.

It was just this spending so much for so little that amazed the Prophet Isaiah, while it broke his heart. He could not look on and keep silent. So he confronted the people of his day, as he does those of our day, flinging at them this question, "Why do you spend money for that which is not bread and your labor for that which satisfieth not?" He saw that they were spending their all for prizes that were unworthy. Paul had a purpose that was worthy.

What was this purpose? He was seeking to lay hold of that for which he had been laid hold of by Christ Jesus. He was seeking to live his life according to the plan of God. That is a purpose that is really worthwhile. To choose the will of God before all else is always to live grandly. We all ought to make that choice in the realization that what God chooses for us is far, far better than anything that we can possibly choose for ourselves. To make a lesser choice is surely to allow ourselves to be cheated.

> I bargained with life for a penny,
> And life would give me no more,
> However I begged at evening
> When I counted my sorry store.
>
> For life is a just employer,
> It gives us what we ask,
> But once we have set the wages
> Then we must bear the task.
>
> I worked for a menial hire,
> Only to learn dismayed
> That whatever I had asked of life,
> Life would have gladly paid.[1]

[1] "My Wage," from *The Door of Dreams* by Jessie B. Rittenhouse. Used by permission of Houghton Mifflin Company.

Not only did Paul have one purpose and that a worthy purpose, but he went about attaining that purpose in the wisest possible fashion. He determined that he would throw away, would forget everything that hindered him in attaining his high purpose. He determined that he would keep those things and only those that helped him in the realization of his purpose. That is, he did what Jesus is constantly calling us to do. He put first things first.

While there are things of yesterday that we ought to keep, there are others that we must throw away or be heavily handicapped.

If you propose to make progress in your Christian life, make a habit of throwing away the petty slights, even the injuries that come your way. Two people may walk through the same garden but with vastly different results: One will gather a handful of flowers, the other a handful of nettles. I am thinking of a young woman who used to live in our home. She was not a stamp collector, but she was a diligent collector of slights. Almost every day she came home from work with a new one that she seemed to keep as if it were a treasure. Therefore, she had a growing number of enemies, a lessening number of friends, and a constant increase of wretchedness.

We ought to throw away our slights because, if we keep them, they will make us angry. If we keep our anger, it is likely to harden into hate. That is the reason Paul urged, "Let not the sun go down on your wrath." Brood over your wrongs and you will come to hate the one who has wronged you. And just in proportion as you harbor hate, in that proportion do you harbor hell.

Throw away your mistakes. Some of you are perhaps thinking with bitterness of some blunder you have made. You keep looking back at it. That only spells weakness and wretchedness. When you pass through a gate, the only sensible thing to do is to shut it. More than thirty years ago, in the course of a sermon, I undertook to quote a poem which I forgot. For at least a year after that whenever I started to quote anything, I would have to fight with terror as I said to myself, "What if I should forget again?" If I had kept looking at that failure, I would soon have thrown away my power to remember.

What is more important, turn your back not simply upon your failures, but upon your sins. We all have soiled chapters in our lives of which we are rightly ashamed. Maybe you have been guilty of doing somebody an ugly wrong. Right the wrong if you can. If you cannot, forget it. We have a right to forget our sins when we accept the forgiveness of God because He Himself forgets them. There is only one something about you and me that God ever forgets—that is our sin. "I will forgive their iniquities and their sins will I remember no more." Bear in mind that remorse may be as ruinous and as damning as hardness of heart. The only help for any of us is to accept God's forgiveness and forget the sins of our yesterdays. When God forgives you, be wise enough to forgive yourself.

"But," you ask, "how can I do that? I have tried to forget, God knows I have, but I cannot." But the truth is, you can. How?

There is a so-called remedy that will not work. You cannot forget by merely clenching your fists and squaring your jaw. When I was a boy, a man of outstanding ability came to take charge of our village school. The most blind of us could see that he was equipped for a far superior place. Why was he there? One day I overheard him talking to my father and he said desperately, "You wonder why I am here, Mr. Chappell. I am here because there is something in my life that I have to forget. I must forget." But in his effort to forget, he lost his mind and the last time I saw him he was being taken away to an institution for the insane.

There is only one remedy that results in a cure—we can forget the past only by fixing our attention upon the future. We cannot make our minds a vacuum, but we can forget one thing by remembering another. How did you forget your first love affair, if you can remember back that far? It was not by determining to forget, but by falling in love with somebody else.

You remember how Silas Marner, broken of heart, gave himself to the love of gold. He used to come home at night to run his fingers through his golden hoard and fairly worship it. But by and by he lost that hard and hardening love altogether. How did it come about? "The gold was stolen," you answer. No, that was no cure. He loved his gold as much after he had lost it as he did before, even more. Here is how he was cured.

One evening he came home to see something that sparkled in the firelight. Thinking that it was his gold come back again, he hurried forward to run his miserly fingers through it and to hear once more its metallic music. But he found that what looked like gold were the silken tresses of a little girl who was sleeping by the warmth of his fire. This girl grew into his heart little by little and so filled that heart with a tender, human love that the old love was crowded out. We are to forget these things that are behind by fixing our gaze upon those that are ahead.

"But what," you ask, "is there ahead for me? I have already run past so much. I have thrown away so many fine opportunities." That may be true, even for you who are still in life's springtime. But in spite of this, whosoever you are, and however much you have squandered, the best possible is still ahead if you will only dare to claim it.

What were some of the things that Paul kept?

When he tells us that he forgot the things that were behind, he did not mean, of course, that he forgot everything that was in the past. To forget all the things of yesterday would be a great calamity. It would also be at once impossible and immoral. There are some things that we ought not to forget.

First we ought to remember our unpaid debts. If you contracted a debt yesterday, remember that while there is such a thing as a statute of limitation in the laws of men, there is no such in the laws of God. "A promise made is a debt unpaid."

I heard of a man some time ago who was converted in a revival meeting. The next morning a friend who had heard of his high adventure met him and said, "Jim, I understand you were converted last night." "Yes," said Jim, "I was converted." "Well," continued his friend, "I suppose that now you will pay me that twenty-five dollars you owe me." "No," said Jim, "the Lord forgave me of that along with my other sins." But God does not do business that way.

We need, therefore, to remember our unpaid debts in terms of money, also our unpaid debts in terms of obligations—our vows taken, our promises made. There are those who feel that they have a right to break up their marriage and forget their solemn vows any time they desire. Others seem to think that the vows they made to God when they joined the Church can be set aside when they leave the home Church. But you cannot get rid of an obligation by merely pushing it aside.

Do not throw away the kindness that have been shown you. If somebody has stretched a hand to you when you were about to sink; if somebody has sent you some lovely flowers when you felt yourself forgotten; if somebody has written a love letter that put a new sparkle in your eye, don't throw these treasures away. Keep them and let them make your heart tender, not only toward those who have been thoughtful of you, but toward others who need such help as you have received.

Do not forget the wounds you have inflicted that you might heal. I daresay I am speaking to some who will never find peace with God until they make right certain wrongs against their fellows. There is an apology that you ought to make; a tear of your own causing that you ought to dry. There is such a requirement as restitution. To be a Christian is not only to stop tearing your neighbor's fence down, it is to build back the panels that you have torn down if such is within your power. Remember that you cannot cover up filth with snow and make God call it white.

Finally, do not forget the mercies of God. Paul was constantly rejoicing in the kindnesses of his friends. He was constantly thrilled by the memory of the mercies of God. We find him in many trying situations. Sometimes he is in prison; sometimes he is without his books; sometimes he is without enough clothing to keep him warm. But however hard his circumstances, we never find him without his song of thanksgiving. Paul kept green the memory of the kindnesses of men and of the mercies of God.

Look then at some of the priceless treasures that are ahead for everyone of us.

God is ahead. We have not run past Him yet. We may have run past many privileges and many opportunities. Granted. But we still have not run past the eternal God in "whose hand our breath is and whose are all our ways." It is said that when the old geographers used to draw their maps, they would picture the known world, then out beyond its borders there would be wide stretches where such entries as these were made: "Here be demons. Here be dragons that devour man."

But the author of the 139th Psalm had a far sunnier reading of the riddle. He said, "Out in the unknown is God." Here is his confession of faith:

"Whither shall I go from thy Spirit or whither shall I flee from thy presence? If I ascend up into heaven, thou art there. If I make my bed in hell, behold, thou art there. If I take the wings of the morning, and dwell in the uttermost parts of the sea; even there shall thy hand lead me and thy right hand shall hold me."

You, my young friends, are going out to futures that will not be easy. You will have to contend with many a demon and many a dragon. In the face of these difficulties and dangers you may be tempted to play the coward. You may whine with Hamlet:

> The world is out of joint, O cursed spite,
> That I was ever born to set it right.

But if you face your tomorrow with faith in God, you will find His grace sufficient. He will steady you by enabling you to say, "Because He is at my right hand I shall not be moved." Remember always that God is still ahead.

Eternity is ahead. That is true for all of us regardless of how few or how many birthdays we may have had. That is a fact we need to keep in mind every day that we live. Always, however old we grow, we have still a whole eternity ahead. We are destined to live as long as God. Whether this fact means heaven or hell depends upon what kind of folks we are. Some of us are perhaps not finding it easy to live with ourselves even now. It is going to grow harder with the passing of the years unless we face in a different direction.

> I have to live with myself and so,
> I ought to be fit for myself to know.

Now, because God is ahead, because eternity is ahead, perfection is also ahead. However little progress we have made, we still have the privilege of becoming increasingly Christlike; both in the life that now is, and as we climb one Alpine height after another with him in eternity. "We know that when he shall appear, we shall be like him for we shall see him as he is." Therefore, the wisest decision that we can possibly make on this, our Commencement Day, is to join with this fine word of Paul our very own: "Forgetting those things which are behind and reaching forth unto those things which are before, I press toward the mark for the prize."

The Power of His Resurrection

REVEREND JAMES S. STEWART, D.D.

*Professor of New Testament, New College, Edinburgh and formerly
Minister, North Morningside Church (Church of Scotland)
Edinburgh, Scotland*

James Stewart's great preaching gift is one of the spiritual treasures of Scotland today. Men and women find faith in Christ at the altar when Stewart preaches! "Stewart of Morningside" is able to preach and also to teach other ministers how to preach with more effectiveness.

In his church in Edinburgh he was so successful that men thronged to church even on Sunday nights. It was worth a pilgrimage to his city to hear him. As he enlarged his work at New College to impart his preaching secrets and plans to others, he joined a long line of great men who have made New College trained men world famous.

His books have enriched our contemporary religious literature: A Man in Christ (the vital elements of St. Paul's religion), The Life and Teaching of Jesus Christ, The Gates of New Life, The Strong Name. His latest book, Heralds of God, is a study of preaching and practical advice to preachers. Those who read the book will find part of the secret of his great success in preaching.

There is something of the profound, a deep spiritual insight, and a persuasiveness in all his sermons. The sermon given here was chosen for its inspiring interpretation of the meaning of Christ's Resurrection. All of James Stewart's preaching brings the Gospel near men's hearts and shows God's redemptive love and Christ as the hope of the whole earth. This sermon was preached at St. George's West Church, Edinburgh, on Easter Sunday, 1948. His preaching is popular in America as well as in England and Scotland and he had promised at the time this sermon was selected to visit America during 1949 for a series of preaching and speaking engagements.

Sermon Sixteen

TEXT: Now the God of peace, that brought again from the dead our Lord Jesus, that great Shepherd of the sheep, through the blood of the everlasting covenant, make you perfect in every good work to do His will, working in you that which is well pleasing in His sight, through Jesus Christ; to whom be glory for ever and ever. HEBREWS 13:20, 21

THE most characteristic word of the Christian religion is the word Resurrection. If you had to choose one word to gather up and focus and express the very essence of the faith, would this not have to be your choice?

For this is what Christianity essentially is: a religion of Resurrection. This is what every worshiping congregation is intended in the purpose of God to be: a community of the Resurrection. And this is what the Gospel offers today to this dark and ruined world, where men peering into the future are daunted by the well-nigh impossible task of creating order out of chaos and life out of death: the power of Resurrection. In short, this is the essential Gospel. Rejoice that the Lord is arisen!

It is true, of course, that for us Christians the cross must ever stand at the very heart of things. If we bungling, sinful creatures lose sight of the cross even for a day, we are done for—and we know it. But a man may gaze at the cross, and miss the Gospel that saves—for he is still on the wrong side of Easter. This is Christianity's symbol—not the dead figure of the crucifix, but Christ risen, trampling a broken cross beneath his feet: "neither is there salvation in any other."

Far too often we have regarded the Resurrection as an epilogue to the Gospel, an addendum to the scheme of salvation, a codicil to the divine last will and testament—thereby falsifying disastrously the whole emphasis of the Bible. The fact is there would never have been a New Testament at all, apart from the burning certainty of all its writers that He whose mighty deeds they were recording had conquered death and was alive for ever. This was no mere appendix to the faith: this was, this is, the faith—the overpowering, magnificent good news. Rejoice that the Lord is arisen!

There is no darkness which does not illuminate, no despair this does not smite with sudden hope. Test it and see.

For example, many in these tense, tumultuous days are trembling for the ark of God, haunted by the fear that the powers of darkness may ultimately defeat the dreams for which Christ died. Many are paralyzed by that terrible doubt. But Easter means that God has already taken the measure of the evil forces at their very worst and most malignant, that He has met the challenge precisely at that point and routed the darkness and settled the issue. Rejoice that the Lord is arisen!

Or the trouble may be more personal. Many are feeling strained and depressed and tired out, and quite inadequate for life, worried by the failure and the muddle of their own experience. But Easter means a living, radiant Christ walking at your side on the weariest Emmaus road. Rejoice that the Lord is arisen!

Or the burden of the mystery may be heavier still. It may be that some one whom you loved the best has left you and passed out of sight for ever across the river, journeying away to the country from whose bourne no traveler returns. But Easter means One *has* returned, to tell you of the glory yonder. Rejoice that the Lord is arisen!

Test it and see. Here is an evangel to scatter every darkness, and to exhilarate every broken spirit with strength and courage. This is the only Gospel the New Testament knows. He is risen indeed. O magnify the Lord with me!

Let us take one of the most moving and memorable expressions of the Easter truth ever penned. In Hebrews 13: 20, 21, we read: "Now the God of peace, that brought again from the dead our Lord Jesus, that great shepherd of the sheep, through the blood of the everlasting covenant, make you perfect in every good work to do his will, working in you that which is wellpleasing in his sight, through Jesus Christ; to whom be glory for ever and ever."

Notice particularly how the writer puts it. He says, speaking of the Resurrection—"It was God who did this thing. It was God's mighty act that brought up the Lord Jesus from the dead."

This emphasis is characteristic of all the men of the New Testament. It is immensely significant that these first Christians never preached the Resurrection simply as Jesus' escape from the grave, as the reanimation of One who had died, or as the return of the Master to his friends. They always proclaimed it as the living God in omnipotent action. It was God's hands that had taken the stone which the builders rejected, and made it the head of the corner. "This is the Lord's doing," they declared, "and it is marvellous in our eyes."

Their insight taught them that it was what lay behind the Resurrection that mattered. And what lies behind it is this—God vindicating the dreams for which Christ died, God ratifying righteousness, justice and truth against the evil powers that hate these things and seek to crush and crucify them, God announcing His invincible divine determination to make Christ Lord of all.

It is at this point that the Resurrection fact strikes right into world history as it confronts us today. This is the dramatic relevance of Easter to our own confused, bewildered age. For if the power that was strong enough to get Jesus out of the grave, mighty enough to shatter and confound the whole hideous demonic alliance of evil, creative enough to smite death with resurrection— if this power is in action still (as the basic proclamation of Christianity declares), why then, you and I can lift up our heads, knowing and rejoicing that "God is in the field when He is most invisible." He shall not fail nor be discouraged till He have established truth for ever in the earth, and brought in the kingdom of heaven.

But the message comes home to us more intimately than this. For see how this writer to the Hebrews continues. "Now may God, who brought again from the dead the Lord Jesus, make *you* perfect in every good work to do his will, working *in you* that which is well pleasing in his sight." That is to say, the same divine creative energy which resurrected Christ is available for you, for me: and that, mark you, not only at death to raise us up, but here and now to help us to live.

Who could realize this, and not be thrilled by it? Here is the apostle praying for those Christians and for that Church, that the identical force which God had exerted in taking Jesus out of the grave might operate on a similar scale in their own lives, might go inwardly to work to make them strong and pure and brave and vital—to make them, in short, resurrected personalities, throbbing with new life!

I sometimes wonder if we have ever really comprehended that this— nothing less—is what the Gospel offers: the power which shattered death for Jesus, to help us now to live!

It is surely worth our pondering. Here was the Lord Christ, wounded and burdened and bowed down with human sin, cut off from the land of the living, with everything apparently lost, and all his hopes and dreams (so the world thought) dead and done for and defeated—and God by one mighty act of power, by the sheer energy of grace, had brought him through and set him on high: and now for ever that some power—not something different, but that identical energy—available for you, for me, for all who will receive it!

Too often we are like the man with the rake in Bunyan's dream, gazing permanently downwards, obsessed with such poor sticks and straws and dust as our own weak efforts of will, our own ineffectual resolves and insubstantial, wistful longings: never dreaming that the Lord God who resurrected Christ is standing there beside us, with that gift of supernatural power—ours, if we would have it!

It is this that explains the irrepressible excitement of early Christianity. They went, those followers of Jesus, to men who had been morally and spiritually defeated scores, hundreds of times, and they said—"Here is a way of victory! God has brought again from the dead the Lord Jesus. With such a power at work, what may not happen—for you?"

That was the message. And lest any of their hearers should think they were being merely rhetorical and romantic, always, these men of the New Testament went on to say—"We know it, for we have proved it. It has worked for us!"

The truth of that claim is apparent. How was it that a little group of men in an upper room—ordinary, fallible, blundering men—were able to go out and turn the world upside down? It was not that they were commanding personalities—most of them were not. It was not that they had official backing, impressive credentials, or illustrious patronage: of all that they had less than nothing. It was this—that they had established contact with the power that has resurrected Jesus, or rather, that this unearthly power had laid hold upon them.

And still today they accost us, saying—"It is abroad now in the earth, the power of the Resurrection. Why not for you?" And they look at us with absolute assurance: "Why not for you?"

But we are so slow to take it in. We are like our forefathers who lived all their days in a world containing the marvel of electricity and never guessed it was there. Dr. Johnson once said a striking thing about Oliver Goldsmith: "He would be a great man, if he realised the wealth of his internal resources." If only we Christians would come awake to that!

But we hesitate. "It can't apply to us," we say. "Our lives are not the stuff out of which God's Easter victories are made. And as for hoping to live on Christ's level, with that new risen quality of life, why, what's the use? All very well to talk like that, but we stopped trying long ago. It can't be for us— our problems are too many, our thwarting frailties too baffling, our chains of defeat too firmly shackled on our souls. We have toiled all night, and taken nothing." And so we go on our way with what Thomas Carlyle noted in Coleridge—"a look of anxious impotence in his eyes."

But those men of the New Testament will not accept that denial "You surely don't imagine," they cry to us, "that the power which took Christ out of the grave is going to be baffled by you? That the God who did that terrific thing is going to find your little problem too hard for Him to deal with? That the God who, in the mighty act of Easter broke through the last darkness of the universe is going to confess Himself impotent on the scale of your life, and say—'No, I cannot work any miracles here: this is too intractable for Me'? But that just does not make sense," these writers say, "that doubt is utterly irrational! He that brought again from the dead the Lord Jesus, shall He not—today if you will ask Him—revive and quicken you?"

This, however, must be added: there is one condition. Before the creative God can come into our life, before this dynamic reality can lay hold of us, before our spirits can know the baptism of power and of eternity, one thing is needful. Self-surrender. Self-commitment.

And this writer to the Hebrews has very dramatically reminded us of that. For did you notice that even this magnificent, triumphant verse has a streak of blood across it? Did you hear, through this shout of Easter praise and the trumpets of victory, the diapason note of sacrifice? "The God of peace, that brought again from the dead our Lord Jesus . . . *through the blood of the everlasting covenant.*" There was no road to Easter for Jesus except by Good Friday; no way to that risen eternal quality of life except by life laid down. And that being so, this, too, is axiomatic: there is no road to the power of

Easter for any of us except at the cost of self-commitment; no way to the experience of having God's energies loosed and set free into our life except through the discipline of self-surrender. That is the condition.

Here then, is the question each of us must face. With the supernatural force waiting to be used, this power that resurrected Christ and energized the Church and made life new for multitudes—with this available, why should my life ever be helpless and maimed and impoverished and defeated? Is it that I have been unwilling to travel the road that Jesus went and all the saints —the exacting road of consecration?

The ultimate secret of Resurrection power was given by William Cowper in the lines we often sing:

> The dearest idol I have known,
> Whate'er that idol be,
> Help me to tear it from Thy Throne,
> And worship only Thee.

That is the streak of blood. That is the Good Friday sacrifice. And beyond it—all the power of Easter, all the efficiency of a conquering soul, all the thrill of being risen with Christ, all the marvel of life blossoming red from the dust of self's defeat.

EASTER

The Meaning of the Resurrection

His Eminence Edward Cardinal Mooney, Ph.D., D.D.

Archbishop of the Roman Catholic Archdiocese of Detroit, Michigan

Cardinal Mooney has served the Church on three continents—Europe, Asia and North America. As is characteristic of the greater part of the American hierarchy, the Archbishop is a native-born American, was born in Mt. Savage, Maryland, May 9, 1892, but grew up in Youngstown, Ohio. When he decided to enter the priesthood, he returned to his home state of Maryland to attend St. Charles College in Ellicott City, and St. Mary's Seminary, Baltimore.

In 1905 he went to Rome for advanced theological studies for four years. On April 10, 1909, he was ordained to the priesthood and he received both the Ph.D. and D.D. degrees the same year. On his return to America he became professor of dogmatic theology in St. Mary's Seminary, Cleveland, until he was appointed as head of the Cathedral Latin School in that city in 1916. His boyhood home town called him to be Pastor of St. Patrick's Parish in

Youngstown in August, 1922. Only a few months later, in January, 1923, he was called to a new assignment in the Eternal City as Spiritual Director of the North American College, where he had lived as a student in his first years in Rome.

He was given the title of Monsignor in 1925, and in 1926 he was named by the Vatican as Apostolic Delegate to India. This year was the turning point in the Cardinal's career, a year of brilliant success and recognition, for on January 8 he was created Titular Archbishop of Irenopolis and was consecrated January 31 by Cardinal Van Rossum. After five years in India he was appointed Apostolic Delegate to Japan in 1931. Two years later, following a visit to the United States, just as he was returning to Japan he was appointed as Bishop of Rochester, New York, in October, 1933. He became active with the Administrative Board of the National Catholic Welfare Conference and was made the Episcopal Chairman of the Department of Social Action. On the death of Bishop Gallagher of Detroit, announcement came from the Vatican that Detroit was raised from a diocese to an Archdiocese and Archbishop Mooney was named as the first Archbishop of Detroit.

Under his guidance the Archdiocese has taken a lead in labor problems, the Association of Catholic Trade Unionists was organized and was a factor in fighting communism in unions. He also organized a Labor Institute and Workers' Schools. During the war years a great increase in population brought a need for more churches and His Eminence led the way in organizing new churches for Catholics where they were needed. He also provided religious instruction for children attending public schools in free or released time.

Archbishop Mooney was created a Cardinal by Pope Pius XII early in 1946 to the great joy of the people of his Archdiocese. "The Meaning of the Resurrection" was preached in the Cathedral of the Blessed Sacrament in Detroit on Easter Sunday morning, 1948. It is marked by simplicity of style and language, brevity and its sound Christian faith. His message on eternal life is much needed in our day. It will be noted that this sermon does not have a text, although His Eminence quotes the Scripture in the body of his sermon; it is not his practice to use a text unless the major portion of his sermon is definitely an explanation or exposition of that very text.

Sermon Seventeen

TO YOU who are gathered in this Cathedral Church for Easter Mass and to those who, through a marvel of modern science, even at a distance follow by eye and ear the age-old ritual of the Church, I would like to speak a brief, plain and definite word on the meaning of this day. The Church ranks

Easter first in the calendar of her feasts. In the decisive importance of the event it commemorates, it even outranks Christmas, deeply as the sentiment that beautiful feast evokes is imbedded in the varied traditions and customs of Christian nations. Christmas strikes the note of joyful hope, for it speaks of a beginning. Easter strikes the note of triumphant certainty, for it speaks of a fulfillment. Christmas touches the heart, but Easter makes its impact on the mind. If what began in Bethlehem had ended on Calvary, the whole story of the Gospels would have been but another of the world's bright dreams—as the discouraged disciples on the way to Emmaus so dramatically illustrate. But Easter makes us look into an open and empty tomb and hear the living words: "He is not here. He is risen as he said and gone before you into Gallilee." This is the event the Christian world commemorates today— the most significant miracle, the most portentous sign in human history. For Christianity is the greatest fact in all the world's history, and the Resurrection is Christianity's most telling evidence.

Practically, then, we can best consider the Resurrection for its value as evidence of the validity of Christ's unprecedented claims, as a vindication of Christ's assertion of a divine mission and personality, as final and compelling proof that the message He brought to earth is true, that the authority He gave His Church is divine, that the ordinances with which He endowed the Church are spiritually effective—and we glory in the Resurrection as a confirmation of our Christian faith.

This view of the Resurrection was foremost in Christ's mind. When Christ's authority was challenged by the leaders of His people, He answered that challenge by formally citing His Resurrection as the sign that would be given. To note only one instance, I refer to the twelfth chapter of St. Matthew's gospel. When the scribes and Pharisees were trying to misinterpret and malign the miracle by which Christ cured the man who was dumb and blind, they said to Him: "Master, we would see a sign from thee." Their evident bad faith drew these biting words from the lips of Christ: "A wicked and adulterous generation seeketh a sign, and a sign shall not be given it except the sign of Jonas the Prophet. For even as Jonas was three days in the belly of the whale, so shall the Son of Man be three days . . . in the heart of the earth." I might multiply the instances, but the fact stands out in the gospel story that when Christ felt He was called upon for a test that could not be gainsaid, that could not be evaded, that could not be explained away, He pointed to His own Resurrection. Christ's other miracles have their value for men of good will, but this was to be the supreme test. The shadow of the cross falls on all the others, but it is the glory of the resurrection that makes the cross a radiant symbol and forever confirms the faith of those who believe in a Crucified Saviour.

Nor is there any vagueness about the broad sweep of the faith in Christ which the Resurrection confirms. In the Gospels we see a Christ who spoke with authority, who called men to join Him and gave them a commission to teach others the things He had taught them, who laid the foundations of an organic spiritual society in the authority He gave the apostles with Peter at their head, who made His speech and touch carry into men's souls supernatural grace of enlightenment, strength and forgiveness, who gave His apostles the power the Father had given Him, and promised to be with them all days even to the consummation of the world, who prayed for and provided for unity of faith and practice amongst His followers, who, in mysterious dispensation, promised His Very Self under the appearance of bread and wine to be the sustenance of souls, who, at the Last Supper, in fulfillment of that wondrous promise connected the solemn Eucharistic rite we here observe with the offering and perpetual commemoration of the sacrificial death He was freely to endure.

It is this faith, confirmed by the Resurrection, that inspires the individual not only to follow Christ in the observance of His supreme law of love for God and neighbor, but to play an active and generous part in the work of the Church Christ established to carry on His saving mission among men.

It is this faith, confirmed by the Resurrection, that gives men the courage to suffer, yes and to die, rather than forswear their allegiance to God through Christ. I fear that we pass over too lightly the record of Christian martyrdom in our own world of today. As a matter of fact, within the life span of any adult amongst us, godless and brutal totalitarian governments in Europe have made more Christian martyrs than all the Roman emperors from Nero to Diocletian in more than two centuries of intermittent persecution that marked the beginnings of Christianity in the West. We must not forget to pray for the millions who live under a terror that is more bitter than death. I ask you to pray, too, for the Christian faith and courage of the common people of Italy who stand guard today on the most menaced frontier of Christian civilization.

It is this faith, confirmed by the Resurrection, that will give Christians here at home the light and strength to oppose the mounting tide of secularism in our own country with its practical disregard of religion in everyday life. No vague, formless and merely sentimental Christianity will be equal to the task. It is precisely the prevalence amongst us of that type of Christianity that has brought on the crisis and made us as a nation defer meeting the issue until it is almost too late. It is only the convinced Christian, the informed Christian, the Christian with a will to make his faith count in every aspect of his daily life, who will be effective in giving Christ His place in the sanctities of the home, in the education of his children, the theory and practice of economic life, in the philosophy of law and government, in the dealings of group with group in the market place and the factory, in the relations that govern international life, in building up the kingdom of God for time and for eternity. For to the Christian, Christ is the way, the truth and the life. No other teacher ever spoke words like these: "I am the resurrection and the life; he that believeth in me, even if he die, shall live; and he that liveth and believeth in me shall not die forever." It is precisely the Resurrection—which Easter Day recalls—that enables us to say with St. Paul: "I know whom I have believed, and I am certain that he is able to keep that which I have committed unto him." With that certainty it is easy to commit unto Him our faith, our love, our loyalty, our life.

EASTER

On the Road to Calvary

REVEREND WALTER ARTHUR MAIER, PH.D., D.D., LL.D.

A Minister of the Missouri Synod of the Lutheran Church, Preacher on the Lutheran Hour; Professor at Concordia Theological Seminary, St. Louis, Missouri

Walter A. Maier was born in Boston, Massachusetts, October 4, 1893, the son of an organ builder. His earliest memory, he has said, is of his father at prayer; and "the most influential human factor" in his life has been "the devotion, prayers, support, and outstanding example" of his parents. He received his elementary education at the Cotton Mather public school in the Dorchester section of Boston, and from his thirteenth to his nineteenth years attended Concordia Collegiate Institute, a Lutheran high school and junior college, in Bronxville, New York. It was at the latter that a professor's call for Christian workers influenced him to devote his life to the ministry; Dr. Henry Stein of the Bronxville school, he recalls, had the profoundest influence on him scholastically.

In 1913 he graduated from Boston University, entered Concordia Theological Seminary in St. Louis, Missouri. In the later years of his schooling in Bronxville and Boston he earned his expenses by washing dishes, mimeographing, and selling typewriters and books. His one extracurricular activity at the seminary was a year's presidency of the Concordia student association.

From 1916 to 1920 he continued his preparation for the ministry on a four-year fellowship at Harvard University, until 1918 in the Divinity School, and from 1918 to 1920 in the Harvard Graduate School, specializing in Semitic languages, literature, and history, with emphasis upon the Assyrian and Babylonian. To fulfill the conditions of his fellowship, he assisted Professor James Richard Jewett in the Arabic department.

From 1917 to 1919, while at Harvard, he was also Lutheran pastor to the German internees quartered on Gallup's Island in Boston Harbor and to the German prisoners of war at War Prison Camp No. 1 at Still River, Massa-

chusetts. In the summer of 1918 he was the representative of his church at the United States Army at Camp Gordon near Atlanta, Georgia. His first full-time work with the Missouri Synod of the Lutheran Church came in 1920 as executive secretary of the International Walther League and editor of the Walther League Messenger. In 1922 he became professor of Semitic languages and Old Testament interpretation at Concordia Theological Seminary in St. Louis; he retained his editorship. He began the International Lutheran Hour in 1935, as a gospel message and counsel to solve the problems of thousands. The Hour grew so that in 1944 he was granted a leave of absence to devote his full time to the radio program. In September, 1945, he resigned as editor of the Messenger while his leave of absence from Concordia Seminary, he reported in 1947, is likely to be extended indefinitely by the Missouri Lutheran Synod. In April, 1947, he went to Europe as a special consultant on educational and religious matters to the United States Army.

A fundamentalist, the radio pastor is, in his delivery, an old-time evangelist. He spares no one in his denunciations as he urges all to repentance and confession. He usually broadcasts from within the locked confines of Station KFUO on the Concordia campus, without the presence of a studio audience. His delivery is impassioned and accompanied with emphatic gestures. The radio engineers do not try to modulate his voice: once when a cold forced him to soften his style, his mail dropped off as many as a thousand letters a day, and solicitous followers called to learn if he were ill.

When he goes on a speaking tour he fills the Chicago Stadium, the Cleveland Auditorium, the St. Louis Arena, or the Detroit Coliseum to overflowing. On such occasions the broadcasts originate there. He is the author of many tracts and pamphlets and about fifteen books, most of them compilations of his weekly sermons. His For Better, Not for Worse, on marriage, is a best seller, running into several editions. He writes each sermon with a possible change of introduction in mind. A recognized scholar, he is concluding a commentary on the prophet Nahum, which has occupied him for more than ten years. Among his favorite recreations are fishing, hunting, and swimming, collecting rare books and stamps, and model railroading.

This sermon represents Dr. Maier's preaching at its best and he is representative of a large group, perhaps of the majority, of the ministers of the Missouri Synod of the Lutheran Church.

Sermon Eighteen

TEXT: And he bearing his cross went forth into a place called the place of a skull, which is called in the Hebrew Golgotha.

JOHN 19:17

CHRIST'S entire earthly ministry was packed into three years—years that came to a seeming triumph on Palm Sunday, but for the disciples turned to tragedy on the days following the hosannas. On Thursday the fury of hell itself seemed to break loose around Christ and his followers. After he had instituted the Sacrament of the Lord's Supper he, resolutely setting his face toward Jerusalem, predicted, "All ye shall be offended because of me this night." And everyone with him in the Garden of Gethsemane on Thursday night was offended—especially his enemies who had come to arrest him. Jesus had healed and helped them; he had fed their bodies and fortified their souls; he had performed miracles in their midst. Perfect in his walks and works, he could challenge his opponents, "Which of you convinceth me of sin?" and not even the poison of perjury could advance a single valid charge against him.

Millions of Americans who have never had enough interest to join any church are offended because of Christ, are ashamed of Jesus. They think they have no sins to be forgiven, no penalty to pay, no guilt to be removed. Proudly they conclude that they do not need Christ, that they do not want a Saviour like Jesus. To them our Lord speaks one of the hardest and most crushing sentences his divine lips ever uttered: "Whosoever . . . shall be ashamed of me and my words in this adulterous and sinful generation, of him also shall the Son of Man be ashamed, when he cometh in the glory of his Father with the holy angels." God shake our souls with grief and repentance!

From the Last Supper Christ and the disciples walked to Gethsemane. "Then cometh Jesus with them unto a place called Gethsemane, and said unto the disciples, sit ye here, while I go and pray yonder." When he went a few paces off to himself, great agony began to crush him and he threw himself headlong on the ground. Anguish, such as mortal never endured, made him cry out into the night. Full realization came to him that he alone could reconcile man to God. In this hour he craved human companionship and returned to his disciples but found them asleep. A second time he returned to them, but they still slept on. And a third time he came to them, but their eyes still remained closed. The weight of the woe burdening his soul was so crushing, that, tormented almost unto death, he cried, "O My Father, if it be possible, let this cup pass from me." Three times that appeal rang through the night, but three times his love triumphed over that lingering dread, and

[107]

in a prayer which should be the model for our petitions, he added resolutely, "Nevertheless not as I will, but what thou wilt." We speak of the heavy inner anguish of soul that men have endured in the last hours of their lives; but where is there an agony like the scourge of sorrow Christ endured in the garden? It is written of him that as he prayed there with an intensity of pleading, "his sweat was as it were great drops of blood." At this point, as the Gospel records, there "appeared an angel unto him from heaven, strengthening him." As the moonlight pierced the foliage of the olive trees in Gethsemane the Saviour was alone in his soul-moving supplication and we find in him all history's Sufferer!

However, we see in Christ far more than a victim of spiritual torture. We ask ourselves, What was the cause of these heartbreaking sorrows? He was sinless perfection itself. Did Jesus in the Garden of Gethsemane fear death? Was he afraid, as some are, in life's last moments, to face the grave? How could he be, when, at the same moment he told his disciples that they would be offended because of him, he also comforted them with the assurance that after his resurrection he would meet them in Galilee? Jesus knew his own divine truth that though they might crucify him on Friday, nevertheless, on Sunday he would be restored to life. The only way you can have full freedom from the fear of death is to trust Christ completely and to believe the guarantee of the Gospel: "I am the resurrection, and the life: he that believeth in me, though he were dead, yet shall he live. And whosoever liveth and believeth in me shall never die."

Only one explanation can truly account for Christ's grief in the Garden. He there began his vicarious suffering for the sins of the world, to give himself as the one sin-offering for all the ages, a substitute for us in paying the penalty for our transgressions and in atoning for our iniquities. Truly he is "the Lamb of God, which taketh away the sin of the world."

Only a few days before this solemn Thursday in the Garden, Jesus was welcomed to Jerusalem with enthusiastic acclaim; now a mob, armed with swords and staves, came to take him! Only a few hours earlier the Saviour held his final meeting with the disciples in the upper room and at that last supper instituted the Holy Communion, with the blessed gift of his own body and blood. Now that time had arrived when that body, scourged and wounded, should be given to death for our sins. Now the silence in the garden was suddenly broken. From all sides an armed mob swarmed into Gethsemane. In this crisis it was a different Christ who stepped before the mob to ask, "Whom seek ye?" When they answered, "Jesus of Nazareth," the Saviour unhesitatingly identified himself, with the words, "I am he."

Bow humbly before the Lord Jesus in His unflinching courage! He knew the agony awaiting him, but he faced it all with unflinching bravery. There was nothing accidental in his anguish; it had been planned before the beginning of the world; and though long prior to Calvary he stopped to shudder at its shame and suffering, yet he went straight to the cross. The agony of the

Garden was followed in rapid succession by a series of mock trials before Annas, Caiaphas, the Sanhedrin, Herod and Pilate. Yet their combined verdict pointed to the sinless, stainless Son of God and declared: "He is guilty of death!" The unerring record of the Gospels continues: "And he bearing his cross went forth into a place called the place of a skull, which is called in the Hebrew Golgotha."

On the road to Calvary there are remarkable lessons. When you are called to bear a cross of affliction, you will know that our Saviour carried an unspeakably heavier load than may burden you. He endured every grief which can ever grip us; only he suffered immeasurably worse sorrows. We have a Saviour who was "touched with the feeling of our infirmities." He knows our pains and problems because he endured them all in a degree which the human mind cannot fathom.

Are you poor? The Son of God was so destitute that his only possessions were the bloodstained garments with which he was clothed—and even these were soon taken from him. He suffered personally, although immeasurably much more, the miseries under which you groan. Take every fevered anxiety to him, "casting all your care upon him; for he careth for you."

Are you lonely? Think of him, carrying his heavy cross alone through the crowded streets, with no one to wipe the blood and the sweat and the tears from his face! Hear him, as in earth's and hell's deepest loneliness he cried, "My God, my God! Why hast thou forsaken me?" He knows the turmoil of your soul, and though he was forsaken, even by his disciples, he promises you through faith, "I will never leave thee, nor forsake thee."

Are you opposed and beset by enemies? See how Jesus was surrounded by soldiers, was mocked on the cross, and then find comfort in the guarantee of his grace, "If God be for us, who can be against us?"

Are you burdened by sin, tortured by transgressions which once seemed trivial and attractive, but which you now recognize as damnable and destructive? Behold your Saviour once more as he bore his cross! He had no sins of his own; yet, on the way to Calvary he bore the transgressions of all mankind. Was he not "the Lamb of God which taketh away the sin of the world"? Had not God laid on him "the iniquity of us all"? Now if our sins trouble us —let us follow Christ on the Calvary road and learn that before seven hours passed he will have declared from the cross, "It is finished!" and died in complete atonement for our sins, in eternal defeat of death and hell!

When President Truman visited our good neighbors across the Rio Grande, the Mexican government and the Mexican people gave him the warmest welcome any foreign guest has ever received in that hospitable country. Mexico City was beflagged as never before, and this is particularly interesting—the houses on the street along which lay the presidential party's route were freshly painted.

When Marie Antoinette traveled through France, beggars and cripples, the poor and the disfigured were removed from the path of her procession weeks in advance. When Ibrahim Pasha visited Palestine, squads of laborers were assigned to widen the road, to smooth its surface, to fill its deep declines. Indeed, years ago, when a Russian czar wanted to impress a visiting ruler, he had entire make-believe cities and villages erected along the shores of the Vistula River, thousands of house fronts, make-believe stores, shells of public buildings and churches. As the royal guest floated down the river in the czar's barge, he was to be impressed with the picture of a flourishing, fertile countryside.

How different the procession in which Jesus Christ, the King of kings, went from Jerusalem to his cross at Calvary! Here marched the Son of God and the Saviour of the world, not on any diplomatic errand, promoting good will between nations, but on the holiest mission this earth can ever know—reconciling mankind with God! He suffered crushing sorrows; agony, not applause; burning grief, instead of warm welcome; cries of hatred instead of "Hurrah" met him as men showed Christ their worst side, rather than their best, hatred in place of loyalty and love.

Jesus after less than a single day had to drag Himself to Golgotha along the *via dolorosa,* the way of sorrows, every inch of the way marked with pain. General Wainwright and thousands of young men had to make the death march in islands in the Orient during World War II for following the American flag against tyrants. Let us follow Christ the Saviour on the Calvary road! See his deep devotion to our souls on that death march! The Son of God suffered humiliation and agonies beyond description—for us.

Go out to Golgotha and see with your mind's eye what happened at a crucifixion. First, the upright timber, usually about ten feet in length, was firmly planted in the ground. Second, the victim's hands were tied, one to each side of the crossbeam, and then nailed to the wood. Third, that beam was then raised, often with the help of a ladder, and affixed to the upright timber. Fourth, to complete the barbaric cruelty, the feet, placed on a rest, were likewise pierced through by one nail or two, and thus the whole body was nailed to the cross.

It takes only a few moments to recount this heaviest miscarriage of justice in all history, which the Bible summarizes in these simple words: "When they were come to the place, which is called Calvary, there they crucified him." Crucifixion in the ancient world was the form of capital punishment which would make its victim suffer most and longest. Often those punished in this way languished on the cross for days, until increasing pain mercifully made them unconscious. The exposure to the sun and wind, raging fever, the inflammation of the festering wounds, the tension of the suspended body, combined to produce increasing torment.

Far greater, however, than these physical agonies were the soul sorrows that tortured Christ. Only in this light can you understand the true meaning of Calvary. Jesus was torn and crushed by the guilt and punishment of our sins, by the appalling aggregate of human iniquity. Thank God, our blessed Saviour gave himself as a ransom for many; Christ is evermore the Lamb of

God that takes away the sins of the world. Christ was truly Christ for you and me. The gloom of Golgotha was followed by the splendor of Easter and the Resurrection! The way of Christ is the road to eternal life.

"A God on a cross," cried the great Lacordaire, "that is all my theology!"

PRAYER: *Christ, our crucified Redeemer: Accept the repentance, the faith, the thankfulness—weak and imperfect as they are—which we bring thee on this day of thy death, for the atoning love which sent thee to the cross as our Substitute! As we behold thy pain in the final agony, let every one of us say, "It was for me, precious Saviour, that thou didst endure these tortures!" Have mercy upon us despite all our sins! As thou didst plead from the cross, "Father, forgive them," so do thou now pray for us, "O forgive them!" O Christ, thou Lamb of God that takest away the sin of the world, have mercy upon us! Grant us thy blood-bought peace! Amen.*

EASTER

The Meaning of the Cross

REVEREND HAROLD E. JOHNSON
Minister, First Methodist Church, Oceanside, California

Harold Johnson is one of the rising young ministers of the Methodist Church in California. His preaching has enthusiasm, sincerity, and conviction, and he has the ability to work hard and to meet people with friendliness. He was born in Kansas City, Missouri, in 1918, took his undergraduate degree at the University of Redlands, and his divinity degree at Boston University School of Theology. He was ordained in the Methodist Ministry in 1943.

He served as youth director of First Methodist Church, Santa Anna, California, then as co-pastor of Saint Paul's Methodist Church, San Bernardino, and is now pastor of First Methodist Church, Oceanside, California. This sermon has an excellent message of several meanings of the Cross to Christians and shows promise of further homiletic ability.

Sermon Nineteen

TEXT: We preach Christ crucified, unto the Jews a stumbling-block, and unto the Greeks foolishness; but unto them which are called, both Jews and Greeks, Christ the power of God and the wisdom of God. I CORINTHIANS 1:23-24.

FOR twentieth-century Christians, the cross, the symbol of Christ's eternal victory over the forces of evil and of death, is one of the most perplexing and baffling aspects of modern theology. The teachings of Jesus men can understand. At times, they even try to put them into practice. But, for the most part, modern Christians stand before the central symbol of their faith—the cross—and, although they may be amazed and transfixed by its glory, they are utterly powerless either to explain or to understand its real meaning.

In an attempt to put into words the meaning of the cross, a great many hymns have been written, but for the average Christian, they are just so many words. The central meaning of the cross is not to be found here. For example: "In the Cross of Christ I glory, towering o'er the wrecks of time. All the light of sacred story gathers round its head sublime." "I must needs go home by the way of the cross, there's no other way but this." "When I survey the wondrous cross, on which the Prince of Glory died, my richest gain I count but loss and pour contempt on all my pride." These hymns are beautiful and deeply spiritual. They stir fond and precious memories within our souls. But they do not speak to us of the central and basic meaning of the cross.

Many modern Christians find themselves in the same intellectual and spiritual confusion, and faced by the same inability to put the real meaning of the cross into mature words, as was John Milton, the great English poet. In 1629, he wrote his ever lovely "On the Morning of Christ's Nativity." A year later, he attempted to write a companion poem to it on "The Passion." After only eight toilsome verses had been written, he gave it up. Sometime later, he wrote these words about the unfinished poem: "This subject the author finding to be above the years he had when he wrote it, and nothing satisfied with what was begun, left it unfinished." Today many Christians are also powerless to explain or to put into words the meaning of the cross. But we cannot leave the matter unfinished as did John Milton. There is something haunting about it which will not let us put it aside. Rather, we must deal with it as best we can.

If we are to understand the meaning of the cross for our day, we must see it under three major ideas. First, we must see the cross as an historic fact in the history of mankind, the most difficult historic fact in Christianity to understand. We preach *"Christ crucified . . . a stumblingblock and . . . foolishness."*

The fundamental basis for our understanding of the cross must be in terms of human tragedy, in the truest and fullest sense of that word. Human life could hold no greater tragedy than that Jesus should die a violent death upon the cross. He lived a pure, beautiful and wholesome life. He was motivated by only the highest ideals. He gave us a truer insight into what a Godlike life might be than any other man the world has ever known. Nevertheless, they killed him. They crucified him upon a cruel, hated Roman cross.

Here are the factors and the sins which crucified Jesus. A corrupt priesthood was crafty and unscrupulous, seeking to hush a haunting voice which would rob them not only of their religious position as leaders, but would also take from them their "economy of graft." Under the guise of religious piety they obtained outrageous amounts of money from the people. Religious intolerance, covetousness and commercial privilege threw their weight against him. A superstitious and cunning politician, caught between Rome and the howling mob, finally sold his honor for his office. He could not make up his mind concerning the guilt of Jesus until it was too late. Political expediency, intellectual dishonesty and personal indecision were there also. A callous and morose mob sought to crucify a man who they thought had played with their highest religious emotions and expectations—the coming of the Messiah—and then thwarted them by refusing to follow through as they thought he should. Revenge and public apathy nailed him to the tree.

All of these sins, incorporated with a single purpose and motivated by an unholy desire, threw themselves with vengefulness at Jesus' head. It was a black and total tragedy showing the worst that man is capable of doing to man.

Death by the cross was the most ignominious that could have been inflicted. The Roman citizens were exempt from it. It was reserved for murderers, slaves and common criminals. Yet, the gentle Jesus, a teacher of love, an advocate of peace and good will among men, who lived and spake as man had never lived or spoken before or since, was innocently and, perhaps, even illegally, sentenced to die. He was severely scourged with a leather whip with pieces of sharp bone tied in the ends of thongs. He was driven to the top of Calvary's hill and there nailed to a rough wooden cross. He was left to face not only the raging elements, the milling and hostile crowd, but a slow and agonizing death.

In the year 500, when men still lived by the sword, Clovis I, king of the Frankish Empire, was converted to Christianity. The first time he heard the story of the crucifixion of Jesus, he was intensely moved by it. He jumped to his feet, unsheathed his sword, and shouted, "If I and my Franks had been there, they never would have done that to him." That should also be our reaction to the crucifixion of Jesus. It was a diabolical crime, a complete human tragedy, alike in its ignominy, malignity and stupidity. The crucifixion of Jesus was the greatest human tragedy the world has ever known, and we must see it fundamentally as a tragic fact in the history of mankind, if we are ever to understand its real meaning.

However, there is one element in that tragedy of death which, although it does not completely sanction it, at least goes a long way toward redeeming it. That element is this: Jesus chose to die. He was acting in the upper realm of the spirit, in the area of what we might call unenforceable obligations. He could have gone down the back side of the Mount of Olives and taken the highroad east of the Jordan and been back in the little town of Nazareth in the morning, had he chosen to do so. That would have solved the whole matter from all angles—all except his own. But what then? What of the message he came to preach? What of the abundant life he came to bring to man? It is only when a man dies for his convictions that anything is wrought out of life. And Jesus knew it. "Unless a grain of wheat falls into the earth and dies," he said, "It remains a single grain. But if it dies, it bears rich fruit. He who loves his life shall lose it, and he who cares not for his life in this world shall preserve it for all eternity." Jesus chose to die. In spite of the fact that the historic crucifixion of Jesus was a stumbling block to the Jews and foolishness to the Greeks and is a seemingly meaningless fact to modern Christians, it is the fundamental basis of our understanding of the cross.

William L. Stidger, in a poem entitled "I Am the Cross," has made the transition from the historic fact of the crucifixion to the spiritual symbolism of the cross. In that transition we can see ". . . the wisdom of God."

> I am the Cross of Christ,
> I bore his body there on Calvary's hill.
> Till then I was a humble tree that grew
>   beside a rill;
> I think, till then,
> I was a thing despised of men.
>
> I am the Cross of Christ,
> They say I tower o'er wrecks of time.
> I only know, that once a humble tree,
> This was not so. But this
> I know—since then
> I have become a symbol for the hopes of men.[1]

In "the wisdom of God" the cross becomes a spiritual symbol of redemptive and creative conflict. In it we can see the Almighty's method of overcoming evil. Hegel makes this observation in the introduction to his *Philosophy of History*: "We may affirm absolutely that nothing great in the world has been accomplished without passion." Arnold Toynbee, in his *Study of History* is advocating the same thesis when he says, "Nothing worth while in the world is won without a struggle." Bach's great B Minor Mass has as its essential

[1] Used by permission of the author.

[114]

theme the glory of creation coming into its triumphant fulfillment by way of the passion of the cross.

What these men are saying is this: Life is no easy road. Rather it is a road of majestic re-creation and redemption. It is literally a continuous recreation of discord into harmony, of tragedy into triumph. One of the eternal purposes of God is to make life into a great symphony or a great drama in which the central theme is the transformation of the discordant and the ugly into the beautiful and the harmonious.

Now, take this same idea of redemptive and creative conflict and apply it to Jesus and his cross. Look at Jesus there in the Garden of Gethsemane, with the shadow of the cross falling across his very path. What did he do with it? You know what he did. He laid hold of it. He wrestled with it. He lifted it up into his mighty passion. He transformed it. He recreated it. He redeemed it. And he made it an integral part of the life of all mankind. Jesus accepted the cross, thinking that it would prove to be a stumbling block for sin. He hoped it would eternally thwart sin's downward drag in the life of man. Our Communion ritual has a prayer which expresses this very idea: Jesus Christ suffered "death upon the cross for our redemption, and made thereby the offering of himself, a full, perfect and sufficient sacrifice for the sins of the whole world." The conflict there upon Calvary was not only one of personal redemption, but it was also one of creative suffering. For in that tragic and lonely hour there upon Calvary, "God was in Christ, reconciling the world to himself."

Let us carry this idea one step further. If it is true for the individual, then it is true for society as well. Therefore, we can apply this threefold idea of "creation, passion, and redemption" to it also. The crucified Christ is the living statement of God's demand upon all society. The cross stands as the symbol of the way of redemption for society as well as for the individual. And that society may mount the path to a higher glory than she has ever known before, she, like her crucified Lord, may have to give up her life for humanity. As Reinhold Niebuhr says: "The Kingdom of God must still enter the world by way of the crucifixion." Surely here is God's way, and the only way of making anything out of life: a humble and self-abasing presence at the foot of the cross, a grateful self-fulfillment through the redemptive and creative conflict which culminated upon the cross of Calvary.

If we are to understand the total meaning of the cross, we must see it not only as a historic fact in the history of mankind, and as a spiritual symbol of redemptive and creative conflict, but we must see it as an eternal challenge in its transforming power. For in the cross of Christ we come to the zenith of ". . . the power of God."

Dr. Lucius Bugbee tells of one of the great medieval altars built with panels on both sides on which are paintings of Biblical scenes. One altar represents, on the outside, a very depressing portrayal of the crucifixion. Against a dark and dreary background, the heavy cross bears the body of Jesus. To one side stands a figure with an outstretched arm, indicating that there is something beyond, something not seen. As if in response to this urge, the panels are flung open. There is a flood of light and color. In the center of the inner panel stands the radiant figure of the Risen and Triumphant Christ. Certainly that is a picture of reality. On Good Friday, there is darkness covering the face of the earth. Hopes are blasted. Dreams are shattered. It all seems like a lost cause. But, as someone has said: "Lift up your heads, ye sorrowing ones, and be ye glad of heart, for Calvary and Easter Day were just three days apart."

Even on Good Friday we realize that there is something beyond, something that is not yet seen by mortal man. It is the Easter morn, the empty tomb, the Risen Christ which give to the cross its transforming power. It is the Easter fact that transformed biography into religion. James Warnack, in *The Conqueror,* says: "Jesus they slew—but Christ they could not kill." In his redemptive conflict, he has been creatively transformed. A great man has become a living Lord. A prophetic voice now carries the overtones of the divine. Gracious words now take on the cadences of love spoken by the heart of the universe. The Jesus who walked and talked and preached and prayed and died becomes the Christ who walks and talks and preaches and prays and lives within our hearts eternally. The broken seal on the empty tomb thus becomes a seal of truth: God's certification upon the word spoken by the side of the Jordan, "This is my beloved Son, in whom I am well pleased."

It is this transforming fact of Easter that rescued the Christian movement from simply becoming a historic fact in mankind's history and set it free as a living redemptive and creative power in the world. On Easter morn, the Jesus of Nazareth became the Christ of faith—our eternal contemporary. On that glorious day he burst the bars of death. He now walks all the highways of the world, and meets man on the level of his own needs. Thus, the local became the universal, the momentary became the eternal. This transforming power of the cross, symbolized in the empty tomb, should be to us an eternal challenge, a challenge to live our lives in the shadow of the cross, and to see the world in its radiant light.

One morning after breakfast, Elizabeth Barrett Browning left her husband and went upstairs, while a servant cleared the table where he expected to work. "After the servant had left, soft footsteps sounded behind him and his wife's hand on his shoulder kept him from turning so he could see her face. She slipped a manuscript into his pocket saying, 'Please read this, and if you do not like it, tear it up.' Then she fled back upstairs while Robert Browning sat down to read the noblest love sequence ever written by a woman to the man of her choice." Hidden in one of these *Sonnets from the Portuguese* runs this line: "The face of all the world is changed, I think, since first I heard the footsteps of thy soul." In a far more significant sense, those disciples who loved the Lord, hearing his footsteps again in their souls, found that the face of the world was changed for them. Realizing what he had meant to them, they went out to change the face of all the world. If we are to be true to the genius of Christianity, we must do the same. For the plain fact is that the Risen Lord will not let those who love him glory in that love. Such vague mysticism would never have satisfied him. The promise of his comradeship and presence is a blessed thing indeed, but it is meant to be something more than that. It is meant to be a transforming power. It is meant to be an inner compulsion which drives man forward to accomplish the tasks which he sets before them.

For two thousand years the cross of Christ has transformed men's lives. It transformed Simon, the fisherman, into Peter, the prince of the apostles. On the road to Damascus Saul, the persecutor of the Christians became Paul, the "Campaigner for Christ." In a little garden in Milan, Augustine of Thagasta became the saintly Bishop of Hippo. In the Chapel of St. Damian the roguish son of Pietro Barnadone became the beloved St. Francis of Assisi. Upon having his heart "strangely warmed," John Wesley went out and saved all England from revolution. Under the compulsion of Christ, Albert Schweitzer resigned as the head of a great theological school to become a "jungle doctor." These men saw the cross of Christ in its total meaning.

For those who thus see it today, there is one inescapable conclusion: The Risen and Triumphant Christ, working in and through us, is seeking to accomplish God's creative and redemptive purpose in the world. Armed by this faith, impelled by this transforming power, take your stand and work for that day when the kingdoms of this world shall become the kingdoms of our God and of His Christ, and He shall reign forever and ever.

FAITH

Answer to Futility

REVEREND CLAYTON E. WILLIAMS, D.D.
*Minister, The American Church in Paris, France,
and a Presbyterian Minister*

The full French flavor of this sermon, preached in The American Church in Paris, makes it fruitful for men who want to know what is being preached by Americans in foreign lands today, for Clayton Williams is an American at home in Paris. Since 1926 he has been helping Americans to find themselves in Paris and has had a brilliant part in keeping faith alive for diplomats and G.I.'s, for artists and teachers, for students and people of wealth.

Born in Peoria, Illinois, he is the son of a Presbyterian minister and studied at Butler College and the University of Pittsburgh. He went into war service in France as a Y.M.C.A. secretary in 1917-18, and became an officer in the air service of the United States in 1918-19. He studied at the University of Paris in 1919, did social work at Château-Thierry in 1921, and later in that year came to the United States as assistant at the First Presbyterian Church in Indianapolis. From 1921 until 1925 he attended Western Theological Seminary and had the highest standing in his class. During 1925-26 he was assistant pastor at the First Presbyterian Church in Poughkeepsie, New York.

Upon the termination of that year of service he was asked to go to Paris to join Dr. Cochran at the famous American Church as the assistant minister in charge of religious education and young people's work. This position he held until 1933, when Dr. Cochran resigned and the full charge of the church went to Dr. Williams. The American Church in Paris was founded by Americans and is largely supported by Americans in the United States and in Paris. It is the oldest American church outside of the United States.

When World War II came and the evacuation of Paris by most Americans took place, the church committee urged Dr. Williams to take his wife and children to America, so that they would be out of the danger zone. This he did, returning at once to France in the hope that he might continue the work in Paris, if it proved possible. However, it did not. In France and in the south of Spain and Portugal, he assisted in many ways with relief and rescue work.

He finally had to return to the United States, and while here, he served as pastor of the Seventh Presbyterian Church, Cincinnati, Ohio, from December, 1941, to May, 1945. In June of 1945 it was possible for Dr. Williams to secure transportation to France. He immediately resumed his pastorate in Paris. The church was the one American church in the war zone which was able to continue to hold services in English all through the conflict. In 1937 the French government made him a Knight of the Legion of Honor for his work for Franco-American relations, and in 1948 he was made an officer of the Legion.

Clayton Williams makes faith a glowing and glorious matter, shows the futility of pessimism and cynicism. His use of history, his knowledge of man and the application of his message to the United Nations then meeting in Paris is a touch of genius. "An Answer to Futility" was also preached in New York.

Sermon Twenty

TEXT: What doest thou here, Elijah? I KINGS 19:9

ELIJAH had been the conscience of his people. He had denounced both kings and false prophets. He had challenged and destroyed the leaders of Baal who had corrupted the faith of Israel. He had done his utmost in the defense of his faith but instead of finding his efforts crowned by the final and complete victory for which he had hoped, he found himself facing forces of evil greater than ever.

His magnificent venture of faith and heroic effort had gone for nothing. He knew well enough that life could not go on halting between two opposing forces, Yahweh and Baal, a godly and an ungodly regime, and yet he saw no answer to the situation, nothing that he could do. The pressure of events was too great for him. The forces which he faced were too strong for a single man to cope with and he felt alone, frustrated and helpless.

There are many today who are haunted by that same feeling. A mood of disillusionment has taken possession of them. The vast reserves of courage and effort expended during the war crisis have issued only in further tension and confusion. Instead of peace and victory have come apprehension and fear. A sense of futility has overlaid their hope and captured their courage. Things are too much for them. Forces beyond their control are determining the course of events and they feel that there is nothing they can do about it. Destiny is no longer in their hands.

A recent visitor to Berlin reports that the people of that great city live in a state of cynic paralysis, convinced that their life and future are being determined not by anything they can do or by any decision they can make, but by forces completely beyond their control.

That mood is prevalent today. There are many who feel that we are in the grip of great world movements, gigantic social, political and physical forces which are cataclysmic in their effect and are determining our destiny. Autonomous man, so confident a few years ago, today feels powerless and frustrated. He has lost both his point of cosmic reference and his sense of destiny. And when the citadel of men's cosmic faith is destroyed life becomes meaningless and effort futile. Existential realism may serve life for a time as a measure of extremity, but it cannot feed man's courage for long.

So, haunted and harassed by his failure to achieve any lasting result and discouraged with both life and God, Elijah fled to a cave on Mount Sinai and flung himself down in despair, ready to give up.

But that was not the end of things. In the midst of his despair the Word

[119]

of the Lord came to him. Whether it was through the residue of his conscience that God spoke to him, as the story suggests, or through some other means we do not know, but we do know that the Divine Interrogater demanded of him what he was doing in such a state of mind.

Elijah began by justifying his depression. Life was not worth the living, he said. All of his efforts had come to naught, Israel was facing a policy of apostasy, her rulers pursuing a program of extermination and of all their God-fearing men he alone was left.

It seemed like a desperate situation, but God would have none of it, and as Dr. Sizoo says, in terms of common parlance, God said to him, "So what? Even if it were true, Elijah, would that change your essential situation? Even if you were alone, and the odds were all against you, and all your previous efforts were in vain, What of it? Does that lessen the challenge to Godly living and invincible faith? Not at all! Great problems call for great faith and great living!"

And today the same question is put to us. Granted that the situation is grave, suppose the worst does come to worst, suppose war breaks out and social upheaval reaps its chaotic consequence and economic ruin descends upon us, What then? Does that change the nature of our responsibility? Does that vitiate the quality of Christian character?

Suppose the world is falling to pieces? So What? Is there anything better to live by than Christian faith? Is there anyone better to follow than Christ? This is not a time to relinquish our great convictions.

"If we are all going to be blown up," as President Hutchins says a friend wrote in a recent letter, "at least we can be blown up as Christians."

Don't misunderstand me. I am not suggesting this outlook as a counsel of desperation but rather to reaffirm the cosmic orientation of our life and faith. It can face the worst. As St. Paul said, at another time when everything seemed threatened and the world doomed to disappear, "I am persuaded, I am confident, that nothing that can happen, even the worst of things, can separate us from the love and care of God, vouchsafed to us in Christ Jesus."

We need to see life in those terms today. We need a sense of Christian destiny that is greater than anything that can be imposed upon life: atomic destruction, social upheaval, economic disaster, anything! The future is still ours and we are Christ's.

We can take our stand there! First and foremost we can orient our life in the eternal love and purposes of God that are beyond all vicissitude. We can do that, every one of us.

And now having oriented our faith and life in our divine destiny, we can consider the question of what we can do today in the face of such stubborn and overwhelming forces as confront us.

The great danger, as Halford Luccock once said, is that of "Living a minimum life in a time of maximum demand." We tend to do the least when we feel we cannot do the most. The magnitude of the problem before us paralyzes all action. Bonaro Overstreet has written a poem entitled, "To One Who Doubts the Worth of Doing Anything If You Can't Do Everything." The modern temper is often like that, to think it futile to try at all because we can't do all the situation requires.

We have seen that recently in Paris in the feeling about the United Nations which is prevalent among people in certain circles. They think that because it has not yet solved all its problems, may not even be able to solve some problems at all, it is worthless and a failure.

There is a grave danger here. Such an outlook reflects a fatal lack of faith. To lose faith in any best possible but limited constructive effort because it does not solve the whole problem is fundamentally to deny one's faith in a God of Goodness. The heart of faith is to trust the broken effort as of the quality of perfect goodness, partial though it may be; to believe as Browning insisted, "that there shall never be one lost good"; to maintain one's faith in the invincible indestructibility of goodness, however small; to persist in one's belief in the force of goodness, however fragmentary.

Faith is faith in the essential power of broken and even defeated goodness because it is part and parcel of the eternal and really triumphant goodness which finds its source in God.

In the presence of overwhelming forces the temptation is always to say, *A quoi bon?* ("What good is it?") but Jesus answers by insisting that even a gift of a glass of cold water has power. Every gain is a true gain. Every bit of goodness is dynamic. Nothing that is good is futile. The fallacy of our judgment of obscure and limited goodness lies in our quantitative evaluation, which should rightfully be a qualitative evaluation.

Jesus never belittled any goodness that was an honest effort, no matter how small, and no man has a right to be discouraged because the field of his effort is small or his capacity limited. The providence of God can multiply the effectiveness of our effort a thousand times if it is in line with His purposes. It is the intensity of our loyalty and the quality of our goodness that gives our effort effectiveness. The consummation may be unseen and unrecognized but that does not change the situation.

The poor widow who cast her two mites into the temple offering box hadn't the faintest notion that her simple loyalty was ministering to the spirit of Jesus, much less that it would speak to the hearts of men through the ages. Ann Irvine, the little "Lady of the Chimney Corner," who lived in the obscurity of a mud-floored hut in Pogues Entry, County Antrim, Ireland, had no remote idea that the loveliness of her spirit would move the hearts and renew the faith of thousands through the touching chronicle of her life written by Alexander Irvine, her son.

All the destiny of nations is not decided at peace conferences or on battlefields. The lives of loyal devoted men and women play a large part.

There is a well-known passage in Romans which—according to newly found manuscripts—we are told should read: "We know that in everything

God works for good with those who love him." God is everywhere at work using the fragmentary goodness and faith of our lives to effect the consummation of His purposes for good.

But let us bring the matter a little closer home. Granted that nothing which I as an individual can do will change the decision of Mr. Vishinsky or bring the franc back to par, or stem the tide of war, what is there I can do? What can one man do?

In reality one man can do a great deal. The individual is the creative and constructive unit. It is not the state or the scheme but the man. That is the Christian faith and that is our democraic faith as well. All constructive action is born in the heart and the mind of some individual man or woman and is empowered by the decision of the other individuals who respond to it. Individual character and individual action are what count for all effective enterprise. If these are lacking the scheme no matter how well conceived will fail.

Dr. Fosdick tells us that the building of the great wall of China was a tremendous enterprise of gigantic proportions, involving the labor of hundreds of thousands of workers. It was the largest and strongest wall of history, a mighty safeguard against invasion, and yet, it was breached three times by the enemy within a few years after its completion, not because the wall itself gave away, but because the gate-keepers were bribed. It was the human element that failed.

The success or failure of any project rests upon the action of the individuals associated with it. The responsibility is yours and mine to do what we can do.

What can we do? We can begin where we live. There is a Chinese proverb that says, "If one would have a clean city, let every man sweep clean the snow before his own doorstep."

A man coming away from a lecture on international affairs, so Halford Luccock tells us, was overheard to say, "Well, I can't do anything about Berlin; perhaps I can do something about myself."

We cannot save democracy in Czechoslovakia, perhaps, but we can save it where we are. We can lift our living to the level that can make democracy effective where we live, by our tolerance, by our faith in our fellows, by our insistence on equal rights and liberty of action for others, by our fundamental faith in the dignity of man. The frontiers of democracy are not alone in the Balkans, and Berlin, but where you and I live; and the frontiers of Christian missions are where the Christians live their faith.

We can bring the impact of our faith to play upon life by the attitude we take.

Linderman says that the minister's biggest task is to give men the courage for living, but that is every man's task. The fact is that we touch many more lives than we know. We radiate pessimism or inspire courage by the very attitudes which we assume, the stands we take, our reactions for or against a matter. Over and over again I have sat in committee meetings where on some vital issue, the general tone had bogged down to sordid selfish indifference, and I have seen the courageous conviction of one man change the whole atmosphere and resensitize the consciences of all the others. It is remarkable how when one man strikes a strong constructive moral note the others will rally to his stand. The contagion of courage is real.

Not long ago I was among a group of men of the Paris-American colony who heard Secretary Marshall speak on the present crisis in world affairs. He had no formula for its solution, no new factor to inject into the situation, no new arresting information to communicate to us, and yet we all went away from that gathering cheered and hopeful.

What was the secret? It lay in the invisible courage and profound faith of this man who spoke to us out of his experience in the center of the crucible of conflict. He spoke "off the record" but there is one phrase which I am sure can be quoted. "I am confident," he said "that we shall win in the end for you cannot beat the truth."

Secretary Marshall is a realist but he talked the language of hope. That too is something which we can do. We can talk a new language, the language of faith. The reiteration of an idea in current phrases like "the inevitable next war," "the impotence of man," "the indifference of God," "the hopelessness of the future," "the meaninglessness of life" creates an atmosphere of futility and tends to increase man's despair.

Language shapes thought as well as thought language. Cynicism thrives on the negative quality of modern news. We need to accentuate the positive, as the popular song suggested. It is high time that we Christians should assert the great constructive convictions that are native to our faith. God forbid that we should resort to a cheap and easy optimism that refuses to face certain desperate facts, but even in the face of those facts, certainly we of all men have cause for hope. We walk in the light of a triumphant faith and we should let that light fall upon life if we would interpret it truly.

The fact is that we have seen man's despicable aspects so vividly portrayed in war and conquest, occupation and concentration camp, and history's intransigent and retributive side so sharply etched in the events of the past two decades that we have forgotten that man is really a potential son of God and history still in the hands of a Sovereign Ruler. In many circles the doctrine of the depravity of men has been given far too large a place and has almost completely obscured the gospel of men's sonship.

To be sure, we must recognize the quagmire that our selfishness and willful pride have created, but that does not mean that we must wallow in it. We must see it and turn from it and center our faith in the power of God to turn prodigals into sons, sinners into saints and the world into a kingdom of heaven.

It is folly to let the gloom of the day determine the color of our observations. We should think and speak in terms of the great positive convictions that have made the Christian faith the redemptive power it has been through the centuries. It was the vital dynamic of a creative minority's faith that made the early Church the redemptive force that it was, sending it out to penetrate

[123]

and transform the pagan world through the faith and loyalty of men convinced of the persistent redemptive purposes of God as revealed in Jesus Christ. The Christian gospel is replete with hope and convinced of triumph! Our conversation should reflect our faith.

And finally, we can repolarize our thinking about the inexhaustible resources of a purposeful God. The trouble with Elijah was that he had let his faith in the power of the sovereign will of God be eclipsed by the magnitude of his troubles. He was so strife-worn and so struggle-weary that his vision was out of focus. He was too close to his problem and too dependent upon himself to see that God had other means at his disposal than his own efforts. He could see no future for Israel because in his preoccupation with the intricacies of his situation and his conviction of his inability to meet it he had lost his vision of God's invincible purposes and illimitable resources. He needed a new perspective born of a larger reference.

There is always the danger that we be too impressed with the world's problems, too concerned with the roar of the passing wind, the convulsion of the earthquake and the desolation of the fire and so miss the message of the still, small Voice and forget the Anointing Hand—concerned with God's judgments and unaware of His mercy and power to save. When that happens, like Elijah, we always underestimate the resources of God.

But God had no intention that His cause should fail. His purposes and His resources were far greater than the little orbit of Elijah's discouraged and distorted outlook. He challenged the prophet with a new vision of His resources.

"Get thee up," he said, "Go back to the desert, for in the desert of your disillusionment you shall find Hazael and Jehu and Elisha, the men whom I have chosen to be the instruments of my will. Anoint them for my service."

The lesson is clear. The purposes of Almighty God shall not lack for instruments; the kingdom is sure; God has planned a great future. His resources are not exhausted by today's limitations. If Benhadad will not serve His purposes He will anoint Hazael; if Abab will not be His instrument, He will anoint Jehu; if Elijah fails, Elisha shall carry on. The purposes of God are not to be thwarted by Jezebel's wrath or Ahab's folly, by atom bomb or communist intransigence. He is still the master of creation.

Science tells us that it has taken over sixty million years for God to bring life up from the protozoan cells wriggling in the slime of the primeval swamps to Shakespeare's sonnets and Lincoln's Gettysburg address! Centuries of patient progress, and not all progress either, because there were times when life failed Him and slid back into blind alleys and dead pockets. But He would not let it give up. There were always some forms, which in His providence, were equal to life's demands and kept on; until one day man stood erect upon his feet and looked up into his Creator's face with faith.

Sixty million years of patient purpose! Do you think God is going to let it fail now? Surely not unless we fail Him. Too great pains have gone into the process to let it be wiped out by the turn of events of one century in six hundred thousand. We must not fall a prey to spiritual astigmatism.

The final basis of our faith is not in the passing scene, but in the eternal purposes of Almighty God, not in the exhausted prophet in the barren wilderness but in the triumphant prophet in the chariot of fire, not in the awesome spectacle of the tempest and the earthquake but in the finality of the still, small Voice, not in the broken, defeated figure on a cross but in the Triumphant Living Christ of God. When we realize that, our situation is never desperate nor our effort futile.

Christian Faith Confronts the Modern Mind

REVEREND C. PENROSE ST. AMANT, TH.D.

A Minister of the Southern Baptist Convention and Professor of Christian History and Theology, New Orleans Baptist Theological Seminary, New Orleans, Louisiana

Dr. St. Amant is active in Southern Baptist work and preaching and represents a fine type of religious thinking in the South today. Born at Gonzales, Louisiana, in 1915, he became a member of the Baptist Church in the community when a child, and was graduated from Gonzales High School in 1932. From 1932 to 1936 he attended and graduated from Louisiana College, Pineville, Louisiana, during student days was active in the religious life of the campus and served one year as president of the Louisiana Baptist Student Union. He was also on the debating team, entered Louisiana State University at Baton Rouge for graduate work in history and philosophy. He spent 1937-42 in the New Orleans Baptist Theological Seminary from which he received the degree of Doctor of Theology with the predicate summa cum laude in 1942. He also studied at Union Theological Seminary and Columbia University in New York and is particularly interested in the thought of Reinhold Niebuhr, whom he considers the dominant influence in the formation of his theological perspective.

Immediately upon graduation from the Seminary in New Orleans he spent one year as Professor of Religion in Hannibal-LaGrange College in Hannibal, Missouri, and in the fall of 1944 returned to the New Orleans Seminary as an instructor in theology and has taught there from then until now; he was elected Professor of Christian History and Theology in 1948. He is the author of A Short History of Louisiana Baptists, *a popular treatise written for the*

[125]

commemoration of the one hundredth anniversary of the Louisiana Baptist Convention. He writes for various Baptist periodicals, and an address before the New Orleans Protestant Ministerial Union entitled "Prophetic Preaching in a Secular World" is now being published. He has preached in many churches in Louisiana and during the summer of 1949 served as supply pastor of the St. Charles Avenue Baptist Church in New Orleans. His main recreational interest is golf. He plans a trip to Europe in 1950-51 on sabbatical leave to study at the University of Edinburgh.

Sermon Twenty=one

TEXT: We are troubled on every side, yet not distressed; we are perplexed but not in despair. II CORINTHIANS 4:8

READINGS: II CORINTHIANS 4:5-8, 5:17-21

AN EDITOR of one of our literary journals has stated bluntly: "The Christian attitude toward life can no longer be presupposed as a datum; it has been completely forgotten by everybody." This generalization, like all generalizations, is too sweeping and reflects a presumptuous finality in its facile disposition of the Christian faith which ill befits the fine mind of its author, but the fact that it could be made at all should give us pause. The Christian faith has been completely forgotten by everybody! Well, hardly. Many of us are still impelled and intrigued by it. T. S. Eliot and W. H. Auden are two among many modern intellectuals who have at last found in the Christian faith the solution to the spiritual disease of our time. But it is nevertheless true that hosts of people live without any conscious reference to the Christian attitude toward life.

The Christian faith confronts the modern mind, which, broadly speaking, neither understands nor accepts it. Reinhold Niebuhr has said: "For the past two-hundred years the Christian church has been proclaiming its gospel in a world which no longer accepted the essentials of the Christian faith." Perhaps this generalization is also too sweeping but let us face the fact: our culture is secular and many of our contemporaries conceive of the Christian faith as a kind of superstitious hangover from antiquity which is irrelevant in the modern world. John Dewey's *Common Faith*, the creed of many modern men, traces the crisis of our time to a "cultural lag," as it is phrased, and treats Christian faith not only as irrelevant but as a factor which actually aggravates our difficulties. Most modern education—that messiah that has displaced the Christ—is informed by Dewey's purely humanistic conception of man's plight.

[126]

You see, the assumption is that our problems are all reducible to an ignorance that education can allay. There is little understanding of man's spiritual depth and the essential problem which is deep within us. Man tends to be treated as a higher animal who can be saved from personal and social disharmonies through the critical use of his mind. This is an implicit denial of man's spiritual stature and the Christian doctrines of sin and grace. This is secularism.

Since the dawn of modern history the Christian faith has fought a running battle with the secular spirit, a view of the human situation which has no place for God. This enemy of Christ, this antichrist, has assumed various forms. Art, music, literature, our common life, and even religion show the stultifying effect of secularism.

Modern art is often the fusing of color (if color has not been discarded) to form an ephemeral picture of an ephemeral experience. It has lost the sense of universality and depth. The function of the artist is said to be to catch the moods of modern men, and these are often moods without faith. Modern art is sometimes only a meaningless smudge of figure and color understood only by the artist, the esoteric few, and God—and one might legitimately wonder whether God understands it. . . . There is no great glory or tragedy because man is no longer glorious or tragic. He is an animal—with enough "mind" to know his lowly state—but still an animal, largely determined by a fate which seems alternately beneficent and demonic. The conscious and unconscious streams of his mind are thrown on canvas, and there is no glory. The modern artist, held firmly by earthbound ties, is a symbol of contemporary man.

If we turn to music, a similar situation confronts us. The really great music is music which reflects man's deeper struggles with himself and his God and the attendant despair and peace. This is not to assert that all the masters were men of faith. Some were tragic figures who could not capture life's deeper meaning. But they struggled with it. Some, like Beethoven, shook their fists at fate or yearned for human brotherhood, but behind their tragic faces was a quest for meaning. Man was still the figure of mystery, he was still made in the image of God, he still lived by or struggled against great Christian affirmations. Some, like Handel and Bach, created deathless music that has the depth of eternity in it because it throbs with the Christian story of man's pilgrimage. The stark superficiality of Shostakovich is a pitiful example of modern music which merely reflects passing experience—in this instance a passing political experience; it is rather interesting but has no depth.

Our literature has deteriorated. There is often no genuine plot but only a description of streams of consciousness without meaning. Modern novels usually possess no plot because many of the people who write them see no plot in life; there are only meaningless experiences piled high. Many of our books and plays reflect not only a lack of plot but a lack of genuine respect for personality. There is little struggle for either meaning or morality in contemporary writing because the God from whom truth and goodness come has been relegated to the limbo of the past. Edmund Wilson has spoken of "the moral

[127]

disease that has invaded the contemporary world," and Raymond Mortimer, literary critic of the London *Times,* commenting upon the current "best" Broadway play, has stated: "Didn't it reflect a lack of a desire for happiness? A feeling that life wasn't worth living?"

In a recent novel one of the characters, Kay, speaks of "that frozen twentieth century mask of a face," to which Vic replies, "Why twentieth century mask of a face?" "Because it's a godless face," she said, "that's a characteristic of true twentieth century men and women. Godlessness. Don't you see it in their faces? They have nothing outside themselves to go to." Christian faith faces this secular mind imprisoned within itself. It confronts the world with a live alternative that promises salvation and hope. It offers to mankind, hovering on the brink of cultural suicide, a diagnosis of its plight and a message of hope.

Let us observe that Christian faith keeps alive our confidence in the value of the individual. Today the individual tends to be lost in the group: a man assembles automobiles and becomes a part of the assembly line. A recent novelist has described man as a "cellular mass on his way to become manure." How can we go on with faces toward the future in hope if this be true? Man, a cellular mass, a physiological process. What a contrast this is to the daring words of the Apostle John: "Beloved, now we are the sons of God and it does not yet appear what we shall be." Cellular mass or sons of God! Christian faith pushes the horizons back, gives a man room to breathe, to smile, to believe in his Divine possibilities, to go on.

But there is a darker side. Christian faith declares not only that man is made in the Divine image destined for the life eternal but also that he is a sinner. This assertion seems incredible to the modern mind. Maladjustment, antisocial behavior, neurosis perhaps, but surely not sin. A psychologist recently called sin "a psychopathic aspect of adolescent mentality." This is not an unusual estimate. Man is really good, it is held, and is corrupted by evil institutions. Salvation waits upon more enlightenment. But how did the good men of previous generations create the evil bequeathed in institutions? And how can mere ignorance give rise to the demonic fury that frequently appears in history? In opposition to the prejudices of modernity concerning man's plight, Christian faith declares that man's inordinate love of himself, from which he cannot save himself, is the crux of the problem. This is not primarily a matter of ignorance which education can cure; it is a situation of spiritual dimensions. The failure of modern culture to do justice to the Christian doctrine of sin is one of the most disastrous errors of our time.

It is clear that the secular spirit overestimates man's virtue, even as it underestimates man's stature. This is why the Christian doctrines of grace and sin are not understood. Knowledge of the natural world is assumed to be all the power man needs and there therefore seems to be no need for grace, which is the power of God. Psychology and psychiatry, guided by secular predilections, tend to surrender the Christian doctrine of sin. The modern man is saved from sin, not by grace, but by having his guilt explained away. There is, of course, morbid guilt which needs even psychoanalytic treatment. But there is also an ultimate goodness with whom man seeks relentlessly to be reconciled; there is a Divine healing of which many moderns do not know; there is a void which only God can fill; there is a grace that is greater than all our sin.

Let it be said to all who despair: man is no mere cellular mass; he is made in the Divine image, he is meant for an eternal destiny with his God, with whom he may share a present fellowship. How we need this confidence to-day! Kirkegaard was right: "Whoever is without God in the world soon becomes tired of himself and expresses this loftily by being bored with life; but he who has fellowship with God lives with one whose presence gives even the most insignificant an infinite significance." That's it! Something that gives the insignificant an infinite significance. How desperately we need this today to displace the futility that haunts the world. The high hopes of the nineteenth century, centered in the harmony which was to grow out of man's control of nature, have not come true. We smile today at Victor Hugo's prophecy: "In the twentieth century war will be dead, the scaffold will be dead, hatred will be dead, frontier boundaries will be dead, dogmas will be dead, man will live." The failure of the fruition of these dreams has led to widespread disillusionment. Thus an optimism which did not understand the demonic possibilities within man has led to despair in some of our most capable minds. There are still many brave humanists who continue to worship man, as if man were God, but there is widespread despair. Professor Hocking has caught this mood: "Everyone today knows not by rumor but by introspection that modern man is tired of himself." To too many, nothing is significant. The insignificant having an infinite significance; far from it. Nothing is significant. This modern temper has been described by Joseph Wood Krutch, who states it simply: "Now we know that man is petty."

Man—this conquering hero out to subdue the earth and himself, with all the glittering magic of science; this brave, self-sufficient man, emancipated from the taboos of religion—now finds himself a futile cynic, baffled by the persistence of evil and by the demonic fury which intrudes to upset his vaunted rationality, baffled because he possesses a stature given by God, deny it though he may, and finds all historical fulfillments unable to satisfy his ultimate concern; baffled because the lust for power breaks through the thin veneer of culture and manifests an incredible cruelty; baffled because "critical intelligence," that God of modern man, is so easily subservient to the terrifying class and political ideologies of our time.

Let us go on in our thought to say that the fundamental doctrines of the Christian faith are the grace of God and the reality of sin. The grace of God, manifested supremely in Jesus Christ, which provides power, wisdom, and forgiveness for man, and the reality of sin, a rebellion of spiritual dimensions that defies the customary psychological explanations: this constitutes the basic intellectual structure of the Christian faith. St. Paul has succinctly defined the spiritual disease which infests man down at the very roots of his being: "They changed the glory of the incorruptible God into an image made like to corruptible man." This self-deification; this claim that "my culture," "my class," or "my anything else" is ultimate and final is the essence of sin.

These doctrines of sin and grace have little meaning for the modern mind because of the strange blending of self-sufficiency and despair which constitutes the spiritual temper of our time. Help from God is spurned by those who are self-sufficient because they think human problems are entirely tractable to human wisdom and by those who despair because they do not believe in God. This secular mind fails to see man's true depth and discards the idea of sin. But look at the chaos of our time. Are we really self-sufficient? We actually are not. Our problem is precisely that we try to think we are when we are really not. If the chaos of our day could drive us to contrition—contrition for our presumed self-sufficiency—instead of to the despair to which many are tempted, we could hope for a better tomorrow. Mark these words: contrition is the condition which must be met before there can be harmony within ourselves and the world. Modern man is not contrite because he tends neither to believe in the God of justice and mercy disclosed in Christ, though he may believe in many gods, nor does he believe in the sin of which he needs to be contrite.

Christian faith confronts the modern mind which has overestimated the wisdom and power of man and underestimated the wisdom and power of God. One may be redeemed from sin, not by merely extending the range of his mind and not by simply changing corrupt institutions, but by the grace of God manifested in the cross. In the cross of Christ is salvation for those who repent of their sins. To what extent God went to redeem us! "For none of the ransomed ever knew how deep were the waters crossed, how dark was the night that the Lord passed through ere he found the sheep that was lost."

St. Paul cries: "Who will deliver me from this body of death?" He answers, "God will. Thanks be to Him through Jesus Christ our Lord." This is likewise the cry of our time but there is today no clear answer. There are those whose pride keeps them from contrition and salvation. Man who has been worshiping himself since the Renaissance does not find it easy to worship God. But there are many whose self-sufficiency has been shattered and who have turned to despair and there are many who move from pride to despair and back again, at last finding despair. Many of our finest minds have given up. There is no hope for man, they say. Still they cry: "Who shall rescue me?", for no man can live on sheer futility. Is this not the cry of our time: who shall rescue me? We hear a thousand voices: who shall rescue me? Who shall rescue me from my despair, my preoccupation with myself, my sin? And there are many answers. Education continues to assert its claim to be man's deliverer. Others turn to Marxism. Rebecca Pitts, writing in the *New Masses*, states the Communist faith: "Men become sincere and incorruptible as they identify their aims with those of the working class as a whole." Others believe in psychiatry, particularly psychoanalysis, with its promise of release from haunting fears.

To him who is proud, who still clings to Swinburne's faith: "Glory to man in the highest for man is the master of things," one needs only to say that this faith does not square with the facts. That man is not the master of things is one of the clearest lessons of modern history. Man has tried to build a world without God and has failed. He has worshiped false gods of his own making, and they were idols and the supreme idol has been man himself. Man's "titanism," to use Karl Barth's word, has been actually demolished and he stands now amid the shambles. Man has been worshiping himself and is tired of himself. He has worshiped his mind, his body, his nation, his blood, his race. And he has created confusions within himself and his world. Man is not the master of things. This is obvious unless our minds are caught in the vicious circle of pride, which makes us unable to see this simple truth about ourselves.

To him whose pride has turned to despair but who wistfully hopes that something will turn up that some modern messiah will appear—let it be said: you will be disillusioned. To him whose pride has turned to despair without hope, to him who, as Auden has put it, is "tired out, his last illusions have lost patience with the human enterprise," let it be said: there is mercy and meaning in Christ.

The phrase St. Paul used to describe the intolerable burden of sin, "this body of death," may be a reference to a hideous method of punishment practiced in the ancient world. A corpse was strapped to the back of a criminal. It could not be removed. It was carried day and night. Thus does the Apostle symbolize the burden of sin as something of which man cannot rid himself. This burden is described by St. Paul with penetrating psychological insight: "The wish is there but not the power of doing right. I cannot be good as I want to be, and I do wrong against my wishes. . . . I want to do what is right, but wrong is all I can manage. I find another law in my members which conflicts with the law of my mind and makes me a prisoner. . . . Miserable wretch that I am? Who will deliver me from this body of death?" He knew despair but he went beyond it to victory: "Who will deliver me? God will. Thanks be to him through Jesus Christ our Lord."

This is a profound analysis of the actual human situation and the answer to its deepest problem. I actually love myself. I pretend to be self-sufficient and then I despair. Who shall deliver me? Human love, friendship, music, psychoanalysis, Marxism, science? Ah, no. If there is any genuine redemption which goes to the very roots of a man's being the self must be drawn out of itself from beyond itself. As St. Paul said also: "I am crucified with Christ"; this is Christian conversion. This is to break the vicious circle of selfishness within which man is imprisoned. This is the antidote to secularism. God will deliver us! Thanks be to Him through Jesus Christ our Lord.

And now the concluding word. "The nineteenth century," declared Andre Malraux recently, "faced the question, is God dead? The twentieth century now faces the question, is man dead?" But God is not dead. Christian faith confronts this secular creed with the living God, whose mighty acts may be seen in history and whose glory may be seen in the face of Jesus Christ. The world has an intelligent and loving creative source. It is no mass of energy going its own way blindly. It is not derelict drifting helplessly upon a wind-swept sea. Even human tragedy has meaning because it is seen against the background of belief in a loving God. God has stooped in Christ to redeem mankind from sin. And man is not dead either—he need not be—for God's grace, mediated through Jesus Christ, offers salvation, peace and power.

Let us lift our eyes to see the light of Christ shining in the darkness of the world; this will lift our horizons and give us hope. We shall still have our perplexities but with St. Paul we shall say: "We are perplexed but not unto despair." People might well be divided into those who are not perplexed, those who are perplexed unto despair, and those who are perplexed but not unto despair. Those who are not perplexed have dissolved the mystery of life by some simple scheme of meaning, such as Marxism or scientism, but it is too simple to do justice to life in its deeper dimensions of beauty and terror, and optimism eventually gives way to despair, serenity becomes perplexity— a perplexity unto despair. Christian faith does not promise to solve all per-plexities. It confesses that we sometimes "see through a glass darkly" but it is convinced that we do see. It escapes the disillusionment which always over-takes utopianism because it knows that life has dark demonic depths which have a cruel way of blasting our highest hopes, but it escapes despair because it clings to the goodness of God as revealed in Jesus Christ and is therefore "persuaded that neither life nor death, nor things present nor things to come, are able to separate us from the love of God, which is in Christ Jesus our Lord."

FAITH

My Duty to Doubt

REVEREND FRANK BENJAMIN FAGERBURG, D.D., L.H.D., LL.D.

Minister, First Baptist Church of Los Angeles, California

Dr. Fagerburg has held just two pastorates and has been a builder of the church in both churches. Upon his ordination to the Baptist ministry in 1923, he became pastor of First Baptist Church, one of the largest churches in Spring-

field, Massachusetts, and remained there for seven years. In 1930 he was called to the First Baptist Church of Los Angeles. The debt on the church at that time was over $300,000. The mortgage was burned September 6, 1944.

He was born at Slater, Missouri, May 30, 1898, spent most of his life in Bloomington, Illinois, and was graduated from Illinois Wesleyan University. He took his divinity degree at Newton Center, Massachusetts. In 1931 his alma mater honored him with a D.D. degree and the University of Southern California in 1934. He received the L.H.D. from Denison University, Granville, Ohio, in 1940 and the LL.D. in 1943 from the College of Osteopathic Physicians and Surgeons of Los Angeles.

Dr. Fagerburg has written The Sin of Being Ordinary, The Questioning Age, and Is This Religion? Articles, devotional guides and lesson helps by Dr. Fagerburg have appeared in The International Council of Religious Education Journal, The Baptist Leader, and The Secret Place.

He is a member of the Board of Managers of the American Baptist Foreign Mission Society, member of the Protestant Film Commission, and a member of the Board of Trustees of the Berkeley Baptist Divinity School. He broadcasts over KFAC Saturday evenings at 7:30.

This sermon on doubt and faith is especially suited to the disturbed world of our day.

Sermon Twenty=two

"DOUBT" has been for most of us an ugly word. "Faith," "belief"—these words express what we want. It is good to keep in mind, however, that doubt is the other side of faith; they are two faces of the same shield. In other words, we believe certain things because we seriously question their opposites. The man of faith is a man of doubt. He believes in God because he doubts the credibility of atheism. The man of doubt is also a man of faith. Remember that the atheist is a believer; he accepts quite tremendous beliefs about the universe. Often the religious man believes not because he finds his faith easy; he believes because he finds its opposite incredible. When you stop for a moment to think it over, it is a bit amusing that we Christians have so often imagined that we are on the defensive. Sometimes we have felt frustrated or embarrassed because we did not have all the answers; because we did not have proof or conclusive demonstration. Do not forget that the pagan and skeptic have also made great claims. Let them defend their position. They would be equally put to it for proof or conclusive demonstration.

A good illustration comes to us from Peter's great sermon in Acts 2. It sounds like an eloquent statement of confident faith. It is; but see here at its

[133]

heart how this man of faith expresses his doubt. He is talking about the resurrection of Jesus, a thing incredible to many of his audience and to many of our own day. He says, "It was not possible that he should be holden of it [death]." In other words Peter is saying, "You are sure that wicked men could permanently destroy this Man of God. I doubt it! I cannot accept that great assumption. It was not possible that such a Person could be held by the tomb."

This, one of the Christian's cardinal doubts, is a good place to begin our list of serious questionings. Someone insists, "After the crucifixion Jesus remained dead. There is no reality behind our belief in eternal life." I doubt it. My faith in immortality is the other side of my doubt that a good life can end in the grave. Only the other day I expressed this basic doubt to my barber. Questioning immortality, he was making assumptions which were too great for me to accept. I said to him, "I simply cannot believe that this chair at which you work will always be in the universe, but that you, the real you who thinks, speaks, works and loves will entirely disappear. Science holds to the position called *the conservation of energy*, contending that no unit of energy can be destroyed; somewhere in some form it will always exist. Personality is the highest thing I know; but it must disappear? I doubt it."

I am not saying that there are no problems connected with our faith in immortality. There are serious problems. What saint does not have his moments when he asks troublesome questions? For me there are greater problems connected with faith in the perishability of the human soul. I doubt it. That doubt grows as one comes in touch with noble persons. In them he sees here and now qualities revealed which he feels must be eternal. That was at the bottom of Peter's doubt. He had known this Jesus; he had heard him speak; he had seen God in him; then "it was not possible that he should be holden of death."

Peter's doubt brings into focus the whole problem of the life and message of Jesus. Again and again we Christians are challenged concerning our faith in Christ. Such great claims we make for him? Such claims he made for himself: "I am the bread of life. . . . I am the way, the truth, and the life. . . . He that hath seen me hath seen the Father. . . . Come unto me, all ye that labour and are heavy laden, and I will give you rest. . . . I am come that they might have life, and that they might have it more abundantly."

See for a moment the other side. If he were not what he said, if he were not what we believe, then what? I see two other explanations: He was then either self-deceived, indeed, a madman; or he was a deceiver, a mountebank. I doubt it. This question about Jesus turns into a tremendous assumption, a stupendous credo: "I believe that Jesus was a good man with strange delusions," or "I believe that Jesus was a benevolent fraud." I doubt it.

There are many who make similar claims about the teachings of Jesus. Read again the beatitudes explaining the quality of character which he said that men can and should live. Hear Him again describe the way of good will, of nonretaliation, of mercy, and love. The world says, "Impossible moonshine and air castles!" I doubt it. This is a tremendous assumption that the pagan makes. He says that instead ill will and hate will work, that "an eye for an eye, and a tooth for a tooth" is the only basis on which to run the world. I doubt it. I doubt it not only because I cannot believe that the greatest Person who ever lived could be so badly mistaken. I doubt it, too, because of the ugly hell that the anti-Christ spirit has made of our world. I doubt it, because again and again I have seen men respond to understanding and good will who only acted like beasts in response to injustice and hate.

It is perhaps too much to expect governments to be interested in Christian qualities. Precedents, principles of the past, rule the actions of diplomats. We have been wrong, too, in calling America a Christian country when even nominal Christians constitute but a bare majority, and so many of them do not care about taking the teachings of Jesus into practical affairs. I cannot resist the conviction, however, that because they are people, even Russians would respond to utter good will. Suppose that we should say, and prove that we mean it, "We will destroy our atom bombs of which you are naturally so fearful. We promise never to use them. We will join all nations in abolishing conscription. We will do any sensible and honorable thing to make peace real and lasting." Before you close your mind to what that might do in changing the climate of international relationships—and nothing can happen until the very climate is changed—look realistically at the road upon which the other attitude is taking us. It is taking us into a war which scientific and military leaders together insist no one can possibly win. On the road which I have mentioned there is a ray of hope for our children and grandchildren. On the road which we are traveling no one has any hope at all; friend and enemy alike must wilt and die in a withering radioactive universe. I should rather fail trying something that might work than to succeed in working something that we know must fail.

It would be very misleading if you should imagine that these are simply the suggestions of an unrealistic preacher. If you have read something more than the daily newspapers you know that responsible people in high places have been saying similar things. I wish that everyone of you might read the little article in the April, 1948, edition of the *Atlantic Monthly*. It is written by Thomas Finletter who was the chairman of the five-man commission appointed by President Truman to inquire into all phases of aviation and to aid in the drafting of a national air policy. Characteristically, the newspapers reported only one part of this committee's recommendations. They did, indeed, urge the enlargement of our air forces, and Congress is busy at work implementing these suggestions. Let me read these sentences which tell something of the other part of the report which you probably did not find in the newspapers and which you do not hear congressmen talking about:

> But we also said that we did not like this preparedness program which we recommended. This is only a second-best way of doing things, forced

on us by the international situation and by the current fantastic developments in the military art—especially in the fields of atomic energy and biological agents, of aircraft and guided missiles. We said that real security for this country lies only in the abolishing of war under a regime of world law and that it is high time that the United States got busy to create such a world of peace. I wish to elaborate on this latter part of our report, which I am sorry to say was not stressed in the press.

It is my faith that the number one foreign policy of the United States must be to establish world peace. . . . Considerably more can be done in this respect than is being done. Our military policy is, however, only the negative side of our foreign policy for peace and by its nature it can only be a temporary policy. It will give us only a short time to do the possible things which will produce peace, for it is inflammatory. Time is running out, and we must make haste with our politics for peace, for we cannot long endure a world racing with itself to build new ways of destroying itself. Some day the weapons will go off if we have not first created the institutions which will let us put these weapons away and use their power for other purposes.

Behind all these impossible credos about Jesus and his teachings is a deeper and more serious anti-Christian faith. It is that God does not exist and that all we are and see just happened. I doubt it. Sometimes I want to say to the atheist—if I could find one; atheists are rare, you know, for few intelligent people care to go to the end of that limb—"I congratulate you, my friend, for your faith—or is it credulity? You have made an amazing stand. You hold that basically the universe as a whole has done what we never find in any of its parts—the stream has risen higher than its source! In a universe behind which no mind exists, mind has developed. In a universe behind which no love exists, love has grown. In a universe behind which no character or purpose exist, we have character and purpose. My belief in God has grave problems, but your belief in atheism is incredible. I doubt it."

Indeed, our belief in God is not always easy. It is fraught with most difficult problems and innumerable questions. In the Bible we find many good men asking such pointed questions as this one from Jeremiah: "Why is my pain perpetual, and my wound incurable, which refuseth to be healed? wilt thou be altogether unto me as a liar, and as waters that fail?" (15:18); or this one from Habakkuk: "O Lord, how long shall I cry . . . and thou wilt not save!" (1:2). These questions and others found in the Bible, which aim at the very heart of faith in God, express what has always been the theist's greatest obstacle: How can there be a good God in a world of so much pain and trouble? It is called the problem of evil. Men who raise this question seldom stop to realize that there is yet another problem, the problem of good. There is evil. Why, we cannot explain; but there is good too. Let the atheist attempt to explain that.

God is nowhere? I doubt it. I feel like the little girl who took the words of the atheist and by rearranging the spaces made them say, "God is now here!"

Then there are those who are not atheists who, indeed, accept this position,

"God is now here," in a general sort of way, but who, nonetheless, do not believe that He has any day-by-day dealings with men. Prayer, for instance; it is simply superstition or autosuggestion, they insist. I doubt it. The other side of my faith in prayer is a deep doubt that God is a kind of absentee Creator, such as the deists of the eighteenth century believed in—a God who set His world to going and then went away and left it to run by itself.

What mind would not be open to the reality of prayer in our modern world where by radio and television man's mind can reach man's mind—yes, and influence his conduct too—across vast distances defying time. Frequently in notes from our radio audience, I am told by people that something I said has changed their thinking or their living. This means that a part of me went out through the ether and became a part of someone else; yet God is unable to reach my life; my prayer goes only as high as the ceiling? I doubt it; therefore, I believe beyond my understanding—indeed, radio is beyond my understanding—that the personality of God can deal intimately and effectively with my personality, and my personality can reach out and come into relationship with God. This is prayer. I believe it because I doubt its opposite.

Last, there are proud, self-sufficient men who say, "Every tub must stand upon its bottom." They are quite sure, in other words, that they can save themselves, that their own bootstraps, pulled by their own hands, will lift them. They need no divine arm extended from above. I doubt it. Few of my doubts are more deep-dyed than this one. I need only to look about me and see the mess that most men make of their lives as they attempt to live them in their own strength. The downdrag of one's instinctive equipment is too much. The temptations and bafflements of each common day are too great. Indeed, I need but look into my own heart honestly. I cannot handle life alone. Christ is the answer to anything and everything in me that has been decent. Without him life would be a desert, a disappointment, a tragedy. Such doubt of yourself is a wholesome thing. It is the first step to God. William Ernest Henley prated,

> I am the master of my fate:
> I am the captain of my soul.

I am not "the master of my fate." I say instead:

> My faith looks up to Thee,
> Thou Lamb of Calvary,
> Saviour divine!
> Now hear me while I pray,
> Take all my guilt away,
> O let me from this day
> Be wholly Thine!

The Escape from God[1]

REVEREND PAUL JOHANNES TILLICH, PH.D., D.TH., D.D.

A Minister of the Evangelical and Reformed Church, and Professor of Philosophical Theology, Union Theological Seminary, New York

Dr. Tillich speaks especially to other ministers who must think and feel and preach. He is a theologian, philosopher, educator, author and preacher of great ability. He helps to mold the theology of men who will go out from Union Theological Seminary to become leaders in churches everywhere.

Professor Tillich was a student at the University of Berlin, 1904-05, University of Tübingen, 1905, University of Halle, 1905-07; University of Berlin, 1908. He served as war chaplain with the German Army, 1914-18. Honorary Ph.D. University of Breslau, 1911; honorary Doctor of Theology, University of Halle, 1926; D.D., Yale, 1940.

He was born in Starzeddel, Kreis Guben, Prussia, August 20, 1886. After extensive study in several German universities, he returned to the University of Berlin as a Privatdozent of Theology, 1919-24, went to the University of Marburg as Professor of Theology, 1924-25, University of Dresden, 1925-29, University of Leipzig, 1928-29; Professor of Philosophy, University of Frankfurt-am-Main, 1929-33 (all Germany). He came to the United States in 1933, where he has been Professor of Philosophy and Philosophical Theology at Union Theological Seminary ever since. He was naturalized in 1940.

He is the author of The Religious Situation, The Interpretation of History, *several books published in Germany on philosophy, philosophy of religion, and numerous articles in religious journals. "The Escape from God" is included in Dr. Tillich's newest book,* The Shaking of the Foundations, *as one of the sermons in this fine collection. It gives part of Professor Tillich's theological and spiritual outlook. This sermon was first published by* The Protestant *and attracted considerable attention when it was delivered by Dr. Tillich. The entire series of sermons contained in* The Shaking of the Foundations *are worthy of careful reading by ministers and laymen for their definitive view of the "Tillich Theology."*

Sermon Twenty=three

TEXT: O, Lord, thou hast searched me and known me.
Thou knowest my downsitting and mine uprising,
Thou understandest my thought afar off.
Thou compassest my path and my lying down,
And art acquainted with all my ways.
For there is not a word in my tongue,
But, lo, O Lord, thou knowest it altogether.
Thou hast beset me behind and before,
And laid thine hand upon me.
Such knowledge is too wonderful for me;
It is high, I cannot attain unto it.
Whither shall I go from thy spirit?
Or whither shall I flee from thy presence?
If I ascend up into Heaven, thou art there;
If I make my bed in hell, behold, thou art there.
If I take the wings of the morning,
And dwell in the uttermost parts of the sea,
Even there shall thy hand lead me,
And thy right hand shall hold me.
If I say, Surely the darkness shall cover me,
Even the night shall be light about me.
Yea, the darkness hideth not from thee,
But the night shineth as the day.
The darkness and the light are both alike to thee.
For thou hast possessed my reins;
Thou hast covered me in my mother's womb.
I will praise thee, for I am fearfully and wonderfully made;
Marvellous are thy works; and that my soul knoweth right well.
My substance was not hid from thee, when I was made in secret,
And curiously wrought in the lowest parts of the earth.
Thine eyes did see my substance, yet being unperfect;
And in thy book all my members were written, which in con-
    tinuance
Were fashioned, when as yet there was none of them.
How precious also are thy thoughts unto me, O God!
How great is the sum of them!
If I should count them, they are more in number than the sand.
When I awake, I am still with thee.
Surely thou wilt slay the wicked, O God:
Depart from me therefore, ye bloody men.
For they speak against thee wickedly,
And thine enemies take thy name in vain.
Do not I hate them, O Lord, that hate thee?
And am not I grieved with those that rise up against thee?
I hate them with perfect hatred.
I count them mine enemies.
Search me, O God, and know my heart;

Try me and know my thoughts;
And see if there be any wicked way in me,
And lead me in the way everlasting.

PSALM 139

W HERE could I go from thy spirit, and where could I flee from Thy
Face?" These are the central words of the great 139th Psalm. They
state in the form of a question *the inescapable Presence of God*. Let us consider this statement, and the powerful images in which the psalmist tries to
express it. God is inescapable. He is God only *because* He is inescapable. And
only that which *is* inescapable is God.

There is no place to which we could flee from God which is outside of
God. "If I ascend to the heavens, Thou art there." It seems very natural for
God to be in heaven, and very unnatural for us to wish to ascend to heaven
in order to escape Him. But that is just what the idealists of all ages have
tried to do. They have tried to leap towards the heaven of perfection and
truth, of justice and peace, where God is not wanted. That heaven is a
heaven of man's making, without the driving restlessness of the Divine
Spirit and without the judging presence of the Divine Face. But such a
place is a "no place"; it is a "utopia," an idealistic illusion. "If I
make hell my home, behold, Thou art there." Hell or Sheol, the habitation of the dead, would seem to be the right place to hide from God. And
that is where all those who long for death, in order to escape the Divine
Demands, attempt to flee. I am convinced that there is not one amongst us
who has not at some time desired to be liberated from the burden of his
existence by stepping out of it. And I know that there are some amongst us
for whom this longing is a daily temptation. But everyone knows in the depth
of his heart that death would not provide an escape from the inner demand
made upon him. "If I take the wings of the dawn and dwell in the midst
of the sea, Thy Hand would even fall on me there, and Thy right Hand,
would grasp me." To fly to the ends of the earth would not be to escape from
God. Our technical civilization attempts just that, in order to be liberated
from the knowledge that it lacks a centre of life and meaning. The modern
way to flee from God is to rush ahead and ahead, as quickly as the beams
before sunrise, to conquer more and more space in every direction, in every
humanly possible way, to be always active, to be always planning, and to be
always preparing. But God's Hand falls upon us; and it *has* fallen heavily
and destructively upon our fleeing civilization; our flight proved to be vain.
"When I think that the darkness shall cover me, that night shall hide me,
I know at the same time that the darkness is not dark to Thee, and that night
is as bright as day." To flee into darkness in order to forget God is not to
escape Him. For a time we may be able to hurl Him out of our consciousness, to reject Him, to refute Him, to argue convincingly for His non-exist-
ence, and to live very comfortably without Him. But ultimately we know that

it is not He Whom we reject and forget, but that it is rather some distorted picture of Him. And we know that we can argue against Him, only because He impels us to attack Him. There is no escape from God through forgetfulness.

"Where could I go from Thy Spirit? O, where could I flee from Thy Face?" The poet who wrote those words to describe the futile attempt of man to escape God certainly believed that man *desires* to escape God. He is not alone in his conviction. Men of all kinds, prophets and reformers, saints and atheists, believers and unbelievers, have the same experience. It is safe to say that a man who has never tried to flee God has never experienced the God Who is really God. When I speak of God, I do not refer to the many gods of our own making, the gods with whom we can live rather comfortably. For there is no reason to flee a god who is the perfect picture of everything that is good in man. Why try to escape from such a far-removed ideal? And there is no reason to flee from a god who is simply the universe, or the laws of nature, or the course of history. Why try to escape from a reality of which we are a part? There is no reason to flee from a god who is nothing more than a benevolent father, a father who guarantees our immortality and final happiness. Why try to escape from someone who serves us so well? No, those are not pictures of God, but rather of man, trying to make God in his own image and for his own comfort. They are the products of man's imagination and wishful thinking, justly denied by every honest atheist. A god whom we can easily bear, a god from whom we do not have to hide, a god whom we do not hate in moments, a god whose destruction we never desire, is not God at all, and has no reality.

Friedrich Nietzsche, the famous atheist and ardent enemy of religion and Christianity, knew more about the power of the idea of God than many faithful Christians. In a symbolic story, when Zarathustra, the prophet of a higher humanity, says to the Ugliest Man, the murderer of God, "You could not bear him to see you, always to see you through and through. . . . You took revenge on the witness. . . . You are the murderer of God," the Ugliest Man agrees with Zarathustra and replies, "He *had* to die." For God, according to the Ugliest Man, looks with eyes that see everything; He peers into man's ground and depth, into his hidden shame and ugliness. The God Who sees everything, and man also, is the God Who has to die. Man cannot stand that such a Witness live.

Are *we* able to stand such a Witness? The psalmist says, "O, Lord, thou hast searched me and known me." Who can stand to be known so thoroughly even in the darkest corners of his soul? Who does not want to escape such a Witness? And who does not want to become one who can deny God in theory and practice, an atheist? "Thou knowest when I sit down, and when I stand up. . . . Walking or resting, I am judged by Thee; and all my ways are open to "Thee." God knows what we *are;* and He knows what we *do.* Who does not hate a companion who is always present on every road and in every place of rest? Who does not want to break through the prison of such a perpetual companionship? "Thou discernest my thoughts from afar . . . Lord, there is not a word on my tongue which Thou knowest not." The Divine Presence is spiritual. It penetrates the innermost parts of our own spirits. Our entire inner life, our thoughts and desires, our feelings and imaginations, are known to God. The final way of escape, the most intimate of all places, is held by God. That fact is the hardest of all to accept. The human resistance against such relentless observation can scarcely be broken. Every psychiatrist and confessor is familiar with the tremendous force of resistance in each personality against even trifling self-revelations. Nobody wants to be *known,* even when he realizes that his health and salvation depend upon such a knowledge. We do not even wish to be known by ourselves. We try to hide the depths of our souls from our own eyes. We refuse to be our own witness. How then can we stand the mirror in which nothing can be hidden?

Is the Ugliest Man right? The Ugliest Man is a symbol of the ugliness in each one of us, and the symbol of our will to hide at least something from God and from ourselves. The Ugliest Man seems to be right, when we consider the support he receives from saints, theologians, and reformers. Martin Luther was as strongly grasped as the psalmist by the penetrating Presence of God. He stated that in every creature God is deeper, more internal, and more present than the creature is to himself, and that God embraces all things, is within all things. But this most intimate Presence of God created the same feeling in Luther that it did in Nietzsche. He desired that God not be God. "I did not love God. I hated the just God . . . and was indignant towards Him, if not in wicked revolt, at least in silent blasphemy." Following St. Bernard, the great master of religious self-observation, he continued, "We cannot love God, and therefore we cannot will Him to exist. We cannot want Him to be most wise . . . and most powerful." Luther was terribly shocked when he recognized this hatred for God within himself. He was not able to escape as shrewdly as his theological masters, who recommended that he not think constantly of the searching Presence of God, and thus avoid the blasphemy of hating God. Luther knew with the psalmist that no escape is possible. "Thou art behind and before me, and on every side of me, laying Thy Hand upon me." God stands on each side of us, before and behind us. There is no way out.

The pious man of the Old Testament, the mystical saint of the Middle Ages, the reformer of the Christian Church, and the prophet of atheism are all united through that tremendous human experience: man cannot stand the God Who is really God. Man tries to escape God, and hates Him, because he cannot escape Him. The protest against God, the will that there be no God, and the flight to atheism are all genuine elements of profound religion. And only on the basis of these elements has religion meaning and power.

Christian theology and religious instruction speak of the Divine Omnipresence, which is the doctrine that God is everywhere, and of the Divine

Omniscience, which is the doctrine that God knows everything. It is difficult to avoid such concepts in religious thought and education. But they are at least as dangerous as they are useful. They make us picture God as a thing with superhuman qualities, omnipresent like an electric power field, and omniscient like a superhuman brain. Such concepts as "Divine Omnipresence" and "Divine Omniscience" transform an overwhelming religious experience into an abstract, philosophical statement, which can be accepted and rejected, defined, redefined, and replaced. In making God an object besides other objects, the existence and nature of which are matters of argument, theology supports the escape to atheism. It encourages those who are interested in denying the threatening Witness of their existence. The first step to atheism is always a theology which drags God down to the level of doubtful things. The game of the atheist is then very easy. For he is perfectly justified in destroying such a phantom and all its ghostly qualities. And because the theoretical atheist is just in his destruction, the practical atheists (all of us) are willing to use his argument to support our own attempt to flee God.

Let us therefore forget these concepts, *as* concepts, and try to find their genuine meaning within our own experience. We all know that we cannot separate ourselves at any time from the world to which we belong. There is no ultimate privacy, or final isolation. We are always held and comprehended by something that is greater than we are, that has a claim upon us, and that demands response from us. The most intimate notions within the depths of our souls are not completely our own. For they belong also to our friends, to mankind, to the universe, and to the Ground of all being, the aim of our life. Nothing can be hidden ultimately. It is always reflected in the mirror in which nothing can be concealed. Does anybody really believe that his most secret thoughts and desires are not manifest in the whole of being, or that the events within the darkness of his subconscious or in the isolation of his consciousness do not produce eternal repercussions? Does anybody really believe that he can escape from the responsibility for what he has done and thought in secret? Omniscience means that our mystery is manifest. Omnipresence means that our privacy is public. The centre of our whole being is involved in the centre of all being; and the centre of all being rests in the centre of our being. I do not believe that any serious man can deny that experience, no matter how he may express it. And if he has had the experience, he has also met something within him that makes him desire to escape the consequences of it. For man is not equal to his own experience; he attempts to forget it; and he knows that he *cannot* forget it.

Is there a release from that tension? Is it possible to overcome the hatred for God and the will that there be no God, that there be no man? Is there a way to triumph over our shame before the perpetual Witness and over the despair which is the burden of our inescapable responsibility? Nietzsche offers a solution which shows the utter impossibility of atheism. The Ugliest Man, the murderer of God, subjects himself to Zarathustra, because Zarathustra

[143]

has recognized him, and looked into his depth with divine understanding. The murderer of God finds God in man. He has not succeeded in killing God at all. God has returned in Zarathustra, and in the new period of history which Zarathustra announces. God is always revived in something or somebody; He cannot be murdered. The story of every atheism is the same.

The psalmist offers another solution. "I praise Thee for the awful wonder of my birth; Thy work is wonderful. For Thou didst form my being, and weave me together in my mother's womb. None of my bones were hidden from Thee, when I was made in secret and molded in the lowest parts of the earth." Using the old mythological idea that men are formed in the abyss below the earth, he points to the mystery of creation, not to the creation in general, but to the creation of his own being. The God Whom he cannot flee is the Ground of his being. And this being, his nature, soul, and body, is a work of infinite wisdom, awful and wonderful. The admiration of the Divine Wisdom overcomes the horror of the Divine Presence in this passage. It points to the friendly presence of an infinitely creative wisdom. It is this mood which runs generally throughout the Old Testament. A great scholar, with whom I conversed once on the will to death in every life, exhibited the same mood, when he said, "Let us not forget that life is also friendly." There is a grace in life. Otherwise we could not live. The eyes of the Witness we cannot stand are also the eyes of One of infinite wisdom and supporting benevolence. The centre of being, in which our own centre is involved, is the source of the gracious beauty which we encounter again and again in the stars and mountains, in flowers and animals, in children and mature personalities.

But there is something more to the psalmist's solution. He does not simply consider the creative Ground of his being. He also looks to the creative destiny of his life. "Thine eyes saw the sum total of my days, and in Thy book, they were all written. They were counted before they ever came into existence." The psalmist uses another old mythical symbol, which is the record of earthly events in an heavenly book. He expresses poetically what we today call the belief in an ultimate meaning of our life. Our days are written and counted; they are not merely accidental. He Who sees us most intimately looks at the vision of our whole life. We belong to this whole; we have a place of the utmost importance within it. As individuals and as a group, we have an ultimate destiny. And whenever we sense this ultimate destiny, whether or not it appears as great or insignificant, we are aware of God, the Ground and centre of all meaning. We can join in the psalmist's cry of admiration: "How mysterious Thy thoughts are to me, O God! How great the sum of them is! If I were to count them, they would outnumber the sands; and if I were to come to the end of them, the span of my life would be like Thine!" The psalmist thus conquers the horror of the all-reflecting mirror and of the never-sleeping Witness by his recognition of the infinite mystery of life, its Ground and its meaning.

But suddenly, at the climax of his meditation, the psalmist turns away from God. He remembers that there is a dark element in the picture of his life—enmity against God, wickedness, and bloody deeds. And since this element disturbs his picture, he asks God to eradicate it. In sudden rage, he shouts, "If Thou wouldst but slay the wicked, O God, and make the men of blood depart from me, who oppose Thee in their thoughts, and utter Thy name in their crimes! Should I not hate them that hate Thee, O Lord? Should I not despise them? I hate them with the deadliest hatred. They are also my enemies!" These words should disturb anyone who thinks that the problem of life can be solved by meditation and religious elevation. Their mood is quite different from that of the previous words. Praise turns into curse. And the trembling of the heart before the all-observing God is replaced by wrath towards men. This wrath makes the psalmist feel that he is equal with God, the God from Whom he wished to flee into darkness and death. God must hate those whom he hates; and God's enemies must be *his* enemies. He has just spoken of the infinite distance between his thoughts and God's thoughts; but he has forgotten. Religious fanaticism appears, that fanaticism which has inflamed the arrogance of Churches, the cruelty of the moralists, and the inflexibility of the orthodox. The sin of religion appears in one of the greatest Psalms. It is that sin which has distorted the history of the Church and the vision of Christianity, and which was not even fully avoided by Paul and John. Of course, we whose religious experience is poor and whose feeling of God is weak should not judge too harshly those whose lives burned with the fire of the Divine Presence and spread this fire ardently all over the world. Nevertheless, the sin of religion is real; and it contradicts the Spirit of Him, Who forbade His disciples again and again to hate His enemies as the enemies of God.

Yet, a change of thought and feeling brings the psalmist suddenly back to the beginning of his poem. He feels quite obviously that something may have been wrong in what he has uttered. He does not know what is wrong; but he is certain that God knows. And so he concludes with one of the greatest prayers of all time: "Search me, O God, and know my heart. Try me and know my thoughts. And see if there be any false way in me; and lead me the perfect way." At this moment he *asks* God to do what, according to the first words of the Psalm, he does relentlessly anyway. The psalmist has overcome his wavering between the will to flee God and the will to be equal with God. He has found that the final solution lies in the fact that the Presence of the Witness, the Presence of the centre of all life within the centre of *his* life, implies both a radical attack on his existence, and the ultimate meaning of his existence. We are known in a depth of darkness through which we ourselves do not even dare to look. And at the same time, we are seen in a height of a fullness which surpasses our highest vision. That infinite tension is the atmosphere in which religion lives. In that tension Luther conquered his hatred for God, when he discovered in Christ the Crucified the perfect symbol for our human situation. It is the tension in which modern man lives, even though he may have lost the way to traditional religion. A human being can be ultimately judged by whether or not he has reached and can stand that tension. To endure it is more horrible and more difficult than anything else in the world. And yet, to endure it is the only way by which we can attain to the ultimate meaning, joy, and freedom in our lives. Each of us is called to endure. May each of us have the strength and the courage to bear that vocation. For it is to that vocation that we are called as men.

FORGIVENESS

The Fate of the Forgiving

REVEREND RALPH W. SOCKMAN, PH.D., D.D., LL.D.[1]

*Minister, Christ Church, Methodist, New York City, and
Preacher on the National Radio Pulpit*

Robert Browning is often referred to as the "poets' poet." Ralph Sockman is in the same sense the "preachers' preacher," yet he speaks the language of the multitude.

Recently selected by New York University as the new director of the Hall of Fame for Great Americans, Dr. Sockman is one of the great preachers of our day. At ten o'clock every Sunday morning he has a nation-wide radio audience on the National Radio Pulpit of the National Broadcasting Corporation and the Federal Council of Churches. At eleven and five each Sunday he preaches to his own congregation at Christ Church, where many New Yorkers go week after week for a spiritual message and visitors from all over the country fill all the remaining seats.

Dr. Sockman was born in Mount Vernon, Ohio, graduated from Ohio Wesleyan University, took graduate work at Union Theological Seminary and holds his Ph.D. from Columbia University. The honorary doctorate has been conferred upon him by Ohio Wesleyan, New York University, Wesleyan University, Dickinson College, Rollins College, Washington and Jefferson College, Florida Southern College, and Northwestern University.

While he was still a student, he became associate minister of the Madison Avenue Methodist Church, and has been minister of this church since 1917.

[1] Sermons by the members of the advisory committee were contributed at the special request of the editor and are included on his responsibility.

He served with the Army Y.M.C.A. during 1918 and from 1927 to 1929 was president of the Greater New York Federation of Churches. In 1933 the present new church building was erected at the corner of Park Avenue and Sixtieth Street and the name was changed to Christ Church, Methodist. Strangers who attend the church soon find that New York has a warm heart and that the minister of this church has warm friendship to give them all.

In 1941 he was the Lyman Beecher Lecturer on preaching at Yale University, is on the Harvard University Board of Preachers, and gave the Fondren lectures in 1943. He is a director of Union Theological Seminary in New York, and of New York University, a trustee of Drew Theological Seminary, of Ohio Wesleyan University, also Syracuse University, Goucher College, and Santiago College in Chile. He has served on the Board of Foreign Missions of the Methodist Church, is president of the Church Peace Union, and is one of the most far-sighted churchmen today.

He is widely known for his excellent books, including Suburbs of Christianity, The Unemployed Carpenter, Paradoxes of Jesus, The Highway of God, Date with Destiny, The Lord's Prayer, Now to Live, Live for Tomorrow, Recoveries in Religion, Morals of Tomorrow, and Men of the Mysteries.

During 1947 to 1949 he was visiting Professor of Homiletics at the Divinity School of Yale University, giving the brilliance of his homiletic insight and his creative impulse to the men who come from all over America and other lands to perfect their preaching technique. "The Fate of the Forgiving" presents one of Christ's messages usually overlooked; it was preached in his own church, February 6, 1949, and was preached on the National Radio Pulpit March 6, 1949.

Sermon Twenty=four

I N SOME of our churches today, the people will pray, "Forgive us our debts as we forgive our debtors." In others the worshipers will say, "Forgive us our trespasses as we forgive those who trespass against us." A cynic might say sarcastically that at least the churches should agree on the same version of Our Lord's Prayer. But this difference in translation indicates no real basic disunity of desire.

In the sixth chapter of Matthew, the twelfth verse, Jesus teaches his disciples to pray, "Forgive us our debts." Then two verses later, he says, "If ye forgive men their trespasses, your heavenly Father will also forgive you; but if ye forgive not men their trespasses, neither will your Father forgive your trespasses." Perhaps we might draw a distinction between the terms by saying that the word debt suggests a sin of omission, leaving undone what we ought to have done; and the term trespass connotes a sin of commission, doing what we ought not to have done.

Deeper thought, however, reveals a value in the twofold translation, for it serves to remind us that a trespass is a form of indebtedness and a debt is a form of trespass. When I break a moral law, it is not merely my own affair. Somebody has to pay for it. I incur a debt. And when I leave a duty unfulfilled, a day wasted, a talent cast away, a holy relationship neglected, I trespass on the rights of others, for they have a right to expect me to do my duty as a member of society.

And while our debts and trespasses involve one another, they also involve God. We cannot forgive and be forgiven on a purely human level. Suppose that I owed one of you a thousand dollars; and you in the goodness of your heart said, "I'll forgive that debt. Forget it." And suppose you owed your neighbor a thousand dollars, and you went to him this afternoon and said "I have just forgiven a man a thousand dollars. Will you not forgive my debt?" And suppose such generosity spread from neighbor to neighbor, would that guarantee a satisfactory and stable society? No, such goodness of heart, divorced from a sense of divine justice, would play havoc with business transactions and society generally. Mercy and forgiveness cannot be mere unregulated human emotions. They are jewels of the spirit, but they have value only in a setting of justice.

This matter of forgiving, therefore, calls for study. Aye, it calls for prayer: "Forgive us our debts, as we forgive our debtors."

What, first of all, is involved in forgiving? Well, of course, it means to forego all private revenge, to remit the right to retaliate. To forgive is somewhat different from excusing. We excuse a person's deed when we exempt him from the imputation of blame. For instance, we may say, "I excuse his conduct, considering the extraordinary provocation under which he acted." But I may forgive a person for behavior which I cannot excuse, because I still believe it is blameworthy. Nevertheless, so far as my relations with him are concerned, I will not hold his action against him.

Also, to forgive is not the same as to pardon. Pardon is always from a superior; from one who has the right to sit in judgment. A judge on the bench may pardon a prisoner for his crime; but though I am the one who has been wronged, I cannot pardon the fellow. Legally, only the authorized government can pardon a crime; morally, only God can pardon a sin. But I can forgive the man who hurts me, even though I cannot pardon him. Forgiveness is a change of attitude within the one wronged.

If, however, I am to forgive in the spirit of Christ's teaching, I must go on to pray for God to pardon. I may abhor the wrong, being unable to excuse it or to pardon it; but if I call myself a follower of Christ I go on praying for the soul of the wrongdoer.

Charles Kingsley once pointed out with sharp irony how we may refuse to seek revenge for a wrong done us, and yet cherish such a lingering resentment against the wrongdoer that if he hurt himself, or if he lost his money, or if he made a fool of himself, or if his children turned out badly—well, we just would not be too sorry. In fact, we might even find a secret satisfaction. As long as such feelings remain in our minds, we are not good enough.

Christian forgiveness involves not only remitting the right to retaliate, and removing resentful feelings, but also the effort to revive friendly relations. Christlike forgiveness is not fulfilled by just calling it quits. Sometimes our attitude is something like this: "Yes, I forgive him, but I hope never to see him again." That's not good enough. Christ would have us go on to try to correct the wrongdoer. And in our effort at correction, we should make it clear to ourselves and to him that our motive is one of sincere good will. We should be sure to aim at winning him and not humiliating him.

From ancient Greece comes the report that Aristippus went to his enemy Aeschines and said, "Shall we never be reconciled until we become a table talk to all the country?" Aeschines answered that he would most gladly be at peace with him. Then Aristippus said: "Remember that though I were the elder and better man, yet I sought first with thee." Aeschines replied: "Thou art indeed a far better man than I, for I began the quarrel and thou the reconcilement." Aristippus started the process of forgiveness by going first to his enemy. So far so good. But he almost spoiled the reconciliation by reminding Aeschines that he had been the first to forgive. It is not good enough to say, "I'll forgive but I can't forget." That keeps resentment alive in my mind. And it is even worse to say, "I'll forgive but I won't let him forget." That keeps the resentment alive in both minds.

Forgiveness is just about the most beautiful note in the music of living, but it is spoiled when we keep harping on it. Tennyson suggested the proper use when he said:

> Love took up the harp of life, and struck on all
>   the chords with might,
> Touched the chord of self, which, trembling, passed in
>   music out of sight.

Having seen what a high and difficult attainment forgiveness is, let us ask now what can make us able to forgive?

The Gospels make it pretty clear that we must look to God for the power to forgive before we look at the people to be forgiven. When Jesus said to his disciples: "Love your enemies, bless them that curse you, do good to them that hate you," he added: "That ye may be the children of your Father which is in heaven; for he maketh his sun to rise on the evil and on the good, and sendeth rain on the just and on the unjust."

When we look at people on the sidewalk level, with their greed and grabbing, the whole idea of forgiveness seems silly and impossible. But when we look up to our heavenly Father, his character conditions the atmosphere of our thinking, just as the good character of an earthly father colors a son's judgment. On the wall of a business office in downtown New York is the picture of the executive's father, a fine rugged type of man, with integrity and benevolence reflected in his face. One can well imagine how often that face of the father has steadied and restrained and strengthened the son amidst the frictions and factions of our city's competitive life.

Look up from the crowd, with its selfish struggle to get even and to take advantage, and behold your heavenly Father, who magnanimously sends His rain on the just and the unjust—aye, more, who "so loved the world that he gave his only begotten Son that whosoever believeth in him should not perish but have everlasting life." And as you fix your thought on the heavenly Father, you will see His Divine Son loving, serving and at last dying for his fellow men. And as the breath leaves his body you will hear him pray for his crucifiers, "Father, forgive them for they know not what they do." When we think of the people around us, we so often think of the bad things being done to us; when we think of God and Christ, we think of the good things done for us. And our hearts begin to mellow.

This contrast in attitude was seen that day when Jesus was dining at the home of Simon the Pharisee. While he was at a table a woman of the street came in bearing a precious bottle of perfume which she broke, and then she proceeded to anoint his feet. Simon, the very proper and pious host, was shocked and thought that surely Jesus would see what an impure person the woman was and send her away, Jesus, divining Simon's thoughts, told a parable of a moneylender who forgave two of his debtors, one for five hundred shillings and one for fifty shillings. Then Jesus asked Simon, "Which of them therefore will love him the most?" Simon answered and said; "He, I suppose, to whom he forgave the most." Jesus replied, "Thou has rightly judged." Then he added, pointing to the woman; "Her sins, which are many, are forgiven, for she loved much; but to whom little is forgiven, the same loveth little."

How much do we feel that we have been forgiven? Do we, like Simon the Pharisee, look around and think ourselves about as good as the average and hence not much in need of forgiveness? Or do we, like that penitent woman, feel overwhelmingly indebted to God in Christ for His mercy toward us, and therefore, gladly pour out our gratitude? Only as our hearts are mellowed by the thought of the mercies shown to us are we able to forgive others.

And when we start with the thought of God's forgiving love we begin to get an understanding of those human frailties which make men forgivable. We see what Browning's "Rabbi Ben Ezra" had in mind when he talked about the "instincts immature" and "the purposes unsure," and those factors in our human make-up which "the low world from level stand" does not properly appraise.

> All I could never be,
> All men ignored in me,
> That I was worth to God,
> Whose wheel the pitcher shaped.

The French have a saying, "He who understands all, forgives all." The kernel of truth in that saying is very large. It can be made too soft. But a great truth is there. When we try to look with God's compassionate understanding, we withhold our hasty judgments. Jesus said, "Judge not that ye be not judged." I do not understand our Lord to mean that we are not to make judgments about other people's conduct. He judged. So must we. But I think that Jesus meant, "Judge not except as ye are willing to be judged." Turn your judging gaze on yourself first. Take the beam out of your own eye first. See what your own temptations and weaknesses are. Then you will be merciful in judging others.

In Nathaniel Hawthorne's "Transfiguration" the very human Miriam says to the puritanical Hilda: "You have no sin nor any conception of it; therefore you are so terribly severe; as an angel you are not amiss, but as a human creature you need a sin to soften you."

Well, I suppose, angels would be rather difficult for us human creatures to live with. That is not an immediate problem for most of us, because not many of us are housed with perfect angels. But the persons I would call most angelic are not severe and unforgiving. They do not need sin to soften them, as Hawthorne's Miriam suggested, but they have an understanding of, and sympathy for, sinners. And in that they are like Our Lord.

Of him, the Epistle to the Hebrews says, "We have not an high priest which cannot be touched with the feeling of our infirmities; but was in all points tempted like as we are, yet without sin." Then he adds: "Let us, therefore, come boldly to the throne of grace that we may obtain mercy and find grace to help in time of need."

Ah, now we are catching the secret of the power to forgive. We look away from the wrongdoers and what they are doing to us. We look up to God and Christ and what they have done for us. And we see our heavenly Father ruling from a throne of grace. In His presence we feel our own need for mercy, and we find grace to forgive and help those in need.

Having considered what is involved in forgiveness and what can help us to forgive, let us ask our final question, what happens to those who do forgive?

At least, we can say that the person who forgives purges himself of the poison produced by hatred and resentment. He gets a peace of mind and health of spirit not enjoyed by the unforgiving. The Nazi party in Germany, seeking a slogan for their rise to power, found one in "Death to the Jews." They held that hatred in their minds until some six million Jews were liquidated. But in doing so, they poisoned their own minds and developed unspeakable cruelties which were the product of their perverted thinking.

In contrast with such self-poisoning through the unforgiving attitude, think of the cleansing and calm which come through forgiveness. Sir Thomas More, Lord Chancellor of England, having been condemned to death in a high-handed court on specious grounds, addressed his judges thus: "More have I not to say, my Lords, but that Saint Paul held the clothes of those who stoned Stephen to death, and as they are now both saints in heaven, and shall continue their friends forever; so I verily trust, and shall most heartily pray, that though our lordships have now here on earth been judges to my condemnation, we may nevertheless hereafter cheerfully meet in heaven in everlasting salvation." When a man can say that to men who have just condemned him to death, he is showing a strength of faith and a magnanimity of spirit which are the divine fruits of the forgiving spirit.

And such a spirit of forgiveness is bound, as a general rule, to beget a change of spirit in others. As Henry Churchill King of Oberlin was wont to remind his students, there is a law or reciprocity in life. It is the one Jesus stressed when he said: "Forgive, and ye shall be forgiven. Give and it shall be given you, for with the same measure that ye mete, withal it shall be measured to you again."

> Be noble! and the nobleness that lies
> In other men, sleeping, but never dead,
> Will rise in majesty to meet thine own.

That is the law and the gospel as given in our Scriptures. Oh, I know we are always hearing about exceptions to this general rule. We are ever being reminded that there are persons and peoples who will not respond to forgiveness and magnanimity. But, my friends, we are going to make ourselves bitter by looking always at the exceptions to God's laws, or are we going to make ourselves better by looking at God's law of forgiveness and obeying it?

Forgiveness, of course, cannot result in reconciliation until the wrongdoer repents. But the question for you and me is whether we are going as far as Christ would have us go in trying to awaken repentance. As I search the gospel, I cannot find any exception to the rule laid down by Jesus that our heavenly Father forgives us our trespasses as we forgive others their trespasses. It is His law and I cannot get around it. But thank God, it is also His gospel and I do not want to get around it. For my only hope of salvation lies in God's forgiving love.

> In the course of justice none of us shall see salvation.
> We all do pray for mercy
> And that same prayer doth teach us all
> To render the deeds of mercy.

PRAYER: *Almighty God, whose mercies toward us are beyond number, may the thought of Thy goodness make us more penitent for our own sins and more forgiving toward others. Multiply our high moments of faith and deliver us from our low moods of doubt. Be with us in our silence and in our speech, in fellowship and in solitude.*

We thank Thee, O God, for the noble dead whose labors have made our lives richer. We bless Thee for Thy servant James Rowland Angell, who has now entered into the reward of his rich service; and we pray that his ideals and achievements may inspire those who carry on his work here and throughout the world. Grant us all a firmer hold on Thine invisible kingdom; through Jesus Christ our Lord.

Discipline for Freedom

REVEREND LYNN HAROLD HOUGH, ThD., D.D., LITT. D., LL.D., J.U.D.

Sometime Dean, Drew Theological Seminary, Madison, New Jersey

Lynn Harold Hough is a distinguished Methodist minister, author and teacher. As dean and professor of Homiletics and the Christian Criticism of Life at Drew Theological Seminary, Madison, New Jersey, he influenced the future career of hundreds of men who attended the Seminary.

Dr. Hough laid a sound educational foundation for his brilliant career, took his A.B. at Scio College, his B.D. at Drew Theological Seminary, did postgraduate work at New York University, and took his Th.D. at Drew in 1919. He received the D.D. from Mount Union-Scio College, Garrett Biblical Institute, Wesleyan University, the Litt.D. from Allegheny College, the LL.D. from Albion College, the University of Detroit and the University of Pittsburgh; the L.H.D. from the University of Vermont, and the J.U.D. from Boston University.

Beginning his pastorates in 1898 in a small church in New Jersey, he rose through his preaching ability to be the pastor of churches in Brooklyn and Baltimore. Then from 1914 to 1919 he was professor of Historic Theology at Garrett Biblical Institute, Evanston, Illinois, and in 1919 he became president of Northwestern University.

In the following year he was called to be pastor of Central Methodist Church, Detroit, where his preaching attracted wide attention. In 1928 he was called to the American Presbyterian Church in Montreal. In 1930 he took the chair of Homiletics at Drew and was dean from 1934 to 1947. In the last forty years he has written forty books, including In the Valley of Decision, The Significance of the Protestant Reformation, The Civilized Mind, The Christian Criticism of Life, *and* Patterns of the Mind.

He gave the Cole Lectures at Vanderbilt University (1919), the Merrick Lectures at Ohio Wesleyan University (1923), the Fernley Lecture, Lincoln, England (1925), the Fred J. Cato Lecture, General Conference of the Methodist Church in Australasia, Brisbane, Australia (1941), and half a dozen other famous courses.

In 1918 he was sent to England by the Lindgren Foundation of Northwestern University to interpret the moral and spiritual aims of the first World War. At the invitation of the British Ministry of Information, he spent eleven weeks in England during the summer of 1942 preaching to the congregation of The City Temple, London, and making addresses in army camps and to the general public. He is as popular in the British Isles as he is in America.

Since his own freedom from administrative duties at Drew, he has preached widely in Canada, England, Scotland, and the various cities of the United States, and has given several important series of lectures. This sermon shows his concept of true freedom in our world and the need for disciplined living and thinking. Dean Hugh's fine mind penetrates to the rich ore of spiritual wealth and his language brings his message clearly and convincingly to every audience.

Sermon Twenty=five

TEXT: Oh how love I thy law! PSALM 119:97

THE study of human life reveals a constant interplay of the forces of discipline and the forces of freedom. Discipline without freedom always leads to tyranny. Freedom without discipline always leads to anarchy. Disciplined freedom holds the secret of the good life. It holds this secret for the individual, for the state, and for mankind. But a form of words, even when it is a good form of words, has a way of becoming ineffective when we turn from the formula to living experience. A man may know all the good watchwords and miss all the vital experiences. To think correctly is important enough. But how shall we turn from correct thought to adequate living?

The totalitarian state has discipline and it discards freedom. And so intolerable tragedy comes upon the world. The democratic state may easily secure its freedom precisely by failing to secure that disciplined loyalty without which freedom becomes impotent at best and disintegrating at the worst.

It is a claim properly made for Old Testament religion that it solves the problems of loyalty and spontaneous action by maintaining both. And it does this by making loyalty itself a creative experience, by making discipline itself an experience of joyous and spontaneous zest. The secret is put in the 97th verse of the 119th Psalm. The great words read, "Oh how love I thy law!" Law itself is thus seen to be most regal when it is suffused by love, and love has this creative quality because law ceases to be an abstract principle, and is found concretely glorious in a living person. The transformation of law through joyous love is seen in its full meaning in the New Testament, where all goodness and truth and excellence are alive in that great person Jesus Christ. Loving him we love all that is excellent. And what might have become a hard and slavish obedience becomes a living joy.

The Marxian dialectic would be sure to come to failure at last, if for no other reason, because it never brings us to the great person at the heart of the universe and it never brings us to that great person in history who made God

[154]

articulate in the very life of mankind. So its disciplines begin by being abstract and end by being cruel.

Everything falls into noble meaning when we see living men meeting the living God as He comes to them in Jesus Christ.

André Maurois in a recent Phi Beta Kappa address declared: "In politics, in economics and even in personal life, the present generation attempts to apply scientific methods to problems which cannot be solved by such means. The regions explored by science are limited: beyond stretch the territories of religion, poetry and the arts in which the humanist alone is the guide." What André Maurois said is true because the mathematics of science— marvelous enough in the proper fields—can never touch that region of the free man choosing, where all values come to have their just meaning. Impersonal laws come to have meaning for persons in a world of living beings. In any other world you do not have values; you have only hard, cold facts. And the loyalty which is creative must always be loyalty to those great values which emerge only in a world of living persons. Each social pattern which has betrayed men in our day has been the expression of a loyalty which could not go beyond impersonal formulas to living persons. So loyalty can never become love. It ends in hard rigidity and never becomes a creative joy. It is a discipline for despotism and never a discipline for freedom. It is living men confronting the living God who can say: "Oh how love I thy law!" and when the saying of the words is the expression of living experience, discipline has already become a form of joyous freedom. The personal reference makes all the difference. It makes all the difference on man's side. It makes all the difference on God's side. And in the great New Testament figure the discipline which is freedom attains a rapturous and creative energy not found elsewhere in all the world.

Social action which is always moving between the two poles (to call them so) of living men and the living God never becomes cruelty, never becomes sheer scholastic frittering away of energy, never becomes a lifeless convention. Even its indignation is all the while roused by the sight of individual men and women and little children, and its furious energy comes from a consciousness of the character of the living God whose face we see in the face of Jesus Christ. So even hate of evil is the love of the good of living beings in the reverse form of the repudiation of that which would deform and disintegrate their lives.

The Church itself may lose the understanding of its central insight. And then there are evil days indeed. But when it is suffusing the world with love of the living person in whom all perfection eternally dwells, it is releasing a creative force which becomes irresistible.

But this love of a perfect person, which transforms all discipline into free action, is the very experience which men in our dark and bewildered age, with its confusions and its cruelties, need more than anything else. We come upon moral and social decay when the inner sources of joyous action are dried

[155]

up. The man who can say, "Oh how love I thy law," is forever safe from this dark end of his human story.

Life as the experience of human persons with the divine person in whom all goodness dwells, gives virtue all the joy of happy impulse, and gives joy all the disciplined integrity of permanent loyalty. It is this insight and this experience which the Christian religion is to bring to the modern world. So will be found new clews to all the various meanings of the ancient and modern culture. So will be found that which will give a soul to politics and spiritual meaning to social action. So the university and the Church may meet in an experience of a living energy greater than that of fifth century Athens or the Renaissance. And so the individual may find his soul in the very moment when all principles are transfigured in the light of a great devotion to one person who walked the ways of men, in order that loyalty might find its fulfillment in love, and faithfulness its completion in living fellowship. No tragedy is too dark for the illumination this disciplined liberty may bring. And so at last it may be seen that all the wonder of poetry, the rapture of religion, the skills of action, and the relationships of politics can be apprehended as a creative joy only in the presence of that one divinely human person to whom nothing is foreign and in whom all noble meanings find their final fulfillment.

FREEDOM AND RESPONSIBILITY

Responsibility: A Red Mass Sermon

THE MOST REVEREND JOHN J. WRIGHT, D.S., TH.,
Auxiliary Bishop of Boston and Titular Bishop of Aegea
(Roman Catholic)

Bishop John J. Wright's Red Mass Sermon at Catholic University, Washington, D. C. Sunday, January 16, 1949, emphasized the philosophy of responsibility for men of our own day. In the midst of the hopeless and loose living and free thinking in much of the modern world, the Bishop's message has a high spiritual challenge.

The Bishop attended Boston Public Latin School and Boston College. After spending one year in St. John's Seminary, Brighton, he was sent to the North American College in Rome and was ordained December 8, 1935. For six years he pursued graduate studies at the Gregorian University in Rome where he received his Licentiate and Doctorate in Sacred Theology. The thesis for his Doctorate, "National Patriotism in Papal Teaching," was pub-

lished in two editions and is an authoritative work on Catholic, social and moral teaching.

In 1939 he returned to St. John's Seminary as professor of dogmatic theology. He was consecrated Titular Bishop of Aegea on June 30, 1947. Bishop Wright preaches chiefly on the identity between Christ and His Church and enjoys preaching retreats on the Love of God, on the Communion of Saints and on the spiritual life in terms of living close to the Church.

Sermon Twenty=six

TEXT: God made man from the beginning, and left him in the hand of his own counsel. . . . He shall have glory everlasting. He that could have transgressed, and hath not transgressed; and could do evil things, but hath not done them.

I HAVE taken these words from two places in the Book of Ecclesiasticus. In the name of the Father and of the Son and of the Holy Ghost. Amen.

The trials of the so-called war criminals have been subjected to thoughtful criticism by a few commentators, legal philosophers and historians. The opinion has been expressed that they may eventually cause our nation and our allies very real embarrassment because the courts which conducted them functioned without previous written law and with the doubtful competence of conquerors. Quite possibly, too, apart from these considerations undoubtedly the cases of individual "war criminals" involved injustices or inequities because of passion or partisanship or misrepresentation.

Whatever of all this, there was one refreshing aspect to the determination to bring to trial the "war criminals" and to demand an accounting before some bar of justice from some of those who by deliberate plan and conscious choice brought about the appalling evil that was World War II. This determination constituted a dramatic affirmation before all the world and under the most solemn circumstances of a seriously neglected truth, the truth that political, social, and other moral disasters do not merely happen. They are not the blind results of inexorable fate. Even the most complex of these calamities are not the work of irresponsible, mechanical forces alone. Just as great movements forward in the social history of mankind may be accurately attributed to the honorable actions of upright men, so the moral disasters which overtake men and nations must be attributed to the unfortunate use by responsible men of that freedom in which God created mankind from the beginning.

[157]

In the rise and fall of societies as in the personal salvation or damnation of individual men, the old truth enunciated by the Sacred Scripture remains valid. It is a law of social history as well as a condition of individual salvation: "He shall have glory everlasting who was free to transgress, but did not; who was free to do evil things, but did not do them." This is the clue to a man's perfection: "Before man is life and death, good and evil, that which he shall choose shall be given him" (Ecclus. 15:8). "Behold I set forth in your sight this day a blessing and a curse: a blessing if you obey the commandments of the Lord your God, . . . a curse, if you obey not. . . ." (Deut. 11:26-28). This is the key to a nation's progress, its use of the freedom in which God made man from the beginning: "Jerusalem, Jerusalem, thou who killest the prophets, and stonest those who are sent to thee. How often would I have gathered thy children together, as a hen gathers her young under her wings, but thou wouldst not" (Matt. 23:37).

The determination to bring to justice the so-called "war criminals" constitutes, I repeat, a dramatic reaffirmation of the reality of free will and of personal responsibility for the moral consequences of individual actions. I speak of a "reaffirmation" because the philosophy of responsibility had lost something of its appeal, certainly in social thinking and possibly in legal thinking, in the generation immediately preceding the war.

There had always been the temptation to shuffle off accountability for moral defect. Shakespeare described and refuted it: "This is the excellent foppery of the world, that, when we are sick in fortune,—often the surfeit of our own behaviour,—we make guilty of our disasters the sun, the moon, and the stars: as if we were villains by necessity; fools by heavenly compulsion; knaves, thieves, and treachers, by spherical predominance; drunkards, liars, and adulterers, by an enforced obedience of planetary influence. . . ." But, "The fault, dear Brutus, is not in our stars, but in ourselves, that we are underlings." (*Lear* and *Julius Caesar.*)

The philosophy of responsibility in modern times has further suffered from the impersonal, collectivist theories of society and of history which found favor during and since the last century. These linked human action more often to material forces and mass controls than to spiritual personality and individual responsibility. An earlier generation of devout and God-fearing people had recognized the challenge of some environments and the limitations of certain heredities, but they still acknowledged that the generality of men remain free to make conscious choice between life and death, good and evil. But then social theory followed new lines along which it has attempted to lead legal theory and application. As against the old philosophy of responsibility there has grown up the theory that misconduct is always abnormal, that what the law calls "crime" and what conscience calls "sin" are to be explained largely in terms of causes beyond the control of the "sinner" or the "criminal." The philosophy of responsibility has been replaced by the philosophy of excuse.

Under the newer concept, it is no longer a question of being able to transgress, but refusing to do so; it is more often a question of acting in accordance with the characters which, without our asking, we have received. Character is considered a product of circumstances, and delinquency and crime are simply other names for conflict and maladjustment. Criminals are sick people, like the insane. They should be dealt with as sick people and far from seeing in their criminal actions anything for which they are responsible, we must learn to recognize in criminality the existence of something for which society is responsible. Hence the familiar captions under pictures of young criminals: "Who is the real delinquent, this boy or society?" Hence, too, the frequent statements of sociologists and other experts who announce: "We believe in the responsibility of society, not of the individual."

Recently I listened to a broadcast over a national network of an extremely effective radio drama. It was clearly conceived by its author and presented by its broadcasters as setting forth a profound and cogent point. Its scene was the cell of a condemned murderer. Every device of skillful radio theater drove home the idea of the play as stated by the players: "Tonight I am sitting on the edge of a prison cot in the cell of a condemned murderer. Between him and the rope which will break his neck and choke the breath from his throat are nine hours of tortured darkness. Soon the collective hand of society will reach out and pull the lever that will spring the trap and send his feet kicking in mid-air in the death struggle. Perhaps the collective conscience of society will permit itself a slight qualm. As I write—the murderer watches me. He is nothing more than a big-boned, hulking, somewhat dull kid who continually trembles. He will die in the first light of the morning. I shall write then . . . about the court which should have tried him. It is a purely imaginary court—(a court which sits in judgment on ordinary people who lead what might be called a blameless life. A court established by a law which reads in part:)—'Whereas the state decrees that no one lacking twenty-one full years in age, can now alone be held responsible for any murder, it is ordered that a minimum of six shall then be hanged if one such minor is condemned to die'. . . . And so this court's been called to quickly find the necessary five; the *five* additional nooses which await along with the *one* society's decreed for the young murderer."

The five extra nooses, as the play developed, were fashioned for the necks of the boy's school authorities, his parent, a political leader in his community, a representative of organized entertainment and an average member of the general community. The broadcast was extremely effective. It undoubtedly left in the minds of millions the impression that thus responsibility was placed where it always belongs: not with the individual criminal, but with the total society—and therefore with no one. It was a dramatic example of the philosophy of excuse as opposed to the philosophy of responsibility.

Judge John Perkins, former Justice of the Boston Juvenile Court, tells how one morning a probation officer came into his courtroom and said: "I went to the prison association dinner last night. The principal speaker made a moving address. At the end of it, after describing how a parolee had committed an atrocious murder, he burst into a dramatic peroration. Raising his eyes to the ceiling and with his voice trembling with emotion he exclaimed dramatically: *'Somehow, somewhere, some one of us failed this man.'* " The judge remarked ironically: "You musn't object to that argument. As a matter of fact, it is a wonderful idea for us, too. All these cases we have been worrying about, because they turned out badly, were not our fault. . . . We never failed. Whenever we thought we had failed, someone else had always failed us."

This is the philosophy of excuse—the philosophy of ultimate irresponsibility. For more than a generation it has undermined the moral and legal and individual social responsibilities upon which the stability of society must repose.

The linking of misbehavior to maladjustments and to forces beyond the control of the individual offender may frequently be justified, but not so often as to warrant a general philosophy of law which loses sight of the normal facts of individual responsibility and of personal freedom. Misbehavior, whether sinful or criminal, always includes an element of "maladjustment," but sometimes there are adjustments which the individual must make on the level of the spiritual in order to meet the test of the material and the trial of the evil.

We must ameliorate bad conditions. We must strive by social action to lighten the load where it is unjust or unsafe, but we must recognize that in all this adjustment there are adjustments expected of the individual as well. We have rationalized too many ruthless tyrants in terms of their adolescent frustrations. Too many "maladjusted" criminals have been explained in terms of the "conflicts" and "tensions" of potentially great artists who were forced to be obscure paper hangers in Austria; potentially great leaders of social movements who were destined to become gangsters and leaders of antisocial rackets which tore American communities apart. Too much gangsterism and sheer criminality on the obscure levels of the underworld and on the higher levels of international action and diplomacy have been encouraged by this philosophy of excuse in the realm of conscience and on the level of courts. The war-crimes trials have caused to resound in our century some echo, at least, of that voice of responsibility which spoke centuries ago with accents divine: "This night do they require thy soul of thee." They have reminded public servants of that accountability which is imposed on every free agent: "How is it that I hear this of thee? Give an account of thy stewardship, for now thou canst be steward no longer."

It is good for civilization that the philosophy of responsibility should be reaffirmed and that the philosophy of excuse should be subordinated to it, "cut down to size." Civilization was not achieved by any such philosophy as that of excuse, by vagueness about accountability. Mankind did not emerge from recurring periods of social decline and even savagery by any such formulas. Social progress has not been accomplished by swinging along with impersonal "destinies," by riding the wave of the future, by the blind operation of uncontrolled, biological, economic or social "forces." It has been achieved by the vision and determination, by the self-knowledge and self-discipline of single individuals and of individuals in groups who have understood the meanings of these responsible, constructive words: "I know. I will. I do."

> "Lord, if thou wilt, thou canst make me clean." And stretching forth His hands Jesus touched him saying: "I will: be thou made clean." And immediately his leprosy was cleansed" (Matt. 8:1-4).
> And returning to himself, he said: "I will arise, and will go to my father, and say to him: 'Father I have sinned against heaven and before thee. I am not worthy to be called thy son: make me as one of thy hired servants' " (Luke 15:17-19).

> It is for us the living, rather, to be dedicated here to the unfinished work which they who fought here have thus far so nobly advanced. It is rather for us to be here dedicated to the great task remaining before us—that from these honored dead we take increased devotion to that cause for which they gave the last full measure of devotion—that we here highly resolve that these dead shall not have died in vain—that this nation, under God, shall have a new birth of freedom—and that government of the people, by the people, for the people shall not perish from the earth. (Gettysburg Address, Lincoln.)

> Poverty is the Northwind that lashes men into Vikings. . . . What we call evils, as poverty, neglect and suffering, are, if we are wise, opportunities for good. . . . If I am left alone, yet God and all the heroic dead are with me still. If a great city is my dwelling place, the superficial life of noise and haste shall teach me how blessed a thing it is to live within the company of true thought and high resolves. Whatever can help me to think and love, whatever can give me strength and patience, whatever can make me humble and serviceable, though it be a trifle light as air, is opportunity, whose whim it is to hide in unconsidered things, in chance acquaintances and casual speech, in the falling of an apple, in floating weeds, or the accidental explosion in a chemist's mortar. (*Opportunity*, John Lancaster Spalding.)

It is easy to satirize these valiant concepts of an age perhaps more rhetorical, but also more resourceful, more self-reliant, more imbued with the philosophy of responsibility, more contemptuous of the philosophy of excuse. But the whole history of human achievement gives meaning to that rhetoric and attests to the worth of those who indulged it, who taught their children and told their fellow citizens and trained themselves to recognize that they could do evil, but must not, that they could transgress, but would not.

So we in our legislation, in our law courts and in our social theory must recognize and make allowance for the inadequate and the unfortunate, but we must not treat their condition as the normal condition of mankind and we must not spin our moral philosophy around their deficiencies. In our sympathy we must not place emphasis on excuse rather than on responsibility and thus spread a demoralizing social philosophy. We must make responsibility the universal norm and excuse the challenged exception. We must state the rules rather constantly, find reasons why they do not apply. We might well return to a bit of the rhetoric that glorified heroism and achievement and tone down the rhetoric lavished on those who lack the moral wherewithal by which to try or who, having it, prefer to serve themselves and blame society rather than serve society and honor themselves. We must recognize how the philosophy of responsibility enabled boys with withered legs to become useful citizens, leaders of their community but above all masters of themselves—while the philosophy of excuse has allowed men of real intelligence and potential parts to become the instruments of society's confusion and of their own damnation. Social stability and individual salvation still depend on the recognition of the central place of individual responsibility in whatever good may be accomplished or whatever evil must be suffered on the face of the earth over which God gave man dominion.

Specifically, it was the philosophy of responsibility that made America great. It is the basis of free self-government as free self-government in turn has been the basis of American greatness. Woodrow Wilson said some wise things about the relationship of self-government to the kind of character produced by the philosophy of responsibility. He said:

> Self-government is not a mere form of institution, to be had when desired, if only the proper pains are taken. It is a form of character. It follows on the long discipline which gives a people self-possession, self-mastery, the habit of order and common counsel, and a reverence for law which will not fail when they themselves become the makers of law.

I offer this as a legitimate social and political conclusion from the moral philosophy of responsibility. If we are to acquire or keep the kind of character which Wilson said was essential for self-government, we must preserve the disciplines by which that character is built and the moral philosophy which dictates those disciplines. Church, state and home must unite in happy understanding to teach each generation the "self-possession, self-mastery, the habit of order and peace and common counsel which will not fail them when they themselves become the makers of law." Thus will our citizenry become the men of glory who could transgress, but will not do so; who could do evil things, but will not do them; who use their freedom, fortified by God's grace, to do God's will on earth unto the temporal stability of their nation and the eternal salvation of their souls.

From Curse to Prayer

REVEREND PAUL E. SCHERER, D.D., LL.D.[1]

*A Minister of the Evangelical Lutheran Church and Professor
of Practical Theology, Union Theological Seminary, New York*

*Paul Scherer has a genius for preaching. He himself insists that it is mostly
a matter of hard work in the preparation of each sermon. His sermons of the
"Great Preacher Series" in Reading, Harrisburg, and other cities; his Lenten
and Easter sermons in Detroit, and his sermon on the 400th Anniversary of
Martin Luther have the elements of greatness.*

*Born in Mt. Holly Springs, Pennsylvania, in 1892, Dr. Scherer studied
for his B.D. at the Lutheran Theological Seminary, Mt. Airy, Philadelphia,
and was ordained a minister of the Lutheran Church in 1916. During 1918-
19 he was assistant pastor of Holy Trinity Church, Buffalo, New York. He
taught at the Mt. Airy Seminary for ten years—from 1919 to 1929—and was
pastor of Holy Trinity Church, New York from 1920 to 1945. In addition
he has preached frequently at colleges and universities along the eastern seaboard, in England during the summers of 1930 and 1931, and on N.B.C.'s
Sunday Vespers program. At the August Conference in Northfield he has
served as vice-chairman since 1937 and as dean since 1942.*

*For years he has been in constant and wide demand as a speaker and
preacher for universities, summer conferences, and Lenten services in leading
cities. His work has been recognized with the honorary D.D. by Roanoke
College, the LL.D. by the College of Charleston (from which he took his
bachelor's degree), and the Litt.D. by Wittenberg College.*

He is the author of several excellent books, including When God Hides
(sermons), Facts That Undergird Life, The Place Where Thou Standest,
Event in Eternity, For We Have This Treasure, *and* The Plight of Freedom.

*This sermon shows his fine ability to analyze a passage of Scripture and
develop its essential meaning for his hearers. A preacher of real ability, he
now gives much of his time to training the ministers and young men who
attend Union. His emphasis is upon preaching methods, sermon construction,
textual preaching, written sermon manuscripts, delivery of the sermons with
criticisms for constructive development. This work is bound to show in improved preaching during the coming years as his students go to important
churches over the country.*

[1] Sermons by members of the Advisory Committee were contributed at the request of
the editor and are included on his responsibility.

Sermon Twenty=seven

TEXT: Then answered all the people and said, his blood be on us, and on our children.   MATTHEW 27:25

ONE of the most extraordinary things that ever happened is what history has done to that. It was once a curse that men called down on themselves out of heaven, thinking it was only laughter! "See ye to it," Pilate had said. They would! Leave it to them! Let him wash his hands if he wanted to, and step out from under, as far as ever he could; meanwhile, they were ready to take it on! With the generations that have followed, poor, wandering humanity, trailing after them ever since, around the world and down the years, the hunger that has never been filled, the tears that aren't dried, and the glory forever past that no future seems able to match! "His blood be on us, and on our children!"

Suppose we take it that way to begin with, as a curse that never was intended, shouldered as lightly as if it had been a jest, and see with what solemn urgency it speaks to us. As I have already indicated, there's something strangely timeless about it. Every succeeding age seems to crowd into the picture with them; and each has its hammer and some nails. "When they were come to the place, which is called Calvary, there they crucified him." Who did?

Nothing that brought it about is dated. Pride was there. "We be Abraham's seed." We are Aryans, God knows, and white men! Do you remember Naaman, the day he came to Elisha to be cured of his leprosy? And the prophet sent down word that he should go and wash himself seven times in the Jordan. But he wouldn't. It wasn't becoming. Who did Elisha think he was? The idea of sending word by a servant! And such a silly thing to do, washing in the Jordan! He was being treated like a child! There were far better rivers back home in Damascus where he came from; and they weren't muddy. So he got on his horse and rode away in a huff. He would have died a leper if he hadn't come to his senses! Try to date that! Eight hundred and fifty years on the other side of Christ, more or less? Wrote a friend of mine from Georgia during the war, "We shall have to bash together the heads of these Nazis, until they find out that they aren't quite so superior as they think themselves." It seemed to him a kind of foreign missionary enterprise, down there in Georgia where they were showing that film, *The Master Race*, in theatres which permitted only the master race to buy tickets! Pastor Niemöller confessed from our American pulpits all the German sins there were to be confessed, and we listened. In large numbers we listened! And forgave, needing no forgiveness! Hiroshima. How many thousand were there?

God have mercy on their souls! Nagasaki. God have mercy on ours! Some have said that the Russians are next. "When they were come to the place called Calvary." The bubbles Jesus pricked don't like to be pricked! "His blood be on us, and on our children!"

Pride was at the cross. And tradition was there. "Art thou greater than our father Abraham? Whom makest thou thyself?" The long centuries were against him. Just as they had been against Isaiah. He too had gone about among these people, favored of God as they thought they were, and told them they were doomed. And they pointed the finger at him and roared. Jehovah's sword at their throat, with the hilt in the hands of Assyria? What kind of nonsense was this? And they were wrong! It was God's sense. He was dealing the cards. They weren't. And death was in the cards! Try dating that. I wish we could leave it with this crowd around the cross, looking up at the man they had placarded there because he wasn't in line with what the founding fathers had said. If we could just be sure that God has nothing to do with any of the other ideas in the world, only with the ideas that have come down to us. Never mind communism and John L. Lewis. Never mind Henry Wallace. Nothing but free enterprise and the American way of life. But God isn't that kind of God! Dr. Toynbee was telling us recently that on the basis of all that had happened in human history the only thing about us that would matter a hundred years from now, five hundred, a thousand, would be whether or not we had kept pace with this God whose very habit it is to stand up out of the ruin of "sacred" things, of ancient and time-honored precedents—though always at the risk of getting Himself lynched—then winning anyhow! "There they crucified him." Look at the world. Who did? Where? When? "Lo," Christ replied, "I come to reap the fields you sow. And now it's dark, Ah, darker far than when I hung at Golgotha two thousand years ago."[1] "His blood be on us, and on our children."

Pride was there, of mind and heart and soul. Tradition was there. And self-interest was there. Sadducees and Pharisees, priests and scribes, he had spoiled too many of the things they wanted—things that meant more to them than people ever had meant. As on the day he healed the maniac over there in the country of the Gadarenes; and the devils he cast out, it was plain to anybody who would look, rushed over into a herd of swine and drove them pell-mell down a steep place into the sea. It was too much. They kept swine in those parts. These healings were all very well, but have you thought of the pigs? "They besought him that he should depart out of their coasts." I wish we could shut it all up where it belongs. And we can't. "Things" are still pretty wrong in the world, but he'd better not fool around with our safety while he's working them out for the Russians; and there are a good many islands in the Pacific that we mean to keep! He'd better not care more for miners than for the coal they mine. Or for the laborer than for the job he does. Or for the Negro than for the suitcases he carries.

[1] Mary Britton Miller, *The Crucifixion* (Charles Scribner's Sons, 1944). Used by permission of the publisher.

You can't locate the cross in space, and you can't fix it in time! I am blood kin to these Jews, and they frighten me! There is the same kind of demonic insanity now about human life—about your life and mine: demonic because it's so unspeakably stronger than just the evil choices we make from day to day; insane because all the evil that men do is irrational at bottom. I know very well that it's wiser to love than it is to hate; but I'll provide you with six good reasons for hating whenever I'm so inclined. We'll salute this Christ, in his niche with the saints, in his stained-glass windows; but out among the nations or on the market place, he'd better not get in our way! No, he's a nuisance and a disturber of the peace. Our hearts may be converted, but our wills aren't! Let him look to himself!

Until on the Temple steps, as on the world's great altar stairs, the judgment of almighty God overtakes the human soul. There was the sound of running, stumbling feet, as one wild vote was cast for Jesus. Thirty pieces of silver rang on the stone floor, with a solitary sob of anguish, that lone ballot for the Nazarene: "I have sinned, in that I have betrayed innocent blood." It was Miserere from the farthest place to which life can get away from God, a Litany in the Desert, a Te Deum Laudamus from hell!

"His blood be on us, and on our children." It was a curse that men called down on themselves out of heaven, thinking it was only laughter. And every generation since keeps crowding in, each with its hammer and some nails!

But the strangest thing of all is that you don't have to take it that way any longer! The years passed and turned the curse into a prayer! Men got down on their knees to whisper it, and crossed themselves, and then set their faces toward the iron gate that led into the arena! "His blood be on us, and on our children." Here is the magnificent reversal!

We may not like the language in our more sensitive day, but the fact inside that language is the throbbing heart of the Christian gospel! Living is not the same since Jesus died. It's like a detective story. You can't read those chapters in the mystery of human life—those chapters marked Good Friday and Easter—then go back and page through all that went before, as if you hadn't read the end! It's different now.

That cross has become the only stalwart hope humanity has ever discovered, and the only stalwart strategy for living that history has ever turned up. We have found out all over again in our time that the death of Jesus wasn't pitted against any enmity that could be driven out and disposed of once for all. If it had been, something less might have served. It was pitted against the violent downward pull of this common life of ours. And we know now that God wasn't startled by that pull, or thrown off balance, as if it had suddenly jerked us all out of His hands. He wasn't dismayed by it, or disconcerted by it. It didn't contradict anything Jesus ever said, or cancel anything he was. He met it straight on then. He meets it straight on still, with the only confidence under heaven that can give birth to any in me.

I don't know just what it was that happened. I don't expect to understand God. It isn't the theory that matters. You can't cover the fact with your explanation of it. I only know that His timeless judgment stands there on that hill, and without moving overtakes me: but when it lays hold on my soul it's mercy! And I know at deeper levels than the wailing music of the Passover ever seems to reach what the Psalmist meant when he wrote, "I will walk before the Lord in the land of the living."

The cross is more than an incident in the past. It's like the continual shifting over to other shoulders of a load that keeps piling up and up—as generations go out from under it, dumb and forgiven and unafraid, even as you and I. "His blood be on us, and on our children." The threat of it, and the promise of it, while the years last. Not as a symbol of something. We talk too much about symbols—as if everything we do stands for something God does, while God Himself doesn't do anything much! The cross is His perpetual act in history: not a deliverance *out* of the process, but a deliverance *in* it; the present coming of more than pardon, of a rescue which no man can work, but which every man is bound to receive as the free gift in Christ of a gracious and mighty God. It isn't the giving up of something, not even of life. It's the achieving of something. Not a fate heroically endured, but a mission deliberately undertaken. Not a plan broken up and shattered. A task finished. So that the issue of it, far from being a sigh, is a shout!

And yet somehow it disturbs my peace; because it won't take its hands off me and leave me alone. It is more than the dawn of hope: it's the pain of God's own strategy. Something evil is still alive inside of me, but it's trying now to die; and out of that death, something is trying to be born. I can hardly tell what, except that it's a better way of treating human life than human life has ever found; so hard for me that I betray it and deny it and turn my back on it, only to come stumbling back, still making the sign of it on my breast!

You see, the ultimate fact of our religion is that we have to deal with a God like this—who doesn't think of Himself, but of others; and won't push, but will die! And the ultimate fact about life is that when we quit dealing with it His way, it quits holding together! Not just putting up with the wrong that's done us, but matching it with something that lies on the other side of forgiveness—as Christ did, in his brave and reckless sortie toward a kingdom for men to live in that's not like this we know; and with nothing to rely on, nothing but God, and the feet that fled, and the hands that nailed him fast, and hearts—so many of them—that weren't even touched with pity.

Of course, as we see it, it's always too late to undertake any such thing. We always argue that it is. Always there is some emergency which makes it impossible to base a policy now on the right choice we should have made a year ago. Always we've got to base it on the wrong choice we did make! You'd think there was something inevitable about it, with nobody to break the vicious circle. The only thing that's inevitable is that such a preparation for tomorrow is no better than it was yesterday as a preparation for today. Sometime we've got to shoulder a cross!

Gerald Heard in one of his books reminds us of Alcatraz, that island in San Francisco Bay which is a very monastery of evil, populated by men we dare not turn loose. They are not insane, he says. They are resourceful and courageous and active and ready and daring. We've simply been unable to produce men at the other end that can match them: match their despair with faith, their deviltry with divinity. Being mildly inoffensive, gentle, in good taste, is just of no use: keeping one's religion to oneself so that no one, not even the Russians, ever notices it, does not avail!

I am bound to this: that God's purpose for His world can come immeasurably nearer some sort of fulfillment. To me the realist is the man who tries to accommodate himself to the shape of what can be, not the other way around, forever "borrowing for an ideal tomorrow the falsehoods of yesterday." From the issue God wants in the years to come we can borrow the current events that alone will bring it.

Only bear in mind that the cross is no incidental privation along the road, no personal misfortune. I've heard everything called a cross, from ill-health to a wayward son, from somebody who pays you no attention to somebody who pays you too much. It's a kind of blasphemy to dress up these private, complaining spirits of ours in the garb of sainthood!

The cross is that place where your saving love goes out to undergird some life and comes back with the hot stab of nails in its hands. It's the place where you try with all your might and have nothing to show for your trying, may be, but the scars, and a heart that keeps stretching away as far as ever your arms can reach. When you've begun to grow that kind of muscle, when you're ready for the defeat life is always trying to impose on you, yet by God's grace can assert your mastery still, striking out toward a lost world through the very floods that have gone over you: then and only then may you begin to talk falteringly of a cross, and grope about unashamed for the feet of him who rules from it.

"His blood be on us, and on our children!" There's a fact inside the language. I wish we'd quit expecting anything to come of anything else in God's world or man's!

PRAYER: *Touch us, O God, here in the shadow of this death which gave life birth; touch us with Thy great compassion; and of that touch let cleansing come, and healing, and signal strength: through Christ, our Lord. Amen.*

The Inescapable God

THE REVEREND HENRY PITNEY VAN DUSEN, PH.D., D.D., S.T.D.

A Presbyterian Minister, and President of Union Theological Seminary,
New York City

Dr. Van Dusen has had a part in the training of ministers at Union Theological Seminary for nearly a quarter of a century. During all this time he has emphasized a combination of sound scholarship and deep religious faith as necessary mental and spiritual equipment for the minister of God.

He was born in Philadelphia in 1897, attended William Penn Charter School, Philadelphia, Princeton University, and took graduate study at New College, Edinburgh, and Edinburgh University, 1921-22; Union Theological Seminary, New York, 1922-24, B.D. (summa cum laude), 1924; Edinburgh University, Ph.D., 1932. He became associate executive secretary, Student Division of the Y.M.C.A., 1927-28; joined the faculty of Union Theological Seminary as instructor in systematic theology and the philosophy of religion, 1926-28; assistant professor, 1928-31, associate professor, 1931-36, dean of students, 1931-39. In 1936 he became Roosevelt Professor of Systematic Theology and President of the Faculty in 1945 at the same time that he became President of the Faculty of Auburn Theological Seminary. New York University conferred the S.T.D. in 1945, Amherst College and Edinburgh University the D.D. in 1946; Oberlin College and Yale University the D.D. in 1947.

He is the author of a dozen significant books, including In Quest of Life's Meaning, The Plain Man Seeks for God, For the Healing of the Nations, Methodism's World Mission, What IS the Church Doing? World Christianity: Yesterday, Today and Tomorrow, Het Christendom in de Wereld. He is the editor of Ventures in Belief, The Church through Half a Century, Church and State in the Modern World; and contributor to Dynamic Faith, The Vitality of the Christian Tradition, Religion and World Order, This Ministry, the Contribution of Henry Sloane Coffin, Education for Professional Responsibility. He is on the editorial board of The Presbyterian Tribune, Christianity and Crisis, Christendom, Ecumenical Review.

Dr. Van Dusen has been a delegate to the Oxford Conference on Church, Community, and State, 1937; Madras World Missionary Conference; Whitby Enlarged Meeting of International Missionary Council Committee, 1947; First Assembly, World Council of Churches, Amsterdam, 1948; Chairman, Study Program. Member, Provisional Committee, World Council of Churches, and its Administrative Committee, 1939-48. Chairman, Study

Commission, World Council of Churches, 1939 to the present. He has so many other important appointments that only a few can be listed: Fellow, National Council on Religion in Higher Education; member, American Theological Society; member, American Association of Theological Schools; president, 1942-44; member, Council on Foreign Relations; member Y.M.C.A., National Council and National Board, 1936-1948; Student Department Committee, 1924-1946; chairman, 1940-46; chairman, Interseminary Movement, 1940-48; president, Union Settlement Association; member, Foreign Missions Board, Presbyterian Church U.S.A.; member, Joint Committee on Religious Liberty of Federal Council of Churches and Foreign Missions Conference; member, Federal Council of Churches; Department of Research and Education; president, United Board of Christian Colleges in China; member, board of trustees: Princeton, Smith, Yenching University, Nanking Theological Seminary, the Rockefeller Foundation, and the General Education Board. He is a director of Freedom House, 1941-48, and of United Service to China; Executive Committee.

Henry P. Van Dusen is an important leader in the theological world, yet he is simple, friendly and unaffected in all his contacts with people. His preaching is from the heart as well as the mind, and he tries to make the world of faith meaningful to all who hear him.

Sermon Twenty=eight

TEXT: O Lord, thou hast searched me, and known me. Thou knowest my downsitting and mine uprising; thou understandest my thought afar off. . . . There is not a word in my tongue, but, lo, O Lord, thou knowest it altogether. Thou hast beset me behind and before, and laid thine hand upon me. . . . Whither shall I go from thy spirit? or whither shall I flee from thy presence? If I ascend up into heaven, thou art there: if I make my bed in hell, behold, thou art there. PSALM 139:1, 2, 4, 5, 7, 8

THIS is probably the loftiest declaration of religious faith outside the New Testament: *The Inescapable God.*

When these words are uttered, our spontaneous response is likely to be of one of three kinds: To some these words speak with a strange, and alien accent. There is nothing, *nothing,* in our experience which recognizes them. Under no possible circumstances could we imagine ourselves repeating them as our own. All of us have been present at discussions to which we felt complete outsiders. It may be that the talk focused on technical, scientific matters

[170]

which were altogether beyond our ken, or in the realms of art or literature of which we know nothing. The universe of speech is familiar enough—each of the words we understand. But the universe of meanings is wholly foreign. "It's all Greek to me," we complain. Annoyance, irritation, resentment may stir within us. So, with these statements of the 139th Psalm. They sound like exaggerated, poetic imaginings of a far-off and bygone world. Perhaps we rather distrust them. Certainly we are not comfortable in their presence; we do not like to hear them.

With others of us the spontaneous response is somewhat different. We also listen with ears which do not fully comprehend, but we admit we like to listen. Our experience is somewhat like that of the musically untutored at a first hearing of Wagner's *Parsifal* or Beethoven's Fifth Symphony. We cannot say that we understand it, but in a vague way we recognize its beauty and its majesty and its reality. If we are unable to affirm it ourselves, we recognize its meaning in the faces and voices of others—those who sing or play, and some who listen. Our appreciation is vicarious, but we are glad to be within that vicarious influence. We may envy just a little those who do understand, for whom it is real. Still, we confess ourselves outsiders, but we know it to be great and true, though we could not so declare it for our own inner certainty. Yes, and perhaps there have been moments, dim flashes, even flickers, when we have caught a fleeting glimpse of its reality for ourselves. We know it to be great and true, not solely because of its meaning for others, but because of the faintest promise of its meaning for us. So, likewise, with the affirmations of the 139th Psalm.

But there are some of us who, as these words are spoken, feel their spirits at once at home, and at ease, and at peace. They rest back in quiet satisfaction, as do music lovers at the first bars of the Grail Motif in the *Parsifal* Overture or at the dum-dum-dum-DUM (now so familiar because of its wartime use) of the Fifth Symphony. Not infrequently life takes us into other companies where we feel painfully out of place. The atmosphere is artificial, unreal, insincere; the talk self-consciously clever, strident, crudely self-important. Courtesy demands that we play a part in it all, but we dislike it intensely. At the first opportunity we withdraw—inwardly strained, distorted, exhausted. We make our way wearily to a place or a presence which is home. In a moment we are restored to ourselves. So, our spirits find these words. However far we wander, however little the hurly-burly of our daily preoccupations might suggest it, here is our home. These words say precisely what our spirits would declare, but in words of beauty and power which we could never command. We may repeat them over phrase by phrase: "O Lord, thou hast searched me, and known me. . . . There is not a word in my tongue, but, lo, O Lord, thou knowest it altogether. Thou hast beset me behind and before, and laid thine hand upon me." We know it to be literally true—each phrase.

Yes, but some of us may query: Can we believe these tremendous affirma-

[171]

tions of faith? And how can our spirits appropriate what our minds find incredible?

Here we may well have recourse to a suggestion from the thought of Jesus. We may call it *the logic of common sense*. There is a feature of Jesus' teaching which is too seldom noted. It is his assumption that in the crucial issues of truth, men already know the answers to their questions. His task is not to convince them of what they do not already know or to persuade them of what they cannot believe, but to remind them of what they already know well enough, to make vivid by a figure or a bit of keen insight the truth which they already possess. They brought him their questions—political, ethical, theological: What attitude should men take up toward an overbearing ruler, Rome? What should be done with a grossly immoral woman? Who is to blame for inherited blindness? What will be the conditions of marriage in the future life? Sometimes he gives a direct answer. More often, a story, an illustration or a biting rebuke. Frequently he turns their inquiry back upon them with a question in reply, hinting that their query was gratuitous. Almost always he seems to be saying to them: "Why do you ask me? You already know the answer. Allow your minds to become quiet, your insight poised. There is your answer." Once he put it so bluntly that they could not evade it: "You know well enough how to read the signs of the weather when it is going to rain. Why is it that you cannot read the signs of these times?"

And the sources of this knowledge? Mainly two: acute observation, sheer common sense; and analogy from men's relations to one another to men's relations to God: "If you being evil know how to give good gifts to your children, how much more will your Father in heaven."

Let us apply this logic of common sense to our thought of God. It was perhaps the most learned scholar of the English-speaking world in our day, one of that select company of twelve who were recognized as having understood Dr. Einstein,[1] who suggested: If you were to ask the ordinary man on the street—or, better, the man on the farm, since he lives closer to nature and, therefore, to reality—what it is of which he feels most certain, after a moment's reflection, he would be likely to answer: "Well, of three things, at least: Behind this universe there is a superhuman Power, God; there is a difference between right and wrong; the right deserves the allegiance of my life." It is the first of these assumptions of the plain man with which we are immediately concerned: "Whatever else and more may be true, behind this inconceivably vast and incredibly mysterious universe, there must be an ultimate power, God."

Yes, but the most serious difficulty for our thought of God is not to believe that He is but to be certain that He knows and cares. Here especially the logic of common sense may guide our minds to true insight. It has never been easy to believe that One in whose power the cosmos revolves can possibly give personal attention to the private interests and hopes, the perplexities

[1] Professor A. E. Taylor of Edinburgh.

[172]

and needs, of Tom, Dick and Harry. It has never been easy to think of One whose mighty sway holds the stars in their courses and yet who marks the comings and goings, the fears and frustrations of each creature. For men and women in our day, the difficulty is slightly, if at all, aggravated.

But a moment's quiet thought recognizes that it is incredible that a Power so vast, an Intelligence so profound, should not be intimately aware of, and solicitous for, each of the sons of men. If there be a God at all, it must be true that He is, quite literally, closer than breathing, nearer than hands and feet, One from whose solicitous concern there need be no parting, One from whose enveloping care there can be no escape. That is the only sensible belief. The Sustainer of the cosmos must be One who also numbers the hairs of each head. That is the profounder insight. "Not a sparrow falls to the ground but your Father notes it," declares Jesus. Note the realism. He does not deny that the sparrow falls, whether through the accident of nature or men's cruelty. But God notes its fall, and cares.

If we think of a human friend who understands me far better than I understand myself, so intimate that he senses my thoughts before I voice them; if we expand a human friend's insight to the wisdom and foresight of an Infinite Intelligence; and if we recall that this Friend's sympathies are so inclusive as to embrace every other person with the same measure of interest and concern, and that His imagination is so flexible as to change from second to second with each moment's advance in each life's course, and that that solicitude is at play toward every man and toward each at every moment; if we can so stretch our tethered and faithless imaginations, we may make a beginning at realizing the intention of God for each one of us. Augustine's word is still the truest: "He loves us all as though we were but one, but He loves each one as though He loved him alone."

Finally, how shall these truths which our minds acknowledge become real to our inner certitude, of the warp and woof of our inmost experience? What, as a matter of fact, is the normal route of our painful and stumbling pilgrimage into the inmost sanctuary of every great meaning? Not merely religious faith, but no less, learning, beauty, freindship, love. In each, is it not usually by three stages?

We begin when we hear of it by the hearing of the ears. But it remains to us external, strange, unknown. Its enthusiasts speak in a foreign tongue. Perhaps they seem to us to speak "with tongues." We have instanced music—*Parsifal*, the Fifth Symphony. Has that not been the experience of many of us with these; but also with others of life's deepest realities—intellectual delight, love, parenthood?

And if we advance to the second stage, is it not usually because we have sensed reality in the response of others? If you will, through them we have faith that for us also there might be meaning—deep, rich meaning—here. Or perhaps because there has been just the dimmest reaction akin to theirs within ourselves. The note without, which has stirred them to singing response, has awakened a faint, almost imperceptible echo within ourselves. It is faint, but it is enough to quicken hope and to give a vague confirmation to their enthusiasm, hope that perhaps for us too that meaning might ring clear.

But if we penetrate within, it is because we have permitted ourselves to be exposed repeatedly to the voice of that message—first, meaningless; then, vaguely, exasperatingly suggestive; finally, rich with power—until it can slowly make its reality clear and take us captive. Pointing to one of the greatest passages in the New Testament, the thirteenth chapter of Paul's First Letter to the Corinthians, Henry Drummond used to challenge his audience to read that passage once a week for a month. Then speaking autobiographically he would add, "I knew a man once who really did that and it changed his life." So one might challenge you to read the 139th Psalm each day for a month.

Let us be clear. It wins its way into our souls not by overpowering or overpersuading us, by forcing us, or by superimposing itself upon us. There is no forcing reality upon man's soul. No, but by repetition the reality without may stir the slumbering response in the dumb spirit within, until those first, faint echoes within awake and increase and ring strong and sure. No longer do we hear with the hearing of the ears. We know. It is true—every word of it. "O Lord, thou hast searched *me,* and known me. . . . Thou hast beset me behind and before, and laid thine hand upon me." This is the inmost sanctuary which stands as the goal of our pilgrimage. Here is our home.

Then we are ready with the true response. We cry: "Search me, O God, and know my heart. Try me, and know my thoughts. And see if there be any wicked way in me, and lead me in the way everlasting."

JUSTICE

The Prophetic Tradition

RABBI LEO JUNG, PH.D.
Rabbi of The Jewish Center (Orthodox), New York City

Rabbi Jung is a fearless preacher, a scholar, a leader of his people, and an educator of ability. A professor of ethics, he was born June 20, 1892, in Moravia, the son of Rabbi Meir Jung, later Chief Rabbi of the Federation of Synagogues of London.

After graduation from the Hebrew High School and Yeshiva of his father, Rabbi Jung studied at the Yeshivoth of Eperies and Galanta, Hungary, and at the Hildesheimer Rabbiner Seminar at Berlin, where he obtained Semikhah from the hand of the Gaon David Hoffman. His universities include Vienna, Berlin, Giessen, Marburg, London, and Cambridge. He holds the Ph.D. of London University. In England he was general director of the Sinai League from 1916-1919 and editor of the Sinaist 1916-1919, also a member of the Royal Asiatic Society and of the Executive War Memorial Committee for Jewish Education.

In 1920 he received a call to the Congregation K'nesseth Israel, Cleveland, Ohio, and in 1922 was called to the Jewish Center, New York, where he has been the Rabbi ever since. In 1926-27 he was lecturer on Jewish philosophy and ethics at the Yeshivah Rabbi Isaac Elchanan. Since 1931 he has been pro fessor of ethics at the Rabbi Theological Seminary and the Yeshivah Uni versity. In addition he has been director of the Jewish Center Hebrew School, director of education of the Down-Town Talmud Torah, a member of the executive board and for six years recording secretary of the American Academy of Jewish Research, and governor of the Jewish Academy of Arts and Sciences.

He has been president of the Rabbinical Council of the Union of Orthodox Jewish Congregations of America, 1928-34; a trustee of the Jewish Welfare Board since 1938; a trustee of the Jewish Social Service Association, 1926-33; a trustee of the Fellowship of Reconciliation since 1940; vice-president of the New York Family Institute, 1928-40. He has written in English, Hebrew and German, contributing to The Jewish Quarterly Review, Horeb, of the Yeshivah University; Haderekh; The Isarelite.

He is the author of Foundations of Judaism, Essentials of Judaism, Living Judaism, Crimes and Character, Israel of Tomorrow, and other books, and holds the distinction of being the only American rabbi who participated in the Great Socino Translation of the Talmud into English, the Tractates of Yoma and Arakhin having been translated and annotated by him.

This sermon gives his views on justice, faith and righteousness, and illus- trates the strength and courage of his preaching.

Sermon Twenty=nine

TEXTS: He judged the cause of the poor and needy. . . . Was not this to know me, saith the Lord.   JEREMIAH 22:16

Righteousness, righteousness, shalt thou pursue.
DEUTERONOMY 16:20

ART may stimulate us, the contemplation of nature arouse our esthetic admiration. Beethoven or Schubert may sweep us off our feet, but most of these influences are as transient as they are beautiful. They are not intimately related to the problems of our daily existence, they do not penetrate to the core of our being, they rarely influence our conduct. We can imagine Nazi hordes moving from Wagnerian music to perfectly organized mass-murder, nor has the contemplation of enchanting sunsets been found to be normally productive of philanthropic enterprise. What is relevant to all of us is *mishpat*, justice, the assurance of our personal worth and of universal human dignity. For the first time in human history the Torah emphasized this truth, speaking of all human beings as God's children, of every man as our brother, and of the obligation: *Love thy neighbor, he is as thyself*. Faith in God and brotherhood thus became interdependent.

It is deep faith in God, in the ultimate decency of things, and in the un-limited potentialities of fellow men that goes to our hearts, fills us with deep feeling, develops into spontaneous attitude that expresses itself in the hundred and one actions spelling out our daily way of life. We learn to be guided by divine commandments, the shall's of moral duty, the do's of divinely enjoined loving-kindness, the vision of tears wiped from our fellow men's faces, the radiant joy of slaves emancipated from tyranny or redeemed from disaster. The French philosopher Souvestre is famous for the statement that essentially there are but two ills in human history: the envious hatred of the poor, and the deadly indifference of the rich. But beyond them there is the basic emo-tional peace achieved by people, no matter how poor, who live in a climate of justice. To know that one has an irreducible chance of one's rights being vindicated, one's opportunity unhampered by legal unrighteousness, means to remain possessed of basic hope which prevents all the senseless cruelty and fury of the eternally wronged.

So paramount and pervasive must justice be that not even the poor may be favored in any case before the judge. This is an indication of the astounding high moral level of Judaism. Elsewhere the admonition would read, *"Do not favor the rich in judgment."* The Divine lawgiver, conscious of native sym-pathy with the poor, finds it necessary to extol the duty of uncompromising righteousness, hence *Thou shalt not favor the poor in judgment*, if he be in

[176]

the wrong. The essence of revelation, as our Torah brought it to us, does not have to do with the mystery of the deity or the ultimate theological aspects of psychosomatics, but with God as the source of justice: *The holy God is sanctified by Justice.* Justice is not merely a technical term for law books, it dare not be restricted to logical formulas and heavy tones. The underprivileged must be protected. The imbalance between the power of the powerful and the helplessness of the poor must be corrected, yet justice must be preserved at all costs. Israel is to be God's messenger, the herald of justice everywhere.

These are the laws which thou shalt explain to them—they must be expounded to every layman, they must become the self-evident possession of every man, woman and child, they must be as normal to their thinking, feeling and acting as the breath which they draw and the bread they eat. They must so deeply enter into the very core of their being that righteousness shall be the only foundation for their private homes and public association, that absence of justice shall be unto them like the absence of light and food. So universal, so vital and so consistent shall be their attachment to righteousness as the single basis of their life that the national history, no matter in what media it expresses itself, shall be like a trumpet blast of justice, that the family attitude and each soul's motto shall be unthinkable except in principle, law and approach in accord with justice. Moses was the father of all prophets, and the fountainhead of the prophetic tradition. An Isaiah's heroic irony, a Jeremiah's desperate denunciation, an Ezekiel's awesome picture of inevitable retribution are but the unsullied stream of that tradition.

Righteousness does not imply vague comfortable abstractions like the unity of God and the nature of the Good. It may become a very uncomfortable principle, as it affects our attitude toward customer, patient, competitor, the man whose power we fear, the man whose weakness encourages abuse. The law of Righteousness does and should interfere with our private dealings and with the men we elect to congress. It respects no person, from policeman to foreign secretary, from the council table of a union local to the exalted personages ready to decide the fate of nations at Lake Success. Gently, inexorably, in the still voice of conscience or through the cataclysm of atomic warfare, it points to wrong as self-destruction, to oppression as self-immolation, to righteousness and kindness as the main undergirders of a happier world.

Religion, beyond dogma, doctrine, ritual, ceremony, hymns and parades, must proclaim and promote the primacy of justice. Houses of worship that do not vibrate with righteous indignation, that do not take up the cry of the oppressed and the cause of the wronged minority, are not true houses of God, but horrid delusions. *Place the supreme court of justice next to the altar,* the rabbis urge. Let religion be magnificent in its championing the divine ideal of justice, let it use its powerful damnations and its shocking vocabulary of contempt against any temporal power that would abuse its opportunities. Even as in the animal world, beasts of prey cannot resist the form of any moving object fleeing before them but leap upon it with uncontrollable ferocity, so in the affairs of men, few seem to be able to resist the allure of power, the chance to obtain by violence, cunning or slow persuasive ruthlessness what belongs to their neighbor. King Greed will ever appoint as his ministers public falsehood and the organized lie. His henchmen are experts in arrogance, foul defamation and deceit. Most ingenious are its devious ways of beclouding issues. We Americans are witnessing one of its elaborate stratagems.

Nobody in my congregation needs a sermon on communism. We recognize it as a religion of despair, essentially bereft of a sense of humor, ignoring the average person's normal expectation of private rewards from his effort. Communism in practice denies man basic freedom, and even as its first cousin, fascism, would subject man and woman to the tyranny of the state.

But in America communism is now made to serve another purpose. King Greed has built himself a mighty empire in these United States. The American mother of today is unable to provide essential needs and comforts for her family. Milk and butter, garment and health, not to speak of elemental comforts, due to the insatiable greed of well-protected dealers in, or producers of, basic commodities, are becoming too expensive for the budget of millions of hard-working honorable parents. Flabby legislators or too interested minions of profiteers have remained dumb and deaf. To divert the attention of the people from their rapacious so-called betters, they have drawn the red herring of communism in crimson streamers across the American continent. What threatens the security of America is no wild-eyed foreigner, beset by thick accents, wild-flowing hair and incoherent eloquence. *A king,* says the wisest of men, *establishes a country by righteousness, but the man accepting bribes will destroy it.* The legislator yielding to the profiteer's lobby undermines the American constitution, and defeats the American dream. Such *ish terumot* ("man of gifts") accepts bribes, yielding to threat and pocketing vicious favors which murder his sense of social responsibility. He learns in consequence to look upon the lucre-swollen tycoon as the superior to the common people, and he classes citizens not as equals before the law, but as inferior if their houses are not luxurious, because they have been wronged and because their protests and their indignation render them "troublesome." Nay, to his blurred vision these oppressed and abused fellow citizens become "foreigners," since Americans are only those whose limousines and other luxuries stamp them as of the 100 per cent perfect class. In the mind of the reactionary, as well as of the man, who accepts fees for his conviction, this projection takes place in internal affairs as well as in world issues: Whosoever oppresses, thus shows power, is per se of the higher type of nations. Whosoever has but moral argument, but a righteous cause, is a near-communist, a fellow traveler, a thing to be ostracized, persecuted, kept out of the American country. The net result of this activity is that liberals become frightened and either surrender the citizen's supreme right, that of protest, or in despair are driven to the very corner which their intelligence and conscience would have shunned: that of communistic senselessness.

Communism serves selfish interests as a first-rate bogeyman to divert attention from their cupidity. But the only way to overcome whatever meager though vociferous forces of that creed exist in the United States, is to make democracy work. The real forces for communistic extravagancies are unemployment, high prices, and the cynical attitude derived from a study of a reactionary congress. Cold-blooded executives of food magnates are the real causes of subversive sentiment. Apathy and callousness, abuse of power and worship of mammon, undermine the security of the country. The law of God demands loyalty from both employer and employee; it stands neither for capitalism nor socialism, but for consistent fair dealing in all their relations.

It is easy to preach ideals. A religion presenting impossible standards will gain the attachment of the unthinking and the conscienceless, for all it demands from its devotees is to listen to the day-dreaming of utopian platforms once a week at worship, to have the congregation return to the tasks of daily life, utterly divorced from the spirit and the principles of such idealism. Judaism has ever stood for immediate steps to concretize ideals. The revelation of Exodus 20 is followed by legislation of Exodus 21. The Torah insists in the name of God that we render ideals significant by heeding their voice beyond the hours of worship, by unflinching attachment to righteous principles in its secular hours, by unfailing directness in our attitude to every wrong and by our encouragement of every right move, plan or action.

The United Nations is not solely a political organization. Beyond utilitarian purposes, it is religious in foundation.[1] Beyond the dreams of eternal peace and indeed buttressing it, it is a hope for the realization of the Torah's revealed direction, the planning and completing under God of an enduring edifice of peace based on righteousness, and of felicity undergirt by merciful conduct. When any nation forsakes the path of justice it offends at once against justice, against its own security, and especially against God. We Jews do not use the Divine Name in vain. We have learned to revere it, having lived for it in a thousand moral climates and having in His honor died a thousand deaths. In our Holy Ark we have preserved the very words of the revelation not only for our children, but for the countless generations of His children everywhere. In our history we have defied all the cruelty, cunning, coldness and corruption of the world's immortal clan, the self-deceived tyrants of all ages, and by our deathless tenacity have lived a national kaddish, *yitgadal veyitkadash shmeh rabbah*—that His great Name be magnified and sanctified, for times unending.

We can say to all religions: *tassim sanhedrin etzel mizbeah*, that a nation or a group of nations, even the United Nations, will either remain true to the spiritual vision that begat it, or cause its enthusiasms to evaporate in

[1] Rabbi Jung defines religion from the Latin word *religare* as a system of life and thought that ties up man with God and all his fellow men.

corroding cynicisms, its organization to disintegrate in hypocritical verbiage, heaping insult upon insult upon religious folks and their faith, burying its foundations now under tons of gold, now under oceans of oil, now in grandiose combinations of power politics and other political tricks and stratagems and self-trapping ingenuities.

Thirty-five hundred years have passed since Moses first brought the tidings of the righteous God in the revelation of Mount Sinai, then implemented its general principles with detailed practical rules, inspiring the succession of prophets and teachers to keep before man's eyes and in his heart one promise and one admonition: Justice as the single foundation of man's work, unrighteousness as the cause of inescapable ruin and chaos.

The message of the prayer book must not stay in the synagogue. The achievement of worship manifests itself in the office and the workshop downtown. So take them, my friends, the passion for justice, the pledge of undeviating rectitude from synagogue into life, from Sabbath to weekday. Pray for moral impregnability and offer on the altar of our beloved country this fruit of our faith as the harvest of gratitude and the gift of our happiness.

LABOR

The Church Speaks to Management and Labor

Reverend Ansley C. Moore, D.D.

Minister, Sixth United Presbyterian Church, Pittsburgh, Pennsylvania

With the great interest in the problems of capital and labor, the greatly increased strength of unions, the enormous number of strikes, the rising cost of living, and the discussions of the Taft-Hartley Law and other measures relating to capital and labor, Dr. Moore's sermon is especially timely. It is recommended that one should read this sermon, giving the thinking of an American minister on the Christian way to handle labor-capital situations and the sermon by Pere Riquet on Labor, giving French thought on this subject.

A native of Atlanta, Georgia, he graduated from Emory University, Columbia Theological Seminary, Decatur, Georgia, and was a graduate student at the University of Chicago Divinity School, Union Theological Seminary, New York, and Union Seminary, Richmond, Virginia. He was exchange preacher in Europe in 1939 and holds the honorary D.D. from Southwestern College, Memphis, Tennessee. He held pastorates at McDonough, Timber Ridge, and Thomasville, Georgia, Clearwater, Florida, and was minister of

Government Street Presbyterian Church from 1942 to 1947. In 1947 he was a representative to the World Alliance of Reformed Churches at Geneva, Switzerland. On June 1, 1947, he became minister of the Sixth United Presbyterian Church in East Liberty, Pittsburgh, Pennsylvania.

Dr. Moore appeals to all age groups. He speaks their language, understands their problems, and has an awareness of their needs. He has the art of making a person of any age feel that he is his contemporary and holds the interest of his entire congregation by varying his sermons. His messages range from those which strengthen one's devotional life to those which challenge one to social action.

His activities are broad in scope. He was chairman of Student Work for the Synod of Alabama, is associate editor of the Presbyterian Outlook, is a member of the Board of Trustees for Agnes Scott College, is president of the Council of Churches of Allegheny County (Pittsburgh), Pennsylvania and is deeply interested in all the activities of his church.

Dr. Moore is a minister who makes his congregation proud of him and proud of their church.

Sermon Thirty

TEXT: Finally, brethren, whatsoever things are true, whatsoever things are honorable, whatsoever things are just, whatsoever things are pure, whatsoever things are lovely, whatsoever things are of good report; if there be any virtue, and if there be any praise, think on these things. PHILIPPIANS 4:8

THE preacher this morning is conscious of the fact that he is no expert on labor problems. There are highly technical matters in this area of our common life which are entirely out of my scope of activity. Men sitting before me have training and experience in the field of labor relations which I do not have, and I would not presume to speak of matters in which they are experts and I am a novice. My concern in this sermon is with *men* and *principles*. The schoolteacher does not have to know how to circumnavigate the globe, to build railroads, or to mine iron ore, to teach geography. There are certain Christian principles which, in my judgment, ought to guide men of good will in both labor and management, and it is the duty of prophetic religion to set these forth and to call men to live by them.

Surely no one here will think the Church out of its realm when it speaks on such a theme The Church of Jesus Christ is interested in anything that affects people. The Church perennially is in danger of being a class Church.

The Church *must* be interested in labor and in the laboring man's problems. Unless it is, we are definitely a class Church and our doom is sealed. We must not forget that labor governments now rule great sections of the world's population. The laboring man is on the march everywhere. Edwin Markham's "The Man with the Hoe" is no longer "a thing that grieves not and that never hopes." Labor is on the up and up and the laborer is coming, here and there, to know of "Plato and the swing of Pleiades." While many have cringed at the rise of labor's power, some with the insight of the ancient prophets of Israel see that

> Through this dread shape humanity betrayed,
> Plundered, profaned and disinherited,
> Cries protest to the Powers that made the world,
> A protest that is also prophecy.[1]

Let us remember too that the Church is for *people*, not for labor or management, or whites or blacks, the haves or the have-nots. Men are our concern, their personalities and consciences, their hopes and cares, their successes and failures. Christ is not on the side of labor or management. He is on the side of people and any situation that people find themselves in is the deep concern of our Lord.

Let it be said also that Christian men can disagree in love. You may not agree with the positions the preacher takes this morning, but you can keep on loving me and I can love you and together we can bring our minds to bear upon one of the most complex situations in our modern life. As we think together in love, God's light will break, and His Spirit will lead sincere, seeking men out of the morass of labor difficulties we find ourselves in today.

Henry van Dyke's little verse, "The Gospel of Labor," set me to thinking about this Labor Sunday message:

> This is the Gospel of Labor—
> Ring it, ye bells of the kirk—
> The Lord of love came down from above
> To live with the men who work.
> This is the rose that he planted
> Here in the thorn-cursed soil—
> Heaven is blessed with perfect rest;
> But the blessing of earth is toil.[2]

We begin our thinking by asking: What are labor's *acute* problems? As a minister who deals with men of labor and management, I have tried to see sympathetically the problems of each.

All would agree that one of labor's pressing problems is to get a living wage without asking for too much. The average family income in the United

---

[1] "The Man With the Hoe" by Edwin Markham. Used by permission of Mr. Virgil Markham.

[2] Reprinted from *The Toiling of Felix and Other Poems* by Henry van Dyke; copyright, 1900, by Charles Scribner's Sons, 1927, by Henry van Dyke. Used by permission of the publishers.

States in 1940 was $740, in 1945 it was $1,050. Now it is higher. But suppose it has risen now to $1,500, or even $1,800—what can a man with a family do for them on such wages with prices where they are today? How many children can one send to college, give music and dancing lessons, buy books and concert tickets for, and make other cultural advantages available to on an income of $100 to $150 per month? Here, then, is the laboring man pulled in two directions; the demands of his family increase with the general rise in living standards of our American population; on the other hand, there is the definite ceiling of his earning power. This is one of labor's most trying problems.

Another is how to get decent working and living conditions. One does not have to go far back into the history of the industrial revolution in this country to find the sweatshop. There were exceptions like the Nash Clothing Company, but these were famous because they were rare. Thomas Hood was not writing about an imaginary evil when he wrote the "Song of the Shirt."

> With fingers weary and worn,
>   With eyelids heavy and red,
> A woman sat in unwomanly rags,
>   Plying her needle and thread—
> Stitch! stitch! stitch!
>   In poverty, hunger and dirt,
> And still with a voice of dolorous pitch
>   She sang the "Song of the Shirt!"

Add to this the fact that most of the world today is ill-fed, ill-housed and ill-clothed. O Americans, look at the plenty with which God has endowed us! As I partake of all the good things to eat in this city, I often think of our terrible peril. The danger of this prosperity is that our ears will be deafened to the cries of the world for bread. While we live in abundance here, most of the working people of the world are hungry. This is an ever-present and acute problem facing the laboring men and women of this generation.

Still another critical problem facing the working people of our day is how to be socially responsible, democratic, co-operative. All of us could cite instances of labor's sense of responsibility as its power has grown. All of us likewise could point with equal truth to times when labor utterly failed to meet its titanic responsibility in our American democracy. Labor must be responsible today for keeping out destructive foreign ideas. It must stand for free enterprise, the American way. It must stand unequivocally against communism. It must co-operate with men of good will anywhere to keep the American system. But it must help to purge this business-for-private-gain of its abuses. Labor must help make our way of life thoroughly Christian so that the profit motive may continue as our way but so that men will have a larger motive—that of seeking the kingdom of God.

Labor has another serious problem in the matter of extending the benefits of organized labor to all workers everywhere. Benefits have come to the workingmen of this day in the form of education, child care programs, family case work and personal counseling services, relief, better wages, and unemployment and retirement compensation. Sick benefits, longer vacations, more pleasant working conditions generally have been gains enjoyed by labor in recent years. Some of these benefits, at least, came at the suggestion and with the full co-operation of Christian men in management who have worked unceasingly for the welfare of the men who work for them. It is true that millions are not yet enjoying the fruit of labor's efforts to lift itself. There are many domestic and agricultural workers, teachers in the public schools and others, who as yet are the victims of a system, with no one to speak for them and fight their battle of liberation. An unknown author has protested this injustice, and all fair-minded men can feel the pain he describes:

> We have fed you all for a thousand years,
> For that was our doom, you know.
> From the days when you chained us in your fields
> To the strike of a week ago.
> You ha' eaten our lives and our babes and wives,
> And we're told it's your legal share;
> But, if blood be the price of your lawful wealth,
> Good God, we ha' bought it fair.

All of us in the Church, regardless of which group we belong to, had better try to understand this point of view. If we do not, we prepare the soil for communism, which is not a political theory primarily but rather an economic theory which makes fantastic promises to the worker which are never fulfilled.

All of us have watched the life-and-death struggle of labor and management in recent years, and the rather general feeling often has been that labor leaders have gone after their goals as if there were no other point of view then their own They have given the impression that management had no rights, no problems, no heart, no sympathy whatever with anything but profits. This is an extreme attitude, and we do well to call labor to consider the problems of management, which are as complex and difficult and important as those of the laboring man.

One of management's ever-present and difficult problems is that of how to protect the stockholders and at the same time to be fair to labor. Many men in management are Christian men just as there are many in labor who are fine, upstanding men in their churches. These men in management, many of them, are eager to go the second mile with the man who works for them. Many of these men came up through the ranks themselves and were reared in homes where the father worked with his hands and had the point of view of labor. But there is a limit to which they can go. They represent other people's money. They are employed themselves to make money for others. They cannot give the plant away and be a faithful trustee. There is a stopping place beyond which they must not step in meeting the ever-increasing demands of labor.

Some of these men in management have been members of my church. I have listened to them talk for hours about their eagerness to go along, their desire to put the teaching of the Christian Church into their businesses, but how? They cannot tolerate strikers taking over a plant. No man has the right to take private property which does not belong to him, regardless of the principle he may be fighting for. We call that stealing and we must make it plain to all that stealing is breaking the moral law of God. Management cannot tolerate strikers destroying property. No man has the right to destroy the property of another. I have known men in management in recent years to grow old trying to determine their Christian duty in the face of this pressing problem—how to be fair to the workers and the stockholders at the same time. The student of Christian ethics knows that in a sinful world there is no such thing as absolute justice. Our only hope today lies in Christian men on both sides seeing sympathetically the other's problems.

Another critical problem management faces is how to be conciliatory, how to be open-minded, how to work with labor. Many in management today are older men whose mental pattern was shaped back in the nineties, the age of the giant industrialists and railroad magnates who ran their businesses with a high hand, and who, incidentally, ran the country along with their expanding enterprises. It is difficult for some of these men to think in terms of sitting down with their workers. Theirs is the dictatorial method. They want to speak and have men quake. They do not know how to co-operate, how to listen, how to make their minds fluid enough to adjust to new situations. These men are hindering the coming day when all men of industry will work in a great fellowship of toil without too much distinction between the blue shirt and the white. Ever since *The Social Ideals of the Churches* was issued years ago by the Federal Council of the Churches of Christ in America, the churches have stood for the right of workers to organize just as management has the right to organize. Most of the major denominations long ago recognized that "a slave worker anywhere jeopardized the rights of all free men." Men in management who have not yet adjusted to the demands of workers for a conciliatory attitude will be forced to this point of view. The new day in a democracy demands that management look with the same concern upon the lifeblood of the worker as upon the property and profits of the stockholder.

Still another grueling problem of management is how to handle power. It is fair to say that neither management nor labor has handled power well. Management has had more advantages. This means more responsibility. Labor did not always show up well during the war when it had the power to stop war production. We saw the shameful spectacle of a few labor leaders using this dangerous situation as a time for personal battles for power. Management likewise ofttimes has been drunk with power. All of us need to remind ourselves of one of the dicta of history, namely, that unlimited power corrupts the human heart. The Constitution of our country is based upon this thought, and so the Founding Fathers wisely set up a system of government with checks and balances. The upper house checks the lower; the judiciary the legislative; and all check and balance the power of the executive. This is because of the danger of unlimited power. Perhaps it is in the scheme of things that there should be men of good will on both sides of this great industrial conflict so that none shall have unlimited power.

Remembering that there are good men, Christian men, fair-minded men on both sides, and also keeping in mind that there are evil men on both sides, the Church speaks to both without taking sides with either. Through the Apostle Paul the Church calls all alike in this conflict to think about whatever is true, whatever is honorable, whatever is just, whatever is pure, whatever is lovely, whatever is of good report—to think on these things. Applied to our morning theme, this means that the man of labor has no right whatever to do anything that is not true, pure, just, honorable, or of good report. Conversely, it means that the man of management has no right to conduct himself in any way which is out of keeping with truth, purity, honor, justice or things of good report. This is the word of Christ to both labor and management.

Interpreting this, the Church, in the name of her Lord, speaks to workingmen everywhere, whether they stand in the factory or sit in the office. Specifically the word of the Church boils down to some very simple truths which all must recognize as binding upon us morally.

One clear word of Christ to both is that dictatorial methods are as objectionable in industry as in politics. The world has just witnessed a blood bath for millions because of the dictatorial methods of a few. We hate that in politics. We must come to hate it in industry. Neither labor nor management has any right in a democracy to attempt to rule others without their consent. The power lies in the body of those who are governed, whether in a country or a business. If democracy is valid as a form of government for a state, then it is equally valid for workers in an industry, and men of good will must find ways of making democracy work in their businesses.

Another clear word of Christ to men of both groups is that greed is as dangerous for labor as for management. Selfishness is no respecter of persons, and it is man's shrewdest and deadliest enemy. The size of a man's pay check has nothing whatever to do with covetousness. The workingmen often talk as though the boss is the greedy, selfish or covetous one. This is foggy thinking. Because we are human, we all stand in peril of being corrupted by an unholy desire for more and more and more. Unless we are constantly on guard, we may be eaten up—all of us—by greed, which works like a cancerous growth, slowly but surely until it has brought death.

Christ has still another sure word for men of both sides in this conflict: violence is a sign of weakness and it settles nothing. It may prove who has the strongest right arm or the quickest trigger finger but it does not prove who is right. Just as profanity is a sign of frustration and inadequacy, so violence on the part of either management or labor is a sign of weakness. We must rely in our industrial disputes upon the power of truth and the saneness of an enlightened public opinion. Violent, biased propaganda is also a sign of weakness and in the end will bring only defeat. If your cause is right, keep on fighting cleanly for it, and be assured that if it is on the side of truth, the whole universe will fight for you.

The word of Christ comes again to all the men of earth on this Labor Sunday, and it says that love is the law of life. Whether you work on the assembly line or behind a mahogany desk, whether your income is from a weekly pay envelope or from coupons, you are to love men. That is Christ's will for you. You are to be the light of the world, the salt of the earth, the lover of all men, and especially of your enemies. You are to be reconciled with your brother and to agree with your adversary. This is the word of your Lord in the Sermon on the Mount and it is the law of life. It cannot be set aside even for you in labor, or you in management.

Again the Church in the name of her Lord has a further word for men of labor and management. This word has to do with ultimate goals Utopia has not come when all of labor's dreams come true. Neither has it come when all of management's desires are fulfilled. Life in God is the only thing that brings heaven. There is danger of our thinking that business goals are ultimate goals. The ultimates lie in the realm of the spirit.

The great and final word of the Church on this Labor Sunday is that men of both labor and management need changed lives. The power of the living Christ in the lives of men is the only power that lifts them up above their weakness and blindness and changes them into men who can overcome and conquer the problems of the world. The Christ of the carpenter shop wants to lead the men of our day to a brotherhood of toil in which the true rights of all are respected, the reasonable hopes of none frustrated, and the opportunities of all advanced. Then all of us will be "aristocrats of labor." W. Stewart has written:

> They claim no guard of heraldry,
> They scorn the knightly rod;
> Their coats of arms are noble deeds,
> Their peerage is from God!

The Christian Confronts Authority:
Authority, Creator of Enterprise

REVEREND MICHEL RIQUET, S.J.

*Member of the Society of Jesus and Conferencier
of Notre Dame Cathedral, Paris, France*

Michel Riquet was born in Paris in 1898. A brilliant student, he served in the infantry in 1917-18, was cited for bravery, was decorated with the Legion of Honor in 1945, and was later awarded the Medal of Freedom with Silver Palm.

Father Riquet worked with the French Resistance until the Gestapo arrested him on January 18, 1944. He was first imprisoned at Mauthausen, then transferred to Dachau. He was kept a prisoner until the allied armies released him in May, 1945. After his return, Cardinal Suhard asked him to preach a series of sermons on "The Christian Confronts the Ruins" ("Le Chretien Face Aux Ruines").

Pere Riquet began his series of Lenten Conferences at the Cathedral of Notre Dame in Paris in 1946. A second series was preached in 1947, a third in 1948, and this fourth series during Lent, 1949, on the theme, "The Christian Confronts Authority." "Authority: Creator of Enterprise," was given March 20, 1949, as one of six sermon lectures in the series.

His discussion of capital and labor, of authority and workers, of employers and unions in France, is interesting for its understanding of the problems and needs of labor, and for its honest facing of the employers' responsibilities and opportunities. His emphasis upon the need for both sides to be fair and Christian, to act as brothers to one another for the common good is a fitting word for France, America, England, and all the world in our day.

His plea for all men to live by Christian standards makes this a sermon to keep and read many times. It makes one wonder when man will learn to live in simple brotherhood with the rest of mankind.

The translation was made by the Reverend Camille A. Chazeaud and the French feeling and thought has been retained as much as translation permits. Father Richard F. Grady, S.J., of the University of Scranton, checked the translation for American usage. Appreciation is gladly expressed by the editor for the translation and checking.

The conferences of Notre Dame were established in France in 1820 and the greatest preachers of France were brought to Notre Dame for a course of sermons The Jesuit de Ravignon, the Dominican Lacordaire and the great

Montsabre made the conferences famous. The conferences have continued until now in spite of wars and difficulties. Father Riquet has added new glory to these famous conferences.

Sermon Thirty=one

TOO often in history, when two men, or two nations or two political parties confront each other, the meeting degenerates into a deadly struggle in which victors and vanquished, masters and slaves are involved.

We shall here consider authority as it operates in one of the many human groups, midway between the family and the state. We shall find that there is no successful enterprise, no collective accomplishment, possible without the virile initative of a leader or without the collaboration of other human beings whose labor would remain unproductive except for the leader's vivifying supervision.

But we shall also establish that, in order to avoid conflicts in industry between master and slave, it is absolutely necessary for both leader and worker to adopt, in their mutual relationships, an attitude which draws its inspiration from the vision of a truly brotherly community.

First of all, we find at the root of every collective achievement a virile initiative, a manly aggressiveness, a spirit of adventure, a genius for organization.

Everyone knows Napoleon's formula: "It was not the Roman legions that conquered Gaul, but Caesar! It was not the Carthaginian soldiers who made Rome quake, but Hannibal! It was not the Macedonian phalanx that overwhelmed India, but Alexander!"

And Marshall Foch came to a like conclusion: "The great achievements in the War [of 1914-1918] were made by the Command. Without that Command, no battle, no victory was possible."

But the prime importance of the leader's role is clear not only in warfare. Study the beginnings of the great undertakings, the great enterprises, the great discoveries, which have most powerfully contributed to the ennoblement of man, to the amelioration of his life on earth, to the refinement of his mind, and to the improvement of his condition, and always, at the root, you will find a man, an idea, and the will of a leader.

It was not a nameless and unorganized group of sailors who finally linked together Europe and America, but one persistent man who overcame all the objections, all the indecision, all the intrigues of the Spanish court; and all the weariness and cowardice and fright of his crews: Christopher Columbus.

It was not a government administration, a succession of committees, which established the airline by which today one can fly in a dozen hours or so from Paris to Santiago, over the South Atlantic and the Cordilleras. That took the daring and perseverance, the brilliance and virtuosity, the authority of a Mermoz.

Think of those bright laboratories, those well-lighted, immaculate halls where powerful machines manufacture ointments, serums, vaccines, which, by the millions of tubes and capsules, prepared in a quick and hygienic operation, will cleanse, heal and strengthen countless infected and enfeebled human beings. Now, who is the one who has made these handsome buildings burgeon out of a barren ground, and surrounded them with shrubbery and blossoms, ponds and flowered brooks, which the white-uniformed working girls look out upon from huge bay windows. It was an ordinary pharmacist's helper, the son of a poor winegrower of the department of Charente, and he alone who conceived and planned this whole plant. It was his extraordinary taste for the beautiful, his ever successful daring that brought to realization this plant which, in the magnificence and beneficence of its construction, far outstrips the petty projects and narrow vision of any irresponsible government bureau.

Anonymity has never created anything. Bureaucracy has never invented anything. At the root of every agricultural, industrial and commercial advance there is always some one person, a leader. And more than once there will be, in order to insure the continuity of the work, a family.

In Roubaix, Tourcoing, Bohain, as at Elbeuf and Lyon, and also at Mulhouse, one can list the names of a man and his sons who, by their tireless ingenuity have launched and maintained, reorganized and developed and perfected weaving processes for wool and silk, that have saved thousands of artisans and workmen from unemployment, thus proving to a world so prone to forget the fact, or to verify it, that there still remain in our land some men who are master craftsmen, creators of beauty and fashioners of noble achievements.

Skilled workmen, of whom there is no small number among us, know full well that nothing great, nothing fine can be accomplished save by teamwork, and they know that there can be no teamwork without a coach, without a captain.

Stone, stonecutter, mason, each was indispensable to the building of this cathedral [of Notre Dame] but no less indispensable was he who directed all their movements, all their skills, all their efforts—from manual laborer to specialist—into the production of a monumental, durable and harmonious whole. I mean the master builder, the architect, the prince of the technicians and commander of the work, the one who carries in his mind the overall plan, the scheme of what this will one day be, which now remains hidden from the men who are working on small jobs that are but fragments of the finished structure, but which the master's plan joins together and co-ordinates toward the future achievement that he alone has so boldly conceived and indefatigably carried through.

Should he die before it is finished, the cathedral will not be quite the same, or perhaps not at all as he had planned it from the beginning. Maderno's additions make Michelangelo's style seem heavy.

But please understand that, while I extol the leader's importance in any collective enterprise, I do not mean to forget or underestimate those through whom, in a no less indispensable manner, the genius of a creator becomes incarnate in a work in hand in which is reflected a share of the intelligence, the courage, and the skill of every workman.

When men unite their efforts in a collective enterprise, the final result is in a true sense the work of all. Neither the leader to the exclusion of the others, nor the workers to the exclusion of the leader would have attained their goal, and this is the basis of each one's right to share in the honor and the profit gained from their common effort.

The conspicuous part played by the creative initiative and the will that organizes and brings its plans to completion, does not exclude the share, no less essential, played by the subordinate workers. Without them nothing would ever succeed.

Every employer, every director knows and acknowledges that the best plans, the most powerful machines, the most marvelous organization would produce nothing better than a run-of-mill result, would even meet with disastrous blocks, if the worker did not, on his part, contribute his share of understanding and loyalty and enthusiasm.

Let us say right out, that despite a certain amount of sabotage inspired and carried out by men who are not true Frenchmen, the workingmen of our country—from bricklayer and carpenter to the skilful weaver of silks and woolens—still have a passion for, a devotion to "work well done," the job finished as it should be. Once let his professional motives, his respect for his trade, the reputation of his firm, of his town or his province be brought into dispute, and he will prove that he knows how to work with more speed, more skill and more precision than any other.

Still, to this end, he must not be led to feel that he is being exploited or used as a machine. That is something no employer ought ever forget. Let us admit that more than one of us, even today, needs seriously to examine his conscience on that point!

A hundred years ago, the well-known investigations of Villermé, of Buret and Villeneuve-Bargemont, as did those of Friedrich Engels, revealed in our own country and its neighbors, the material and moral misery, the shameful bondage to which the working people were subjected, at the very same time that the industrial revolution and mechanical progress were providing others with spectacular increases in comfort and luxury. About that, the Encyclical *Quadraguesimo Anno* makes this ironical comment: "This state of affairs was accepted without any difficulty by those who were bountifully provided

[191]

with this world's goods and regarded it only as the necessary consequence of economic laws."

During the past century, the condition of the factory worker has seen some notable improvements; he has won more humane working conditions. More than once, we must admit, certain employers who were truly Christian or were simply philanthropically-minded, took the initiative to make generous and effective provisions; as, for instance, in providing subsidies for their employees' families. But often enough such progressive measures were obtained or made generally applicable only at the cost of a bitter fight directed by the workers' organizations or by the political parties identified with them.

Nevertheless, in spite of these struggles, which were often successful and often renewed, the slums have not yet disappeared from the workers' quarters of our cities. Far from it. Many a family still has to live packed together into a single wretched room devoid of adequate air or light or water. Moreover, though some privileged workers are provided with salaries and advantages superior to those of a college professor or engineer or magistrate, the great majority of workers, day laborers, clerks, and machine operators, receive only a small salary for their hard work in depressing surroundings.

The man who knows that the best and brightest hours of the day wither while he is confined in the unhealthy, sometimes even poison-laden air of a workshop, a department store or a mine shaft, has a right, has he not, to claim more than a minimum living wage in compensation for the sacrifices he is making for others in giving up the best of his time, his health and his whole being?

Has he not the right to desire and even to demand that this best part of his life should serve to make his life brighter instead of wearing him out and leaving him broken and brutalized?

And for that, what is needed? First of all, that his work should be becoming to a human being—that is to say, it should be work fitting for an intelligent and free person!

The worker, and particularly the French worker, likes to know the "why and wherefore" of the jobs and tasks to which he is assigned. As a militant labor unionist has said: "A wage-earner instinctively wants to get a grasp on his job as a whole, from its planning and preparation right through to its finish, and the way it will be marketed. . . . To get a grasp on the sense and direction of his actions, in order to make them more vital, more free, more spontaneous." He wants to know what he is producing; he does not want anyone to use him as a tool and to exploit him against his will, in turning out weapons and ammunition for powers which he, rightly or wrongly, considers hostile or harmful to the working class. He will not permit anyone to make him, under some specious pretext, forge the chains to bind himself or his brethren. But, if he understands that every one of his actions, even the most boringly monotonous, results in increasing the welfare and comfort and joy of humanity, then he will put his whole heart into the work; however hard and tiring and grimy it be, it will be nevertheless, a job worth a man's doing, a labor of love.

In order that this self-sacrifice may remain worthy of a man, it has to be made under the conditions freedom requires. Therefore, let the discipline necessary for the work be freely consented to—a condition that will be the better resolved when the clauses of work contracts, shop rules and production standards are looked upon as law established by democratic process, for the common good of the enterprise and not as the arbitrary dictation of a tyrannical power.

A leading employer has recently written:

> It would be mean, unjust and dangerous to reduce the position of manual laborers, and of clerks, to a state of passive submission given in exchange for weekly or monthly wages. Our employees have the right, we would even say the duty, to organize to defend their own interests, in full freedom according to the methods and procedures that experience and tradition would recommend to them.

And management has to recognize this situation openly and specifically, and should welcome as collaboration any representations, so long as they are constructive and not destructive, which the employees shall think it necessary to present.

In the same vein, the Encyclical *Quadragesimo Anno* noted that it would be "more in harmony with existing conditions to moderate the work contract in so far as might be possible by means of elements borrowed from the contract of association," and encouraged experiments thanks to which "the workers and the employer have been invited to share in some fashion in the ownership of the enterprise, in its management or in the profit it earns."

This brings us back to the concept of association, to those relationships of man to man, for which the family presents the social pattern. And, gentlemen, this is no place to preach a paternalism, which in the mind of the workingman is identified with those condescending attitudes of patronage, that parade of apparent good will and humanitarianism, which serve some employers I could mention as excuse for production estimates and demands that are dictated more by a self-interest of which they are pretty well aware, than by a true sympathy for their fellowmen.

Without endorsing the criticism, often hasty and unjust, that has been leveled against some well-meaning industrialists (whose knowledge of psychology is, also, frequently superficial), we ought to insist that the first prerequisite for humanizing the struggle between master and slave is to transmute it into a brotherly emulation which, in the prosecution of the work both are engaged in, would thus be broadened into a co-operation between father and sons, a collaboration of brotherliness.

First and foremost, all the members of the same undertaking must look upon and accept one another, appreciate and esteem one another as brothers. Let them remember what St. Paul says when he asks Philemon to take back his runaway slave, "No longer as a slave, but as far better than a slave, as a beloved brother"; certainly not in a spirit of condescension, but with the conviction that "nothing is so close to a man as another man," especially when they are toiling and working together at a common task.

Community of effort! With that in mind, employers, directors, technicians, workers, all ought to accept the attitude of mutual responsibility that exists between father and mother. The complete success of any collective enterprise demands that everyone contribute to it, each according to his ability and skill. Some, as leaders, as coaches, will contribute organizational planning, initiative, drive; the others, an intelligent and sustained effort. But the same love, the same pride in their work must animate all of them, each one in the particular function that is to be determined by service to the good of all. What will preserve the dignity of each one in any enterprise, will be this ideal of the good-of-all-those who are giving the common task life and fruitfulness. Now, we have already said that, when men pool their efforts in a collective undertaking, the end product is actually the work of all together. The boss could not have produced anything without the workers, nor could the workers without the boss. And that is the basis of each one's right to share in the honor and the profit of the collective work.

If an airplane or an automobile wins some honor in an international or national exposition, is there a single worker or foreman in the firm who does not look upon it with as much pride as does a father or mother on their child? Each one has put into it a part of his being, something of his intelligence, his skill, his "know-how," his toil. And have not some groups of workers spontaneously offered to give up a Sunday or to work all night so that the success all desired might not suffer delay? It is at such times that the factory is what it ought to be: a brotherhood in the fellowship of work.

Why is it not always thus? Because, as in not a few divorce cases, wrongs have often been found on both sides. Normally, the more responsible one is the one whose intelligence and aptitudes have preordained him to promote, to educate and ennoble, to raise to a higher level his less gifted partner.

The mistake more than one employer makes is to accept without question or criticism the economic regime that was forged by the liberal individualism and capitalism of the past century, with all its disastrous consequences for the masses of the proletariat. These employers are not heartless or stupid; but the pressure of business, and obsession for all-important profits, which are the rewards of the investments, the requirements laid down by boards of trustees or meetings of shareholders, led them finally to subordinate, and sometimes to sacrifice, the worker to the points of view and the interests of high finance, and thus to sacrifice him to the supremacy of money over man.

A leader worthy of the name will not permit his horizons to be limited to the outlook of the market. What should warrant his position as leader is not the profits he makes for himself, but the profits accruing to the community of workers, considered as a body, the head of which cannot separate his fate from that of the members!

To make money is not the first or only objective. Rather must it be, first of all, to guarantee to all those who are working together in the same productive endeavor, humanly decent and happy conditions of life, in which they will be able to contribute by honest and useful work to the common welfare of the entire nation. Consequently, it is important to supply the needs of the human family with products in such quantity and of such quality as will be necessary to satisfy the needs of the productive group and permit it in its turn to receive in exchange all that it requires for the proper support of its members and their families, and at the same time to keep the stocks and buildings and machinery up to date.

But to attain this objective, the leader has to be a man of wide initiative, not constantly hampered by paralyzing controls, by systematic distrust, and by a more or less underhand insubordination among those who ought, on all levels of production, to be his loyal and trusted fellow workers.

Now take a look at the wrongs on the other side.

Marxist literature, starting from the indisputable fact of the exploitation of human labor by a profit-greedy capitalism, has set the working class not only against the loan sharks, the speculators and black marketers and profiteers, and all those responsible for decrease in wages and increase of prices, but against all employers, all captains of industry, all unjustly stigmatized as the Masters, "the idle rich" of Hegel's *Phenomenology,* or as the Capitalists, "the parasitic exploiters" of Karl Marx. Some think that, to be freed from the tyranny of money, all one has to do is to suppress anyone who has the appearance of a boss or a person of authority.

But do away with the leaders, and you behead any enterprise; you deprive it of those factors of its success which are boldness and originality in planning, flexibility in organization, speed in adaptation to changing economic trends, perseverance and persistence in difficult situations. A group can be put in the place of a proprietor who is static and old-fashioned, without immediate detriment to the enterprise; but to put some bureaucrat or other into the place of a leader who is dynamic and passionately devoted to the work which he has himself built up or given new life to, means the death of that enterprise.

It is not my purpose here to approve or to condemn this or that form of appropriation of the means of production. But I do insist on the necessity for every collective enterprise and every community of workers to have a real leader endowed with genuine powers of initiative, decision and command, which should be matched by a loyal self-dicipline on the part of his employees. Or rather, take the word of a responsible head of a national administration: "There are no two ways to manage an enterprise on a sound basis, whether it be private or state-owned. The only way is the one in which unity of responsibility prevails. Every time that men in industry have deviated from this principle, they have run head-on into serious trouble, and their unfavorable results have gone into the record."

In the community of labor, no less than in the political community, democracy does not mean anarchy. It signifies and requires only that authority be exercised for the profit of all, with respect for the individual's dignity, under the control of, and within the limits determined by, those institutions to the establishment of which all have in some measure given their consent. Can anyone point out to me a single democracy in the world in which armies are maintained without officers empowered to enforce obedience, or where factories and agricultural developments operate without effective and energetic management? We know of some people, who call themselves progressive, who enforce so strict a workshop discipline as would not readily be submitted to by those who, while they are among us, complain so quickly of being enslaved. Indeed, proletarian revolutions, no matter in what country they occurred up to the present, have succeeded only in replacing yesterday's bosses with others who have proved themselves no less harsh, no less demanding. Both ancient and modern history teaches us that even the most pitiless, the haughtiest and most tyrannical masters have frequently come up from among the former slaves and outcasts. That is why the Christian believes it wiser to avoid these violent upheavals out of which are begotten fresh disorders and miseries, new slaves as well as new masters.

Does that mean that the Christian should tolerate the injustices of his day? On this question the Church, in the words of Your Eminence as well as those of the Supreme Pontiff, orders us to take a stand that has nothing in common with the passive resignation for which some rebuke us and which others sometimes recommend to us. In a recent statement Your Eminence said:

> Once more we insist on affirming that the major problem of our day is that of the suppression of social injustices. We are profoundly in sympathy with the just claims and legitimate aspirations of the working class. . . . The Church refuses to submit to the tyranny of money. . . . She imposes on the faithful the obligation of working courageously for the elimination of the disorders which stem from the present capitalistic system.

His Holiness, Pius XII, speaking to the Sacred College (of Cardinals) has also exhorted "the Catholics of the whole world not to be satisfied with good intentions and beautiful plans, but to devote themselves bravely to their practical fulfillment."

It is not the prerogative of this pulpit to specify what particular organic reform could best restore to the industrial fabric and the working community the atmosphere of friendliness, the human contact and brotherly relationship which should exist among all those who, whether they be leaders or subordinates, work together in production.

That is up to the Christian laymen: employers, heads of firms, superintendents and shop foremen, clerks, craftsmen, workers It is up to all of them together to look for and to find a common ground of mutual understanding and to study together the technical reforms which will permit both sides to work together with each another and no longer against each other.

Everyone in his own place of work, whether it be great or small, must understand that no life is possible, no progress can be achieved, without sustained effort, co-ordinated by qualified leaders, in an atmosphere of mutual respect and confidence, that is to say in friendship. But friendship cannot be forced upon anyone; it is bestowed and deserved in a give-and-take that is absolutely necessary.

As long as the employer of labor continues to treat his employee as simply a goods-producing machine which has to be used to the maximum and can be speculated with as a piece of merchandise whose value is measured by the price one pays for it, the employer will find his employee holding up production, refusing to give himself whole-heartedly to a job which to him is drudgery, and doing as little as possible for a wage that is never equivalent to his worth as a human being.

For a worker to put his heart into a job, he has to be interested in it, not only as paying a reasonable return for his toil, but as giving him a feeling of being a partner in the work, not as an unfeeling cog, but as a free man working freely, intelligently, at a common task whose purpose and procedures and end products he understands.

Conversely, the trust, the generosity, the good will of the employer must be matched by the confidence, the diligence, the devotion of his employees. Because he is, generally speaking, better educated, more highly developed, more responsible, the employer should make the first advances toward reducing the distance between himself and his workers. He must step out and pledge his interest, but all this on condition that he will not encounter an organized resistance presenting demands that take into consideration neither the actual situation and the special circumstances of this particular enterprise, nor the probable repercussions of such demands upon the economic situation throughout the nation. In short, he ought not to be met by a determination to sabotage every initiative which might create an atmosphere of peace and co-operation, out of a sheer contrary desire to maintain and enlarge the spirit of class struggle and class hatred.

When employers are weary of endless discussion, with concessions immediately made the point of departure for new demands, when trustfulness and kindness are constantly repaid by ingratitude; or, on the other hand, when workers are tired of having their patience and good will frustrated by empty promises or by settlements that are straightway subjected for revision, then employers and employees alike face the same temptation: to break the opposition by force and to adopt that dialectic of the "fight-to-the-death" which crushes all opposition by crushing one of the opponents.

To this superstition of hatred and destruction the Christian can and should oppose only the discipline of love—discerning love which knows that after having given way to the craving for violence, after having multiplied ruins and slaughter, there will finally come the time when men will have to rebuild and recreate human enterprises in which there will always necessarily be found employers and employees who will produce results only in so far as they are willing to accept one another, each in his own respective role and separate sphere. All strikes and revolutions end, as do all wars, in talks and conferences and in coming to terms.

Why can't we start where we always end and save ourselves from devastation, misery and murder?

It is the wisdom of love to prefer a talk to a fist fight, a friendly and brotherly talk, in which one does not slyly try to take advantage of the other, a mutual understanding, an accord based on reciprocal concessions made in the interest of all. This means for the good of all who confront each other, but cannot subsist save at the price of a trusting and loyal co-operation. That is the talk we mean. Nowhere in all the world can you find an enterprise without a leader, without department heads, without foremen. Nowhere in the world will you find a working community happy and prosperous without at least a minimum of confidence and friendliness among all those who, from top to bottom, contribute to the success of the common task.

Let us rather begin, therefore, with love, not hatred. Love alone unites; love alone is constructive; and, finally, only love will triumph over evil by doing good. Amen.

MAN

This Mind In You

REVEREND LISTON POPE, PH.D.

A minister of the Congregational Church and Dean of the Divinity School of Yale University, New Haven, Connecticut

Dr. Pope is a preacher of rare ability, combining understanding, reverence and vision supported by sound scholarship and balanced judgment. As the new dean of the Yale University Divinity School he will exercise a wide influence on the training and thinking of thousands of young ministers who attend Yale.

He was born in Thomasville, North Carolina, September 6, 1909, took his college and theological studies at Duke University. As a student he was president of the Duke University Y.M.C.A. in his senior year. He began his ministry as Associate Pastor of Wesley Memorial Methodist Church at High Point, North Carolina, from 1932 to 1935. During 1935-38 he was minister of the Humphrey Street Congregational Church in New Haven, Connecticut, while he carried a part-time schedule of studies in the graduate school at Yale. In the Fall of 1938 he was appointed Lecturer in Social Ethics at Yale Divinity School, served as assistant professor from 1939-44, associate professor, 1944-47, and in 1947 was made Gilbert L. Stark Professor of Social Ethics.

He received his Ph.D. from Yale in 1940. His doctoral dissertation was awarded the John Addison Porter Prize for that year. Its subject was A Study of the Interrelationships of Religious and Economic Institutions in Southern Cotton Mill Towns. It was published by the Yale Press as Millhands and Preachers. He has served as editor of Social Action. He was a member of the Congregational Christian Commission for Study of World Organization and Chairman of the Committee on Intercultural Relations of the Congregational Christian Churches. He has served with the Federal Council of Churches as a member of the committees of its Department of Christian Social Relations, Department of Race Relations, and Department of the Church and Economic Life. He was chairman of the Industrial Relations Division of the Federal Council from 1944 to 1946.

During the war he held several interim pastorates in three different Congregational churches in Connecticut. On the retirement of Dean Weigle from the administrative duties of the Yale Divinity School Dr. Pope was made the new dean in 1948.

Sermon Thirty=two

Text: I Corinthians 1:10, 18-25

ONE of the most impressive and best-known members of the Yale University faculty resides in the Peabody Museum of Natural History. His name is Brontosaurus—Brontosaurus Excelsus, the thunder saurian. As befits one with a name so distinguished and a podium larger than any other lecture platform in the university, he is a great teacher, and I have discovered that hours spent at his feet are seldom wasted. He says practically nothing—it is reported that only small children and immoderately convivial persons have ever heard him speak. But he gives great instruction merely by standing there and reminding us of some of the lessons of life. Millions of years ago, he and his fellow dinosaurs held undisputed mastery of the Connecticut Valley. His physical bulk has seldom been matched by any other species. More than sixty-seven feet long and sixteen feet high, Brontosaurus weighed, at his peak, about forty tons.

Impressed by such power, I have often pondered over the decline and fall of Brontosaurus, and have consulted some of the authorities on the subject. A layman hesitates to discuss their theories lest he be suspected of belonging, so far as geology and paleontology are concerned, in the same period as Brontosaurus. But the fact that he was overspecialized appears to have been one of the principal factors contributing to the downfall of the mighty dinosaur. Despite his physical bulk—indeed, largely because of it—Brontosaurus could not adapt to changing conditions on a changing earth. You see, he had less than one pound of brain matter to forty tons of weight. So he and his kind became extinct, and they are celebrated now only as museum pieces.

But how did the physical pygmy we call man succeed at last to the domain of the dinosaurs? How did homo sapiens become lord of creation? By what gift do we rule land and sea—and even sky? How is it that we can disinter the bones of Brontosaurus, and build a museum to house them, and write books to explain his fall?

Many theories are offered in reply, and doubtless there are many answers. One of the principal explanations, and the most obvious, is found in the magic powers of the human mind. The human brain, the intricate mind, with its capacity for adaptation to new conditions, has guided man onward in his long struggle on the earth. The ability to remember, to learn from experience, has kept him from making the same blunders too frequently, though often he has been spared by the skin of his teeth. The ability to imagine, to conceive of better ways of doing things, has added to his margin of security and to his power again and again. Man, it has been said, is a thinking animal; therefore, he stands at the peak of the world, bending nature to his will and shaping his own destiny.

On every hand we can see in these latter years fruits of the human mind: in the skyscraper that rends the clouds, in the plane that passes like a flying star, in the music, the painting, the book that probes realms where no plane can fly. We can tell of the marvel of the mind in our own lives, of what Byron called

> the power of thought,—
> the magic of the mind.

Strange filament of alternate dullness and incandescence, it baffles us even as we live by it. We study the brain and nervous system; we count the cells of the cerebral cortex; we analyze the functioning of the cerebellum—but even as we study we puzzle over the mystery that somehow the mind transcends even the study of itself. We use many terms to describe its action: memory, imagination, thought, appreciation, logic, emotion, appetite, the unconscious, the consience, the will—but we do not know the boundaries of any of these. We do know that through the mind, and in it, we possess a vast kingdom, and a bliss excelling all other "that earth affords or grows by kind."

In our paeans of praise to the human mind, however, we had best not forget that it is a very troublesome and dangerous endowment. It is particularly dangerous in two respects.

First of all, the mind is easily stultified. Despite its occasional liveliness, it appears on the whole to prefer inertia, and to be content with automatic routines. The most common tragedy of the human mind does not lie in its occasional derangement—though the increase of mental illness recently is alarming. Mental disease generally evokes in the observer a feeling of pathos rather than tragedy, as in Arnold Bennett's story of the poor creature who thought he was a poached egg and went through life in misery because he could find nobody to put him on toast. But the common tragedy of the mind, deeper and more pervading than pathos, lies in its tendency to stop growing and to be quite content with itself. In most persons it develops rapidly in early years, and then suddenly tends to become dogmatic and satisfied. It is like a man who sets out eagerly to see the world but stops at the first pleasant island, and spends the remainder of his life there making the island his world. This is the tragedy of the mind—the ease with which, in Byron's words,

> Years steal
> Fire from the mind as vigour from the limb,
> And life's enchanted cup but sparkles near the brim.

The most obvious symptoms of a state of arrested, but not abnormal, mental development are found in clichés and catch phrases—in stereotyped verbal reactions by which the mind dismisses problems rather than face them. Examples are legion in number. In the midst of a political campaign, for instance, we are made acutely aware of the lack of deep or creative thought among our national leaders. A candidate for senator from the West in 1948 announced as his platform: "I believe in God and motherhood and will fight fearlessly, on the radio and the platform, to save them from the aggressor." If this definition of the great issues of our time were only a local aberration we might sleep more easily at night. But even the candidates for the Presidency often campaign at approximately this same level. The seriousness of the times calls for

> Tall men, sun-crowned, who live above the fog
> In public duty and in private thinking.

Instead we are given men who deserve the words of Thomas Moore concerning politicians of his day: "The minds of some of our statesmen, like the pupil of the human eye, contract themselves the more, the stronger light there is shed upon them."

It is easy to deride politicians; this in itself is a favorite type of cliché for many of us, by which we escape our own political responsibilities. We like to forget that the successful politician merely reflects, often all too accurately, the mental level of the electorate. Though the reflection may be distorted, the politician holds a mirror up to us. His strategy is essentially that of a character in John Buchan's novel, *Three Hostages*. A candidate for local office in Ireland describes one of his campaign speeches as follows:

> The chief row was about Irish Home Rule, and I thought I'd better have a whack at the Pope. Has it ever struck you that ecclesiastical language has a most sinister sound? I knew some of the words, though not their meaning, but I knew my audience would be just as ignorant. So I had a magnificent peroration.
> "Will you, men of Kilclavers," I asked, "endure to see a chasuble set up in your market-place? Will you have your daughters sold into simony? Will you have celibacy practiced in the public streets?"
> God, I had them all on their feet bellowing, "Never!"

The tendency of the human mind to stop growing, to take refuge in easy clichés that preclude deeper thought and understanding, is aggravated by many forces of our time. Propaganda seeks to steal our minds from us by providing plausible catch phrases. In our day most ideas are ready-made, and produced in quantity for mass distribution. Newspapers, movies and radio devote most of their energy to the effort either to capture our minds or to prevent us from using them independently. It has come to the point that one is not expected to use his own head even in sending personal telegrams; you merely check a little square and your thoughts are conveyed across great distances in a sentiment like this:

> On Hallowe'en
> May you come through.
> I hope the ghosts
> Will not get you.

This, then, is the first danger of the human mind, and this is its tragedy: the ease with which it lies down in pleasant places and goes to sleep, doubtless to be awakened only at the judgment day.

There is a second, and greater, danger of the mind: the tendency of intellect, or reason, to regard itself as all-sufficient, to set itself up as an end in itself—in short, to play God, and to offer itself as an ultimate and adequate object of devotion. If stultification is the tragedy of the mind, self-deification is its heresy. If the former is the peril of the nonacademic man, the latter is the temptation of the intellectual.

For most of the eighteenth and nineteenth century intellectuals, reason was the perfectly adequate guide of life, the ultimate solvent of all human problems, the worthy object of man's highest devotion. As Gunnar Myrdal has pointed out, this worship of reason has produced many of the superstitions which are still cherished in academic circles, such as the myth of immutable natural laws in social affairs, the delusion of pure objectivity and a corresponding scorn of value judgments and of practical reform, the doctrine of folkways and mores as automatic regulators of life, and many others. Modern intellectuals, emancipated by reason from the dogmas of medieval religion, have in turn been reduced to bondage by the new dogmas about omnipotent reason.

Now the tide of rationalism has turned, and men begin to wonder whether intellect alone can save us. Some men are moving frankly to new irrationalism. In desperation most of us continue to formulate grandiose mental constructs for a rational world, but even as we do so we wonder whether we are merely playing a classroom game. And when the intellectual gymnastics are over, we find reality in the world outside to be largely unaffected. We can sympathize with Oliver Wendell Holmes' account of his certainty, while under ether, that he had grasped the key to all mysteries. As he came back to consciousness he hurriedly wrote the formula on a pad; it read, "A strong smell of turpentine prevails throughout."

The mind easily turns on itself when it knows no law or loyalty beyond itself. It appears to be a law of life that self-worship leads at last to self-alienation, and the intellect is no exception to this law. Unless the reason recognizes norms of truth beyond itself, one thought becomes as true as another, and, conversely, no idea is better than any other. The result is sheer confusion; the veil of the temple is rent, and the darkness of skepticism settles over the ruins.

Though, as always, he writes with quiet humor, an editor of *The New Yorker* probes deeply in the October, 1948, issue into the malady of the contemporary mind. Pondering whether to bequeath his brain to his alma mater, which is making a collection, he decides to send this inscription along with it:

> Observe, quick friend, this quiet noodle,
> This kit removed from its caboodle.
> Here sits a brain at last unhinged,
> On which too many thoughts impinged.[1]

Brontosaurus became extinct largely because he was too specialized. It may be that man has similarly become too specialized, relying too exclusively on intellect to preserve him. A professor at Harvard has warned of this danger; one of his colleagues there has proposed a drastic remedy—the extermination of all children who begin to show traces of genius.

But it may be that a million years from now some strange new species will have come to ascendancy on the earth, and its museums will contain the skeleton, including the skull, of Homo sapiens. Edna St. Vincent Millay has captured the irony of this possibility:

> When Man is gone and only Gods remain
> To stride the world . . . when the plain
> Round skull of Man is lifted and again
> Abandoned by the ebbing wave . . . what tongue
> Will tell the marvel of the human brain?[2]

[1] Copyright, 1948, by The New Yorker Magazine, Inc.
[2] From *Wine from These Grapes*, published by Harper & Brothers. Copyright, 1934, by Edna St. Vincent Millay.

You see, the mind can destroy as well as create. It can discover bacteriological warfare as well as penicillin; it can spread vicious propaganda as well as tested knowledge. Unless it is subordinated to a larger law of life, mind may demolish the civilization it has created and the creature it has sustained. In a society where love ruled as the ultimate law of being, those who put their supreme trust in intellect would inevitably be destroyed.

These, then, are the two greatest hazards of the mind: on the one hand, that it will not be used enough; on the other, that it will be relied on too exclusively. Indolence and idolatry: the first is more prevalent; the second may prove at last more disastrous.

How than shall we be saved? Clearly our minds cannot be controlled by statute law or by physical force; stone walls make no prison for them—*Mein Kampf* was written behind prison bars. Indoctrination may warp the mind, and censorship may thwart its ideas, but at length it overleaps all such obstacles.

No external remedy will suffice. The mind can be redeemed only from within—only as it gives itself, fully and joyously, to a Truth greater than itself, to a God greater than it can construct. It can know itself and its own powers most truly only if it is given back to Him who gave it, to the Mind of minds. Christian faith has sometimes lent itself to obscurantism and to glorification of the irrational; more characteristically, it has understood that there are thoughts higher than man's thoughts, and vast designs beyond the power of man to know. These designs, we believe, include the full free play of human intellect, that the mind may come at last to know and to adore its Maker and its Master. This can come to pass only as we confess that the foolishness of God is wiser than men, and that it has pleased God to ordain that the way of salvation, for the mind as for the soul, is the way of the cross, as was in Christ the wisdom of God.

And so for every study desk or laboratory bench, where men sit with humble minds in the presence of mystery or of sudden illumination, the injunction remains: "Let this mind be in you, which was also in Christ Jesus." And for every intelligence devoted to the service of the ultimate Wisdom, the promise holds: "Thou wilt keep him in perfect peace whose mind is stayed on thee: because he trusteth in thee."

The New Look

REVEREND NEIL BURN

Lafayette Avenue Friends Meeting, Brooklyn, New York

Mr. Burn is an Australian, who came to the United States in May, 1946. He studied theology in the Federal College of the Churches of Christ in Australia, and was ordained to the ministry from that institution in November, 1944. While waiting to come to this country to pursue his studies, he served with the Church of Christ in Charters Towers, Queensland, Australia.

Before coming to the Lafayette Avenue Friends Meeting in August, 1947, Mr. Burn served as associate minister of the First Friends Church in Indianapolis. He is working toward a Ph.D. in sociology, and is at present taking courses at New York University in this field. He is only thirty and is studying to fit himself for a place of leadership in the Church. Although it is thoroughly humanist, there is something very moving about this sermon.

Sermon Thirty=three

> Then let us pray that come it may,
> As come it will for a' that,
> That sense and worth, o'er a' the earth
> Shall bear the gree', and a' that;
> For a' that, and a' that,
> It's coming yet for a' that,
> That man to man, the world o'er,
> Shall brithers be for a' that.

THE above familiar words come from Robert Burns' poem, "Is There for Honest Poverty," and in the fashion of the poetic Scotsman they convey impressions that are loaded with meaning. In fact, they get to the very center and core of living; they convey the same message that Jesus, by putting first and foremost this conception of the worth of the individual, taught, and made Christianity to be the most effective religion known to the world.

"A man's a man for a' that" means that it does not matter what a man's station in life; it matters not his wealth, power or influence; it matters not his skin color; it matters not his nationality or creed; for above and beyond all these things a man is a man and should be treated as such.

[205]

We need this emphasis today, for we all too easily lose sight of this one all-important specific principle in the jungle maze of philosophic, economic and political generalities concerning human life. Men are lost in the generalities of such terms as democracy and totalitarianism, capitalism and communism, socialism and fascism, and, being lost, their unstable conduct leads to national and international tension and disruption. The consequence is that the systems devised by man become great monsters of oppression devouring his life.

But, is there anything vague and hazy about "a man's a man for a' that"? Are we apt to mistake the meaning of such words? No matter who the man, or from where, or what his political beliefs, or what his philosophy of life, he is a *man*.

That is the primary thing for us to remember in our world today. The answer to man's disorder does not lie in the deterministic theories put forward by some of the social scientists, or in the fatalistic approach of some theologians. It lies in the simple recognition by every man that his fellow man is a man. That "a man's a man for a' that." The sociologist La Piere says: "Commonly ignored in the relations of group against group is the fact that a negro is not just a negro, a communist a communist, or a German a German, or a Russian a Russian. Each is as a human being unique, and to put him into a type category inevitably does violence to the facts." Yes, every man is a human being unique.

Do you remember the story of Jesus rubbing wet clay over the eyes of the blind man, telling him to open his eyes, and then asking him if he could see? The answer of the man was, "I see men as trees walking." This was only the first stage of the making of the blind man to see, and there was still much dimness of sight. Modern man is able to see much more clearly than formerly the road that leads to national and world harmony, but our eyes are not yet fully opened. In all too many instances we see "men as trees walking"; in the fundamental issues of life we see men as something other than men. We have haziness of sight because of prejudice, hate, ill will, and misconceived ideas. The question for us is, we see men as what?

How dramatically Shakespeare drove home the message that a man's a man no matter what else. In that great plea of Shylock's we have words that go straight to the hearts of men. "I am a Jew. Hath not a Jew eyes? Hath not a Jew hands, organs, dimensions, senses, affections, passions! Fed with the same food, hurt with the same weapons, subject to the same diseases, healed by the same means?" A Jew, yes—but first of all a man. Yes, the great question today is, we see men as what?

Jesus saw men as men. The Jewish people found it easy to hate their conquerors, those who were keeping them in bondage, the Romans. The name Roman was one that made them spit upon the ground as it was spoken. Yet Jesus, a Jew, was able to see a Roman centurion not as a Roman, but as a man, and he said this of him: "I have not found so great faith, no, not in all

Israel." To speak something good about the enemies of your own government could be dangerous, but Jesus was not blinded by national bigotry and saw men as men. That made the difference.

That new way of looking at men needs to be brought into our life relations. Can we cultivate the new look in our dealings with others, and treat all men as men? The way was illuminated by Jesus Christ, with the heart of the message being found in the prologue to the fourth Gospel, where in John 1:9 we read," . . . the true Light, which lighteth every man that cometh into the world." The potentialities that every man has in being a son of God can be realized if we treat men as men in whom there is this light of eternal significance.

How do we deal with men? It depends on how we see men. Do we see them according to their darkness, or according to the light "which lighteth every man that cometh into the world"? The recognition of this light within every man is the duty of Christians, for the recognition of this light leads us to the right treatment of people. It enables us to see men as men. In Jesus' day, an ordinary person would say of another: "How degraded he is. He deserves to be punished." But Jesus always said: "How sick he is. He needs help."

There are still plenty of Matthews in our society today—men who are outcasts, living by graft and extortion; men who are despised by their fellows. They still need people like Jesus who will recognize the light within them, and make them see their own worthiness.

When we begin to look at people with this new look, it revolutionizes many of our old values. We see things more plainly; we see people as people instead of seeing them "as trees walking." Look what happens in the realm of justice. One of the most remarkable places in this world for gruesome memories is Port Arthur in Southern Tasmania. On this small peninsula in southernmost Australia was one of the most infamous convict settlements in the early days of that dominion. As you wander around there you see all the tortuous devices that were employed as instruments of man's justice early in the last century. If you visit Port Arthur, the guide will lock you in a special one of the old cells that still remains. It is a cell with great thick walls, and when the door is closed not a glimmer of light can be seen, with the darkness thick and heavy, weighing the prisoner down with unbearable pressure. A prisoner was confined in this cell in solitary punishment, and more often than not a few hours was sufficient for him to be brought out raving and insane. That was man's justice.

Yet even at this same period of history something else was happening. There were other people in the world taking a new look at man, especially at the men who languished in prisons. Men like John Howard, and women like Elizabeth Fry were looking at these prisoners in a different light. They were concerned with the light within man, rather than his darkness, and thus found themselves acting in accord with a higher type of justice which brought about great changes in the prison system.

There is no conflict between justice and love, for only as we love men, only as we treat a man as a man no matter what his condition, are we really just. Man often treats his fellow man according to the lower nature and calls that justice, but when we treat men according to the light which shineth within every man, we are bringing into force a higher type of justice, because we are dealing with the highest in man. And this new look, this higher justice, is the redemption of man.

Kahlil Gibran in *Jesus, Son of Man* makes Mary Magdalene say:

> It was all that was sod in me and all that was sky in me calling unto him. Then he looked at me and he said, "You have many lovers, and yet I alone love you. Other men love themselves in your nearness, I love you in yourself. Other men see a beauty in you that shall fade sooner than their own years. I see a beauty in you that shall not fade away, and in the autumn of your days that beauty shall not be afraid to gaze at itself in the mirror and it shall not be offended. I alone love the unseen in you." Then he stood up and looked at me even as the seasons might look upon the field, and he smiled and said, "All men love you for themselves. I love you for yourself." On that day the sunset of his eyes slew the dragon in me and I became a woman.

To treat men as men is the secret of making our world a fit place for men to live in. We have the power to make this new look effective, even as the scientist has the power to unveil the secrets of the physical universe. We must become scientists in human relationships. We know where to start. We have the ability to bring to mankind the glorious experiences of living in true harmony and fellowship through recognition of the worth of each individual. We must look again at man. We must look within our own lives and see the light that shines there, see the spiritual forces there, and then crusade in our world for the recognition of this worthiness in all men, refusing to let man surrender and become a puppet to any force other than the light which shines within himself. In the words of Tennyson,

> Follow the stars that light a desert pathway, yours or mine,
> Forward, till you see the highest human nature is divine.

What Is Man?

THE RIGHT REVEREND HENRY IRVING LOUTITT, D.D.

Bishop Coadjutor, Protestant Episcopal Diocese of South Florida, Orlando, Florida

Bishop Loutitt was born in Buffalo, New York, January 1, 1903, attended public schools in Buffalo and graduated from Hobart College. He took his theological work at Virginia Theological Seminary and was ordained to the priesthood in 1929. He began his ministry as vicar of All Saints' Church, Tarpon Springs, Florida, was called to be curate of Trinity Church, Miami, and in 1930 became rector of Holy Cross Church, Sanford, Florida. In 1933 he moved to be rector of Holy Trinity Church, West Palm Beach. He was called to active duty with the Armed Forces of the United States in 1941 and was assigned as chaplain to the Thirty-first Infantry Division. He remained with this division throughout the war and rose to be assistant division chaplain. He was awarded the Bronze Star for his service in the South Pacific.

Elected Suffragan Bishop of the Diocese of South Florida while still in the Armed Forces, he was consecrated May 23, 1945, and in April of 1948, was elected Bishop Coadjutor of the Diocese of South Florida, with headquarters in Orlando.

The Bishop is President of the Florida Council of Churches, a member of the Board of Editors of the National Council Department of Christian Education of the Episcopal Church, and a member of the General Commission on Chaplains. He is also Division Chaplain of the Forty-eighth Infantry Division of the Florida National Guard, and is active in community affairs.

This sermon asks an old, old question: "What is Man?" And then it answers that question with affirmations of faith and fact. His reference to Le Compte du Noüy illustrates the scope and timeliness of his reading and his use of that reading in his sermonizing.

Sermon Thirty=four

Text: What is man, that thou art mindful of him? Psalm 8:4a

WHAT is man? That is the primary question in all philosophy, whether epistemology, metaphysics or ethics. Moreover, put in the terms, "What am I?" it is the basic question that each man must answer for himself. In the answer to that fundamental question is reflected our understanding of the universe, our attitude toward life, and the way we live. And it must be answered. If not formalized in thought or expressed in words, it is betrayed by our daily life.

What am I? From the viewpoint of science, that is, strictly from observation, I am an integral part of the physical universe. Man is composed of molecules, atoms and electrons, like any other physical object in the world. If chemically analyzed, he is found to be composed of some ninety parts of oxygen, thirty of carbon, fifteen of hydrogen, three of nitrogen, two of phosphorus, and small parts of iron, copper, sulfur and the like. But if I were analyzed both quantitatively and qualitatively and an exact formula found for my physical body, and then the right elements in exact proportion were mixed, it would not be I. The result would not even be living matter.

These chemical elements of which I am composed are so arranged and organized that they constitute living matter, a physicochemical machine with properties quite unlike those of the inorganic world. Specifically, I am highly developed living matter, an animal, a mammal, a primate. With all the animals, I share a common heritage and inherit certain instincts. All of us, for example, must eat and sleep in order to survive. All of us have a deep instinctive urge to preserve the species by self-preservation and by procreation.

But our essential difference from other animals is quite as obvious as our essential sameness. I am the most highly developed kind of animal, known as man. I stand erect, have hands fitted for the use of tools, have a tongue and vocal cords that allow me to communicate. I have a more highly developed brain than any other animal, allowing me to think and feel and will—differently in degree, possibly different in kind from the thinking, feeling, and willing of what are called dumb animals. In large part, I am free. I have a conscience, make moral judgments, know right and wrong. I can do right or wrong. Therein lies my essential humanness.

Contrary to general public opinion, science and religion are not mortal enemies; indeed, they are not in opposition; rather they are complementary. Each in its own sphere seeks knowledge of God, known in and revealed through His universe.

So with these observations of science, Christianity agrees. As a matter of fact, centuries ago the Book of Genesis stated the same thing in different words. "I am an integral part of the physical universe" is there stated: "And the Lord God formed man of the dust of the ground." "I am living matter" is written: "And He breathed into his nostrils the breath of life." "I am a man"; what characterizes man as man is stated Biblically: "And man became a living soul."

As a matter of fact, science per se merely asks the questions, What is this? and, How does it function? It remains for philosophy and religion to ask the further essential question, Why? The philosophy which during the past century has spoken the longest and loudest in the name of science is materialism. To the materialist there is no answer to the question, Why? It just happened, that is all. It is a result of just pure chance. To the materialist, human life is without cause or purpose, and hence, without meaning. Man to him is an irresponsible particle of living matter engulfed in a maelstrom of purposeless force. It is that philosophy which in popular form has largely undermined the Christian faith in an age that we are proud to think of as an age of science. It is that philosophy which undergirds fascism, communism, and irresponsible capitalism. It is that philosophy which makes strong men quake at the mere thought of atomic warfare.

And it simply is not true, as prophetic voices have been crying in the wilderness of modern civilization all through these years.

So speak responsible and recognized natural scientists. In the field of biology, Sir J. Arthur Thomson in the Gifford Lectures of 1915-16, entitled *The System of Animate Nature,* argues through some 650 pages that neither nature nor organic evolution can be understood apart from God. He ends his study thus: "But we cannot worship Nature. . . . Happy, then, are those who have what Sir Thomas Browne called, 'a glimpse of incomprehensibles, and thoughts of things that thoughts but tenderly touch.' Shall we not seek to worship Him whom Nature increasingly reveals, from whom all comes and by whom all lives?"

The astronomer and mathematician, Sir James Jeans, takes a similar stand in his *The Mysterious Universe,* published in 1930. Summing up his chapter on "Matter and Radiation," he states, "These concepts reduce the whole universe to a world of light, potential or existent, so that the whole story of its creation can be told with perfect accuracy and completeness in the six words: 'God said, Let there be light.' " The whole work is an attack on the materialistic and mechanistic view of the universe and its thesis might be summed up in his own words, "Today there is a wide measure of agreement, which on the physical side of science approaches almost to unanimity, that the stream of knowledge is heading toward a non-mechanical reality; the universe begins to look more like a great thought than a great machine." Again he states, "If the universe is a universe of thought, then its creation must have been an act of thought. Indeed the finiteness of time and space almost compel us, of themselves, to picture the creation as an act of thought."

More recently A. Cressy Morrison, past president of the New York Academy of Sciences, in his little work published in 1944, *Man Does Not Stand Alone*, brings forcibly to our attention the fact that the narrow physical limits within which any life can exist on earth could not be brought about at one time on one planet by chance alone. His thesis is, "The existence of a Supreme Being is demonstrated by infinite adjustments, without which life would be impossible. Man's presence on earth and the magnificent demonstrations of his intellect are a part of a program being carried out by the Supreme Intelligence."

That is the refreshing refrain of the outstanding scientists of our day. So Dr. Robert A. Millikan writes, "Modern science of the real sort is learning to walk humbly with its God." Sir Arthur Eddington proclaims, "Dismiss the idea that natural law may swallow up religion; it cannot even tackle the multiplication table single-handed." Even Julian S. Huxley, who is hardly orthodox, states, "Science may destroy particular theologies; but it cannot destroy religion . . . because the religious spirit is as much a property of human nature as is the scientific spirit."

The vast majority of philosophers have, of course, been on the side of faith even from Plato to the present time. The scholastic philosophy of the Middle Ages is almost totally neglected in modern colleges and universities, save in Roman Catholic institutions, but in fact that great school did square the philosophy of both Plato and Aristotle with the Christian faith, and few thinkers in the whole history of mankind equal, for example, St. Thomas Aquinas. Royce, Santayana, William James, Hocking, Whitehead, to mention but a few of the moderns, all are theists. Recently an article in *Time* magazine reported the conversion of Professor C. E. M. Joad of the University of London, long bête noire of Christian teachers, and his return to the Christian faith. Only thus, as he states, can he understand and meet the apparent evil in the world.

Given the fact of God, the Christian faith follows naturally, logically and inevitably. That seems to be the conclusion of the epoch-making study of Lecomte du Noüy's *Human Destiny* recently published. Du Noüy, one of the world's outstanding scientists, marshals scientific fact to prove that neither life nor humankind could evolve in the universe by chance alone. The scientific laws of probability forbid that conclusion; "Willy-nilly are we, therefore, obliged to admit the idea of transcendent intervention, which the scientist may as well call God. . . ."

With St. Paul he sees man as a new creature, his progress no longer merely evolutionary, the results of forces outside himself, but increasingly an ascension through his own effort to grow mentally, morally and spiritually. That is not quite the whole story, of course; "his own effort" must be understood as the Holy Spirit stirring within him. So du Noüy ends his work, "And let man above all never forget that the divine spark is in him, in him alone, and that he is free to disregard it, to kill it, or to come closer to God by showing his eagerness to work with Him, and for Him."

As a scientist, and on scientific fact he approximates the Christian position that man's existence, his purpose and his meaning lie in God. That is the meaning of the creation story in Genesis: "So God created man in His own image, in the image of God created He him." That is the vision of our text, "What is man, that Thou art mindful of him? and the son of man, that Thou visitest him? Thou hast made him lower than the angels, to crown him with glory and worship."

That is the Christian faith, its answer to what and why. We like to think that we are in this world to be successful, to love and to be loved, or above all that we may find happiness. That is not the Christian doctrine of the end of man. On the one hand, Protestantism expresses itself in the Westminster Catechism: "Man was made by God, and for His pleasure we were and are created." On the other, the Roman Catholic faith as expressed by St. Ignatius Loyola states: "Man was made to serve, praise, and reverence God his Lord, and by this means to save his soul." In the Early Church before it was divided, the faith was quite the same. So St. Augustine speaks, "Thou has made us for Thyself, O Lord, and our hearts are restless, till they rest in Thee."

The fundamental and ceaseless human struggle, seen in history, in the lives of those about us, and in our own lives, with all the attendant tensions and failures, result from this. This life is an effort to overcome the downward drag of our material and animal heritage as our spirits climb the steep ascent to heaven, as we aspire to the Perfection which is God.

On that journey, which from one point of view is evolution, three stages of development and of growth may be discerned. The first stage of man's development might be called the life of instinct. The foundation of our human organism is material. We are animals. The infant in his crib seeks only immediate satisfaction of his physical desires. The spiritual infant lives likewise by desire, without conscious thought or effort. He does what he wants to do. The second plane might be called the life of law. Man's essential humanity consists of knowing right from wrong, of knowing that some things are good, others better, others best, and of his freedom to choose right or wrong; good, better, or best. By and large, the spiritually immature does what he ought to do, or is made to do it by parental authority, by school discipline, or in adult society by public opinion or the police. The final and highest state is the life of grace. This is the only Christian life properly so called. Here God's presence, His power, and His will are realities. Christ increasingly dwells in our hearts by faith. We are the temples of the Holy Spirit. What we desire to do and what we ought to do more and more blend into one. We have become God's sons.

What is man? "Beloved, now are we the sons of God, and it doth not yet

[213]

appear what we shall be: but we know that, when He shall appear, we shall be like Him; for we shall see Him as He is." "Till we all come in the unity of the faith, and of the knowledge of the Son of God, unto a perfect man, unto the measure of the stature of the fullness of Christ." That is mankind's, ofttimes unconscious, vision. That is our goal.

NATIONAL AND INTERNATIONAL

Christianity and Democracy

THE VERY REVEREND ROBERT I. GANNON, S.J.

S.T.D., D.D., LL.D., L.H.D., LITT.D.

Director of Retreats, Mount Manrisa, Staten Island, New York

The Very Reverend Robert I. Gannon, S.J., was born in New York in 1893. He was educated at Loyola School, New York, and Georgetown University, Washington, D. C. In 1913 he entered the Society of Jesus. From 1919 to 1923, he was instructor of English and philosophy at Fordham College. Soon he founded the "Play Shop" and in 1925 wrote The Technique of the One-Act Play.

After leaving Fordham, he made his theological studies at Woodstock and was ordained in 1926. After his ordination he was sent abroad for special studies, taking his S.T.D. from Gregorian University in Rome in 1927, and his M.A. from Cambridge (Christ's College), in 1930.

On his return from England in 1930, Father Gannon reopened St. Peter's College, Jersey City, which had been closed during the war, and became its dean. He opened Hudson College of Commerce and Finance, of which he was the first dean from 1933 to1935. He remained as dean of St. Peter's until his appointment as President of Fordham University in June, 1936.

In 1937 he went to Venezuela on the invitation of President Lopez Contreras for consultation on school problems, and in 1942, received the Award of the New York Academy of Public Education for distinguished service in the field of Education. He is a trustee of Town Hall, an elective manager of the New York Botanical Garden, a trustee of the New York Zoölogical Society, a director of the Netherland-American Foundation, and a member of the Committee for International Economic Reconstruction.

Father Gannon's most interesting war time pulpit assignment was in air-raided London, where he preached the Lent in 1943 at Westminster Cathedral as the guest of the late Cardinal Hinsley.

"Christianity and Democracy" was delivered by Father Gannon at the

Eighth Annual Red Mass Celebration in New England (The Solemn Votive Mass of the Holy Spirit), given to invoke the Blessing of God upon the judicial year. It was under the auspices of the Boston College Law School, Saturday, October 2, 1948, in the Church of the Immaculate Conception. The name "Red Mass" was probably derived from the ancient custom of the justices of wearing red robes and because the Officers of this Mass have always worn red. The prayer for this special occasion traditionally symbolizes the flaming fire of divine love and wisdom. "The Red Mass" anciently was observed in Rome, Paris and London (Westminster) and was introduced in Boston by the late Cardinal O'Connell and continued by Archbishop Richard J. Cushing. After twelve years of brilliant leadership as president of Fordham University Father Gannon now turns to spiritual leadership as Director of Retreats at Mount Manrisa, Staten Island, only a few miles from where he was born.

Sermon Thirty=five

IN THE summer of 1947 President Truman reassigned Myron Taylor as his personal representative at the Vatican. On this occasion he wrote the Holy Father a beautiful letter which is returning now to plague him. In it he said without qualification, "Your Holiness, this is a Christian nation," and for this unqualified statement he is accused of violating the Constitution by an attack on the sacred white elephant that separates Church and State. The accusation is, of course, fantastic and unimportant except for the fact that it calls our attention to an alarming phase of our national development. After all, was the President right? Are we a Christian nation? The question can be answered several ways.

Certainly, we are not a Christian nation by law established, as England, Sweden and Spain are Christian nations. The First Amendment in the Bill of Rights takes care of that. "Congress," we read, "shall make no law respecting an establishment of religion." The words are clear enough, but the background of that simple sentence is an interesting one. Judging from recent developments, one would think that the Founding Fathers were taking precautions against the Pope and the Catholic Church of 1789. Actually, the poor Holy Father was probably never weaker at any period since the Western Schism than he was in the years between the fall of the Bastille and Waterloo. The same was true of the Catholic Church. It was undergoing one of its periodic burials and most people thought that this was the last. No, the Church which James Madison and the rest did not want established in the United States was the Church which had collected tithes in the colonies for generations—the Church of England. So by the First Amendment, which is now violently twisted to prohibit the mention of God in an American school, the Founding Fathers merely wished to make it clear that the Church of England was disestablished in America and that no other was to take its place forever. Henceforth all religions—Mohammedan, Jewish, Zoroastrian, Rosicrucian, Catholic—would be absolutely equal before the law. Clearly, then, we are not a Christian nation as England, Sweden and Spain are Christian nations. Are we, however, Christian on the basis of population? That point is not too easy to settle, so many people differ on what constitutes a Christian. It is true that the majority would list themselves as Christians, but 56 per cent have no church affiliation and 60 per cent are unbaptized, while many of the rest who talk like Christians, look like Christians, and often act like Christians, quietly ignore Christian doctrine or openly reject it. It would be difficult to prove that the United States is Christian on the basis of population. I think it would be impossible.

What, then, of its ideals, its education, its philosophy, its morality? Would these be Christian enough to justify the President's claim—"Your Holiness, this is a Christian nation"? One hundred years ago the answer would have been "Yes." Our schools, beginning with the founding of Harvard College and continuing almost to the Civil War, were religious foundations; and the only religions with vigor enough to build an educational institution were Christian. But Horace Mann, in his effort to avoid offense against any particular sect, originated the policy that banished Christianity from the public schools, while the private schools gradually succumbed to the Ph.D.'s who had flocked to Europe, to Paris and to Berlin, and had returned eager to spread the secularism they had learned there. As a result, education in the United States is, if anything, anti-Christian today. That being so, what can we expect of our philosophy? All the influences of every school of thought in Europe have been blown across this continent which we call our country. We have had our materialists, our Cornell idealists, our logical empiricists. We have had James and Whitehead and Cohen and Dewey—and Boston's unique Santayana. These, after all, represent the men who have produced whatever is distinctive in American philosophy. So that in spite of a liberal sprinkling of Neo-Thomism, in and out of the Church, our philosophers have not helped to make the United States a Christian nation; much less have those who are the arbiters of our moral standards. The note of warning on the last named point is sounded often enough in America to make us mildly apprehensive, but it shocks us to hear ourselves denounced as pagans in the Soviet press. Granted that ISVESTIA, TRUD, PRAVDA, and *The Literary Gazette* have no ideals of truth to restrain them, their picture of decadence in the United States is too close to reality for comfort. When they speak of bourgeois morality it has a brand new meaning now. Formerly it was used to sneer at clean living, pity, truth-telling and common decency. But today it refers to comic books and radio horrors that incite feeble minds to murder; it refers to our growing army of drunken women—they say we have 600,000 female alcoholics; it refers above all to our national scandal and shame, our disintegrating family life. They point out that by 1960 one out of every two American marriages will end on the rocks, so that half of the next generation will never have known the common blessing of a normal home. It would take an optimist to hold that on the basis of our moral tone the United States is a Christian nation.

And yet, the President was not altogether wrong. We are a country with at least a Christian past which cannot be ignored. The President in his letter mentioned the explorers and early missionaries who were gallant and unselfish Christians. He mentioned the colonists, too, who either came here specifically to practice Christianity or brought some form of Christianity with them. When the time arrived to establish an independent Government of the United States, very few of the leading citizens were Deists or Free-Thinkers. The thirty-nine signers of the Constitution, the fifty-five signers of the Declaration of Independence, plus a few great men like John Jay and John Marshall, were almost without exception practical Christians. Most of them, like Washington, Hamilton and Madison, were members of the Church of England. A few, like John Adams, were Congregationalists; Charles Carroll, Daniel Carroll and Thomas Fitzsimmons were Catholics. And so for the eighty-odd others. Franklin and Jefferson were the two outstanding exceptions. But Franklin was a deeply religious nonsectarian who would not have called himself unchristian—one of those naturally good men we meet even today who are long on morals and short on doctrine. While Jefferson, although he was in reality a conservative materialist who held that God was an "ethereal gas," insisted that he was "a real Christian," better than most. In fact, the tone of that whole generation is found in Washington's message to the governors of the thirteen States on resigning as Commander-in-Chief of the Army. In it he assumed that all the American governors believed as he did that the future happiness of the United States depended on the imitation of Christ.

It is not surprising, then, that the form of democracy bequeathed to us by the Founding Fathers was a Christian form of democracy, a democracy that rests on two distinctly Christian ideals. The first of these is the supremacy of law over the ruler; the second is the equality of all men before the law, based on the God-given dignity of the human person. The first, the supremacy of law over the ruler, was handed down to us with English Common Law, and this, deriving from custom and tradition, rather than from formal codes, rested squarely on the Christian concept of the Natural Law. Before the rise of Christianity, no one recognized the existence of a Divine Law which was knowable through reason; knowable because it could be deduced from our very nature. No one recognized a natural right. All law was positive law. For the Jews it was Divine Law known by revelation and collected into

[217]

codes, the greatest of which was the Ten Commandments given to Moses on Mt. Sinai. For the Gentiles it was positive law known by state edict and likewise collected into codes. But our Founding Fathers presupposed in the democracy they bequeathed to us a Natural Law binding rulers and ruled to which all positive law must conform. This great tradition, which involves every man's right to immunity from the arbitrary, leads back through John Marshall, Hamilton and James Wilson to Edmund Burke, and Lord Somers, Seldon and the medieval lawyers like Henry de Bracton—back beyond Magna Carta to St. Ambrose and St. Augustine. The same is true of the second great principle underlying our democracy, the principle of equality. It is not to be confused with the *égalité* of the French Revolution any more than *fraternité* is to be compared with Christian charity. The French were profoundly affected by the revival of Roman law under Philip the Fair and the subsequent weakening of the medieval tradition. Unlike England, with its common law, France henceforth lived by codes of regulations, many of them resting on pagan principles. *Égalité* was understood in the stoic sense which condemned all inequalities, thus running counter to the Christian principle that all authority is from God. Our Founding Fathers, when they preserved for us the English common law and the constitutional tradition, carried over from the Middle Ages the Augustinian concept that all men are equal under God as persons; as individuals, that is, with spiritual powers; as adopted sons of God and heirs of the Kingdom of Heaven. You will find nothing about personal rights in Aristotle or Cicero or the books of the Old Testament. It was because of the Church's teaching on personality that we fell heir to the tradition that no man has the right to impose his will on another except as God's representative. This is a tradition which may be called unfair to Atheists, which may embarrass Mrs. McCollum's sensitive little boy, but it is difficult to declare traditions which gave rise to the Constitution—unconstitutional.

The President, therefore, should have qualified his statement, saying not that this is a Christian nation, but that the boasts of our country in which we take the deepest pride are Christian still: its origins and its democracy. In its origins it is immutably Christian, but its democracy is seriously threatened with change because of the changing ideals of our Bench and Bar. In the Supreme Court of the United States and in many of the state courts throughout the land we are witnessing a struggle between the old and the new theories of law; between what I might call the scholastic and the realist interpretation of the law. The old theory which is presupposed in the Constitution and the Declaration of Independence, which is part of the tradition of American democracy, rests on the fact that there is a superior law which tests the laws of men and that there are objective standards for weighing the validity as well as the expediency of new legislation. The new theory of law ignores the existence of God as the source of all authority, minimizes principles and precedents, discards the fundamental doctrine of *stare decisis* and makes the judicial process a thing of mere utility tempered with emotion, whim and intuition. The layman may be unable to express his doubts and fears in legalistic terms, but basically his thought is that the sands are shifting under him—there is no more certainty in the law—no more permanent rights—no more unalienable rights—no more natural rights since the Natural Law went out of fashion. If this Natural Law continues to be ignored in our schools and God, the Author of the Natural Law, continues to be excluded from His rightful place on the Bench beside the Judge, the last link that binds us to our Christian past, our Christian concept of democracy, will disappear and the President's critics will be right when they say "The United States of America is in no sense a Christian nation."

NATIONAL AND INTERNATIONAL

Sermon to the Republican National Convention

THE RIGHT REVEREND OLIVER JAMES HART, D.D., LL.D., S.T.D.

Bishop of the Protestant Episcopal Diocese of Pennsylvania,
Philadelphia, Pennsylvania

This sermon is significant not only for what it says but because of the occasion that called for its delivery, the convention of one of our two major political parties meeting to select its candidate for President and recognizing the need for spiritual guidance.

Bishop Hart was born in York, South Carolina, July 18, 1892, attended Hobart College, General Theological Seminary and Union Theological Seminary. Dickinson College, the University of Pennsylvania, and Hobart College have recognized his work with the LL.D., the University of Chattanooga and the University of the South with the D.D., and the General Theological Seminary with the S.T.D.

He was ordained into the ministry of the Protestant Episcopal Church in 1917, was curate of St. Michael's Church, Charleston, South Carolina, 1917-18, assistant minister, 1919-20; rector of Christ Church, Macon, Georgia, 1920-26; St. Paul's Church, Chattanooga, Tennessee, 1926-34, St. John's Church, Washington, D. C., 1934-40, Trinity Church, Boston, 1940-42. In May, 1937, elected but declined bishop coadjutor of the Diocese of Tennessee, Diocese of Central New York, September, 1937; bishop of the Diocese of Delaware, September, 1938. Bishop coadjutor, Diocese of Pennsylvania, consecrated bishop in the Church of the Advocate, Philadelphia, October 16,

1942. He served as chaplain (1st Lt.), United States Army, with A.E.F. 1918-19; chaplain (Captain), Fort Dix, New Jersey, 1941-42.

He is the author of History of Christ Church Parish of Macon, Georgia, 1825-1925. In his preaching he combines vitality, consecration and courage.

Sermon Thirty=six

TEXT: Jehovah reigneth; let the people tremble.   PSALM 99:1

THE two strongest political parties in our country are meeting here within the next few days to nominate not only the next President of the United States, but the leader of the civilized world. If ever there was a time when the world needed first-class leaders as well as first-class followers, it is today.

The developments since July, 1945, have tended to strengthen the uncanny, nightmarish sensation that our moral universe has gone bad. Many today are unmoved by, and unresponsive to, appeals for any constructive effort because it all seems so useless. Their viewpoint is, "Why labor for good, efficient and honest government if all is to be annihilated? Why strive to live nobly in a doomed world? Why work for world peace when God is dead?" But God has not deserted the universe which He created and sustains. *Jehovah reigneth.* The one God is the God of all the earth. His Sovereignty extends over the whole of human life in all its departments, individual and social. The road to security and peace is an extremely difficult one, but we are not driven by an irresistible fate to World War III. If such comes to pass, we should know that it has come because of the lack of spiritual leadership. War is not an act of God, but a crime of stupid and sinful men.

The delegates to this Convention know to what extent God has been ignored or thrust out to the edges of our life. Once in Washington, at a Gridiron dinner, I overheard a group of political leaders arranging for a Sunday morning committee meeting. One of them jokingly suggested that it might interfere with church attendance and the remark brought forth guffaws from the group! It is a hopeful sign that in contrast to their attitude, you desired to start your deliberations with a public service of worship. I hope that it is due to a growing realization that our religion is *not* based upon ideas about God, but upon what God is and what He is doing in actual fact upon the plane of history. The moral order of the world is no mere by-product of human aspiration and feeling. The moral order is a divinely ordained order of life. It is beyond man's ability to challenge or to destroy. Man either obeys or perishes. In the long run men do not prosper when they base their lives on dishonesty and deceit. The same applies to the policies of governments.

The sincere and honest recognition of this truth leads us to the second half of the Psalmist's statement, "Let the people tremble." Instead of resting on our oars, we tremble at the staggering responsibilities laid upon us. The fact that God reigns makes it crystal clear that selfishness can never be the basis of happiness in His universe. God reigns, whether the delegates to the approaching political conventions act wisely or foolishly. This great fact saves us from the most cruel delusion ever perpetrated on men, i.e., the delusion that we can base civilization on selfishness and greed and avoid the consequences of such action.

The fact that this is God's world frees us, on the one hand, from the false assumption that there is no hope, and, on the other hand, that the world has been wound up and will automatically produce a better and better civilization. We are not worshipers of mere progress. Under God we should guide and control it. Jesus Christ faced the possibility of a world that was clean swept of its faith in God. "When the Son of Man cometh," Jesus asked, "shall he find faith on the earth?" Rabbi Liebman, whose recent death brought sorrow to the thousands whom he has helped, said in his book *Peace of Mind,* "The basic fear, upon which all other fears are built, is the fear of being left alone in a hostile world." Jesus made it clear forever that God's grace and power are available to direct man's life and work. We are never the victims of circumstances. We are never left alone in a hostile world. I must bear my witness that without Jesus Christ as the Sovereign Lord of individual lives, and His Spirit animating our relationships with one another, we cannot escape the inevitable workings of the moral laws of the universe. Forget God, and life becomes common and the social order a frightening monstrosity.

On the other hand, our fears would vanish if we could rely upon Christian policy and action in domestic and international relationships. Two world wars in one generation have deepened the feeling that knowledge is inevitably linked with destruction. Knowledge does mean power, but power does not *necessarily* have to be used to kill and to degrade. Power would be used constructively if it were in the hands of those whose lives were under the constant control of the God and Father of our Lord Jesus Christ.

The greatest service, therefore, which the Church can render to the nation and to the world is to develop Christian, public-spirited citizens; men and women, whose conduct in all matters—home and social life, politics, industry, commerce—is dominated by the conviction that Jesus Christ is the Lord of all life. All churches, of whatever name, at their best are laboring for the common good, and we know that the test of a church is the kind of men and women it produces. Often you hear it said that we have more food here in the United States than anywhere else in the world. Civilizations, however, are not remembered for the quantities of food consumed, but for the quality of character produced. The Christian Church would surrender its faith if it became a religion of respectability and political expediency. True Christians have always possessed a scorn of comfortable substitutes for disciplined living and sacrificial service.

Some people feel that we made great sacrifices to win the war, and that now we should be able to glide easily into world peace. The story is told of a guide and an inexperienced climber who had to stay all night in the Pyrenees. Toward dawn there was a tempestuous wind that twisted trees and started rocks rolling down the mountainside. The inexperienced climber was terrified, but the guide reassured him by saying, "This is the way the dawn comes in the Pyrenees." This is also the way in which the dawn of a better world comes—not through softness, indifference and complacency, but through struggle and sacrifice. We must meet toughness with toughness. During the war we showed qualities of courage, alertness, decision, tenacity of purpose and unselfish devotion to a cause. If we are willing to put more faith, more sacrifice, more effort into winning the peace than we did in winning the war, we can under God's guidance and through His grace build a world fit to live in.

The United States is committed to world leadership whether she desires it or not. However we may differ about the policies to be pursued, this is absolutely clear—we cannot withdraw from the world struggle. The years ahead are bound to be years of disturbance and unrest. Strikes abound. Racial and religious tensions, which were held in check by the united war effort, have now flared up openly. These problems call for great qualities of will power, native resourcefulness and reckless daring. World War II has given ample evidence that we have in the American people good material with which to work. The issues of the war quickened in the hearts of our people their sense of the honor and claim of citizenship. They made the cause of the country their own. In the service of their country, even to the supreme sacrifice, they showed what men and women will do for that in which they believe. The pressure of material needs and comforts and pleasures can be overcome if our leaders will not hesitate to summon our people to make the world a better place in which we and our children's children may live in righteousness and peace.

Man is capable of changing his environment by new scientific inventions, but far more important than that, he is capable of being changed himself. Jesus said, "But as many as received him, to them gave he power to *become* the sons of God." We can put righteousness before self-interest. We can seek to discover God's purpose for the world rather than to pursue our own. We can have the abundant life which Christ came to make possible for us.

You, who are delegates, are in a situation in which fateful decisions are necessary. A heavy responsibility rests upon your shoulders. The whole world has the right to demand that you discharge this responsibility to the very best of your ability. May the Holy Spirit guide you as you perform this important duty.

Leadership in the Modern World

THE REVEREND JOHN F. CRONIN, S.S., PH.D.

Assistant Director, Department of Social Action, National Catholic Welfare Conference and a member of the Society of St. Sulpice; Director of the Institute of Catholic Social Studies at the Catholic University Summer School, Washington, D. C.

Father Cronin has written and lectured extensively in the social field. This sermon is one of four which he gave in a series of nationwide broadcasts on the Catholic Hour, discussions of current social problems from the Christian view. He is noted particularly for his textbooks on economic problems, Economics and Society *and* Economic Analysis and Problems. *He has also written many pamphlets and articles on social problems; his articles have appeared in* The Sign, The Commonweal, Common Sense, Survey Graphic, *and in technical publications.*

His lectures have taken him to Chicago, Detroit, Toledo, Buffalo, and many other cities, where he has spoken on social questions and has also addressed conferences on interfaith questions. In 1939 he appeared at the Public Affairs Institute of the University of Virginia at Charlottesville.

In his writings and lectures he particularly stresses the need for national unity in these critical times and suggests programs to solve the social, economic, and political obstacles that would lead to real reform. During the recent war he did volunteer work in the fields of labor and rationing and has been permanent arbitrator to the Clothing Industry in Baltimore, Maryland. He is active in the Catholic Association for International Peace. He was one of the winners of the Papst Post-War Employment Awards, a contest in which most of the nation's leading economists submitted proposals for the best postwar use of resources in men and materials to continue and retain prosperity for the greatest number.

His new book, Catholic Social Action, *gives the thinking of Catholic leaders on social matters. This sermon stresses the place of America in the world today and the economic and Christian obligations laid on all Americans. Leadership has been thrust upon our country: what will we do with it?*

Sermon Thirty-seven

THESE are days of anxiety. Thoughtful persons are much concerned over the problems which face us. We must make great decisions, and it is vital that they be made wisely. America today faces the burden of leadership in regard to the entire world. Our economic strength is such that we must assume the task of restoring prosperity to war-ravaged regions. Our political and military primacy leaves us with the duty of forging peace in the midst of grave tensions between nations. This is an hour of destiny and of duty.

In offering leadership to a world in crisis, America must act on many fronts. Of course, it is vital that we offer economic aid and sound political guidance to nations which look up to us. But, at the same time, we cannot overlook the great force of moral leadership. People abroad will study not merely what we say, but what we do. They will learn more from democracy in action than from thousands of books on the theory of freedom.

If the task of America is to offer moral guidance to the world, surely religion can indicate some of the steps which we must take. The great love of God and of neighbor can be applied here in a way which others will find inspiring. We hope to suggest concrete ways in which America will show the way by its example of the brotherhood of man. Two areas in particular offer us a real challenge: the achievement of peace in labor-management relations; and the fostering of harmony among diverse national, racial and religious groups.

It will not be easy for us to set a world-wide example of peace between labor and industry. This field is complex and intricate, and there are few short cuts which really work in it. However, there are certain constructive ideas which are gaining acceptance today. We would like to stress them here.

A fundamental for industrial peace and harmony is the recognition of the dignity of man. Religion teaches us that we are brothers, under a common Father, God. Regardless of our individual abilities and characters, we have a common quality in the immortal soul, breathed into every human body by the Almighty. We are persons, not merely machines or quantities in an economic equation. We are more than impersonal forces in a labor market; we are human beings with our hopes and fears, our desire to love and be loved, our moments of noble aspiration and our relapses into weakness and sin.

When a man goes into a factory to work, he does not leave his human personality behind him. While he may work with a machine, he does not become a machine himself. On the contrary, he is profoundly dissatisfied and unhappy at his work if he does not receive recognition for his human

[224]

worth. This was well expressed by one of America's industrial statesmen, General Robert Wood Johnson: "As a human being, no worker can thrive and give good advice in the void of loneliness. He must feel that he 'belongs'; that he is a responsible and respected person who counts for something in his group. With this must go dignity and satisfaction in the job beyond the pay for doing it."

Far-sighted industrial leaders acknowledge that the problem of human relations is fundamental today. Mechanical and chemical processes can be changed, but human nature is not so easily altered. Accordingly, it is wiser to build industry around man's needs than to try to force men into a mold for which they are not fitted. Yet, too often the human equation is the last factor considered. We have refined engineering skill to unbelievable degrees, but often have gone backwards in our treatment of human beings.

If certain basic needs of man could be met, we would make great progress in the way of achieving peace and harmony in industry. Among these basic needs is man's desire to maintain his self-respect and dignity. Industry can meet this in many ways. First, there is the matter of physical surroundings, which should be as neat and as attractive as the circumstances permit. Then there is the question of attitudes towards workers. They can be made to feel that they are a respected part of the organization. Their work can be explained to them, so that they understand their contribution to the final product. Their views and opinions should be asked and listened to. In the language of the shop, there is real two-way communication between the top and the bottom. This may seem to be a minor point, but it makes a major difference in the attitudes of workers.

Men desire the respect and appreciation of those around them. They wish recognition and esteem. It is only human to desire praise for work well done. When we do fail, a quiet and private explanation is far more effective than a public rebuke. Such would be the way of Christian brotherhood. Yet, too often men unthinkingly follow the opposite pattern. Achievement goes unnoticed and unrewarded, while failure brings on public and humiliating rebukes. This is not the way to build industrial peace.

Workers wish security at a good wage. Most of them have heavy family obligations. They do not wish to lose their homes and savings through no fault of their own. But industry likewise desires steady, high-level production. There is no conflict here in the basic aim of both groups. Yet, the fear of joblessness or wage cuts is one of the greatest causes of industrial unrest. Why should this common fear be a source of separation between labor and management?

The answer to this question is significant. Fear persists because we have not developed any common ground for co-operation between industry and its workers. Though they have many interests in common, we have too often stressed the points which keep them apart. It is true that disputes exist on the matter of sharing the ultimate product of industry. If the worker gets a wage increase, the stockholder may receive smaller profits. But this point is minor compared to the problem of sustained high production which will bring prosperity to all. Co-operation to achieve this is a real and pressing need today.

If labor and management could join hands to face their common problems, it would be an inspiration to the entire world. Elsewhere bitterness and class strife have divided nations into warring factions. Men have swung to extremes, feeling that capital and labor must fight until one or the other prevails. It is for us to prove that the joined hands of brotherhood are more mighty than the clenched fists of hatred.

We face another great problem in our task of world leadership. This is the specter of intolerance which at times hovers over our land. We could be divided into warring groups on the basis of religion, race, cultural background or national origin. This clash could weaken the unity which has made America great. We were founded as a land of sanctuary for those who fled from intolerance elsewhere. We have become known as the great melting pot composed of diverse racial, religious, and national groups. In our short history we have assimilated millions from every port of the globe and yet forged one nation, loyal and united. Such is our history. Such is the standard which we must preserve today.

Yet, if we are to achieve tolerance and understanding as a national habit, we must face the problem frankly and honestly. There is a right and a wrong approach to this issue. The wrong approach is attractive, because it seems deceptively easy. It is this: Let us base our tolerance upon uniformity. Let everyone in America think the same and act the same. Let us keep our differences to unimportant matters, and make these as few as possible. Then we will have no grounds for quarrels and misunderstandings. This seems simple but, I say, it is deceptively so. Actually, it is contrary to our American tradition. Our forefathers came here to avoid forced conformity in matters of religion and culture. We have always preserved the right to differ, within the framework of our constitutional democracy.

The right approach to tolerance is more difficult. It involves the recognition of differences, and the granting of full freedom to those who differ from us. Americans have not always found this easy in practice. We are usually broadminded about differences when they do not seem important to us. But when they touch on a sore spot, then we are likely to become resentful and intolerant.

Too often today we consider ourselves tolerant when we are merely indifferent or apathetic. Thus, many persons might say that they are tolerant in religious affairs. They say: "After all, religious difference is not important. It does not matter much what people believe. It is what they do that counts. We are all going the same way, even if we use different roads." While this sounds plausible to many, it is not real religious tolerance. Thus, a member of a certain faith might reply: "To me my religious belief is important. What I believe makes a real difference in how I act. I do not feel that it is up to

[226]

us to choose our own way to heaven. On the contrary, if God has revealed laws of belief and of conduct, I must humbly submit to His will. What is more, if I believe a truth on the basis of divine revelation, I must consider any contrary statement to be wrong. I will disagree with others who do not think the same way I do. But at the same time, I will respect their right to follow their own conscience and convictions." This is genuine tolerance.

The importance of a sound approach can be seen from some concrete examples. Thus, several religious groups in this country have their own school systems. They do not send their children to the public schools. This has caused resentment in certain circles. Some feel that these religious groups are setting themselves apart as a distinct and separate group in our democracy. What is vital is the recognition of the right of American citizens to follow their consciences in the matter of religious education of children.

The same principle applies to marriage laws, religious regulations on food, and other points of difference among our people. These distinctions do not spring from spiritual pride or contempt for the general ways of our country. Rather they are laws accepted in humble obedience to the authority of God. If we look at things this way, we are less likely to become intolerant of our fellow citizens.

It takes an effort to achieve real tolerance based on acceptance of differences. Yet our religious belief in the brotherhood of man should impel us to make this effort. This is largely a community problem. It calls for good will and education. If responsible and fair-minded citizens in each city and town were to face this issue openly, much good could be done. They could gather and discuss frankly the sources of tensions and difficulties in their community. From this discussion would emerge patterns of understanding and sympathy. These in turn could be spread more broadly through the school system, through public meetings, and through direct efforts to remove sources of potential trouble. By these devices, each community could translate into concrete deeds its ideals of Christian brotherhood.

It would be too much to hope that peace throughout the world could be achieved only by the example given here. There are broader political and economic issues which must be met. But at the same time, it would be almost impossible to achieve such peace if we are divided at home into hostile camps. It is the duty of this generation to show the world that free men can live together in peace and harmony. We must make clear by our example that force is the wrong way.

This is not a simple path to follow. It calls for patient and sustained effort. It is much easier to indulge in name-calling, or preaching, or passing laws to get what we want. But the easy way is too often the wrong way. May God give us the courage and the faith to face this problem frankly and wisely, so that America will truly be a shining light before the world.

[227]

The Roads We Travel

REVEREND FRANK JOHNSON PIPPIN

Minister, The Community Christian Church, Kansas City, Missouri

Frank Johnson Pippin is known as the poet-preacher of Kansas City. His sermons reflect a love of humanity, deep spiritual understanding, and a love of nature. During his days as a chaplain he served in both the European and Atlantic areas. After the war he assumed the pastorate of the Community Christian Church and preached his first sermon there on February 3, 1946. This is one of the dramatic church buildings in America, having been designed by the architect Frank Lloyd Wright, who planned it for the late Burris Jenkins as "The Church of the Future."

Under Frank Johnson Pippin the church has reached even larger vision and its program of spiritual and social activities has been widened. Mr. Pippin's sermons have a gentleness and understanding about them, a quality that makes men feel music and poetry while they listen. "The Roads We Travel" was preached to an overflow congregation on Christmas Eve, 1947.

Born in Georgia in 1906, he took his college degree at Emory University and his divinity degree at Southern Methodist University, with graduate work at Phillips University. He is co-author of Gordon Carr, *a story of the depression in America, and author of* Only This Throne, *a volume of poems. He was ordained as a Christian (Disciples of Christ) minister, held pastorates in Oklahoma City and Bristow, Oklahoma, then organized and built a large church in Tulsa, where he ministered for seven years before he went to war (he was promoted to be a major in the chaplaincy). In 1948 he attended the World Council of Churches meeting at Amsterdam as a writer for* The Christian Evangelist.

Sermon Thirty=eight

TEXT: Whither have ye made a road today? I SAMUEL 27:10
And as Paul journeyed, he came near Damascus. ACTS 9:3

I HAVE always loved old country roads and the little hidden places to which they lead. Sometimes of a spring day I turn off the large arteries of noisy traffic to explore a sandy lane that runs awhile under an arch of cool trees. From a field in the clearing near by come the tang and smell of freshly plowed earth. Such country roads bid for immortality when their dogwood and wild plum in bloom bear their white, scented glory to the face of a full moon.

I love the holy hush of old country roads at night—the velvet quiet, broken now and then by the silver tinkle of a cow's bell far away or the plaintive call of a night bird to his mate. And when all the russet, gold and scarlet leaves have kissed their autumn trees good-by, these friendly roads stretch out across a winter wonderland of snow and stars.

And often, when that mood has died, I hunger for the wide, famed high-ways that beckon toward great cities, teeming with busy life by day and blazing with lights at night: the roads to Paris, Rome, London, New York, San Franscisco.

Yes, there are roads and roads and roads. There is the road of remembrance "Out to Ole Aunt Mary's," so often traveled by the Hoosier Poet when he was a boy, and dreamed about a hundred times when he was old. There is the road of faithful love that runs out to "Dover through the fields of clover on our golden wedding day." There is the road of rest to Bethany, so often pressed by the weary feet of our Master. There is Kipling's "Road to Mandalay, where the flyin' fishes play." Yes, there are roads and roads and roads. And roads are not only convenient. They are also important, for the roads we travel determine our destination—our destiny. With a catch in his throat, Robert Frost used to say

> I shall be telling this with a sigh
> Somewhere ages and ages hence;
> Two roads diverged in a wood, and I—
> I took the one less traveled by,
> And that has made all the difference.[1]

It does make all the difference. To have good intentions is one thing, but to take the right road is another. Some roads we must travel, if we are to have life and have it more abundantly.

[1] From *Complete Poems of Robert Frost*, 1949. Copyright, 1949, by Henry Holt and Company, Inc.

[229]

The first of these is the Road to Damascus, the oldest living city in the world. This is the Road of Awakening. I name it such, because along its desert stretches, nineteen hundred years ago, Saul of Tarsus was stabbed awake by a blinding light and a condemning yet healing Voice. He was struck blind that he might regain his true sight. He was brought low, that he might be exalted. In short, he was converted: his very name was changed from Saul to Paul, and with that changed name he took on a changed attitude toward his own misdirected life, toward God and toward his fellow men. When he reached Damascus he was no longer the mortal foe of Christians, but one of them and their strongest advocate. For the first time in his life he had been awakened and that made all the difference to him and to Western civilization.

There are many experiences analogous to this one: the young falling in love for the first time, a mother having her first child, the first sight of the sea, or gazing with Katharine Lee Bates upon "America, the Beautiful" from the alpine reaches of Pike's Peak. But these experiences in themselves are not deep and inclusive enough to awaken life to its uttermost depths and resettle life if the awakened spirit searched patiently for the ultimate meaning of all experience—God!

Before his conversion, Paul had witnessed the stoning of Stephen, the first Christian martyr. As he looked on unprotestingly, he held the cloaks of the men who committed the vile deed. Stephen died bravely as a son of God should die. Paul never forgot that. And it is highly probable that he was still searching for the ultimate meaning of that experience when he was stricken on the Damascus road. And, in the great awakening, pattern and meaning and purpose were given, not only to Paul's chilling experience of watching a martyr die, but to all the future events of his stormy life. Thus, if the Road of Awakening is not taken, our experiences lose pattern and meaning in their cold isolation from the warm purposes of God.

The second of these roads is the Road to Jericho. This is the Road of Service. The parable of the good Samaritan has set this road apart forever in the literature and philosophy of the Christian faith. In passage from Jerusalem to Jericho one lone, helpless man fell among robbers and thieves, who beat him, robbed him and left him for dead by the road. The priest and Levite, traveling that way, saw him and heard his cries, but they passed him by on the other side. They were on the Road of Service but they were too callous and busy to travel it through. The mechanics of their religion had robbed them of its spirit—so they left their brother to grovel and die in the ditch.

It remained for a Samaritan, of alien race and religion, to answer his cry of need. The good Samaritan dressed his wounds, lifted him from the ditch, put him on his beast, and took him to an inn for rest and further treatment. Then he paid the bill. Doubtless the good Samaritan was late getting home for supper that night and his wife and children were becoming worried, but I suspect that he slept better than the Levite and the priest. The benediction of white peace must have settled upon his spirit and gently closed his heavy eyelids as the "Amen" of his prayers melted in "the great gift of sleep." For he had traveled the road we all must travel if we are ever to know the regal teachings of our Lord.

Jesus declared that "he that doeth my will shall know. . . ." We learn by doing. When we travel this ancient road, we learn that Christ becomes alive, vital, real. When this happens, we see and feel that unselfishness is the royal highway that runs right into the heart of God. We discover our highest and most real selves by becoming selfless. You see, that good Samaritan actually became that robbed and beaten man groaning in the dust. Like him, the Samaritan became penniless and helpless, and far from home. He became so bound up in this human tragedy that he lost himself in it. The life of the weak and the life of the strong became one, and the only way the good Samaritan could keep forever strong was in the human helpfulness of the weak.

A popular fable tells the story of a good man who died and went to heaven. Upon approaching the Keeper of the Gates, he made the strange request to visit hell a few days before taking up his heavenly residence. Permission was granted, and he was amazed at what he found below. He saw huge banquet tables piled high with delectable foods fit for kings. But all the people were emaciated, lean, anemic. They were starving to death. Knives and forks, six feet long, were strapped to their hands and fingers so that they could never reach their mouths. Try as they did, they could not get one bite of food. The startled visitor had enough. He hurried back to heaven, and on entering there he saw practically the same scene: the same kind of banquet tables, the same kind of long knives and forks strapped to the hands and fingers of the people. But there was one big difference. The saints were pictures of health and strength and they came in to dinner laughing together. As the newcomer stood by breathlessly, they approached the tables and gathered generous helpings of food with their clinking silverware. Then heaven's happy host turned around and began to feed each other! This had never occurred to the people in hell. According to the fable, that's why they were down there in the first place.

The third of these roads is the Road to Emmaus. This is the Road of Fellowship. On the third day after the crucifixion, Cleopas and another disciple were walking along this road in dejection and despair before they heard the glad story of the Resurrection. As they plodded along toward homeless home in the purple stretches of the twilight they felt the night coming on. It was nature's night and, worse than that, the night of the soul. They were suffering from "an old wound and a dream grown thin."

The one Person on whom they had pinned all their hopes had died a felon's death at the hands of blind and brutal foes. This was too much for these disciples. As they tried to reason about it, they trailed off into disillusionment, muttering under their breath: "We had hoped . . . we had hoped. . . ."

Slowly they came nearer their village home in Emmaus and they kept thinking of him. They went on meditating. . . . Then something happened. They felt his presence with them on the dusty road! Straightway their cold hearts burned within them. Their hopelessness dissolved. Their Holy Scriptures came to strange, new life. They got home before they knew it. Then, after a hasty supper, and a moment for recollecting themselves, they sped back to Jerusalem to shout the glad tidings of their redemptive experience with the deathless spirit of their Lord. And lo, they found him there also, imparting faith and power and peace to the larger group of his disciples. They were thus bound together into a beloved community with a heart-warming sense of oneness and joy because of what they shared in common. What an experience! What a fellowship! What a road to travel!

Apart from this road Christian faith can have little or no meaning for our own lives and for the shattering times in which we must live. Love can have no meaning except where others are concerned. Service to self is no service at all. Not until we have become "members one of another" can there be meaning in single membership. Thus, the Church itself is a fellowship or it is nothing.

Those two forlorn disciples actually became members of a saving fellowship as they traveled that road back and forth. They came to possess a genuine faith, and a shining hope; a spirit, at once conquering and tender, that warmed the heart; a mind that gathered up the noblest in their religious heritage; a sense of oneness with, and obligation to, others; and a witness to the bouyancy and splendor of the new life. The story, as Luke the physician narrates it, thus carries the basic elements of a redemptive fellowship.

Once on this road we begin to see that it is not Jesus himself, but Jesus working through a community of believers that transforms individuals and societies into integrated wholes. It was such a community of believers, such a fellowship, that gave us the Christian Church, the New Testament Scriptures, and the testimony of a redeeming experience with God that keeps haunting the common man of every generation with the challenge: "Now are we the sons of God, and it doth not yet appear what we shall be. . . ." It was such a fellowship that pulled down the remaining rafters in the dark house of the Roman Empire, and set about to build a new house that men everywhere, in all nations and centuries, could call their home.

We do not know how far this road carried Cleopas and his companion. We know they rushed away from their house in Emmaus as if it had been an army tent. We know they returned to Jerusalem and from there we lose their tracks. But one thing we do know about the Road of Fellowship on which they set out: it never ends until it spills over into eternity, bearing on its bosom the traffic of all races and all nations, who "seek a city which hath foundations whose builder and maker is God."

On its long perilous way, this road runs through all the divisions which are ruining us. Its mileposts carry the plea: "O be ye reconciled." And such a cry falls on the broken homes along the way; the divided houses of management and labor; our warring racial and religious groups; and upon all the prodigals who are lost on the detours, far from the road that leads to the Father's house. Those who travel this road dare to live and die by a compulsion higher than any human law, and they dare to sing when the heavy night is falling: "We know Someone who has changed all our sunsets into sunrises!"

The fourth of these roads is the Road to Bethlehem. This is the Road of Wonder. Other things being equal, we are born on this road into a world of wonder that leaves us wide-eyed and almost breathless with the thrilling question of childhood—what next? This glad road glistens with new surprises at every turn, and a luring spray of stars is cast overhead. The greatest thing about life is living, and to live is always to keep the sense of wonder, romance and expectancy alive. When we leave this road we die, though our public funeral may not be held for twenty-five years.

This heaven of wonder lies about us in our infancy and in our youth. But all too soon and often our questing spirit of vision, and our appetite for adventure are deadened by what we have been misled to call "the hard facts of life." Wordsworth put it this way:

> The youth who daily farther from the East
> Must travel, still is Nature's priest;
> And is on his way attended by the Vision Splendid,
> At length, the man perceives it die away
> And fade into the light of common day.

This was not true of the Magi from the East. Though they had grown weary and old, these Wise Men from the Caspian Sea still possessed the sense of wonder and awe that belongs to a little child. They left the warmth of their firesides; left the security of their homes; bade their loved ones good-by; mounted their camels, and rode away into the night—all because of the light of a star and the wonder of a little Child. No one knows how long their journey took, nor what privations they suffered on the way, but the wide world knows they finished their long trek to Bethlehem and laid their gifts of gold and frankincense and myrrh at the feet of the little Prince.

They were still chasing stars at seventy. After the long years had done their worst to them—years that leave us bowed and beaten and broken— these old men were young again when they heard the story of that wondrous Child. Their tired hearts beat a little faster and their dim eyes were fired with a forgotten light when they saw that gleaming star. Worry, doubt, self-distrust, fear and despair had left their telling marks upon them, but life had not got them down. These Magicians from the East were still young in spirit. Their youth was still living in the ideal that keeps tempting us all to search for the Everlasting Light that shines behind all the black clouds of the world's heartbreak and woe.

The Road to Bethlehem was probably the last road they ever traveled, or at least the last long journey they ever made. But they made it, and I am sure they would tell us today that the rendezvous they kept with the lure of wonder and the call of the road was worth all it cost, for at long last that road brought them

> To an open house in the evening . . .
> To an older place than Eden,
> And a taller town than Rome.
> To the end of the way of the wandering star,
> To the things that cannot be and are,
> To the place where God was homeless,
> And all men are at home.[2]

A Tender Care That Nothing Be Lost

REVEREND WILLIAM L. STIDGER, D.D., LITT.D., D.H.L.

A Methodist Minister and Professor of Homiletics, Boston University School of Theology, Boston, Massachusetts

There is a wholesomeness and a great deal of homespun sentiment in Dr. Stidger's sermons that appeal to a wide audience. He is probably quoted oftener by more ministers in their sermons than any other living minister-writer. As the editor has read the more than twenty-one thousand sermons received for the four volumes of Best Sermons, he has been amazed at the number that quoted Bill Stidger here and there.

Nature has always been a part of his life—it gets into his poems and into his sermons and books. Born in Moundsville, West Virginia, he attended Allegheny College and Brown University. He was ordained a minister of the Methodist Church in 1914, was pastor of Calvary Church, San Francisco, 1913-16, and was appointed to the Methodist Church in San Jose, 1916-19.

During 1919-20 he made a tour of the Far East for the Methodist Centenary, then returned to be pastor of St. Mark's Church, Detroit, 1920-25, when he was called to Linwood Boulevard Church, Kansas City, Missouri, 1925-29. He became head of the department of homiletics at Boston University School of Theology and for twenty years has exercised a wide influence on the theological students at Boston. For several years he also served as preacher of the Church of All Nations in Boston.

He has done many things and been almost everywhere. In 1918 he drove

[2] From Collected Poems of G. K. Chesterton. Copyright, 1932, by Dodd, Mead & Company, Inc.

a truck for the Y.M.C.A. in France, played football, has been a newspaper writer, has traveled in Java, the Philippines, China, made daily patrols over the Bay of Biscay in World War I, and has written fifty-two books. Among his books are Giant Hours With Poet Preachers, There Are Sermons in Books, God Is at the Organ, Planning Your Preaching, Edwin Markham— A Biography, Henry Ford, The Man and His Motives. His poems have won him a place with preachers and others, especially his "I Saw God Wash the World Last Night" (which has gone around the world in fifteen languages), and "Rainbow—Born to Beauty." There Are Sermons in Stories, Sermon Stories of Faith and Hope, Sermon Nuggets in Stones were eagerly received. The Place of Books in the Life We Live, and Finding God in Books reveal his lifelong love and appreciation of books.

His work has been honored by Allegheny College with the D.D., by Kansas Wesleyan University with the Litt.D., and by Salem College with the D.H.L. In 1925 he had a part in starting the early volumes of Best Sermons, which he edited and to which he contributed. His radio programs have always been popular and he has been honored for them also.

"A Tender Care that Nothing be Lost" represents a distinctly popular type of preaching that attempts to keep close to people with simple language, illustrations from nature and life. He has given this sermon about two hundred times, always varies it some for each audience, and gave it in St. Mark's Methodist Church, Brooklyn, New York, just before this volume was completed. He has a touch of Walt Whitman in his preaching as he piles up words to make his meaning perfectly clear to the last man or woman or child in his congregations all over the country.

Sermon Thirty=nine

TEXT: Are not two sparrows sold for a farthing? and one of them shall not fall on the ground without your Father will it. . . . Fear ye not therefore, ye are of more value than many sparrows.
MATTHEW 10:29, 31

D R. ALFRED NORTH WHITEHEAD, the Harvard philosopher, makes this significant statement in his book, *Process and Reality*: "The image under which the nature of God can best be conceived is that of a tender care that nothing be lost." Here is the very focus of the meaning of reverence for human personality which is at the heart of the New Testament and the spirit which permeates all of Christ's life and teachings. Jesus always had a tender care that nothing of human personality be lost.

[235]

Jesus, who lived constantly in the out-of-doors, knew birds even as some of us who are amateur naturalists have come to know the birds. Through Dr. Robert Breed, an old Allegheny College science teacher, I learned much more than biology. On beautiful spring mornings, as an extracurricular activity, Dr. Breed took us on bird trips and brought a great and lasting richness into our lives; for to this day, in mature life, I love the glorious adventure of watching the birds come back from the south, build their nests and raise their young.

At this moment I can close my eyes in memory and see the swaying reeds in a swamp near Meadville, where I saw my first red-winged blackbird; I can visualize the very oak where I saw my first red-breasted grosbeak; the maple tree in which I glimpsed my first scarlet tanager; the apple tree in which my first Baltimore oriole flashed its golden wings in the sunlight; the white birch tree where I saw my first cardinal in its crimson beauty singing its heart out on a June dawn. It is an enriching experience to know the birds by their coloration, songs, eggs, flight and nests; to know why the whip-poor-will sings at twilight, why the nighthawk and bobolink have the peculiar colorations they have and why the bobolink flies in long, lazy swoops across the sky.

Another thing I know about birds is that the sparrow is the commonest and most universal bird of them all; that it has a habitat around the world, including our own nation and the Holy Land. It is not only the commonest bird of them all but it is the least colorful, being a tawny, dull bird. Of about sixty species not a single one has any beautiful coloration, and only one a beautiful song, the song sparrow.

Certainly Jesus knew the characteristics and habits of birds, and purposely selected the sparrow to teach the eternal truth that the heavenly Father watches over, loves and takes note of every single human being. In the text of this sermon he was saying exactly what Dr. Whitehead has said: that the Father of us all has a tender care that nothing of human personality be lost.

The fact of this important matter is that in every contact Jesus had with human beings: the woman taken in adultery, the woman at the well of Jacob, the blind man whose eyes he opened, or Zacchaeus the tax collector, there is this gentle concern that nothing be lost. You can follow that spirit, like a silver stream through a green meadow, from the beginning of his life to its end on Calvary's cross: up to the tragic end Jesus always had a great reverence for human personality, even for the thief on the cross and for those who crucified him.

Also it will be noted that at the heart of everything he said and did was this tender care: the parables he uttered, the story of the road to Jericho, the miracles he performed, the sick bodies he cured, the anxious hearts he quieted with a word, the things he spoke which he called, "These sayings of mine," the Lord's Prayer, the Sermon on the Mount, and that last word and testament: "That ye love one another."

Jesus had what I like to call a seismographic sensitiveness and sympathy to the needs of other people. He could come under a recent definition of sympathy which I heard from a little child: "Sympathy is your pain in my heart."

The lost coin, the lost sheep, the lost soul summed up this attitude in one simple, understandable parable which once again reminds us of the theme of this sermon "The image under which the nature of God can best be conceived is that of a tender care that nothing be lost."

A tender care that nothing be lost is also at the heart of the whole missionary movement in the Church.

One of my first childhood recollections is that of hearing a returned missionary, Emma More Scott, speak in the old Simpson church in Moundsville, West Virginia. She told us how the people of India had so little reverence for human life that they threw the girl babies to the crocodiles in the Ganges river. Later I heard another missionary in that same church tell how, in China, they tossed the unwanted babies into the cemeteries for the wild dogs to eat at night. Those stories haunted me for years. I did not know then, as I do now, that this was the universal attitude of whole groups of pre-Christian humanity toward the life of a newborn child. But that callous attitude through the centuries changed, because a man came to earth who once took a little child in his arms, blessed it and said: "Of such is my kingdom."

Joaquin Miller, the great California poet, caught the full meaning and beauty of that scene in these lines:

> Then reaching His hands He said, lowly,
>   "Of such is my Kingdom"; and then
> Took the brown little babes in the holy
>   White hands of the Savior of Men.
>
> Held them close to His heart and caressed them;
>   Put His face down to theirs as in prayer,
> Put their hands to His neck and so blessed them
>   With baby hands hid in His hair.[1]

And, after that scene where Jesus took little children and blessed them, those people called Christians went to the ends of the earth to carry the gospel of the sacredness of the personality of a little child to what we then called "the heathen nations."

Most of us know that there was also little reverence for the persons or personalities of women in the world before the coming of Christianity; that woman was often a beast of burden, compelled to pull crude plows, and to do the menial, cruel chores of life in the field and home and shop, until Christ came to teach the world a tender care for the personalities of womankind.

[1] From "Beyond Jordan," from The Poetical Works of Joaquin Miller, Stuart P. Sherman, ed. (G. P. Putnam Sons, 1923).

This new reverence for the vehicle of human life and spiritual power was born into the world on that immortal day of the Annunciation when "Mary pondered all these sayings in her heart." It came to its full fruition when a little child was born in a lowly manger in Bethlehem of Judea. It ultimately found its full expression in the art of the Madonna. With the event of Christianity the whole art world was reborn in the attempt of great artists to depict the Mother of Jesus and the entire world caught a new reverence for childhood, motherhood and womankind. It was that reverence for the personalities of womankind which the world did not have before Jesus came which inspired Christian missionaries to travel to the ends of the world to carry this new idea and this new attitude of reverence for womankind.

Indeed, the whole inspiring motive of the missionary movement can be summed up in the story of Fred Pyke and Frances, his wife, both of whom were born of missionary parents and both of whom spent forty years as missionaries in China. Fred was a graduate of Boston University School of Theology and Frances of Wellesley College.

At the outbreak of World War II they were in Peking. When the Japanese came within a few miles of the city, the Methodist Board of Missions ordered all missionaries home on the *Gripsholm*, which was sailing in two weeks, but Fred and Frances refused to leave.

When they would not go at the order of the board, their Chinese bishop came to see them and to order their return to America.

"Those are my orders! You must leave China!" said Bishop Wong.

"But we are not going to leave, Bishop!"

"You must leave! I am your bishop and I tell you that you must leave! You will be thrown into an internment camp if you stay and you may be killed!"

"Frances and I have thought it through, we have prayed about it and we are not going to leave!"

"Why won't you leave?" the bishop asked.

"Because our people, the Chinese, need us now more than they ever needed us. They will need the prestige that American missionaries can give them when the Japanese take Peking. We have invested forty years in these people and we do not intend to lose that investment by deserting them now in their hour of need."

"Is that your final word, Fred?"

"It is, Bishop!"

Then a strange and beautiful thing happened. That stoical Chinese bishop, normally a rigidly disciplined man, as are all Chinese, stood there, gripping Fred Pyke's hands as he said:

"That's what I wanted you to say, Fred! That's what I wanted you to say! But it was my duty as your bishop to order you to leave!"

And Fred and Frances Pyke stayed, as did Tyler Thompson in Singapore. So did hundreds of missionaries, and, in so doing, bound those peoples of foreign lands to the Church of God with bands stronger than steel. They stayed because they had a tender care that nothing of spiritual value be lost.

Fred and Frances Pyke were thrown into an internment camp at once and remained there for two years. Fred's task assigned by the Japanese generals was to clean out the latrines for two thousand English and American prisoners, the intention being to make Fred Pyke, a man of great power among the Chinese, lose face, as they calculated that lowly, menial task would cause him to do.

But the Japanese miscalculated in that as they did in so many other things. For, instead of making Fred lose face, that heroic, self-sacrificing service made him gain face with the Chinese.

The Japanese miscalculated because they did not know that Fred and Frances Pyke, and all other missionaries, were followers of a lowly Christ who long years ago dressed himself in the garments of a slave, got down on his knees and washed his disciples' feet. And in that drama of service he taught the world that he who is greatest among humankind is he who serves: he who has a tender care that nothing be lost.

This spirit has seeped down from the New Testament and the attitudes of Jesus into the world of philosophy and science.

Dr. Borden Parker Bowne founded a school of philosophy called "personalism" which teaches a reverence for human personality which is the exact antithesis of war, dictatorships, fascism and communism; the complete antithesis of the spirit of a Napoleon, a Hitler or a Stalin. With them the individual exists for the sake of the state; but in personalism and the democracy which grew out of the New Testament the state exists for the sake of the person. It is that spirit which makes this nation great in its service to humanity through the Red Cross, the community drives, the Cancer Week appeals, the Marshall Plan. We may complain, but we give and send our money to the starving and needy peoples of the earth, both at home and abroad, because down deep inside we have a "tender care that nothing be lost."

Perhaps the ultimate expression of this philosophy of "a tender care that nothing be lost" is found in Dr. Albert Schweitzer, who not only has this personalism in his thinking, but goes a step further in his reverence for all life, even the lives of bugs, bacteria, bees and birds.

This spirit has seeped down from Christianity into the world of science. The first great scientist of them all, Galileo, once said: "I have observed that the sun which holds the wheeling worlds in order, also has time to ripen a bunch of grapes on an Italian hillside and to bring a purple pansy to its full flower and perfume."

There it is, spoken by a great scientist, the same thing that Jesus said in his symbol of the sparrows: that God does have a tender concern about individuals.

Perhaps the best illustration of that spirit in science is the fact that research men do not work to make money from their discoveries. What they discover in the laboratories is handed over to the human race for its own good. It is a tradition of research that the scientist does not work for his own betterment or for financial reward. He works in the spirit of Edwin Markham's immortal quatrain, "Christus":

> Why does he make our hearts so strangely still?
> Why stands he out so stately and so tall?
> Because he has no self to serve, no will
> That works against the welfare of the all.[2]

I recently found the ultimate expression of the Christian attitude in a book called *Banting's Miracle*, a story of the discovery of insulin, a control in diabetes. For eight years doctors Banting and Best worked on this research at a salary of about two thousand dollars a year, even though both were married and had children to keep. Neither of them was much encouraged by anybody. They were so poor that they had to go out to catch stray dogs and cats to carry on their experiments. Ultimately they came forth from a narrow little laboratory under the stairway of a Toronto university hallway with insulin, one of the most beneficent discoveries which has ever been revealed to humanity.

I discovered the motive back of this research in a single sentence in *Banting's Miracle*. Banting was a lad on a Canadian farm, where he had a little girl playmate named Janie. He loved her because she could run, romp, play hockey and baseball and skate as well as a boy. Then one day young Banting heard his elders whispering about what they called "sugar in the blood" in connection with Janie. He didn't know what the phrase meant, but from the way they talked he knew it was an ominous phrase. Then he heard the word coma in connection with Janie; nor did he know what that word meant. But he did know what they meant when he was selected to help carry the formerly restless, vibrant, leaping, laughing little body of Janie to its last resting place in a God's acre on a Canadian hillside. He never forgot that dire day. Then the sentence of which I speak leaped up out of that book like a blazing comet across the sky of my reading. This is what that sentence said: "Dr. Banting could not forget day or night, winter or summer, what had happened to his little Janie."

Young Banting first planned to be a preacher but gave that up. Then he decided to be a missionary but gave that up. In both cases it was the spirit of service which motivated him. Then he went into research work to discover a control of that dread disease which had carried off his little friend, Janie, so early in her life. His was a motive that had a "tender care that nothing be lost."

Today, close to two million diabetics—a million known and a million unknown, according to a statement made to me by Dr. Joslin, the great Boston authority in that field—live in this nation alone, including thousands

[2] Used by permission of Mr. Virgil Markham.

of children, all of whom will live normal, natural lives because these two Canadian scientists had a concern about humanity and its needs.

Finally, this tender care that nothing be lost has found its way down into everyday life.

In spite of all our selfishness as a nation, the fact still remains that we do concern ourselves about others; that we have gone to war at least three times to help other people, that we do respond to a need caused by a Japanese earthquake, a famine in India, hunger in Europe and China; that we do have a Marshall Plan to feed the starving peoples of the world; that we do recognize our world responsibility for human needs; that we have caught the spirit of Christian stewardship.

I know a preacher who has a daughter named Betty. When she was seven years old she either wouldn't or couldn't go to sleep at a reasonable hour after she had been sent to bed. Both father and mother tried every known technique to get the child to go to sleep, but, ultimately, both the father and mother knew what had to be done, indeed, what was, each night demanded by that child. That was that the father had to go upstairs and lie down on the bed with her and sing the old hymns of the Church for her until she fell asleep. That was the nightly procedure and ritual.

He would lie there beside his child and sing, "Rock of Ages Cleft for Me," "Softly Now the Light of Day Fades upon My Sight Away," "Nearer My God to Thee." But, invariably the final hymn demanded by that child was, "Softly and Tenderly Jesus Is Calling."

Under the tender imagery of this hymn Betty would drop off to sleep, and the father would tuck her in and creep quietly away with a sigh of relief.

Moved by curiosity, later in life, that father asked Betty why she always demanded that particular hymn, and she said, in the vernacular of her time: "Why, Daddy, I like that softly and tenderly stuff!"

"But just why do you like what you call that 'softly and tenderly stuff,' Betty?"

She was thoughtful for a full minute and then replied: "Why, I guess its because it makes me feel that God must be just like a mother, Daddy!"

There it is. Betty, even though she had never heard of Dr. Whitehead, was saying exactly what he said: "The image under which we can best conceive of the nature of God is that of a tender care that nothing be lost."

She was also saying, without being conscious of that fact, exactly what Jesus said when he uttered those words: "Are not two sparrows sold for a farthing? And not one of them will fall to the ground unless your Father will it. You are worth far more than the sparrows."

Stop Fuming and Fretting: Get Peaceful

REVEREND NORMAN VINCENT PEALE, D.D.

Minister, Marble Collegiate Church, New York City
(Dutch Reformed)

Dr. Peale's preaching attracts crowds at both his morning and evening services every Sunday that he preaches. As minister of the famous Marble Collegiate Church, he is one of the group of ministers serving the oldest existing Evangelical Church in America. The Collegiate Church (Reformed Protestant Dutch Church) was founded in New Amsterdam in 1628 and has had a continuous ministry ever since. This sermon represents Dr. Peale's dynamic attempt to meet the personal religious problems of the people who attend his services, and they are distinctly his, for it is his preaching that packs the balcony and overflows chapels as well as the first floor week after week.

He insists that his sermons do not fit the accepted homiletical pattern, for he limits them to personal problems, employs a style, terminology and approach that is simple, even "free and easy." All his preaching is designed to reach the average man, and in order to accomplish this goal, he painstakingly avoids the so-called scholarly touch and regards his pulpit addresses as "talks" rather than "sermons" in the strict sense of the word.

The Marble Church does not advertise that he will "preach" but that "Dr. Peale will speak." He speaks extemporaneously, using no pulpit or desk, no manuscript or notes; he simply stands on his platform with everything out of his way and talks with his large congregations. His sermons are in such demand by visitors and those who live at a distance that they are usually recorded and published in pamphlet form. He steps beyond technique to reach the heart.

Born May 31, 1898, he attended Ohio Wesleyan University, Boston University School of Theology, and has received the honorary doctorate from Syracuse, Ohio Wesleyan and Duke Universities. He is the author of The Art of Living, You Can Win, *and co-author of* Faith is the Answer. *He is in constant demand as a speaker before many groups and is especially popular with businessmen. He was one of the two technical advisers representing the Protestant churches when "One Foot in Heaven" was filmed several years ago.*

Sermon Forty

Text: Fret not thyself. Psalm 37:1a
Scripture Lesson: Psalm 37:1-11

MANY people today are dissipating a large proportion of their energy in fuming and fretting. Have you ever considered the picturesque quality of some of our English words? The word "fuming" for example; it means to boil up, to blow off, to emit vapor. It means to be agitated, to be distraught, to seethe. And the word "fretting" is equally picturesque. It is reminiscent of a sick child in the night, a petulent half cry, half whine. It ceases, only to begin again; it has an irritating, annoying, penetrating quality. To fret is a childish term but it applies to many adults today.

The topic of this sermon was suggested by the head of a large industry. He is an eminent businessman and also a great soul, with the result that he is constantly being interviewed by his employees both from the office and from the factory for personal counseling. So many are the people who desire to see him for the solution of personal problems that he consulted me about employing a permanent counselor for his company. I asked him what problems were brought to him.

"Oh," he said, "the usual ones. The same ones you get. Have you noticed how many, many people haven't any real specific problem, except the general over-all problem of themselves? They are just fuming and fretting about themselves and everything in general."

Apparently it has always been so, for the Bible had something to say about it in the 37th Psalm. The writer of this Psalm noticed how people were disturbed about one thing or another. So like a great, kindly mother putting her hand in comfort and quietness upon a restless child he says: "Fret not thyself." He says, fix your eyes on God and get His eternal and everlasting peace in your soul, quiet down—"fret not thyself." But how do you do that?

In the first place, it is necessary for most of us to reduce our pace or at least the tempo of our pace. We have no conception of how accelerated we become or the speed at which we are driving ourselves. That is true physically. We are literally tearing our physical bodies to pieces. More than that we are tearing our minds and our souls to shreds as well. It is perfectly possible for a person to be very quiet physically and still live at high tempo. Even an invalid can have too high a pace. It is the mind that determines pace. The mind goes rushing on pell-mell from one thing to another, it does not seem to be content to live today amidst the circumstances that we now have. The mind has an insidious tendency to apprehend and to bring into the present the sinister possibilities of the future.

You have to reduce this debilitating overstimulation and overexcitement. Physically we know that overstimulation and overexcitement produce toxic poisons in the body. We know how it disturbs the equilibrium of the mind. Then what must it do to that deep inner essence of the personality known as the soul? You cannot have God in your soul if your pace is so fast, because God won't go that fast. He will not keep up with you. He just says, "All right, go ahead, go ahead, and when you get all worn out, I will be along by and by and pick you up." God moves imperturbably, slowly and with perfect organization.

This is really a pathetic generation, especially in this city. This is the worst place on earth from the standpoint of an accelerated and excited pace. But go into the country, in the backwoods, you will even find high tempo there because you have the radio, and the airwaves transmit this acceleration. We are not even content with getting it through the airwaves but now we are getting it visually through television. We see it, hear it and feel it.

What are we going to do about it? Start by reducing the pace. Just stop, quiet down, do not fume, do not fret. I heard of a doctor not long ago, who gave what may seem queer but wise advice to one of his patients, one of these modern, up-to-date, aggressive go-getter type of businessman. He excitedly told the doctor about what an "enormous amount of work he had to do, and how he had to get it done right away quick."

"I am taking my work home with me nights," he said with nervous inflection.

The doctor asked quietly, "Why are you taking it home with you nights?"

"I have to get it done."

"Can anybody else do it?"

"No, I am the only one who can do it. It must be done just right and it has to be done quickly. Everything depends upon me."

"If I write you a prescription will you follow it?"

"Well, I will if it is a good prescription."

"I will not write it unless you say you will follow it."

And this was the prescription, believe it or not. He was to cut off two hours of every working day deliberately. Then he was to take one half day a week, and on that half day every week he was to spend the entire time in a cemetery. In astonishment he asked, "Why should I spend a half day in a cemetery?"

"I want you to wander around and look at the gravestones of those who are there permanently, and realize that many of them also thought the whole world rested on their shoulders, and maybe that is why they are there. Meditate on the fact that when you get there permanently, almost everybody will forget about you, and the world will go on, and you are not so important after all. Just sit down on one of those tombstones and repeat to yourself, "A thousand years in His sight are but as yesterday when it is past, and as a watch in the night."

Strickland Gillilan, one of the great humorists of this country, had an article in a magazine about a man who cured himself of "bargitis," which, he says, is one of the great modern diseases. Did you ever watch people on a train coming into New York? On the Pennsylvania Railroad, they start moving to the end of the car when the train passes Newark, and they glare at anybody who tries to get ahead of them. On the Fifth Avenue bus they will get up five blocks before they reach where they want to get off, to get ahead of everybody. Or, like a lot of crows on a telephone wire, they will perch on the end of the curbstone waiting for the lights to change to see who can get across the street first. That is the devastating disease of "bargitis." Now the best way, says Strickland Gillilan, for a man to cure himself of that, is to deliberately get fifth or sixth back in the line and calmly say, "Go on get ahead." Or better still, sit in the seat until the train stops in the station, and wait until the clean-up squad comes and puts you out. "Fret not thyself." Reduce the pace.

"But," you may say, "nobody would ever get anywhere in this highly competitive generation by reducing the pace." Moreover, you may look at me and say, "Why don't you reduce the pace yourself?" This sermon is being preached to me, not to you; you are just listening in on a soliloquy I am having with myself.

The wise man always discovers that the way to make haste is to make it slowly. Easy does it. Easy does it because ease is correlated, ease is lubricated, ease works together properly.

I was talking along this line once when a man came up and told me that he used to be on a university crew and his was a champion crew. They won a regatta on the Hudson River several times in other years. The wise old crew coach used to say to them, "Boys, if you want to go fast and win a race you must learn to row slowly." He pointed out that rapid rowing tends to break the stroke, and if you break the stroke you probably cannot get back into the rhythm again, and the other crews will pass you. To go fast, row slowly.

In order to row slowly, the person who has been the victim of a high tempo has simply got to get the peace of God in his mind, in his soul, in his muscles. Did you ever stop to think of the peace of God in your muscles, in your joints? Maybe your joints would not squeak so much if you had the peace of God in them. "Fret not thyself." Whatever it is you want, it will be there when you get there. If it is not there, it was not supposed to be there. If you miss it, perhaps you should have missed it. If you miss it, you will never know whether you would have liked it or not. So do not fret yourself, walk along with God, and keep pace with the Eternal.

A second way to do this in addition to reducing the pace, is to practice thinking peaceful thoughts. Think peaceful thoughts about everything. I imagine that if we were to throw upon a screen this morning the thoughts of everybody in this place, it would be a sorry picture. Disturbed, agitated, worried, apprehensive, antagonistic, what a jumbled lot of fuming and fretting it would be. But a man can practice peaceful thoughts. Take such a thing as reading the newspaper. We have about seven editions of the newspapers in this city per day. Why? What can possibly happen between edition number two and number seven that makes it so terribly important to get it right away quick? Last summer I experimented, and for one week I did not read a newspaper, not a one, nor did I listen to a radio. I cut myself off entirely, and when I started reading the newspapers again I found exactly what was in the newspaper when I left off reading them seven days before.

One time I was on a university commencement program with one of the greatest newspaper editors in this country. He actually said, on the public platform that day, although he did it with his tongue in his cheek, that newspapers should perhaps be published only once a year. It would give time for the news to cool. Of course he went right back the next day and published seven editions of his paper.

I only half mean what I am saying about the newspapers. I am simply declaring my independence of all this excitable jumble of which we are victims. You would be a lot better off if you read the Bible every morning. The Gospel means good news, hot off the griddle. Hold up any page of the Bible, get it between you and the light, and looking through it you can see in imagination marching troops, the crashing of great temples, the decline of civilizations. But you will also read, "Jesus Christ, the same yesterday, today and forever." And also, "The peace of God which passeth all understanding."

Think peaceful thoughts. If you are disturbed about people, about what Mrs. So and So said about you, or what Mr. So and So did to you, sit down and think peaceful thoughts about Mrs. So and So, or Mr. So and So. Say, "Poor Mrs. So and So, I wonder why she said that? Poor Mr. So and So, somebody must be prodding him. Poor, Mrs. So and So, must not be feeling very well. The Lord bless poor Mr. So and So in order that the everlasting peace of God may get into poor Mr. So and So." Think peaceful thoughts about people. "Fret not thyself." I have practiced this myself and I know it works, I know you can stop this fretting and fuming by the practice of the therapy of peaceful thoughts

Not long ago I went to a certain city to make a speech. I was met by a committee when I got off the train. They rushed me to one bookstore where they had an autograph party. Then they rushed me to another bookstore where they had another autograph party. Then they rushed me to a luncheon, and after the luncheon I was rushed to a meeting. After the meeting I was rushed back to the hotel, where I changed my clothes to go to a reception, where I met three hundred people and drank four glasses of punch. Then they rushed me back to the hotel and told me I had twenty minutes to dress for dinner. I was just getting dressed, when the telephone rang and someone said, "Hurry, hurry, we are ready to sit down for dinner." I said I would be right down. I got outside the door and was so excited I could hardly get the key in the lock. I hastily felt myself to see if I was completely dressed, and rushed toward the elevator when all of a sudden I stopped. I was out of breath. I said to myself, I do not care if I go to dinner, I do not care if I make a speech, I do not have to go to this dinner and I do not have to make a speech.

I went back into my room, locked the door, telephoned the man and said, "If you want to eat go ahead, if you want to save me a place, save me a place and I will be down after a while." I took off my coat, sat in a chair, and put my feet up on the table. I opened the Bible and read the 121st Psalm: "I will lift up mine eyes unto the hills, from whence cometh my help." I sat there and said to myself, "Come on now, start living a slow, relaxed life. God is here and His peace is touching me. I do not need anything to eat. The dinner will probably not be any good anyway, and if I am quiet now I will make a better speech at eight o'clock." I sat there for exactly fifteen minutes. I will never forget the feeling of mastery I had when I walked out of that room. I had the glorious feeling of having overcome something. They were only through the first course at dinner, and all I missed was some soup which by general consent was no loss on my part. This experience gave me a tremendous sense of the healing presence of God, just sitting down and thinking peaceful thoughts for a few minutes.

You ought to do that, at some time every day, preferably when you are the busiest, when you do not have time to do it. Decide what period of the day you are the most pressed, when you "do not have time to turn around," then just sit down for fifteen minutes and think peaceful thoughts. Do not do it when you have leisure. Do it when you do not have the time to do it just to prove that you are master of your own busy-ness and let your mind wander among the great peaceful things of God. Think about the flowers, think about poetry, think about something that is peaceful. Above all think about God and Christ. You will feel the hand of the Great Physician upon your head. "Fret not thyself."

Yet, even that is not going deeply enough into this problem. What is it that drives people? What is it that keeps the human mind in a turmoil? This is not true of everybody, but it is true of so many people that to preach a sermon on this topic and not to mention this would not be keeping faith with our hearers. The human system, as it is created by God, is a well-integrated, well-organized mechanism, it is perfection itself. It comes off the assembly line without an imperfection in it, perfectly balanced, one part working in perfect harmony with the other. The most perfect thing ever created is a new-born baby who is healthy. He is an astonishingly marvelous creation. Now if you could just keep him that way, healthy in his mind and therefore healthy in his soul, he would in the very nature of the case on the basis of natural development, always have a free flow of power, he would have continuous access to energy, he would never get off balance, never. His pace would never be too fast and there would be no disturbance in his mind.

What is this terrible thing that throws him off balance? It is the wrong that he does, it is the sins that he commits, it is the evil that he performs. He commits a sin and tries to isolate it. I really believe the reason the pace gets so fast is that he tries to flee from his sins, unconsciously. "The wicked flee where no man pursueth." There is no man after him, but something else is after him, therefore, he redoubles his energy, both physically and mentally, to get away from this terrible thing that is haunting him, chasing him, reaching out to dominate him. This is an unconscious reaction but it is terrible. Ibsen says the sins we commit are like ghosts and they destroy men emotionally, nervously and physically in the prime of life.

This is as modern as tomorrow morning's newspaper. This is the latest insight into human nature, this is what doctors are finding today, and they are telling patients that if they really want to be healthy they had better be good. The old-fashioned preacher used to stand up in the pulpit and say, "Be good because you ought to be." Nowadays we stand up and say, "You had better be good or you will not be healthy, you will be sick, you will have a nervous breakdown, you will be under tension."

A doctor told me that a very finely set up man about forty-five years of age, debonaire, sophisticated, immaculately dressed came to see him and said, "Doctor, I just do not feel good. I have twinges in my fingers and my shoulder. I get out of breath. I can't sleep nights. My nerves are on edge and I am irritable. The doctors have told me to play more golf but that does not do any good, it just wears me out. I used to be able to play thirty-six holes, but now I cannot play eighteen holes without being tired out. My energy is slipping from me and I am only forty-five years of age. I am in a bad way."

The doctor was very thorough and went over him minutely, took a complete case history, put him through every test, put him in a hospital, took his blood count, his blood sugar, every test was made that a modern competent physician can make, and they all came back negative. So he said to the patient, "There is nothing wrong with you physically that I can discover."

"There may not be anything wrong with me, but still I do not feel good. So now what are you going to do? If it is not in the body, if it is not in the blood stream, if it is not in the nerves, if it is not in the heart, if it is not in the blood pressure, where is it?"

"The answer is in the mind," replied the doctor. But there is no instrument that can go in and probe or x-ray the mind. You only get to the mind by conversation, so this doctor who is a great old soul, shut the door and said, "Now listen, I am a physician and if you resent this tell me so, but I am going to stop being a physician of the body now, and am going to be a physician of the soul—come clean with me, have you any sins on your conscience. I have a hunch you have a conscience-ache."

The man was astonished. "I do not think that is any of your business," he snapped.

"Well," said the doctor, "it is my business that you get well."

"Do you think that has anything to do with health?"

"It has everything to do with health. Tell me about it."

The patient hedged and stammered, but finally confessed. "I lived a moral and upright life until three years ago, then I was unfaithful to my wife. I practiced one infidelity."

"One?"

"Absolutely, one, only one."

"Did you ever get it forgiven, did you ever tell anybody about it?"

"I certainly have not, I have kept this thing to myself."

"All right, tell me all about it."

The man told him all about it and the doctor said, "You have now confessed it to one human being. I am a member of the church. I am a Christian, you have confessed it to me, now confess it to God."

He confessed it to God, told the Lord he was sorry, told the Lord he would not do it any more, and asked the Lord to come into his heart with peace. "The result," said the doctor, "is that after a few months the pain has gone out of his finger, he sleeps nights, he can play thirty-six holes of golf if he wants to, although no man his age should play that much. He is a normal, healthy man, and lives quietly."

Do you see why they call Jesus Christ the Great Physician? There is healing in his touch. So he comes and he says to you, "My son, daughter, why are you fretting yourself? You had better tell me what you have in your heart." You do not need to go to any other man, just go home, kneel down or sit down and quietly talk to him, and tell him what is on your heart. Ask his forgiveness for any wrong done and hear him say to you, "Fret not thyself."

PRAYER: *Our Heavenly Father, come into our agitated, nervous, hard-driven lives and give us, we beseech Thee, the secret of Thine everlasting peace and quietness. Help us that we may not fume and fret but that we may have Thy peace always in our cleansed hearts and lives, through Jesus Christ our Lord. Amen.*

When I Think of Serayë

RABBI MILTON STEINBERG, D.H.L.

Rabbi of Park Avenue Synagogue (Conservative), New York City

Born in Rochester, New York, in 1903, Rabbi Steinberg was educated in the public schools of Rochester and New York City, graduated from City College of New York (Phi Beta Kappa and Summa Cum Laude), and became Instructor of Classical Languages at City College, 1924-25. From 1926 to 1928 he was Instructor of Jewish History and Religion at Teachers' Institute of the Jewish Theological Seminary of America; Rabbi, Jewish Theological Seminary, 1928; attended Columbia University for graduate study. The Doctor of Hebrew Letters was awarded honoris causa by the Jewish Theological Seminary of America in September, 1946. He was Rabbi of Temple Beth-El Zedeck, Indianapolis, Indiana, 1928-33. He has been Rabbi of the Park Avenue Synagogue, New York City, since 1933.

As an author his articles have appeared in The Journal of Religion, The Modern Thinker, The Atlantic Monthly, Common Ground, The Contemporary Jewish Record, The Nation, *and in pamphlets for the United Jewish Appeal. He is a member of the editorial board of* The Reconstructionist; *author of* The Making of the Modern Jew, As a Driven Leaf, *a philosophical novel of Rabbi Elisha Ben Abuyah, set against the background of Jewish and Greek life in the second century of our era;* A Partisan Guide to the Jewish Problem, *and* Basic Judaism.

At present he is at work on a new novel, The Prophet's Wife. *He has several interests, his synagogue, writing, preaching. In the last fifteen years his synagogue has grown from a hundred to 750 families.*

He believes Jews should have two cultures, that they have two heritages, the American and the Jewish, and should enjoy both. He loves music, art, painting, enriches his sermons with wide reading. There is a spiritual quality in all his work. "When I Think of Serayë" was delivered on the occasion of great Jewish efforts to help the Jews of the world; it shows the thinking of a great Jewish heart that is deeply religious and soundly American. In language, thought and construction this sermon is worthy of careful study.

Sermon Forty-one

I HAVE been thinking a great deal of late about Serayë.

What, you will ask, is Serayë?

Serayë is a village situated in the Lithuanian County of Suwalki, just to the east of the old German frontier.

And what—to paraphrase Hamlet—is Serayë to me or I to Serayë?

Serayë, as it chances, is the town whence my family stems, where my father was born, from which he set forth at the ripe age of ten to continue his Talmudic studies at more conspicuous seats of learning—a venture which ended up after many wanderings, physical and spiritual, in this land.

I say that I have been thinking about Serayë a great deal of late, and for a compelling reason. I cannot think about all of Europe's Jews: the six million dead, the one and a half millions of walking skeletons. Such numbers are too large for me to embrace; the anguish they represent too vast for my comprehension. And so I think of Serayë instead.

Now since, in all likelihood, there is not another person in this auditorium who has even so much as heard of Serayë, I would not have ventured to speak of it, were it not that each of us has a Serayë, some place of origin abroad from which, as the case may be, we or our parents, or grandparents or remote forebears set out for the new world.

These Serayës may lie in Germany or France or England or Hungary or Poland rather than Lithuania; they may be large cities rather than villages. In any event they are places toward which we feel some personal bond, and constitute therefore a handle by which we may the more readily and vividly lay hold of the agony of Europe today and of the even deeper agony of Europe's Jews.

Let me then speak to you of Serayë, and do you as I speak translate it into its equivalent in your own lives. So we will make real and concrete for ourselves the largest and most terrible tragedy in all recorded time.

Let me confess here and now that, having been born in America, I have never seen Serayë let alone set foot in it. And yet I am sure I am well acquainted with it. I know it from the tales told me by my father, from descriptions of similar towns in books like Irving Fineman's *Hear Ye Sons* and Maurice Samuel's *World of Shalon Aleichem*, from the writings of its inhabitants, and most of all, from the kind of people it produced.

I know, for example, of Serayë that though it was a tiny town, it made up in poverty for what it lacked in size. Even in its best days it was so poor that black bread and herring brine often made a full course dinner.

I suspect too that physically Serayë also left something to be desired. Its houses were ramshackle, its streets unpaved. It was, all in all, a slum.

[251]

It had its limitations, Serayë did; but it had its virtues also, and quite extraordinary virtues. . . .

There was piety in Serayë, intense, pure and exalted.

There was learning in Serayë, and reverence for learning. Bread might be scarce there, but not books. That village of near beggars supported a system of universal schooling and maintained a scholarship at Volozin, the great Talmudical Academy of the district.

What is more, the townspeople of Serayë, as befitted disciples of the Scriptural prophets and rabbinic sages, had a keen sense of justice, so keen that, according to an ancient practice, anyone who had been wronged was entitled to interrupt public worship, holding it suspended until the inequity had been righted.

And it was a merciful place. The poorest of Serayë, even those who themselves lived on alms, gave something regularly for sweet charity's sake. Nor was its philanthropy merely formal. It sprang rather from spontaneous compassion, from that sense of *weltschmerz* which created the Hebrew phrase: *tsar baale hayim*, "the pain of all living things."

And it was a place of a great spiritual earnestness.

Do not smile when I say this, but Serayë was very much like Boston and Concord in the days when New England was in flower.

The Kabbalist of Serayë, probing the mysteries of transcendentalism, what was he but a Hebraic Emerson? And the *Parush*, the scholarly recluse, was he not another Thoreau whose Walden chanced to be a corner of the *Talmudic Academy*.

That is why Jewish immigrants to this country came so quickly to understand Americanism. They needed only to translate the spirit of Serayë into English.

And now Serayë is gone, expunged by a ruthless hand almost to its last trace. After all, when evil men went about destroying a whole world, would they be likely to spare one corner of it, especially evil men so efficient in their wickedness?

Serayë is no more.

Its old, old synagogue where my ancestors for uncounted generations worshiped God is in ruins.

Of its Academy, where my father studied, nothing remains.

The books it composed and treasured, for which it dreamed, scrimped and saved, are now ashes.

Even its cemetery where my forefathers sleep has, I suppose, been erased.

And as for its Jews, of whom there were about two thousand in all—men, women and children, some saints, some sinners, some learned and some untutored, some wise and some foolish—but all eager to live, all undeserving of the fate which overtook them—I do not want to think of them. Especially I do not want to think of how most of them were done to death.

Yet think of them I must.

For, some of those Jews still live.

How many?

I do not know, of course. No one knows. Perhaps no one will ever know.

But there are probabilities and presumptions on which one can calculate.

We have learned, for example, that Jews in small towns fared much worse than those in the cities. They were so much more easily detected and apprehended; their opportunities for concealment were fewer. Besides, the non-Jews of Serayë, long schooled in anti-Semitism, would seem to have helped the Nazis in their job of extermination.

Let us, however, be optimists and say that, of two thousand Jews, as many as twenty came through alive.

These twenty Jews haunt me.

In the first place, I cannot figure out why they are they and I am I. Through what merit of mine am I safe, secure, free and light in heart whenever I watch my wife going about her household duties or hear my children laugh as they play? And what was their offense that they are cold, naked, hungry, haunted by horror? I simply cannot puzzle out what sin they committed so horrible as to merit the torments meted out to them: to look on while one's wife disappears into a death train or gas chamber, to see one's children spitted on bayonets, or to ponder their slow starvation, their bellies waxing great with bloatedness, their arms and legs turning match-stick thin, their bodies growing feeble with lassitude until life and death can no longer be told apart.

That is what haunts me: the thought that there but for the grace of God and a capricious decision made by my father, but in any case through no virtue of mine, there go I, there my wife, there my children.

This thought, this morbid vagary if you prefer, takes on further poignancy when I reflect that though I did not know them, some of those twenty Jews may very well be my remote kin. Who knows? Perhaps they bear the names common in our family—the Samuel to which my father answers, the Shraga Feivel, or Philip of one of my American cousins, the Jonathan of my son. What is more, being kin to me they may actually resemble members of my family in both appearance and character. Perhaps one of them is short, limpid eyed and gentle like my father. Perhaps another, a little girl, is fair haired, blue eyed, and delicate as my Aunt Sarah was said to have been in her childhood, as her little American granddaughter Alice is today.

That is why these Jews haunt me; I feel that I know them and their lot.

After all, are they not flesh of my flesh, and blood of my blood?

Twenty out of two thousand are still alive—if a word so suggestive of joy, vigor and hope can be applied to human wreckage.

Twenty out of two thousand, and these scattered to the four winds. A few are in Salzburg in the American zone of occupation, several in Bergen-Belsen in the British, one or two in Italy, a couple in France, one in Siberia, and one, of all places, in Shanghai.

[253]

And not so long ago a strange wonder occurred. Two Jews of Serayë wandering the streets of an internment camp unexpectedly came face to face with each other and cried out in one voice, "Merciful God, are *you* still alive?" And then they wept heartbroken with the joy of a familiar face and the inconsolable grief of memory.

But the dispersion of the townspeople of Serayë is the least of their ruin.

Not one of them is sound in body. The starvation, torture and terror that wasted their frames, have ulcerated their stomachs, poisoned their kidneys, hardened the arteries of their brains and hearts, rotted the teeth out of their mouths. Only one or two among them are actually insane. But every one of them is at least touched with madness—and some cannot sleep for the terrors that come in dreams by night.

Until recently no one of them had a single garment beyond the rags on his back, the broken shoes and burlap wrappings on his feet.

No one had a single possession—neither watch, nor fountain pen, nor scarf, nor coin.

No one had a home, or shop, or a tool of his trade.

No one had a newspaper to read, a prayerbook from which to worship God, a religious calendar to tell him which days are Sabbaths and Holy Days, a synagogue in which to pray.

Their children are unschooled, their young people untrained in crafts and skills.

Mention anything pertaining to life and its graces and they do not have it.

Of the twenty Jewish survivors of Serayë, three went back. After all, one cannot stay in an internment camp forever. And who knows, perhaps in Serayë by some miracle one will come upon a dearly loved and long-despaired-of wife or mother or child or friend. Perhaps something remains of one's former home, or shop, or library or synagogue.

Then too, there is the unfinished fight for freedom in Serayë—including freedom for Jews.

Besides, Serayë is home.

And so they went back—a tottering old woman from Switzerland, a young man from Lublin, a girl from a camp in Germany, half labor camp and half brothel.

When they arrived at Serayë, the odds are, the husband, wife, brother, friend were not there. The home was gone, the shop gone, the synagogue gone.

Wherefore they have required our help in earnest for houses, shops, books, tools, and since not so many as ten Jews are left to form a congregation, for a synagogue at least in Suwalki, the county seat.

That help they will continue to require into the indefinite future, until they again enjoy the status of human beings.

Of Serayë's Jews, seventeen have refused to go back to Serayë.

They have refused for any one of many reasons: because they know that nothing remains in Serayë to which to return; because they can never again trust their neighbors who joined with the Nazis against them; because the streets of Serayë cry aloud of rape, murder and torture; because, despite all the efforts of the Red Army, there is as much anti-Semitism in Serayë today as ever; because they are tired of defending themselves and apologizing for themselves; because they want to live normal lives.

Of these seventeen Jews, three have set their hearts on America, though thanks to the quota system only three or four will be so fortunate as ever to get here.

But for those few, American Jewry must be prepared, not only for their own sake but so that other lands may be encouraged also to open up their doors to homeless Jews.

And as for the rest, fourteen out of twenty, they are going to one place, and one place only—to the land of their fathers, the place where refuge was promised them by the nations of the world, to the Jewish Homeland, Eretz Yisroel.

Some are going to Palestine because there is literally no other place on earth for them; others because that is the only place where they are really wanted; still others, because long before the World War most of them had been made Zionists by the Jewish tradition, by the dream of a Judaism reborn and of historic Jewish ideals incarnated in the land which first gave them birth.

Observe I do not say that they want to go to Palestine. I say they *are* going to Palestine.

They are going and nothing has been strong enough to stop them.

They have not been stopped by broken pledges.

They have not been stopped by force of arms.

They have not been stopped by investigations, inquiring into facts that are matters of public knowledge; investigations that are time-consuming and therefore life-devouring.

They have not been stopped. And I am proud of them for that.

One of them, a young vigorous man, journeyed on a schooner to Palestine. An old couple who wondrously not only survived but remained unseparated, trudged their way to a Yugoslav port, where passage was found. Two orphaned children in France schemed by day and night to make contact with the underground railway.

They got through because they had to, because the alternative was slow death. They got through because the right was on their side, and right will not forever be denied. They got through because they were homeward bound.

They got through; wherefore, we may rest more easily concerning them. Not only are they safe at last; not only do they know what it means to be welcome and wanted; they have become participants in one of the most brilliant, creative and idealistic enterprises of modern times—the rebuilding of the Jewish National home in Palestine—an enterprise which has revived, enriched, cleansed and modernized a land long poverty stricken, sterile, retarded and disease ridden; which has established an outpost of political and economic democracy in the feudal medievalism of the Near East; which has blazed trails toward more equitable and co-operative forms of group life; which has evoked an infinitely rich and colorful revival of Hebraic culture; which has converted Jews like the survivors of Serayë from pauperdom to stalwart self-reliance, from a burden to themselves and a problem to the world into a social asset for all mankind.

Such are my thoughts of Serayë.

With them and in their wake come all sorts and conditions of feelings.

Sometimes, when I think about Serayë, I am ashamed to be a human being, ashamed to be a member of a species which could perpetrate the evil done to Serayë, and almost as much ashamed of the supposedly good people of the world who stood by when the evil was being perpetrated, and who stand idle now.

Sometimes, when I think of Serayë, I burn with indignation against the British statesmanship which, having sworn to encourage Jewish immigration into Palestine, kept the doors of that country so nearly closed through the terrible years of Hitler that tens of thousands of Jews who might today be alive are dust and ashes.

Sometimes, when I think of Serayë, I want to hurl hard words at God, that terrible saying of Abraham: "Shall the Judge of the whole earth not do justice," that soul-searing inquiry of the prophet:

Thou, too pure of eyes to behold evil,
Thou that canst not look on oppression,
Wherefore hast thou looked on when men did treachery
And didst hold Thy Peace when the wicked swallowed up the righteous?

Sometimes, on the other hand, I want only to slip into some synagogue and say Kaddish, the prayer for the dead, not the familiar Kaddish but the *Kaddish shel Hassidim*, the Saints' Kaddish, as solemn as the other but with its grief more brightly illuminated by hope. I want to stand up and cry out over Serayë, over its dead, over its handful of living:

Yisgadal v'yiskadash shmeh rabbah b'olmo di hu atid lithadata. . . .
Magnified and sanctified be God's great name, in the world which He is to create anew, in which the dead will live, and life be eternal, and Jerusalem be rebuilt, and its shrine restored and heathenism be uprooted and the worship of the true God be set in its place, when the Holy One blessed be He, will establish His Kingdom. . . .
Baagoloh uvisman koriv vimru amen. . . .
Speedily and at a near time, and say ye, Amen.

Such are the mingled emotions that attend my thoughts of Serayë. But beneath them all, like contrapuntal themes, move a resolution, a hope and a confidence.

The resolution is this: I am determined, all American Jewry is determined, that so far as lies in our power, justice and mercy shall at last be done to those Jews of Serayë; that those of them who are coming to America shall experience at our hands the fullest measure of brotherly assistance and understanding; that those who have gone back shall enjoy security, freedom and an honorable civic status in the countries of their citizenship; and that those who have already reached or are now headed for Israel shall lack nothing they require, not alone for the rehabilitation of the land and its inhabitants, actual and potential, but also for the rebirth of the Hebraic tradition they strive to effect.

The hope is that to the "few in number" of Serayë who have been left of the sword, who have so long been afflicted and storm-tossed, there is soon to be spoken the words anciently promised, yearningly awaited through the weary centuries but never more anguishedly than in the last decade, darker than any Dark Age which went before: "Comfort ye, comfort ye, my people."

Aye, it is my hope that the events of the latest days, especially in Israel, may yet prove to be like the morning star, of which a rabbi said of old: "Such will be the Deliverance: at first but a single ray, but thereafter growing apace unto the full light of day."

As for the confidence of which I spoke, it is that Serayë and the ten thousand places akin to it in all except name are not dead; that their bodies may have been broken, mutilated, murdered, but not their souls, which are, I profess, unslayable, inviolable, immortal.

This I know from the evidence of my own senses, from the fact that when I gaze into my own heart or my children's eyes I find Serayë there, in whatever is best within us; and when I look abroad, I discern in the courage of Europe's Jews struggling to rebuild their world and, even more clearly, in the magnificent heroism, creativity and idealism of the new Israel, that Serayë lives in other souls as in mine.

But I know it yet more certainly from the faith by which I live, which tells me that since God is and all things are under the sway of His economy, nothing good perishes altogether. Is it not written concerning the soul that over it the grave shall have no victory? And can that into which many souls have poured themselves in dedication be of less account than the individual soul itself?

Wherefore I am persuaded that to Serayë the Destroying Angel will have no choice in the end but to say what, according to rabbinic legend, he said to an ancient saint:

"Over thee and such as thee I have no dominion."

The More Excellent Way

REVEREND JOHN MALCUS ELLISON, PH.D.

*A Minister of the National Baptist Church and President of Virginia
Union University, Richmond, Virginia*

Dr. Ellison was born in Northumberland County, Virginia, where he received his early training. He received part of his high school education at Virginia Normal and Industrial Institute, now Virginia State College at Petersburg, Virginia, and completed his preparation for college at Wayland Academy (of Virginia Union University). In 1917 he was awarded the Bachelor of Arts degree from Virginia Union University; in 1927 he received his M.A. from Oberlin College, and in 1933, Drew University awarded him the Ph.D. degree in Christian Education and Sociology. He has also studied at Columbia University and Union Theological Seminary in New York.

He was pastor of the famous Shiloh Baptist Church in Northumberland County, Virginia, moderator of the Northern Neck Baptist Association, principal of Northern Neck Industrial Academy, founder and principal of the Northumberland County High School, college minister at Virginia State College, pastor of Zion Baptist Church, Washington, D. C., special research assistant in rural sociology at Virginia Polytechnic Institute, Blacksburg, Virginia. After teaching at Virginia Union University for about four years, Dr. Ellison became president in 1941.

He is co-author with C. Horace Hamilton of The Negro Church in Rural Virginia, 1864-1934, author of Negro Organization and Leadership in Rural Virginia, The Art of Friendship, and the following brochures: "The Christian Minister and His Preparation," "The Church Associations—Their Programs and Tasks," "A Century of Negro Baptists and their Achievements," and "Christian Education in a Day of Crisis." His recent writings include two new brochures, "Abiding Influence of a Faithful Minister," and "Achieving Character Through Christian Education."

He is a member of the American Sociological Society, American Teachers Association, Virginia State Teachers Association, Virginia Council of Churches, Southern Regional Council, and the Southern Education Foundation.

He is particularly interested in Human Relations and the way to help his own people to solve their problems. This sermon on "The More Excellent Way" was preached in the Alderson-Broaddus College, February, 1948, and shows the combination of thinking in two races and two cultures in one Christian faith.

Sermon Forty=two

TEXT: But covet earnestly the best gifts: and yet shew I unto you a more excellent way. I CORINTHIANS 12:31

THE problem of difference remains today the world's greatest problem. Men of any culture or community seem not to know how to find an adequate basis upon which to build a program of living together in peace and good will. The problem is an old one. Paul was baffled by it as he faced it in the Church of his day, for the early Christian movement saw and suffered from many dissensions, schisms and antagonisms, just as we witness and suffer from them in our religious and secular life today. These differences continued to multiply so rapidly in the Early Church that it appeared at times that a disastrous collapse of the whole structure of Christian faith was imminent. The sin was not that they differed one with the other; that was not only natural, but might have been regarded as a reasonable right. "We all have the inalienable right to be different; and the expression of it is every artist's dream."

God's world is always one of variety. Stars, fields, rivers, mountains, and people of many tongues help to form that variety. Such variety not only delivers our world from monotony, but contributes to its beauty and makes it interesting. But then as now, it was the spirit of antagonism, bitterness, bickerings and hatreds that brought the Church and community of Paul's time upon evil days. That was the sin. In truth, the particular belief that was held might have been legitimate and tenable. But when one claimed and contended that only his opinion was right and all others wrong, destructive situations developed. That always happens. It was the sins of narrowness, intolerance, selfishness and bigotry that Paul condemned and warned against. His explanation and argument are very simple and realistic. He compares the body of religious beliefs and practices to the human body which has many members that have different functions. Yet all are needed for the complete and wholesome functioning of the body. They work not independently, but together interdependently and harmoniously for the good of the whole. "In the same way," Paul says, "ye are the body of Christ and members in particular." However, any attempt at understanding differences and appreciating and reconciling them must be done in the spirit of Christ and love. One thing above all is important, Paul urged. Out of this maze of beliefs and practices, choose and appropriate unto yourself the best, remembering that "all are yours." But you are God's trustee, holding them in trust for others and God. Then with revealing insight he adds, "Yet I show unto you a more excellent way." In interpreting that "more excellent way," Paul gives us his beautiful and familiar exposition on "love." "Though I speak with the tongues of men and angels and have not love, I am become as sounding brass or tinkling cymbal."

Differences in people and in their thinking are difficult to handle when the spirit of love does not prevail. Just as in the faraway days of Paul, our world needs the spirit of love in these days. All about us our world is also torn by strife, contentions, hatreds, and bigotry. These divisive and destructive attitudes are exhibited and felt in almost every area and segment of our life —within national groups, in international relations, in labor organizations and in politics.

Religion and the Church do not escape. Some of the most bitter and almost never-ending conflicts and feuds arise and persist within churches of any persuasion. Paradoxically, Gandhi's assassin was an avowed religionist. On a college campus as well as in many other educational circles, conflicts and clashes persist to no good or wholesome end. Now the sin is not in the fact that there are units and divisions in our society, but rather in the violent intolerance, selfishness and hostility that invariably accompany them. Is there hope for peace, good will, harmony, and deliverance from these terrifying divisions? Paul believed that the way of love, which he called "the more excellent way," was the way to peace and good will among men, because it is that high quality of living that sets men in right and wholesome relations with themselves and others. In making clear his conviction about the quality and power of love, he describes it with almost matchless beauty and insight:

> Love is very patient, very kind. Love knows no jealousy; love makes no parade, gives itself no airs, is never rude, never selfish, never irritated, never resentful; love is never glad when others go wrong, love is gladdened by goodness, always slow to expose, always eager to believe the best, always hopeful, always patient. [I CORINTHIANS 13:4-7, MOFFATT.]

To come into that conviction and achieve that faith is the great challenge to Christians in our day. It seems fully possible when we know that notwithstanding all the disintegrating tendencies and devastating hatreds, there is deep down in the human heart a longing for fellowship, love and good will. That is man's higher destiny. We were made for fellowship. Of this truth man is constantly aware. The growth of mind and morality in human relations is a new kind of reality. As Herbert Alden Youtz puts it, "It is the development from animal beginnings to richer and complex capacities of experience." The facts in that story "constitute the romance of becoming human beings." It was for the resurgence of that faith and hope that Jesus petitioned the Father in that great prayer for unity: "That they all may be one." We cannot ever doubt, then, that Jesus cared most deeply for the beloved community, the unity and fellowship of all those who believe in him. He thought of this society of friendly people as inspired by the highest motives and dominated by the tenderest love, and with eagerness whose energy is clear enough, but the depths of which we can only surmise. He believed in a society held together by the closest ties of fellowship and capable of the most unhesitating sacrifice and expression of good will.

There are revealing signs of hunger for fellowship and the way of love, that men of all persuasions are wearying of conflict. It is reassuring to look back and find what the efforts and anxieties of the years have been yielding. Though often the gains may appear meager and uncertain in the light of the needs and conflicts, yet slowly but surely progress is being made. Christians of many communions and creeds are happily finding a common denominator for their faith and working together in building a world of understanding and good will. In many states, interdenominational organizations are maintained. The merger of churches of different creeds is taking place. Community churches are being organized. Interracial churches are meeting the needs of Christian fellowship and mutual understanding. Ecumenical conferences and literature are broadening the concepts and giving a new impetus and outlook to Christian faith and responsibility. The Fellowship of Southern Churchmen, the Southern Youth Conference, and the Southern Regional Council are a few of the new movements to break down barriers. Young college people of different races in all sections of the country are enthusiastically initiating plans to meet and to know each other. One of the most encouraging signs in recent years is the integration of scholars of various racial groups in the teaching programs of institutions of higher learning. Here students of college and university levels have the opportunity to know the mind and intelligence of other races in a way they have not known them, and thereby lay a basis of understanding and good will. This is particularly significant in reference to Negro scholars such as Dr. Frazier. Other groups representing the interests and vision for brotherhood are vigorously vocal in exploding outmoded and nonsensical myths regarding human relations. The Federal Council of the Churches of Christ and other international alliances tell an eloquent story of the effort and progress toward Christian fellowship.

In the presence of such a compelling and uncompromising ideal, one is persuaded to ask how it can be kept a living and masterful concept in the midst of the vicissitudes and contradictions of our modern life. How is it to be made and kept demanding and authentic in the midst of the bitter and cumulative disillusionments of the years? Contemporary men of faith have no more serious responsibility than that of finding a secure foundation for their belief in the beloved community in which all men can live together in mutual understanding, good will and warm fellowship.

Despite persistent disillusionments we are not without hope. The moral history and achievements of man are always the story of a faltering, wondering search for life's meaning and enduring values. Here and there, guided by some noble philosophy of life, an ethnic culture of great and ever-increasing beauty has arisen. Slowly but surely the philosophy of living together and sharing with each other is winning its way into men's souls, shaping their vision, and satisfying their hunger for the eternal.

This new recognition of the need for human fellowship is touching almost every phase of our life. It meets us in our economic and social life, in efforts to secure justice in the community, in matters of making a living or finding a home for loved ones. It meets us in the experiments of education as it seeks to make religious teaching and knowledge available to school children that they may grow up in an atmosphere of sympathy, and where the philosophy of good will is stressed as a virtue of religion. More and more men are coming to know that, as the late Dr. William Adams Brown very appropriately pointed out, the "art of living, as we of the democracies aspire to practice but don't, is to live in peace with those with whom we differ because we and they alike have given first place to those basic human interests which we share as men."[1]

There are many approaches, as Dr. Brown added, to the attempt at achieving this faith and practice:

> One approach may be the way of history. . . . As the story of the way in which men of different faiths have been trying to master the difficult task of living together. . . . The way of literature—the great classics . . . as they have survived sum up the wisdom of the ages with simplicity and a beauty that outlasts their own generation because they speak to each succeeding generation of matters which it recognizes as germane to its own.[2]

Langston Hughes and Arna Bontemps' recent anthology of poems by Negroes, *The Poetry of the Negro, 1746-1949,* is informing and inspirational for all people. Then, there is the way of music. They who sing, quickly and surely become the ambassadors of good will because they speak a universal language. Marian Anderson, Roland Hayes and other great artists belong to no time or race. They belong to the ages and to the world. Confucius uttered a great truth when he declared: "When men learn courtesy and music there will be no more war."

Then there are the devious expediencies to which so many men turn in their feeble attempts to answer somehow the demands of conscience. These may be illustrated by certain interracial committees and occasional brotherhood days. But any attempt, however plausible it appears, is futile if it is not undergirded by love and a controlling conviction that no man is completely moral who does not yearn and pray for the spiritual unity of mankind. With revealing insight, Paul said to the dissenting members of the Early Church, "I shew unto you a more excellent way," the way of love. We, too, must find our faith and our salvation in that conviction—that the way of love is the sure way.

> Come, brothers, from the ends of earth
> This is the trumpet call
> To understanding, tolerance
> And liberty for all.[3]

[1] William Adams Brown, *The New Order of the Church* (Nashville: Abingdon-Cokesbury Press, 1943), p. 113.

[2] *Ibid.,* p. 112.

[3] From "Tomorrow's World" by Georgia Douglas Johnson.

"The more excellent way" makes inescapable demands upon all who would accept it. It demands the recognition of the dignity of human personality. They who would become pilgrims of the "more excellent way" must enter it on the basis and merits of character. They must have been born again and into the kingdom of new and abiding values. Religious commitments must have been revised, and religious convictions reclothed with the essential qualities. The recognition of the dignity and worth of human personality necessarily becomes a dominant quality in the newborn soul. In a recent preaching mission in a southern city in which several noted clergymen participated the late Dr. Peter Marshall declared that our civilization needs "spiritual surgery" to cut out stubborn pride and give a new life under God's management; for goodness lies not in keeping laws, but in character. This quality of life is the fruit of a new spirit, a new birth, a complete change in life under a new management. For Christ can do little for us, save as we let him change us inside.

In urging the importance of recognizing the dignity of human personality, Dr. Clovis G. Chappel, a member of the same commission, declared: "Some folks enjoy putting a man in his place." Then he warned, "When I see this being done, I know I am dealing with hard-hearted men. When I look down on a man for being the color God made him, I don't reflect on the man, I reflect on God." The kingdom of God is a moral kingdom of human relations to which all men are inwardly aware. There is no race or creed in Christian ethics.

> In Christ there is no east nor west
> In Him no south or north
> But one great fellowship of love
> Throughout the whole wide earth.[4]

Here is the dramatic motive at the heart of the gospel of Jesus which gives depth to the ideal of brotherhood and gives powerful appeal to the imaginations of men.

The "more excellent way" demands the quality of sincerity. Jesus repudiated as severely as anything the parading of insincere religious practices and pretences. Hear his stern warning: "Take heed that ye do not your alms before men, to be seen of them. . . . Therefore when thou doest thine alms, do not sound a trumpet before thee, as the hypocrites do in the synagogues and in the streets, that they may have the glory of men" (Matt. 6:1-7). Perhaps the apostle was voicing some such feeling for the need of sincerity when he exclaimed: "And though I bestow all my goods to feed the poor, and though I give my body to be burned, and have not charity, it profiteth me nothing" (I Cor. 13:3).

No, one cannot play false and have the reward of the sense of approval and acceptance of God, or have the feeling of warm fellowship with his fellowmen. Always "the treacherous provoke treachery." And it cannot be

[4] From "In Christ There Is No East nor West," from *Bees in Amber* by John Oxenham. Used by permission of American Tract Society.

other than a dark moment in the soul when in the quiet of reflection one must recall and remember his acts of insincerity. Such a one the poet reproves:

> To have gone from home with the confidence of friends
> And then return, a thing that has price;
> To know within his heart that this is so;
> To have sold honor, yet to take men's hands
> To meet the honest merchant on the street
> The humble workman clean beneath his grime
> To face the Sabbath in the little church,
> And after service feel the press of friends
> And hear sincerely spoken words of praise
> While wife and children stand admiring by—IS NOT THIS HELL?[5]

They who accept the "more excellent way" must come to know and to be moved by the passion of love. Over against the aristocracy of birth, wealth, opportunity, leisure and power, Jesus sets the wide democracy of goodness, service and love. Whosoever is capable of committing himself to this trinity of virtue becomes thereby a member of the kingdom of the choicest spirits to be found on earth or in heaven.

Again, they who would enter the "more excellent way" must have a religion that is God-centered. The man whose religion finds its roots in his belief in God always holds fast to a few positives: "I know." "I know in whom I believe." "All things work together for good to them who love God." "I know he is able." "I am persuaded that nothing can separate me from his love." He knows that the good will which is eternal in the life of God made it possible for Jesus to believe in good will among men. What God was made it possible for Him to have glorious views of what man might become.

The final inescapable demand of the "more excellent way" is that our religious forces and movements—churches and Christian institutions—must produce a regenerate and courageous leadership to lead the world to peace, harmony and brotherhood. In a moment of great inspiration, Paul said, "I am debtor both to the Greeks and to the Barbarians." He felt that his message was a debt which he owed every human being in the world. He had no reservations in paying it. The authenticity of religion is vindicated and strengthened every time a moral battle is fought to a finish in any human soul. In the adventure of such a faith we are surrounded by a great cloud of witnesses. Let us lift our hearts in gratitude to God for the thousands of heroic men and women in every land and age, who, by their faithfulness, have become pilgrims of the "more excellent way," the way of love.

[5] Quoted from a sermon, "Great Motives for Service," by the late president Henry Churchill King of Oberlin College, delivered to the graduating classes June, 1927. The author and publisher are unknown.

The First Day of the Week

REVEREND DUKE K. McCALL, PH.D., LL.D., D.D.

A Minister of the Southern Baptist Convention, and Executive Secretary of the Southern Baptist Convention, Nashville, Tennessee

Dr. Duke K. McCall is a preacher, educator, and religious leader of great ability. As executive secretary of the Southern Baptist Convention Executive Committee, he holds a position of strategic importance in the leadership of more than six million fellow Baptists. As a member of the Baptist World Alliance Executive Committee, his influence touches the world's fifteen million Baptists.

He is a native Mississippian, the son of Judge and Mrs. John W. McCall of Memphis, Tennessee; took his college degree from Furman University, his divinity and Ph.D. degrees from Southern Baptist Theological Seminary. He also holds the LL.D. from Baylor University. From the pastorate of Louisville's historic Broadway Baptist Church, Dr. McCall went to New Orleans in 1943 to become president of the New Orleans Baptist Theological Seminary, being one of the youngest graduate school presidents in the country. He was recently given the D.D. by Furman University.

In May, 1946, he succeeded Dr. Austin Crouch as executive secretary of the Executive Committee, where he leads six million Southern Baptists in their world-wide evangelistic, educational, and benevolent work. His first major undertaking in his new post was the raising of $3,500,000 in three months for the relief and rehabilitation of the war-torn countries of Europe and Asia.

He led a successful campaign for the enlistment of "A Million Southern Baptist Tithers." He spent the summer of 1947 in a tour of Europe, following attendance at the Baptist World Congress in Copenhagen, toured the Canal Zone and portions of South America in late January of that year. He returned to Europe in 1948 for a tour of Baptist work in Germany.

The theology and dogma in this sermon will do much to stimulate many to renewed thinking of some of the basic religious and philosophical beliefs of the Church. It is important for men to believe and to know what and why they believe.

Sermon Forty=three

EASTER Sunday! What a contradiction of terms on the lips of a Christian. The word "Easter" is the slightly mispronounced name of Eostra, the Norse goddess of spring. According to legend, Eostra transformed her pet bird into a rabbit. Thus we have the Easter bunny who builds nests like a bird and fills them with colored eggs. It is all a relic of the Norse worship of the goddess of spring. How Christianity has changed the meaning of Easter for us—or has it?

Easter Sunday! Why Sunday is the day for the worship of the sun, Monday is the moon's day, and Tuesday belongs to the Greek god Zeus, and Wednesday belongs to Woden, while Thor, the god of thunder, claims Thursday, and Friday is dedicated to the goddess Frigg, wife of Odin, and Saturn takes over the last day in the week. Not a single day in our week is Christ's day, or at least the names do not indicate it.

No . . . This day of all the days in the year belongs to Jesus Christ. Today we celebrate the Resurrection of the Son of God, who thereby gives evidence that he is able to keep every promise and every pledge he made. Lowry wrote:

> Up from the grave He arose,
> With a mighty triumph o'er His foes;
> He arose a Victor from the dark domain,
> And He lives forever with His saints to reign.

Well, I wish I could believe that every one of us who attended a sunrise service this morning or who will go to church any time today is motivated entirely by the Resurrection of Jesus Christ. I fear that the old Norse goddess Eostra would find more to her liking in our hearts than would Jesus Christ. Our lips sing adoration for a risen Saviour, but in our hearts is only the joy of the spring festival.

You see, if Jesus Christ is in truth risen from the grave, it makes a difference, not only for today but also for every day. No day in the week belongs to the pagan gods of pleasure and passion, and power and pride. The Apostle Paul, who met the risen Master on the Damascus road, cries across the centuries to us, "Therefore we are buried with him by baptism into death: that like as Christ was raised up from the dead by the glory of the Father, even so we also should walk in newness of life" (Romans 6:4). It is a newness of life which throbs through us today because by faith we have become partners in the Resurrection.

Too often we think of the Resurrection simply as an incident which affected Jesus Christ in the past and which gives us hope for life beyond our own death in the future. We fail to realize that his resurrection reclaims from

Zesus and Thor and Woden every day in every week. What a difference Christ's resurrection ought to make in the way we live today! As Paul wrote to the Roman Christians, "If we have become united with him in the likeness of his death, we shall be also in the likeness of his resurrection; . . . Even so reckon ye also yourselves to be dead unto sin, but alive unto God in Christ Jesus" (Romans 6:5, 11, A.S.V.).

We must not dull the edge of the assurance which the Resurrection of Christ gives to every man concerning life beyond the grave. We need, however, to drive the wedge in deep to separate us from those secular and sinful pagan points of view and practices which still permeate our lives. The Resurrection changed the day we worship from the last day in the week to the first. The Resurrection changed the way we worship from pagan sacrifices on the altar of the sun god to reverent adoration of the Son of God. We ought to change the way we spell Sunday from "Sun" to "Son"; but such a change on the calendar is unimportant compared to a change in our character, which would indicate that we meet him in worship on the first day of every week to walk the remainder of the week in his fellowship. The words of the old song must be set to the musical rhythm of our own heartbeat:

> And He walks with me, and He talks with me,
> And He tells me I am His own.

There are too many spiritually dead church members. They were neither united with Christ in his death nor did they rise with him. For them the conventional phrases about the Resurrection slide glibly across their tongue, but they would not understand the bracing admonition, "If ye be risen with Christ, seek those things that are above."

They have set their affections on things beneath. Their lives are organized around low motives, not high ones. They are the so-called realists who keep their feet on the ground. For them Easter has much more connection with the new look than with the new birth. Easter marks a change in the style of their costumes but not of their character. Christ would describe them as whited sepulchers—all dressed up on the outside but full of rottenness and decay within their souls. In churches all over our country today ministers will repeat the mirthless jest of wishing these members of their churches a joyous Fourth of July, a happy Thanksgiving, and a merry Christmas because they do not expect to see them again until next Easter.

Thank God, however, there are those who celebrate the Resurrection every Sunday with worship which prepares the mind, and heart, and will to walk the high road of the resurrected life throughout the week. The purpose of the Resurrection of Christ was not to make possible an annual pilgrimage to an empty tomb but to provide fellowship with a living Saviour every step of every day. Something tremendous ought to happen to each of us as we worship this Easter Sunday and on every other Sunday. It will, if we can recover the day from our pagan expectations and habits.

The first thing to do is to get rid of the sacrament of the Sunday suit, and the ritual of the ride on the open road, and the ceremony of secularized amusements, and the ordinance of the opening game. Emperor Constantine had a good idea when he declared the first Sunday blue laws in A.D. 321. He required all courts, towns, and workshops to be at rest on the Lord's Day. It is about time for the clergymen of our country to stop smiling sweetly over the excuse, "I can't come to hear you preach because I have to work on Sunday." The proper answer is, "You do not need an excuse to avoid my sermon, but the Word of God says, 'Six days shalt thou labour, and do all thy work: but the seventh day is the sabbath of the Lord thy God: in it thou shalt not do any work'" (Exodus 20:9-10).

The cogs of the acquisitive machinery of our society are grinding to bits the spirits of men. While men cannot be made to worship by law, they can be unshackled from the wheels of our economic machinery. Christian employers must come to have a conscience about the Lord's Day. All Christians must come to have a new sense of the importance of worship even above their work.

The recovery of worship as an experience at the very center of life's resources is one of the urgent necessities of our day. While Kipling wrote of the region east of Suez, "Where there ain't no Ten Commandments and a man can raise a thirst," now most of the region west of the Suez, as well as north and south, has no Ten Commandments and no respect for pledged word and no regard for sacred compact and no concern for the aspiration of human souls and no sense of the value of the life of a man. Employers keep their businesses open seven days a week and then complain because their extra profits disappear into the pockets of dishonest employees. It never occurs to them that they have themselves pulled out the main support of character. Governments relegate worship to the category of a luxury and then wonder why any international agreement is a scrap of paper and crime wave after crime wave beats against the foundations of society. Men and women change the holy days into holidays and try to get recreation for the body instead of re-creation of the spirit. Then they wonder why the remainder of the week drags by in purposeless futility where every task is a trial.

Does God demand worship as a duty or offer worship as a gift? The answer to that will be determined by whether you go today to glance into an empty tomb or seek to find a risen Saviour in order to fall in step with him. On the one hand, you fall to your knees in wonder before an empty tomb, while on the other, you rise up to go to meet him who is risen and goeth before thee.

True worship introduces us to the difference between the push and the pull of life. Too many of us are pushed around by the duties and responsibilities of the day. We are driven by circumstances. We would like to rest for a while, but things keep pushing us on. We pause in worship and hear the Master say, "Rise up and follow me." Then it happens—there is a new gleam in our eyes and a new spring in our steps. We are going ahead because we want to go ahead. There is a goal which beckons us on. Thus an anonymous poet wrote:

> Heaven above is softer blue,
> Earth around is sweeter green,
> Something lives in every hue,
> Christless eyes have never seen.

The worker goes to his task, not pushed by vicious competition but pulled by the vision of service he can render his fellow men. The housewife goes to her tasks, not pushed by the obligations and responsibilities, but pulled by the opportunities and possibilities of her home and household.

Those upon whom life has laid the heavy hand of suffering and sorrow pass the days, not as quarry slaves driven sulking to a dungeon, but climb a difficult trail knowing that the Guide has gone on before them and found at the end of the way the glories of heaven. You see, the One whom we worship has tasted all the bitterness of disappointment and felt the pang of loneliness, yea, even the separation of a sinner's death from his holy Father, but he arose as the first fruits of them that sleep.

As a consequence, we are not unlike eight-year-old Jack Keely from the East End of London. He was bound for the United States when the *Benares* on which he was sailing was struck by an enemy torpedo and went down in the Atlantic. It was ten o'clock at night, and the wild waves flung their young victim back and forth in almost complete darkness. Finally three men pulled young Jack up on their little life raft. Immediately he asked, "Which way is America?" No whimpering, no begging for attention, just, "Which way is America?" His imagination was gripped, not with the wind and the waves, but with where he was going. Fear had no place in his concern, for his present plight was unimportant compared to his destination.

We, too, with the weight of cynical unbelief sucking us down in the crush of competition which would crowd us off the little raft we have found in the sea of life, in peril of temptation or tragedy, with the valley of shadows not far ahead—we pause in worship and take courage even as we ask which way is heaven. We know there is a way because the Son of God came from thence and has returned to sit down at the right hand of the throne of the Father. Christ's Resurrection assures us that even death is not our goal but a gateway, not the end but an entrance, not a terminus but a thoroughfare. We are on our way. Today we pause for direction. Which way is heaven? Within our hearts we hear the Son of God say, "I am the way—come, follow me."

The Ministry of the Son of Man: A Ransom for Many

REVEREND NED BERNARD STONEHOUSE, D.TH.

A Minister of the Orthodox Presbyterian Church and Professor of New Testament in Westminster Theological Seminary, Philadelphia, Pennsylvania

From the foundation of the Westminster Seminary, in 1929, Dr. Stonehouse was associated with Dr. J. Gresham Machem, and succeeded him as professor of New Testament.

Dr. Stonehouse is a graduate of Calvin College and Princeton Theological Seminary. He went abroad in 1927 on a fellowship from Princeton and pursued graduate work in the New Testament in Amsterdam and Tübingen. In 1929 he received the degree of Doctor of Theology from the Free Reformed University of Amsterdam.

He is the author of The Witness of Matthew and Mark to Christ, *and co-editor of, and contributor to,* The Infallible Word. *He is serving as editor-in-chief of* The International Commentary on the New Testament, *several volumes of which are now in preparation. Other literary activities include his editorship of* The Presbyterian Guardian *and contributions to* The Westminster Theological Journal.

He was ordained to the ministry in 1932. Since 1936 he has been active in the Orthodox Presbyterian Church and served as Moderator of its General Assembly in 1946. This sermon is "fundamentalist" in outlook, represents a group of dissenting churches today.

Sermon Forty=four

TEXT: Even as the Son of man came not to be ministered unto, but to minister, and to give his life a ransom for many.
MATTHEW 20:28

MANY people today are seriously troubled about the question of the nature of Christianity. The march of the centuries since the time of Christ has brought into existence so many diverse expressions of Christianity that we can well sympathize with the proverbial man in the street in his bewilderment. How shall he find certainty in his quest for the truth in the face of all the differences in theology and creed among the numerous sects and denominations?

We shall make progress in this situation only if we direct men back to the Scriptures. Only the Scriptures provide an objective standard for the determination of the question as to what Christianity really is. But men are likely to object that this appeal to the Bible does little to remove the present confusion. The Bible is so large, and its contents so complex and diverse, that the answer is thought by many to remain virtually unattainable.

Relief from this difficulty can be found, it is frequently said, only if Christianity is reduced to simpler terms. It is high time, it is claimed, that the creeds which separate Christians from one another be set aside. It is insisted, moreover, that we may no longer rely upon the Bible as a whole. We are told, for example, that it is harmful to maintain the authority of the Old Testament. And frequently the authority of Paul is scouted. The way of true enlightenment is declared to be found only if we get back to Jesus, the simple Jesus of the Gospels. This approach, however, is guilty of extreme oversimplification. Moreover, it also breaks down because the Jesus discovered by this method has turned out to be a merely human Jesus, of whom, in the last analysis, the Gospels know nothing.

Nor can we be satisfied with the approach of evangelicals who have found the solution in terms of a few great texts of the Bible or in terms of an elementary creed. The historic creeds deal more solidly and basically with the question at issue. And we must insist above all that the answer will escape us unless the Scriptures be considered in their grand comprehensiveness, unless we receive the whole counsel of God.

Nevertheless, for all of our insistence upon the relevancy of the whole counsel of God, we recognize that not all of Scripture is on the same level. There are passages which bear more directly and immediately than others upon the question, What is Christianity? Among such passages none has greater pertinence than my text: "Even as the Son of man came not to be ministered unto, but to minister, and to give his life a ransom for many." We shall see that this saying characterizes the ministry of the Son of Man in three particulars: it tells us that his ministry was (1) an act of self-humiliation, which points to the divine character of Christianity; (2) a work of self-sacrifice, which displays the redemptive character of Christianity; and (3) an example of self-denial, which intimates the ethical demands which Christianity makes upon us.

Christianity is divine. It is supernatural in its origin and character. It cannot be explained in terms of the development of forces within history. Rather, the God who made the world, and upon whom all of life and of history depend, has made himself known in word and deed in this world. And this revelation in history has found its ultimate expression in Jesus Christ, the eternal Son of God who became incarnate. It is through the divine words and deeds in history, which find their culmination and center in the entrance of the

Son of God into this world, that the redemption of the people of God has been accomplished. Hence, too, salvation is by the grace of God. It is his work from beginning to end. It is the Lord's doing, and it is wondrous in our eyes.

You may perhaps be ready to acknowledge that Christianity is divine, that Jesus Christ, the author and finisher of our faith, is the eternal One who, without ceasing to be God, has become man. But, you may ask, is this the teaching of Jesus? How, in particular, does this saying of Jesus support that view of Christianity?

My answer is that the divine nature of Jesus finds expression in his claim to be the Son of Man! But you will say, Isn't that a strange proof of the deity of Christ? Does not the title Son of Man establish rather his perfect humanity? So, indeed, some have supposed. Actually, however, it has become clear that this is a quite mistaken view of the meaning of that title. The key to its understanding is to be found in the vision of Daniel 7:13, 14, where the prophet says: "I saw in the night-visions, and, behold, there came with the clouds of heaven one like unto a son of man, and he came even to the ancient of days, and they brought him near before him. And there was given him dominion, and glory, and a kingdom, that all the peoples, nations, and languages should serve him: his dominion is an everlasting dominion, which shall not pass away, and his kingdom that which shall not be destroyed."

It is this language which provides the background for the title "Son of Man" and for the understanding of the significance attached to it by Jesus. Clearly, the one described in this vision is not a mere man. Indeed, he is not described as being a man at all, but only as having the appearance of a man. Nor is he depicted in terms of humiliation. Rather, we behold a most glorious figure, who is in the most intimate relation to the Ancient of Days, and shares in the sovereignty and glory of the Ancient of Days. To him belongs everlasting dominion. He belongs to heaven rather than to earth, to eternity rather than to time.

And when the title is applied to himself by Jesus, as it is in our text and in many other passages recorded in the Gospels, it serves to express the coming of a celestial being to earth. Nothing short of pre-existence is in view when Jesus speaks of the coming of the Son of Man. Some scholars have indeed not generally allowed this conclusion. But this has been due basically to the fact that their starting point is that Jesus could not possibly have been more than a mere man. On this view the name "Son of Man" as applied to Jesus must be deprived of its distinctive force or must be conjectured to be the creation of the Early Church. Such interpretations are arbitrary and must lead to skepticism. They demand that we desert the witness of the evangelists who stood closest to the events which they described.

In the words of our text, then, Jesus is saying: "I, who belong to heaven, whose is the glory and sovereignty of God, have come to earth in order to die." There was, therefore, nothing in his person nor in the external circumstances which he encountered which made it necessary for Jesus to die. He died because he came into the world to die. His death on the cross was a voluntary humiliation of himself. And this self-humiliation makes the cross not a tragic event which might better not have occurred, but a wonderful disclosure and manifestation of the redeeming love of God.

We have thus been brought to the second characteristic of the ministry of the Son of Man. It is a ministry of redemption. Jesus describes his work in terms of the self-sacrifice of himself for many.

Men have resisted this conclusion concerning the purpose of Jesus as they have resisted his supernatural claims. If we ask why men have found the doctrine of redemption uncongenial, an answer may be found in their evaluation of its implications for the doctrine of man. Modern man, proud of his creative ability and accomplishments, often charges that the doctrine of redemption is unacceptable because of its pessimism. The evaluation of man in terms of sin and guilt, of blindness and death, is said to be too impossibly pessimistic to make it acceptable.

On this background the effort has been made to distinguish between Paul and Jesus. Paul, it is acknowledged, had such a doctrine of sin and redemption. But Jesus is judged to have had a far more optimistic conception of human powers and character, and hence Paul's doctrine of redemption is regarded as an innovation, perhaps introduced through the influence of pagan religion.

But the effort to hold Paul responsible for the Christian doctrine of redemption is doomed to failure. This is apparent from the consideration that this doctrine is at the center of the teaching of the Bible from beginning to end. As the Epistle to the Hebrews emphasizes, under the old covenant as under the new, "without the shedding of blood there is no remission of sins." But my main concern now is to point out that Jesus himself taught this very doctrine when he declared that the Son of Man came to give his life a ransom for many. If this language is taken at face value, it must be recognized as teaching the Christian doctrine of the atonement.

What is the meaning of the word "ransom"? It is a word that has been used all too frequently in recent years in newspaper headlines. A ransom, we have been reminded, is the price that must be paid to set free one whose life has been declared a forfeit. But we do not need to depend on our newspapers for our understanding of this term. It is a Biblical concept which must have been quite familiar to Jesus' hearers.

You will recall the provisions which were made for the redemption of the first-born at the time of the Exodus. Pharaoh refused to let the children of Israel leave Egypt until the final terrible plague was visited upon his land— the slaying of the first-born of man and beast in the entire land. Only the first-born in Israel escaped. But ever after, in acknowledgment of this deliverance, the first-born in Israel were set apart unto Jehovah as belonging to him in a special sense. They were forfeited to the Lord. But, to be sure, this forfeiture did not bring about the destruction of the first-born. For gracious provision was made whereby the first-born might be redeemed by the sacrifice of a substitute. An ass might be redeemed by a lamb. And the first-born sons were always to be redeemed (Exodus 13:15; 34:20). In pursuance of this command, Joseph and Mary brought Jesus to Jerusalem to present him to the Lord and to offer the required sacrifice (Luke 2:22-24).

A still broader application of this language of substitutionary sacrifice finds expression in the 49th Psalm. This is a Psalm which treats of the folly of trusting in riches. And the high point is reached in the declaration that "no man can ransom the soul of his brother." The clear implication is that every man's life is actually forfeited to the Lord, and that, no matter how much of this world's wealth one might acquire, it can avail nothing to effect a ransom or exchange when man appears before his God.

And the striking fact is that Jesus, as he began to speak solemnly concerning his death, employed the same thought in describing man's condition. "What shall a man be profited, if he shall gain the whole world and forfeit his life? or what shall a man give in exchange for his life?" This language of Jesus has often been appealed to as if it taught the infinite value of the human soul, and thus to support an optimistic evaluation of human nature. But as the context shows, Jesus has in view the day of judgment, when "the Son of man shall come in the glory of his Father with his angels; and then shall he render unto every man according to his deeds" (Matthew 16:27). The point of Jesus' words, then, is not to say how valuable the life of man is or how noble his outlook, but rather to remind men how desperate their condition is as they come face to face with God. The question with which each man must approach God is, What shall I give in exchange for my soul? Man must confess that there is nothing that he can offer as a ransom.

But thanks be to God, our Saviour himself supplies the answer and provides the remedy. As he is on his way to Jerusalem he declares that "the Son of Man came . . . to give his life a ransom for many." What man could not do for himself the Son of Man came to do. He came to take the place of many. As a substitute for many it was necessary for him to humble himself, to suffer and to die upon the cross. He teaches, then, not merely that he died to make the salvation of men possible, but actually to accomplish the salvation of many.

To men who have not come to a realization of their dreadful sin and guilt, such a doctrine may be uncongenial. It may be scorned as a doctrine of pessimism. But to those who, through the grace of God, have come face to face with their sin as transgression of the holy law of God, this message of Jesus spells "good news." It puts a new face upon life.

But we may not stop at the recognition of the supernatural and redemptive character of Christianity. Jesus indeed describes his ministry as an act of self-humiliation and as a work of self-sacrifice. But he also demands that we recognize that his ministry is set before us as an example of self-denial. Christianity, in brief, is more than history and doctrine. It is also a life.

Many modern interpreters of Jesus have insisted, indeed, that the entire point that Jesus is making is summed up in his ethical demands. Jesus is not concerned with a doctrine of the atonement, it is frequently charged, but only to rebuke the ambition and pride of his disciples.

Let us consider this claim on the background of Jesus' words. The episode took place, as we have noted, while Jesus was on his way to Jerusalem. His face was set steadfastly toward Jerusalem. Even in his manner something ominous might be detected, and the disciples were filled with fear and amazement. And Jesus added greatly to the solemnity of the situation by repeating from time to time the necessity of the program of suffering and death and resurrection. The disciples do not comprehend his message. Yet their faith in him as the Christ does not fail. The sons of Zebedee desire places of honor when Jesus enters upon his messianic reign. Jesus replies, "Ye know not what ye ask," and shows that his thought is concentrated upon the cup which he is called upon to drink. He assures them that they too will be called upon to suffer because of him, and adds that the positions of honor are not his to bestow but are for those for whom they have been prepared by his Father. Then the other disciples become indignant at James and John, and prove that they likewise are not prepared to take the places of humble service and self-denial. It is this distressing situation which Jesus makes the occasion for as remarkable a lesson in Christian service as he ever taught.

Have you observed the tremendous climax which Jesus reaches in the words of our text? He has said, "Whosoever would become great among you shall be your servant." Then, as if to say that if one is not satisfied with being great and wishes to be chief, it is necessary to take a place of even greater humility, Jesus adds: "Whosoever would be first among you shall be your slave." And the whole lesson reaches its amazing climax when Jesus calls attention to his own humiliation and service, that of the Son of Man, the glorious heavenly Son of Man, whose service was about to bring him unto death. For Jesus says, "*Even* as the Son of Man came not to be ministered unto, but to minister, and to give his life a ransom for many."

In this lesson in self-denial, however, how shall one dare to allege that the reference to the death of Jesus as a ransom is only incidental to the lesson concerning the service we are to perform? It is far nearer to the truth to say that the lesson of service is incidental to the story which the Gospels tell of the march to Calvary where Jesus went alone to die for many. Others might engage in service, but only the ministry of Jesus took the form of his giving up of his life as a ransom for many. The cross in which the Christian glories is the cross of Christ. Though other crosses stand alongside of it, it alone is *the cross* because of who was there and what he accomplished there. Our service did not contribute in the slightest to the payment of the ransom. It is a service that is possible only because of the price that has been paid to set us free.

In the last analysis, therefore, we must distinguish between the self-denial of Christ and our own self-denial. The two are quite distinct. He could deny himself only in the sense of a condescending humiliation of himself. He made himself of no reputation. And even in his self-humiliation he remained Lord. Our self-denial, on the other hand, is that of men. It is the self-denial of sinful men. It is not, and can never be, identical with that of Christ. At best it finds only its prototype and analogue in the unique and incomparable sacrifice of Christ.

Yet, the fact remains that we who may find our ultimate basis of comfort in life and death in the knowledge of our redemption through Christ may not for one moment allow that the Christian life is a matter of incidental or secondary significance for us. It is our divine Redeemer who calls upon us to deny ourselves, take up our cross and follow him. Although we cannot accomplish by our self-denial and humble service what he wrought by his ministry, yet the Christian life is unthinkable unless we, in imitation of him and in obedience to him, are made conformable to his pattern. We too must be ready to say, "My meat is to do the will of him who sent me."

In this simple statement from Jesus' lips we have found reflected several of the basic ingredients of Christianity. Christianity is a religion of supernatural redemption through Jesus Christ, a redemption which carries with it and calls forth profound changes in the life of men. Shall we, then, attempt to unite on these fundamentals and regard all else as nonessential? Shall we cease our insistence upon the proclamation of the whole counsel of God? To these questions, we believe, the answer should be "No!" To follow such a course might well cause us to lose our hold on Christianity. For its truth is an organic whole, and must be seen as such to be truly understood and appreciated. Only as we contemplate the living God of the Bible in his majesty and sovereignty will we grasp something of the meaning of the supernaturalism of Christianity. Only as we give further thought to the Biblical teaching concerning sin and guilt and grace and salvation will we do justice to the doctrine of redemption. Only as we relate the significance attached to the example of Christ to the glory of God, the law of God and the motive of love, will we begin to see the Christian life in its integrity.

On the other hand, in our understanding of the Christian faith, it is imperative that we contemplate its unity as well as its comprehensiveness. In preaching the whole counsel of God we must ever be proclaiming Christ and him crucified. There is no other name under heaven by which we must be saved.

Do you, my reader, so receive Jesus Christ? Have you asked, What shall I give in exchange for my soul? And have you come to Christ as the one who is the only Redeemer? Do you acknowledge that he is divine, and so is One whom you should worship, and so is mighty to save his people to the uttermost? Do you acknowledge his life and law as the standard for your life, and purpose, in reliance upon him and out of love to him, to follow in the way of self-denial? This is the way of true peace and joy and action. This is the way to bring honor and glory to the Name of the Triune God.

Out of the Shadows

THE MOST REVEREND JAMES E. KEARNEY, D.D., LL.D.

Roman Catholic Bishop of Rochester, New York

Bishop Kearney was born in Red Oak, Iowa, October 28, 1884, attended New York public schools, Teachers College, New York City, 1901-03, St. Joseph's Seminary, Dunwoodie, Yonkers, New York, 1903-08, and Catholic University, Washington, D. C. He was ordained in 1908 and after a year of graduate study at Catholic University, he was assistant at St. Cecelia's Church, New York, 1909 to 1928. He was the founder and Pastor of St. Francis Xavier Parish, Bronx, New York, 1928-32. Professor of Apologetics, Good Counsel College, New York, 1928-32.

He became Bishop of Salt Lake City, 1932-37, and was appointed Bishop of Rochester, New York, in 1937. He has been Episcopal Moderator of the Newman Club Federation since the Federation has been part of the Youth Bureau of National Catholic Welfare Conference (1940). He holds the LL.D. from Fordham, Niagara and Canisius universities.

This was Bishop Kearney's Newman Club Convention Sermon at the Pontifical Mass celebrated at the National Convention of the National Federation of Newman Clubs of America in Houston, Texas, July 12, 1947. The Bishop gives the story of Cardinal Newman's years of intellectual and spiritual struggle, discusses the difficulties of the man of modern mind, shows the impasse between two cultures in our day, and discusses the significance and meaning of history. He insists that holiness alone transcends all barriers and quotes Newman himself to show how he came out "from the shadows and figments into truth." His discussion of the absolute value of truth as opposed to pragmatism, the search for truth, gentleness, courtesy, revelation and rationalism, the world of ideas, and the birth of new ideas make this a sermon for consideration.

Sermon Forty=five

TEXT: What I was born for, what I came into the world for is to bear witness to the truth. Whoever belongs to the truth listens to my voice.

JOHN 18:37

ONE hundred years ago last Memorial Day, John Henry Newman, our patron, was ordained to the priesthood of Christ, in the little chapel in the Eternal City. I am sure that as the great churchman knelt in meditation that morning, he would never have imagined this scene; that one hundred years later a group of young college men and women would gather in this great progressive city of twentieth century America, to seek from him inspiration and encouragement in their efforts to make Christian ideals effective on their college campuses.

The century that has spun out its length since Newman's ordination has wrought innumerable changes and none more remarkable than those which have affected and modified religious thinking. It is difficult for us today to recapture the precise mood and feeling of the times that witnessed the slow pilgrimage of the leader of the Tractarian movement to Rome.

We open the pages of his superb *Apologia Pro Vita Sua* with a consciousness that the particular problems which tormented his soul have largely lost their meaning for us. It is a rare scholar indeed for whom the historic controversies of the Arians and the Donatists have more than an academic interest. The Branch theory, which for a time seemed to offer him a safe anchorage in the Anglican "Middleway," has largely been relegated to the lumber room of forgotten things.

For all save Anglo-Catholics the argument of Newman's celebrated "Tract 90" has lost its pertinence to the theological debate of the mid-twentieth century world. In this sense, Newman's capitulation has gradually been stripped of the peculiar significance which it held for men of his own generation. To clarify this point: If another Newman were to repeat the conversion of his great predecessor today it would hardly cause a ripple of astonishment. His thinking would be so completely foreign to what we call "modern thought" as to be regarded as merely quaint. For Newman, history had a decisive importance; for us history has degenerated to the ignominy of a minor branch of the social sciences.

Obviously, our position is hardly enviable. Our sophomoric disdain for the past has already committed us to mistakes and errors of judgment for which we are paying bitterly, and the fact that scarcely any of our contemporaries

[278]

so much as suspect this as the source of our discontents offers pitifully little to cheer our forward view.

Newman emerged into the clear light of faith (he chose as his epitaph the phrase *Ex Umbris et Imaginibus in Veritatem,* "Out of the shadows and figments into truth") from a background where the historic continuity of Christianity was fully recognized as of ultimate importance to the whole question of belief.

He realized perfectly that the moment he established in his thinking that the See of Peter was the divinely designated guarantee of orthodoxy, his personal duty was plain.

In a word, he possessed the concept of Christianity so deeply ingrained in his mind as to reduce his problem to the relatively simple one of determining its proper vehicle. It was not, of course, a simple problem for him in the sense of being easy to solve. It cost him years of intellectual struggle and spiritual anguish, but the stages on the road were definitely marked. He knew at any given moment precisely where he stood.

The difficulty of the modern mind is suggested with reasonable adequacy in that one sentence. It does not know where it stands, either with reference to the past which it has forgotten or to the future which it has peopled with such portentous figures of doom. Its skepticism has resulted in an intellectual and moral impasse, out of which it can discern no gleaming thread leading to salvation.

The Catholic apologist, attempting to grapple with this protean antagonist, is tempted to cast a backward glance of envy toward the era of John Henry Newman, when controversy proceeded along lines laid down by common agreement upon rules of historical evidence and logical sequence. If he is aware that in some important respects his apologetic must cut deeper and rest upon the finer bases of reason itself, he is also conscious of the intellectual impoverishment which this implies.

The world is no longer Christian even for purposes of debate. Newman, with his historical certitude, could give only a dusty answer to the hot questioning of the centennial generation.

All this, however, does not mean that Newman is nothing more than a Victorian period piece catalogued for the benefit of the curious. Far from it. On the intellectual side, he is of special value to us today. In one respect he recalls to us our own St. Thomas Aquinas. That is to say, he fulfilled for an intellectual movement, which was the antithesis of the scholastic movement, the function performed by the Angelic Doctor in reference to thirteenth century scholasticism.

St. Thomas effected that assimilation of Aristotelianism with the teaching of Aristotle's great enemies, the Fathers, which has come to be known as the Scholastic Theology. The great agitation of medieval thought which accompanied the introduction of Aristotle's metaphysical and physical works from the East, by Frederic II, and the skepticism which it produced, were first dealt with satisfactorily from a Christian point of view by the Angel of the Schools.

The movement was unquestionably a dangerous one. It was rationalistic, and in some instances, under Arabian influences, it became pantheistic. What was needed was a thinker steeped in the Aristotelian culture, competent to hold his own in the dialectical tournaments of the day, and at the same time steeped in the traditions of the Church and the teaching of Holy Scripture.

Such a mind alone could save theology from a false position—that of a necessarily ineffectual rejection of the characteristic culture of the time.

The work of fusion was completed by St. Thomas. So, too, Newman, intensely sensitive by temperament to surrounding intellectual influences, and yet from early years a close student of the Fathers, coming upon a critical time when the divergence between many traditional theological forms and modern culture could no longer be ignored, laid down the lines of the synthesis which was a crying need to thinking minds.

In history his special studies of one period—of the ecclesiastical history of the first three centuries—made this perception still more acute. Under circumstances of exceptional difficulty he pointed out the path to conciliation, which to his successors is likely to prove a boon simply inestimable.

In the essay on "Development" and the sermon on "Development," in the lectures on the "Relations between Science and Theology," delivered at Dublin, in the last chapter of the Apologia, in the introduction of the Via Media, he has laid down principles which must quite inevitably guide Catholic thinkers of the future, however much short-sighted men may attempt to retard their frank acceptance.

He saw truly that the questions raised, the modes of thought determining men's deepest convictions, were largely different from those which obtained in the thirteenth century. The historical and scientific sense has come into its own with a force equal to the passion for logic and syllogism dominant in the twelfth and thirteenth centuries.

Writing at a time when it needed infinite tact to suggest so grave a reform without offending, Newman achieved its lines, so courageously, so surely, yet so gently, that many have not yet seen the magnitude of the task he accomplished; while some of those who are most sensitive to the requirements of the time, have felt that no more is needed than the full and detailed adaptation of the principles he sketched, to meet the successive challenges of scientific and historical inquiry as they arise.

Above the barrier separating his intellectual interests from those of today looms the quiet dignity and graciousness of his personality. Holiness is the argument which transcends all barriers and levels all differences. Absolute honesty and complete integrity are qualities which even we, with all our deplorable lack of this historical sense, can still recognize and admire.

Perhaps it is because of these things that Cardinal Newman now as never before exercises that astonishing influence over youth so intimately associated with his name. The deathless spirit of the man who fought his war without rancor and without regret from the "shadows and figments into truth," has captivated the imagination of thousands of young men and women, themselves incapable of appreciating the intricacies of his historical theology.

The unwavering courtesy of his bearing, the instinctive gentlemanliness of his carriage, even under the provocation of deliberate misunderstanding and when goaded by unbelievable pettiness, these have enshrined him forever in the hearts of those to whom greatness is inseparable from dignity. And because it is youth today that is again seeking the foundation of its lost heritage, the historical treasure which the generation of materialism so lightly cast aside, it may well be that his ascendancy may be restored to its proper setting and his *Grammar of Assent* become again a textbook of belief.

What a lesson for the world today, in the career of a man devoted solely to the quest for truth, in the courage of a man who gave up all he held dearest for the possession of truth, and then devoted his life and exceptional talents to the defense and dissemination of truth. Against the all too popular pragmatic interpretation of religion, he would oppose the absolute value of truth and goodness. Against the popular fallacy that religion is a sentiment, not to be confined by creed and dogma, he would oppose the Divine Revelation that religion must have definite doctrinal content, that religious truth has its principles, natural and revealed, which are more exacting in their logic than mathematics.

It is childish intellectual surrender to say, "It makes no difference what one believes or accepts in religion." Any thinking man does violence to his own intelligence, if he cannot sit alone with his thoughts and say, as Newman did, "I am convinced that I have found the truth." That, of course, demands that he admit that, in conflicting religious creeds, truth must be somewhere. It is worth the search!

Pilate said to Jesus, "Thou art a King, then?" And Jesus answered, "It is thy own lips that have called me a King. What I was born for, what I came into the world for is to bear witness of the truth. Whoever belongs to the truth listens to my voice."

The world needs that truth today. The Newman Club on your campus keeps faith with Cardinal Newman, in keeping God and the things of God in the life of the Catholic student.

Unfortunately for us and for the world, this land of ours has become a bit strange to God and the things of God. Once we were a religious people. It was primarily because we understood the necessity of religion for human happiness and well-being that we established our schools and means of education. In the Declaration of Independence we claimed for ourselves the rights that belonged to us because God had created us, and we came forth free and equal from His hands. Our forefathers went to church on Sunday and realized that their fundamental obligation in living was the worship of their Father Who is in heaven.

In recent years we have strained in our moorings to the Divine, and too frequently we have sundered them completely. Our education is no longer rooted and founded in religion; we no longer consider it an obligation to go to church; literally millions of us are utterly illiterate in matters religious. We do not know God and hence we do not glorify Him or give Him thanks. The visible things all around us bring to our foolish minds no meaning whatever of things that are invisible. We profess ourselves to be wise. Yet we are vain in our thoughts; and, if we but knew it, darkness broods over our hearts.

All of this must, of necessity, handicap us most seriously in the mission we have undertaken to bring about universal acceptance of those fundamental principles of truth and justice that must govern the actions of individuals and nations if there is to be peace in the world.

What America professes to stand for, what America strives for, what America is fighting for, what America dreams, has neither reality nor substance apart from belief in God. We talk of the brotherhood of man, but men are brothers only because there is a common Father in heaven. We dilate on the sacredness of the human personality; but human beings are sacred, not because we say so, but because they are creatures whom God has fashioned according to His image and likeness, redeemed by the precious blood of His Son, and destined for eternal union with Him. We make strong pronouncements in favor of religious freedom; but some of us are so befuddled in our thinking, so obtuse to the dictates of right reason, that we justify on this score of the freedom of government to attempt to destroy religion.

We would break asunder the shackles that tyranny has forged to enslave mankind; but we fail to take due cognizance of the fact that human liberty can be guaranteed only on the condition that we recognize the authority of God and submit our wills to the yoke of His Commandments.

A nation that is forgetful of God, that pays Him occasional lip service, could easily enough become a nation that is godless, and godlessness never created anything of lasting value. It is a deadly virus that enervates, debilitates, and eventually devastates all that is fine and decent and noble and sacred.

Highest time it is that we got down on our knees, made full confession of our disloyalty to Our Maker, and acknowledged that we are not sufficient unto ourselves. If we have gotten off our course, it is because we have refused to steer according to the compass of His Holy Will. We must rediscover the America our fathers founded and in which their hopes were vested, the America of faith in God, the America of churches and church-going people, the America of men and women and children who pray and walk in the Divine Presence, the America that feeds its intellect on Heavenly Wisdom and not on the husks served up by the shallow-minded teachers and writers who lack the education and the mental stamina to understand the American soul and to cling to the American tradition.

"There is only one Name under heaven in Which men can be saved."

This is a fact which remains immutably true. There is only one possible center for the universe of mankind and that center is the Heart of Jesus Christ. The peace that the world can give is at the very best an armistice; lasting peace can be achieved only under the banner of the Prince of Peace. In Him alone will God gather up the things that are scattered. In Him alone can all things be restored. America can become an effective instrument for this Eternal purpose only in the degree that she accepts His leadership and moves and has her being in His Grace.

What the Newman Club stands for, what we strive to accomplish, the nation needs. We have the truth, the truth concerning Christ and Him Crucified; that truth lights our way in our search for all other truth.

Our faith is for us the key to the riddle of life, and living. It enables us to glimpse the unity that underlies all variety and to understand the meaning of what would otherwise be meaningless. Our faith is the yoke that emancipates our minds from the thralldom of ignorance and error and doubt. We are not as children tossed about by every wind of doctrine. We are rooted and founded in reality—the reality of the supernatural.

Our mission is to make the power of the supernatural felt and insistently felt in whatever we are doing. We will have failed in the degree that we conform ourselves to the spirit of the world. It is our duty, not only our religious duty but our patriotic duty, to translate our education into a quality of living worthy of the vocations into which we may be called. The charters of our Newman Clubs are not just bits of parchment; they are marching orders from the Prince of Peace. Essentially, every Christian is another Christ going about doing good and bringing salvation to his fellow man.

The Kingdom of Heaven is like unto a leaven; that leaven must work through us, each one of us making Christ's power felt in our own particular spheres. This thought was never more tersely expressed than by your own patron—John Henry Newman.

"A man finds himself in a definite place; he draws persons around him; they know him, he knows them; thus it is that ideas are born which are to live, that works begin which are to last. Let each approve himself in his own neigborhood; if each portion is defended, the whole is secured. This is a great principle to keep in view. Make yourselves and your religion known more and more, for in that knowledge is your victory."

God's Laboratory

BLISS FORBUSH

Chairman, Friends General Conference (Quakers), and Headmaster,
Friends School, Baltimore, Maryland

This thoughtful sermon has a large scale view of life and faith. It has inspiration for our day and a hope that would be good for some of the pessimism abroad. As a sermon it is an excellent study of a thoughtful, prayerful, positive and progressive message.

Bliss Forbush was born in Yarmouth, Nova Scotia, attended Oberlin College, Johns Hopkins University, and graduated from the Divinity School of the University of Chicago. In 1939 he was awarded the Geneva Travel Fellowship for study in Europe. He became the executive secretary of the Baltimore Meeting of Friends in 1921, and was made a recorded minister in 1925. Three years later he became responsible for assisting the Friends meetings in Maryland, Virginia and Western Pennsylvania. Through the years he served as instructor in Bible and religion in Friends School, Baltimore, and became headmaster of the School in 1943.

After serving the Friends in the fields of young people's activities, leadership training and religious education, he was named chairman of Friends General Conference in June, 1941, an office he still holds. He is a member of the board of directors of the Maryland-Delaware Council of Chuches, and the American Committee of the World Council of Churches; he is a trustee of several schools and a Regent of Morgan State College. His book, Towards Understanding Jesus, *is widely used in courses in Bible and religion in independent secondary schools, and a later book,* With Cymbals and Harp, *has found an appreciative audience.*

Sermon Forty-six

SCANNING the pages of a technical journal will bring forcibly to mind the extent to which our twentieth-century civilization is dependent upon the modern scientific laboratory. Such words as radar, nuclear, plastic, lucite, bakelite, carbonic, ethylene, molybdenum, nylon, thiamine, riboflavin are but a few which indicate our indebtedness to the research worker. The prospectus of a new American weekly journal published in 1827 carried this paragraph at the top of its editorial page: "At no former period, has the human intellect been so intensely and variously occupied. We can scaic 'v turn our eyes to a corner of nature, respecting which, during the last thirty years, there has not been some important discovery. Within that period, new sciences have been created, and all the old ones enlarged their boundaries." The editorial amazement at the pushing outward of the scientific horizon in 1827 was but a prophecy of things yet to come. Today, over two hundred thousand marketable products exist which saw their beginnings in the scientific laboratory created by "that human intelligence intensely and variously occupied."

Remarkable as are the tools at the service of our laboratory technicians, there is a greater laboratory than any constructed by man, a laboratory in which each of us is a participant. In Walt Disney's motion picture *Fantasia* there was portrayed in vivid color the successive eras through which our earth passed from the Archeozoic through the Mesozoic times. His audiences saw those primeval orderings when the surface of the earth was still in flux, when mountain ranges were thrust up and volcanoes spread their lava over entire countries. On the screen he delineated the colossal struggle that continued for untold ages between fire and water until the heat of the earth was chained and the waters of heaven found their resting places. Then was pictured the warfare between water and land for domination. Great floods swept over much of North America, opening a passageway from the Gulf of Mexico to Hudson Bay, while coral reefs were formed far up the Mississippi River. The floods retreated and land bridges were thrown across the liquid barriers between Labrador and Great Britain, between Brazil and Africa. *Fantasia* ended its story with primitive life struggling from tiny single-celled animals up to the day when flying dragons sailed far over the chalk seas of Kansas, and forty-ton monsters struggled with armored dinosaurs.

We can carry the story further than did Walt Disney. We know that somewhere along the line of development a new spirit entered flesh. "And the Lord God formed man of the dust of the ground, and breathed into his nostrils the breath of life; and man became a living soul." This coming of the divine spirit into man is symbolized in the temples of ancient Egypt. Their colonnades of pillars and pictured walls were so designed that the direct light of the sun reached the inner sanctuary only on the longest day of the year. These temples were the symbols of ascending life. It was as though life were feeling its way through the pillared courts of time, washing the walls of lesser forms, and seeking the inner sanctum of personality, at last to find the end of its search in the sanctuary of the human soul.

Throughout the story of man's development there are innumerable questions. What does the story mean? Why are we here? For what purpose were we made? Many answers have been given by philosophers and theologians in the past. There is a simple answer. This is God's laboratory in which He is fashioning the character of men according to His design and purpose.

In God's laboratory there is beauty to charm us. There is no person with seeing eyes who cannot recall some scene of transfiguring beauty. Perhaps it is a glorious sunset, the soft velvet of a rose leaf, a majestic mountain vista, the moon mirrored in the quiet surface of a forest-hemmed lake, a mass of tulips blooming in May. Beauty is scattered indiscriminately for all to see, from microscopic wonders to the most sublime spectacles in nature. Everything from the dewdrop to the mountain glacier is a bearer of beauty. As Rufus M. Jones once declared, "Beauty has no function, no utility. Its value is intrinsic. It is its own excuse for being. It greases no wheels, it bakes no puddings. It is a gift of sheer grace, a gratuitous largess." Beauty is present in the most commonplace things. A drenching shower once swept the surface of a grimy-coated city street. When it passed a child ran out and saw the sun reflected in a pool of mingled oil and water on the asphalt pavement. Held in astonished surprise, she exclaimed in glee, "Mother, see the rainbow gone to smash." God must have a tremendous preference for beauty to have made it in such measure to be enjoyed by each of his children.

In God's laboratory there is mystery to intrigue us. In spite of the constant enlargement of the boundaries of science, we live, as it were, on an island of knowledge in the midst of an ocean of unknowing. Dr. Compton, the Nobel prize winner in physics, lectured a few years ago at the University of Chicago. The students came in large numbers to hear the famous scientist speak about the cosmic rays. They learned that cosmic rays exist, that they probably come from outside our solar system, that the rays now entering our atmosphere began their journey some five thousand million years ago, and that further knowledge about their origin and composition may disclose to us the ultimate composition of the universe. But from whence these rays came, and what started them on their way, and to other baffling questions the students received no answers.

There are fish which swim a mile or more beneath the surface waves of the ocean. These fish are equipped with light organs that attract their prey. But why these linophryne arboifer live where the waters are purple black and the temperature only slightly above freezing we do not know.

Tools used by primitive men have been found under Mexican lava which flowed down the sides of volcanoes more than seven thousand years ago. The origin of these implements and the destiny of those who fashioned them is still a mystery. In the Middle Ages skilled craftsmen built a cathedral in Greenland and forwarded their tribute to the Church at Rome. These men disappeared in an unexplained manner, and at the present time Eskimos wander among the ruins of long ago. No doubt a hundred years from now other men will look back with indulgent smiles on our boasted knowledge, just as we read of the "new sciences created" and "the enlarged boundaries" of 1827. In a thousand places we have but turned back the hem of the curtain that covers the mysteries of God's laboratory.

At no point are we so perplexed as when we attempt to plumb the mysteries of the human mind. Centuries ago the author of the Book of Proverbs wrote:

> There are three things which are too wonderful for me,
> Yea, four which I know not:
> The way of an eagle in the air;
> The way of a serpent upon a rock;
> The way of a ship in the midst of the sea;
> And the way of a man with a maid.

Nature has not yet disclosed to us her secrets, and though the sons of God may have shouted for joy long ago "when the morning stars sang together," more often they are forced to cry with Job, "I have uttered that I understand not; things too wonderful for me, which I knew not." There are depths within the human mind from which come strange obsessions, base cruelties, and cowardly deeds; but from which also come unclouded hopes, great idealisms and magnanimous courage. Jacob lied to his blind old father. David, too late, went into his chamber over the city gate and cried, "O my son Absalom, my son, my son Absalom! would God I had died for thee, O Absalom, my son, my son!" Judas betrayed his master for silver and at the sign of a kiss. But Jesus went to the cross crucified between two thieves. We are as little children opening a shuttered door. Filled with intellectual pride, we are like the eight-year-old child who asked his teacher at the end of the school year, "Now do I know as much as I don't know?" We are just at the threshold of God's laboratory, what lies beyond is still to us a mystery.

In God's laboratory there are many ways to test us. In the scientific laboratory of today there are vast numbers of measuring, weighing and testing machines. There are ponderous hammers which measure the tensile strength of huge steel beams; and there are other instruments so delicate that they can calibrate to the thousandth of an inch. So in God's laboratory there are means by which He molds and tests the character of men. Hardships, handicaps and dangers try the quality of men's souls.

Sometimes the tests are the measure of a man's stature. A biographer of Handel writes, "His health and fortunes had reached the lowest ebb. His right side had become paralyzed, and his money was gone. His creditors seized him and threatened him with imprisonment. For a brief time he was tempted to give up the fight—but then he rebounded again to compose the greatest of his achievements, the epic Messiah." Louis Braille, blind at the age of three, taught himself to read by touching raised type with his finger tips. At twenty-five he had perfected the system of raised letters which has brought light to the blind all over the world. John Bunyan wrote *Pilgrim's Progress* in Bedford jail while in misery at the thought of his fatherless family "especially of my blind one." Charles Reade declared, "Not a day passes over the earth, but men and women of no note do great deeds, speak great words, and suffer noble sorrow." They are meeting the exacting tests in God's laboratory.

The rough steel would complain if it could feel, at the buffeting of the grinding wheel; but it is by this rendering process that the steel is polished until, like a mirror, it reflects the sunlight. Human personality is also buffeted into shape. Like the abalone shell it would be drab and gray were it not polished until every color of the rainbow is reflected.

We can expect no miracles to solve our problems in God's laboratory. The testing, weighing and refining go on year after year. The Master Scientist, the Keeper of the Laboratory has given us ample resources with which to face our difficulties.

He has given us a body and brain, perfected over countless centuries, with which to work. There are certain major problems which continually recur, sometimes in new guise, to baffle us. Among these are the production of sufficient food to provide for mankind, the reasonable distribution of economic goods, international co-operation and peace, and the enhanced realization of the inherent dignity in all human personality. These problems will never be solved by chance, nor by men and women insufficiently prepared, intellectually lazy, or selfishly motivated. God has given us the bodily strength, the intellectual acumen, and the moral sensitivity to solve if we will these age-old difficulties which block human progress.

There are those who are pessimistic as to man's ability to conquer such age-old plagues as war. Many still believe that war is inevitable and that such efforts as the League of Nations, or the United Nations, will be no more effective than the medieval truce called "The Peace of God." Jesus answered these doubters when he said, "With men it is impossible, but with God all things are possible." And God works through men. In the summer of 1948 representatives of one hundred forty-seven denominations, drawn from forty-four nations, met in Amsterdam in The Netherlands to establish the World Council of Churches. Among the delegates were those who had lived through the war years in constant danger of their lives; others were present who carried on their bodies the scars received in prison camps. They were realists, and yet they proclaimed, "War is a sin against God and a degradation of man. War is not inevitable if men will turn to Him in repentance and obey His law. There is no inevitable tide that is carrying men to destruction."

Jesus said there was one eternal sin, the sin of blasphemy against the Holy Spirit. This is still the sin which can bar us from building the kingdom of God on earth. An ancient rabbinical legend relates that when Moses had climbed Mt. Pisgah and taken a last look beyond Jordan and toward the Promised Land, he asked the Lord why he could not enter into the inheritance of his people. According to the legend, the Lord replied, "You doubted me, and I forgave that doubt. You doubted your own power to lead the people. And I forgave that doubt. You lost faith in this people and doubted the divine possibility within human nature. That I cannot forgive. That loss of faith makes it impossible for you to enter the Promised Land."

God will give us courage to tackle our unsolved problems; he will give us courage according to our faith. There once lived an American whose greatness is legendary because of the handicaps which he overcame and the defeats

[288]

out of which he built his final success. He enjoyed little formal education. His first partner caused their joint project to fail and left him with a mass of debts. He turned to surveying to help retrieve his losses, but his instruments were attached by the sheriff for the payment of the debts. He ran for a minor political office and was defeated. He enjoyed a brief term in the House of Representatives and was then retired by his constituents. He was named a Vice-Presidential candidate, lost the campaign and was shortly afterwards defeated in an attempt to secure a seat in the Senate. After each defeat, however, Abraham Lincoln refused to retreat, to lower his standards, or to betray his message. His faith in himself and his dauntless courage make him one of the world's great heroes.

The story is told that when Christopher Columbus was about to sail westward in his little cockleshell, an old Admiral called from the dock, "What will you do when the winds rage against you?" Columbus is said to have replied, "We shall catch the wind in our sails." Brave men have always found that when life comes to a barricade and there is no going on, new resources are given to men of courage.

God has given us a pattern to follow. There lived one, centuries ago, through whose life more of the unexplored and mysterious goodness of this universe showed than has elsewhere been revealed to men. As strength is given to them, workers in God's laboratory must strive to follow where he leads. Harry Emerson Fosdick once said that Christ "played his life like music meant to be played over again." One need not be a Beethoven or a Bach to reproduce the beautiful harmonies of such composers. Once the great strains have been placed on record a man need not be a master musician to repeat the melodies. They can be played again and again. The tenderness, pity, love, majesty, righteousness and holiness of Jesus, his reverence for human dignity, his devotion to the ideals of the kingdom of God have all been demonstrated for us. It was his desire that such qualities be reproduced again and again, "Until the whole earth should be full of the music."

The world without and within is God's laboratory. It has been long in preparation. It contains beauty to charm us, mystery to intrigue us, and means by which our souls are measured and tested. God's laboratory is not a playground—it is a school. Thus we need not expect to solve the problems put to us in this laboratory in any easy fashion. Yet the Great Technician has given us resources of body, brain and spirit with which to solve our difficulties. Furthermore, He has sent one ahead who could say, "I have given you an example, that ye should do as I have done."

We need not be in a panic when we read the daily headlines, or listen to the solemn voice of the radio announcer. As James Russell Lowell once said, "I think He would not let us get at the match box as easily as he does unless He knew that the frame of His universe were fire proof."

The spirit required of men who would go forward from Mt. Pisgah is that symbolized in the portraits of Rembrandt. Out of a dark background there shines an illuminated face.

Love Thy Neighbor As Thyself

THE REVEREND RICHARD F. GRADY, S.J., PH.D.

The University of Scranton, Scranton, Pennsylvania

Father Grady received his college degree at Saint Joseph's College, Philadelphia, in 1924, entered the Society of Jesus the same year, and pursued studies in philosophy and theology at Woodstock College. Ordained in 1935, he studied abroad, receiving the Ph.D. from Gregorian University. On his return to the United States, he was appointed dean of Canisius College, Buffalo, then transferred to Loyola College, Baltimore, as head of the English department.

He entered the army as a chaplain in 1942 and served three years overseas in European headquarters. In 1946, on his return from the army, he was named to head the new Department of Communication Arts and supervise the construction and management of FM radio station WFUV at Fordham University. After completion of this work, he went to the University of Scranton as dean of the Evening School and head of the English department. He is the author of several articles and many book reviews in national publications.

This sermon was given for the students and faculty at the University of Scranton at the Annual Mass of the Holy Ghost in Watres Armory, Scranton, on October 5, 1948. It gives Father Grady's philosophy of education for our modern world, a distinctly religious and Christian educational viewpoint so much needed today.

Sermon Forty=seven

TEXT: You, my brethren, have been called unto liberty: only make not liberty an occasion to the flesh: but by charity of the spirit serve one another. For all the law is fulfilled in one command: Thou shalt love thy neighbor as thyself.

GALATIANS 5:13, 14

THERE is no need for me to elaborate the reason for this occasion. It is truly meet and just, right and profitable unto salvation that we should begin a new year of studies, as we ought to begin all our days and all our daily tasks, with prayer. A prayer, honest and sincere, to the Holy Spirit, the Third Person of the most blessed Trinity which is God; the Paraclete, promised us by Christ, who would teach us all things and confirm us in faith. A prayer for wisdom and understanding, for knowledge and counsel and fortitude, for piety which is godliness, and reverence for God our Father, addressed to the Spirit of Wisdom shared by the Father and the Son, the Eternal Light of infinite Understanding and Love, which arcs between the Father and Son in an inestimable bond of divine Charity.

Our prayer is this solemn Sacrifice of the Mass—celebrated here and for this hour making this place a temple—and by it we dedicate our labor to learn; and dedicate our studies to the only purpose worthy of such dedication: to better know and love and serve God by better knowledge and love and service of our neighbors who are, all of them, our brothers.

Given this occasion, as a member of the faculty of this University and as a friend sincerely interested in your welfare, I should be derelict in my duty, I should betray the loyalty I owe you, did I not remind you now that, if you prefer any purpose before this of which I speak, you will be making a grave mistake, one that will do serious harm to you and the happiness you hope for, and to the community of which you are inevitably and inescapably a member. Put yourself and selfish aims as the gauge and guide of your studies, and you will be perverting those studies. Reckon these years in college as merely an investment that will pay a dividend to be measured in dollars and cents, to be gathered from preferred positions in professional or administrative fields, and you will be deeply disappointed; you would be better advised to spend this time in earning experience in those fields. Value your college education only as it benefits yourself in social prestige, in bargaining power in the employment market, and as a means of making more for yourself, and you are a traitor to the community of your fellow citizens, who, in the last analysis, are the ones who make your education possible. Greater responsibility is imposed upon those who have received more. You are more fortunate than many of your fellow citizens, and they have a right to demand more of you. More than that, this duty is laid upon you by your faith, which establishes the first and all-inclusive law of Charity.

What is the purpose of formal subjects? Your study of history is not a memory exercise, to make you facile in the parroting of dates and names and events. History is a study of the past achievements and the past mistakes of the men who went before you, so that you may better understand the world you now live in, and the men who with you make that world. You study Latin and Greek and modern languages, not for their several excellences only, but to better acquaint you with the mind and heart of men of other nations and other times; to help you better understand and communicate with them, to aid you to express your thoughts and ideals more clearly. You do not study chemistry to learn the prices of the various salts and compounds; but to know better how they can be put to better use to serve mankind; your study of physics and biology is not intended merely to amuse you or to satisfy your curiosity, but to prepare you to make your contribution to the progress of mankind in harnessing the forces of nature and in fighting disease. Your study of philosophy is not an academic exercise in dialectic; but to equip you for more clear and balanced judgment, to aid you to counsel and advise your fellow men; to stimulate your thought and deepen your appreciation of moral worth.

Even your studies of accounting and business administration are intended primarily to fit you better to serve your fellow men in commerce and trade, rather than to give you yourself a higher market value as an employable citizen.

The whole purpose of your collegiate studies is thus to make you better able to serve the community of citizens of which you are a component part. Your success as a citizen and as a man, and no less your happiness in life, depends on your appreciation of this purpose, your recognition and acceptance of this responsibility which you must accept, and cannot avoid without danger to yourself and to the community.

Every one of you has lived through a war which laid heavy burdens upon you; which demanded sacrifices of your time and energy and comfort which you can still recall and number. And every one of us here must be aware that the times require of us yet more unselfish sacrifices, the while we fear that even greater demands may yet be laid upon us. And for what purpose? To preserve or extend our pleasures? To guarantee greater profits? To enlarge comfort? Not at all! Guadalcanal and Kasserine Pass and Bastogne were not endured to protect the great American privilege of buying an electronic blanket, nor to safeguard the Saturday evening ice cream sundaes and the Sunday afternoon automobile trips. They were major engagements in a continuous struggle to defend the liberty in which you were born . . . a liberty to work together in harmony, a freedom to co-operate freely with your fellow men for the greater good of all. Not to protect your own or any other individual's privilege to expand himself at the expense of others.

The citizen who works only for himself is of no worth to the community. On the contrary, he is an active danger, a center of disaffection, a contamination of the commonweal. For such a one will betray the community to profit himself. You despise and complain of doctors and lawyers, of businessmen and merchants whose only standard, whose sole measure of service is: "What's in it for me?" You condemn and despise men in public affairs, politicians, who are venal and self-centered, who compromise principles for personal profit. Yet, too frequently, you envy them their opportunity to grow fat at the expense of the community; and you tolerate them, knowing that they are destroying your freedom, wishing you could, like them, have the chance to take advantage of your fellow citizens that you yourself might enjoy their scope, their lack of scruple. And yet you know that to do so is to pervert liberty by making it an occasion of sensuality, or selfishness.

This college, this university is not ashamed to acknowledge graduates who earn their living with their hands. The bachelor's degree is not intended to disbar a man from labor in the fields, in factories, in mines. There is nothing incongruous or shameful in a man with a college education earning his livelihood as a plumber, a truck driver, a carpenter. But a man with a college degree—which represents four years of added opportunity to learn how better to understand and to assist with counsel and wisdom, his fellow man—will rightly be expected, be required to serve his fellow men in fulfillment of the responsibility which his greater opportunity has given him. He will be looked to for leadership in whatever field of life he walks and works.

This responsibility to serve others, to put the common good above your own, is enriched and redoubled by the Law of Life your faith imposes on you. That Law of Life is a law of Love: Thou shalt love thy neighbor as thyself. The Law of Charity. And it is for the Spirit of Charity that we pray this morning. A spirit that will inspire our studies with a purpose as simple and sincere as that described by the father of Mr. Walter White, when that young man, a Negro, was leaving home after completing his college course:

> Your mother and I have given you the best education we could afford, and a good Christian home training. Fortunately, it is better than most colored children have had. Now it is your duty to pass on what you have been given by helping others less fortunate to get a chance in life. I don't want to see you go away. I'll miss you. But remember always, God will be using your heart and brains to do His will. You will be misunderstood and criticised when you fight so difficult a battle as that created by the race problem. But decide, with the help of God, what's right, and don't falter or turn back.

This advice is the same as that which your own father and mother would and do give you. You have an obligation to yourself and to your family—to make yourself and them a sound and healthy, happy and harmonious segment of the community. But *not* at the expense of others. Rather with justice and charity toward all, and malice toward none.

Now there are varieties of gifts, but the same Spirit; and there are varieties of ministries, but the same Lord; and there are varieties of works, but the same God, who works all things in all. . . . As the body is one and has many members, and all the members of the body, many as they are, form one body, so also it is with Christ. For in one Spirit we were all baptized into one body, whether slaves or free [white or black or red, poor or rich]. The body is not one member, but many. The eye cannot say to the head "I do not need your help"; nor the head to the feet: "I have no need of you." God has so tempered this body together in due portion that there may be no disunion in the body, but that the members may have care for one another. And if one member suffers anything, all the members suffer with it, or if one member glories, all the members rejoice with it. Now you are the body of Christ, member for member. . . .

So it is that Saint Paul explains the need for this Spirit to inspire and guide and direct you: the Spirit of Charity. The Law which is contained entire in this one command: "Love your neighbor as yourself!"

That this may be the spirit that guides and inspires your studies, we earnestly pray. Through our Lord Jesus Christ, who with the Father and the Holy Spirit, livest and reignest, God, world without end. Amen.

SERVICE

Privilege: Getting or Giving?

THE REVEREND CANON MARCUS KNIGHT

*Canon and Precenter of St. Paul's Cathedral, Church of England,
London, England*

Canon Knight has a great opportunity to speak to the people who attend the world famous St. Paul's Cathedral in London. He was born in 1903, was educated at Birkhead College and King's College, took his A.B. with honors in the classics. He was awarded the Caldecott Prize, the Trench Prize and Relton Prize. He was made a Fellow of King's College and was ordained in 1927.

He served many years in the parochial ministry, was vicar of a seaside parish in Torquay and of an industrial parish at Nuneaton. During 1929-30 he held a Fellowship as an English Student at Union Theological Seminary, New York City. Since 1944 he has been Canon Residentian and Precentor of St. Paul's. There is a freshness and penetration about his preaching that matches its brevity.

St. Paul's Cathedral is one of the great religious edifices of the world, and was built by Sir Christopher Wren after the great fire of London. Its dome, organ, altar, and other features make it unique. John Donne and other great preachers have made its pulpit famous.

Sermon Forty=eight

TEXT: Command that these my two sons may sit, one on thy right hand, and one on thy left hand, in thy kingdom. MATTHEW 20:21

THERE is in our own day a growing tendency to misuse the English language. One particular example which is frequently heard in discussions upon the social problem occurs in the use of the expression "the underprivileged." It is a term denoting those persons who for one reason or another are believed to be receiving less than a fair share of what goods are available. Such persons might correctly be described as underpaid or undernourished, but not as underprivileged. For privilege surely means the obtaining of special advantages over the general public. It means that a man is receiving more than his fair share of such benefits as are available. The privilege of one surely means the deprivation of another, at least so far as material goods are concerned. It does not seem as if we have yet succeeded in realizing any social order in which privilege is entirely abolished. Even in Soviet Russia, which to some appears the nearest expression of the kingdom of heaven here on earth, the best seats at the opera and the largest motorcars are reserved for the commissars, and for those who seem to the ruling class to deserve the special privileges associated with their usefulness to the regime. In any social order privilege may be connected with money, birth, tradition or political power; but so long as there are special opportunities available, there are some who will enjoy them.

We should not then be surprised that in the Gospels we find an example of an effort to obtain special privilege. The twelve disciples were on their way to Jerusalem with their Master, who knew that he was to face there the ordeal of the cross. James and John—two of the twelve who were closest to Jesus and most frequently with him—came to him with their mother, who may have been used by them as an instrument to ask for something of which they were slightly ashamed, asking for the two chief places in the new kingdom which they thought Jesus was going to inaugurate. The action was secret and underhand. It was an attempt to cut out the ten and get their request in first. No doubt many people today might admire them for their enterprise and readiness, qualities which seem necessary in a competitive world. But the other ten were hardly better. Their own indignation was a symptom of their own liking for position and precedence. Their annoyance may well have arisen from the fact that they had not thought of anticipating James and John in putting forward their own claims.

We can sympathize with all twelve. They were only human. The normal idea was, and on the whole still is, that the greatest men are those who give the orders and the least are the men who take them. It was a sign of high place to demand obedience and a mark of low place to have to give it. The superior man was to be served; the inferior man was obliged to serve.

Our Lord reverses this whole structure. "Whoever wants to be great among you must be your servant; and whoever wants to be first among you must be your slave." Slaves had no legal rights. They were hardly more than animals. They had to live entirely by the will of another. Our Lord says that only a man whose life is conducted in the spirit of service to others, for which he asks no credit and demands no reward, can hope for a place in his kingdom. He himself gave a practical demonstration of this principle just before the Last Supper, when he insisted on washing the dusty feet of his disciples, and told them "I am among you as he that serveth." Not one of the twelve had offered to wash the feet of the Master. Each was waiting for someone else to begin, and not one of them wished to demean himself before the others, and undertake the task. It was he who was most tired, who carried the heaviest burden and responsibility, who did what had to be done. Never in history has there been a clearer example of the insidiousness of a grave spiritual temptation, and never has it been more devastatingly exposed. For it is these spiritual weaknesses and failings which wreck human relationships even more than the sins of the flesh, and in these areas of human life that Christianity can be felt in its most painful and demanding power over the accustomed natural feelings of the ordinary man.

Why do we all like privileges? It is not easy for any man to avoid a slight feeling of complacency and gratification if he enjoys a privilege. It tempts him to think that he must be rather better than the average run of humanity. Men find that their self-esteem and their self-confidence are enlarged. It is even possible to imagine that if James and John had been granted the special privileges for which their mother asked they might have displayed far more courage when their Master was seized by his enemies. As it was, they first went to sleep, and then they forsook him and fled. But Jesus was not going to buy their courage and loyalty on their terms. It had to be won by a harder way.

We cannot help desiring privilege when we feel tempted to try to break into a circle from which we feel ourselves excluded. Envy and malice so often arise in this situation. Mr. C. S. Lewis once called attention to the strength of this temptation among large numbers of people. The existence of circles from which we are at present excluded makes us over critical of those who are within those groups, and moves us to self-pity for our failure to achieve a recognition to which we feel ourselves entitled. The temptation may present itself in different ways. The intellectual man may feel it in relation to certain groups into which he would like to be admitted; the student may feel it in respect of a club or an athletic group which carries respect in college; the suburban housewife may feel it in respect of the size of a house, or the make of an automobile, trying to gain social standing by a demonstration of the resources which a better income may command.

It is easy to estimate the power of this human weakness in ourselves by the amount of pain which we feel if we lose a privilege which we have enjoyed. The present changes in society in Great Britain have resulted in many losses of privilege among certain groups, and without a Christian attitude to these losses, it is not easy for such persons to accept a new position with cheerfulness. But the whole principle of the Incarnation enables the Christian to enter into a better understanding of the true ends of life. He who was rich for our sakes became poor. He who was Master washed the feet of the disciples. He who was King went to the humiliation of the cross. So also was it with St. Paul. He was born with many advantages. He was a member of the best educated and most influential religious group of his race. He possessed Roman citizenship. Every possible opportunity which a Jew could desire was open to him. But, as he said, he counted all this but dung, if only he could be found worthy of Jesus his Lord. He discovered the secret of how to be abased and how to abound, and so to sit lightly to all power and position and privilege, rejoicing in any chance given him to serve his Master.

One of the impressions left upon the reader of Dr. Iremonger's recent life of Archbishop William Temple brings home this point. Dr. Temple had every privilege: a cultured home, high intellectual gifts, the interest of many powerful friends, and advantages open to very few. But, although he held so many high offices, one feels that he possessed a spirit of cheerful humility which made him able to move freely everywhere, caring nothing for the advantages, but only for the opportunities to be of some use to the Lord Jesus Christ. It seemed to many that he had passed out of that narrow world of self-concern and self-pity which is the mark of the man who is thinking about his own position and prestige. So to each one of us the words of St. Paul come with special significance: "I know how to be abased and I know also how to abound; in everything and in all things have I learned the secret both to be filled and to be hungry, both to abound and to be in want. I can do all things in him that strengtheneth me" (Philippians 4:12).

If Jesus of Nazareth Could Speak to the Christians— If Judah Maccabee Could Speak to the Jews—Today

REVEREND JULIUS MARK, LL.D.

Senior Rabbi of Congregation Emanu-El (Reform), New York City

Dr. Julius Mark's preaching at Congregation Emanu-El is vigorous, appealing, scholarly. In him the Temple has found a worthy successor to Dr. Samuel Goldenson, who was loved by Protestants and Jews alike. As Senior Rabbi of Temple Emanu-El, New York, he is in one of the great synagogues of the world. A graduate of Hebrew Union College, the University of Cincinnati and the University of Chicago, before his call to New York he served as Rabbi of Vine Street Temple, Nashville, Tennessee, and Temple Beth El, South Bend, Indiana.

He is a member of the Board of Governors of the Hebrew Union College, vice-president of the Alumni Association of the Hebrew Union College, and former chairman of the Commission on Justice and Peace of the Central Conference of American Rabbis.

During World War II he served as a chaplain in the United States Navy. For nearly twenty months he was Jewish chaplain to the United States Pacific Fleet on the staff of Admiral Nimitz. The honorary degree of Doctor of Laws was conferred upon him by Cumberland University in 1936.

This sermon was preached Saturday morning, December 25, 1948, and caused much discussion at the time for its courageous view and the clear vision shown in his message.

Sermon Forty=nine

THIS is a sacred day for our Christian neighbors, since it marks for them the anniversary of the birth of their Lord and Saviour. In the spirit of neighborliness and friendship, we may well pause and express to them our heartfelt good wishes and join with them in the prayer that our common hopes for peace on earth and good will toward men may soon be realized.

Tomorrow evening, we Jews will commence the observance of Chanukah, —the Feast of Dedication, which commemorates the heroic resistance of the

Maccabees against the brutal totalitarianism of Antiochus Epiphanes more than 2100 years ago.

We frequently experience the feeling that not much progress has been made since the times when the stirring events, recalled by the Christmas and Chanukah festivals, occurred. Where is the freedom for which the Maccabees fought? Where are the peace and good will which the Man of Nazareth was supposed to have ushered in? Was the Maccabean struggle all for naught? Would the world have been in no worse condition if there had been no Jesus and no Christianity?

We tend to grow cynical and pessimistic whenever we permit ourselves to conceive of civilization as a straight line that constantly advances—forward and upward. This, alas, has never been the case. We go forward for a time—and then, when we forget the lessons that have been learned, frequently at the cost of suffering and bloodshed, we retrogress and go backward. Man's battle for freedom and justice is never permanently won. It must be refought in every generation, unless he makes a genuine and sincere effort to live by the ideals for which he made so many sacrifices. Thus, as we turn back the pages of history, we discover that civilization may be compared, not to a straight line, but to a line that goes forward for a time, then recedes, then goes forward again. The purpose of observances such as Christmas and Chanukah is to stir men's hearts to such an extent that the lessons which they teach will not be forgotten and that the recessions in man's onward progress will be fewer and less painful.

It is of value to note that the Christian Christmas and the Jewish Chanukah originated in periods of history strikingly similar to our own. Try to picture to yourself the Jewish community in Palestine in the second century, B.C. During the early part of the sixth century B.C., the little Jewish state had been conquered by the Babylonians, who carried into exile those Jews who survived. Fifty years later, King Cyrus the Persian, having vanquished Babylon, permitted those exiled Jews who wished to return to Palestine to do so. But the Jews in Palestine remained under Persian rule. In the fourth century B.C., the Persians were, in turn, overcome by the Greeks under Alexander. Judea now became part of the Greek Empire. After Alexander's death, his vast empire was divided among his generals, Palestine and Syria being joined under the reigning family of the Seleucids.

The Jews were not averse to adopting Hellenistic forms of life and thought. In fact, they were attracted by the new culture and charmed by its customs. The Greek language became the vernacular among the wealthy and cultured elements in Jewish society, while Greek names became the rule among all sections of the population. The finer elements of Greek culture, its philosophy, its poetry, its emphasis upon the aesthetic, appealed to the Jews of Palestine as well as to those living in other parts of the Greek Empire. Greek gymnasia and Greek games were introduced into Jewish communities and attracted the younger elements. The Bible had been translated into Greek at the request of the Jewish community in Alexandria. This process had been going on for a long time without arousing any serious opposition.

It was only when King Antiochus, in the second century before the Common Era, attempted to regiment all the tribes and nationalities that comprised the Seleucidian state in accordance with his pagan pattern that he met opposition among the Jews. Other peoples had little objection to adding another god to their pantheon. To the Jew, however, the worship of any God save the Eternal was worse than blasphemy. They resisted Antiochus' decree with their lives, as recounted in the books of the Maccabees. Calling himself the "Illustrious," but surnamed by others the "Madman," Antiochus caused the country to run red with the blood of Jewish martyrs as well as that of his own soldiers.

Not all the Jews, it must be remembered, fought back! There were appeasers, traitors—quislings, we would call them today—who were willing to sacrifice their liberties that they might enjoy their privileges, the cowardly and craven who preferred to live on their knees rather than fight and die, if need be, on their feet. But there were enough courageous and indomitable men and women who valued liberty more than life, and who followed the Maccabean standard to ultimate victory. So far as we know, this was the first struggle for religious liberty in all history. It was a struggle, however, in which, though arms were resorted to, warfare was not glorified. Its motto was: MEE CHOMO-CHO BO'ELIM ADONOI ("Who is like unto Thee, O Lord, among the mighty"); and its watchword a verse from Zechariah: LO B'CHAYIL V'LO B'KOACH, KEE IM B'RUCHI OMAR ADONAI TZ'VO'OS ("Not by material strength nor by physical power, but by My Spirit shalt thou prevail, saith the Lord of Hosts").

Like Judah Maccabee, Jesus of Nazareth—165 years later—came into a world in which brute force was in the ascendency. It was a dark age for those whose hope lay in the emancipation of the human spirit. Nations in which the lamp of reason had been kept burning and the worth of the human personality had been maintained were swiftly passing into the black night of ruthlessness. It was an age of deep recession in human progress. Greece was entering upon the period of her greatest degeneracy. Palestine lay crushed under Caesar's bloody heel and was on its way to the tragedy which Titus was to seal seventy years later with the storming of Jerusalem. All the world was paying tribute to the coffers of Rome. In fact, Jesus—the Greek for his Hebrew name of Joshua—was born while his parents were on their way to Jerusalem to pay a special tax imposed by Caesar Augustus.

The life of the Man of Nazareth could not have been of much significance to a tyrant who ruled by the exercise of brute force. Here he was, a child of humble Jewish parentage—his father was a carpenter—attending school and synagogue, making an impression upon his teachers by his brilliance; then disappearing from the scene of history, to return at the age of thirty, and for three years becoming a kindly teacher of love and a flaming prophet of righteousness. The Romans thought nothing of putting him to death, for to them he was just another rabble-rouser who was becoming too popular among the bitterly persecuted people, who longed for a champion and redeemer. So they crucified him—a Roman form of execution reserved for traitors—as they had crucified thousands before him and since.

And yet this gentle Jewish teacher was destined to become the inspiration of countless human beings. Men were to live and die by him. So devoted did they become to him that they made of him a God. Shameful acts were perpetrated in his name, through no fault of his own. Jesus of Nazareth still remains the greatest of all teachers, the kindliest of all men, the loyal Jew who died for the glory of God. Jews have never rejected Jesus! They rejected the divinity ascribed to him after his death! For divinity, according to Judaism, is reserved only for God. Perhaps the clearest way of stating the difference between the Christian and Jewish concept of Jesus is to say: For Christians, Jesus was born divinely and lived humanly; for Jews, he was born humanly and lived divinely.

It is precisely because our own times are in so many ways similar to those in which Judah Maccabee and Jesus of Nazareth lived that, if they were to appear among us today, their messages would have a timely, modern ring.

Would not Jesus of Nazareth say to his Christian followers: "Never forget that I am a Jew. My father, mother, brothers, sister, were all Jews. I have only contempt for those who would make something else of me. When you hurt the children of Israel, you hurt me! When you persecute and crucify them, you are persecuting and crucifying me! You so-called scholars of Germany who try to disprove my Jewish ancestry by declaring that I am the offspring of an officer in the Roman Legion who seduced my mother, insult my mother and cast shame upon my name! I was born, lived and died a Jew! The Jews are my people, blood of my blood, bone of my bone, flesh of my flesh!"

Would not the Man of Nazareth din into the ears of his followers once again his teaching that "out of one blood hath God created the whole world," that all men are brothers, that in the sight of God there is no distinction between barbarian and Scythian, circumcized and uncircumcized, slave and free, Greek and Jew?

Would he not emphasize anew his magnificent Beatitudes, which form the grandest sermon ever preached, and denouncing the arrogant, the unjust, the brutish, the hateful, declare again:

> Blessed are the poor in spirit, for theirs is the kingdom of heaven.
> Blessed are they that hunger after righteousness.
> Blessed are the merciful.
> Blessed are the peacemakers.
> Blessed are those who are persecuted for righteousness sake.

Yes, his place would still be at the side of the needy, the hungry, the oppressed, the persecuted—and he would charge those who call upon his name to follow his example.

Now, what would Judah Maccabee say to the House of Israel in these trying times, so similar to his own? Would he not again rouse his people to a renewed devotion to the faith of Israel? Would he not implant new courage and zeal into the hearts of those who are in fear and trembling? Would he not lift up those who are in despair with the challenging charge of his father, Mattathias: "Be ye zealous for the law and give your lives for the covenant of your fathers"?

In present-day reborn and resurrected Israel, the Maccabean spirit has taken hold of the hearts of the embattled defenders of their hearths and homes. There indeed they are giving their lives for the covenant of their fathers.

In blessed America, where we live in peace and freedom, we are, thank God, not asked to give our lives *for* the covenant of our fathers, but are challenged to give our lives *to* the covenant of our fathers through a staunch and revitalized loyalty to our glorious faith and sacred traditions.

In our own day, as in the days of the Maccabees, there are those amongst us who are weak of knee and timid of heart, the escapists, those who, if they could, would renounce their ancestry and their faith; who cravenly and pathetically declare: "Woe is me that I am born a Jew, to be hated and persecuted. Since I cannot escape," so they say, "I shall at least bring no children into the world."

Of these betrayers of the Maccabean spirit, I would ask: "Did you ever hear of a Dane, a Pole, a Czech, a Norwegian, who, when their countries were ruthlessly invaded and their liberties taken from them during the recent war, exclaimed that they would not bring children into the world?" On the contrary, while in the depths of their suffering they were more determined than ever to resist their oppressors and to assure the perpetuation of their nations and their freedoms.

For months on end, the skies of England rained down bombs of death and destruction. Thousands were killed, many more thousands maimed; entire blocks of homes in London were destroyed. Coventry was wiped out! Did the English curse the fate which made them Englishmen? On the contrary, from the hands of the dead and dying, the next generation received the torch of freedom and liberty. Let them kill us, let them destroy our homes and hospitals and public buildings; let not one stone be left standing upon another —yet, there will always be an England! We may not approve of the foreign policy of the present government of Britain, but in our hearts there was the highest admiration for the pluck and courage of the British people who were ready to fight on the beaches, on the streets and in their homes.

Shall we of the House of Israel, with our heroic Maccabean tradition, do less? If Judah Maccabee could speak to us today, he would say: "Fear not! Be of good courage! With the God of Heaven, it is all one to save by many or by few."

The history of the Jew is an undaunted, eternal affirmation that physical force must ultimately give way to moral courage and that the triumph of wickedness is but for a day.

Christianity, too, having caught the vision of Jesus, the Jew, will yet inspire its adherents with the glorious dream of "peace on earth, good will toward men."

In this season, when Christians and Jews become conscious of their great spiritual traditions, they may well pray together in the inspired accents of one of God's true noblemen, St. Francis of Assisi:

> Make me, O Lord, an instrument of Thy peace.
>   Where there is hatred, let me sow love;
>   Where there is injury, pardon;
>   Where there is doubt, faith;
>   Where there is despair, hope;
>   Where there is darkness, light;
>   Where there is sadness, joy.
> Grant that I may seek not so much to be consoled,
>   as to console;
>   To be understood, as to understand;
>   To be loved, as to love.
> For it is in giving that we receive.
> It is in pardoning that we are pardoned.
> And it is in practicing good-will toward others
>   that Thy peace comes to us."

WAR AND PEACE

Covenant with the Unknown Soldier

REVEREND JAMES W. FIFIELD, JR., D.D.

Minister, First Congregational Church of Los Angeles, California

Dr. Fifield is a dynamic preacher who draws large congregations to First Congregational Church in Los Angeles Sunday after Sunday.

Born in Chicago in 1899, he studied at Oberlin College, the University of Chicago, and took his divinity degree at Chicago Theological Seminary in 1924. He was ordained in the ministry of the Congregational Church the same year. He was minister at Chamberlin, South Dakota, 1921-22, Woodstock, Illinois, 1922-24, East Church, Grand Rapids, Michigan, 1924-35, and has been at First Church, Los Angeles, since 1935.

In 1937 he was lecturer in the School of Religion at the University of Southern California; is national director of mobilization for spiritual ideals. He is close to young people and contemporary education, and is a member of

Sermon Fifty

TEXT: The gospel of peace. EPHESIANS 6:15

FOR thirteen years, Sunday after Sunday I have preached from this pulpit on the great themes of our Christian faith. Always, and indeed increasingly, I have had an underlying conviction that peace is imperative before most other things. If we do not have peace, I have felt, nothing else matters.

During the recent war, which I vigorously opposed until the tragedy of Pearl Harbor, it became increasingly apparent that civilization is doomed, unless ways are found to eliminate war as the means for settling international disputes. When the atomic bomb was used, my convictions deepened. Humanity's alternatives are peace or annihilation.

I believe the will to peace exists in the rank and file citizenry of every nation. Unworthy leadership leads to war. Rank and file citizens, therefore, must think, talk and act for peace. How can this be gotten under way before it is too late? By each of us making a compact with himself and God—by each of us making a solemn covenant with the Unknown Soldier. Here is mine:

Being a Christian minister of the "gospel of peace," and on behalf of millions who are dedicated to that gospel, and on behalf of other millions who share a sense of debt to you and concern for the things your life's sacrifice was to vouchsafe, I make this solemn covenant with you this day. I make it freely and voluntarily because of my sense of obligation to you and millions more for whom you are the world's symbol.

In imagination I can see you with all the glow of hope and expectancy in your youthful face. I can see the sturdy body God had given and you had developed. I cannot tell whether you are black or white or yellow or brown, nor would that matter. I cannot see your uniform to discern your rank or even your army. You may have been a flier or an infantryman, a paratrooper or a submarine crewman. I don't know whether you volunteered or were drafted, nor do I care.

[304]

The circumstances of your death are, happily, unknown. Was it bomb, bullet or shrapnel? I hope you died quickly, without prolonged suffering, especially if you were alone and if it was dark and cold. I hope you had a sustaining faith in the eternal God, by whatsoever creed. I hope you died believing that in the providence of God, the cause to which you gave yourself would one day be established, earthwide. I hope you died believing that because of your sacrifice and the sacrifices of others not unlike you, this wonderful earth over which God has given man trusteeship, will experience permanent peace, social justice and universal good will. That would seem worth dying for.

I ascribe such hopes to you, whether or not you actually held them. You were justified in cherishing them because of the promises and propaganda amid which you went forth to battle.

It is over thirty years since you left those you most loved, and who loved you most, and went off to camp. Your picture still stands on your parents' piano. Your father and mother, now in their seventies, indulge their imaginations as they look at you in your uniform. They love to think of what might have been. They have not forgotten to remember, nor has your wife, although she has married again and has other children.

Your son is in an army hospital, having been wounded on the Normandy beaches of the same France in which you died. He is making heroic adjustments to his legless life and its cruel handicaps. You'd be proud of your son! His wife and his five-year-old son who bears your name, are his great inspiration and joy. Your picture is by his hospital bed. He hopes and prays that his son will never know the hell of war. It is the same hope you had for your son, but he feels even more deeply about it, if that is possible.

It is humiliating to have to confess that there has been another and a worse war and that the things for which you gave your precious self are still unattained. Moreover, God forbid, some are talking of the next war—as though it is inevitable. It shall not be. I and millions more vow it shall not be. We covenant with you, with your son, and with your grandson, that it shall not be.

Your sacrifice rests heavily upon my conscience. I wore the uniform in that same war. I might have been you! I must take up your torch and I must hold it high. I must help fulfill the hopes of your legless son!

I make solemn covenant with you, Unknown Soldier, to use my fullest influence as a man, as a father, as a Christian minister, whose gospel is peace, to the end that war shall be no more. I dare do no less! I shall not wait till tensions develop and international incidents arise. I shall be aggressively active *now*—now while there is yet time—now before it is too late. I purpose to work and pray for the foundations of lasting peace—social and economic justice. I vow to exert every possible influence for international and interracial good will. I covenant not to be blind to the faults of my own country and its leaders, nor blind to the good in other nations. I pledge to help develop understanding and mutual appreciation between the common people of all nations and to help keep alive both the hope and the determination that there shall be permanent peace. I join the best minds of science and philosophy in the conviction that peace is not only possible but imperative.

Fearful new weapons have been developed since you left us, making it necessary that the nations and the races live together in good will to live at all. It has become as simple as that. Peace is the will of God! I, with others, accept peace as my responsibility. I vow to you, before God, that we shall not fail Him—nor you. So help me, God!

Let us pray.

WORK

The Workman and the Work

REVEREND HARRIS E. KIRK, D.D.

Minister, The Franklin Street Presbyterian Church, Baltimore, Maryland

For forty-eight years Dr. Kirk has been the minister of Franklin Street Church, Baltimore. His sermons and his circle of influence have grown with the years. Born in Tennessee, he graduated from Southwestern University at Memphis, and was ordained to the ministry of the Presbyterian Church in 1897. He was minister of Cottage Church, Nashville, 1897-99, First Presbyterian Church, Florence, Alabama, 1899-1901, and has been at the Franklin Street Church ever since.

He has held many lectureships, including the annual lectures on historical Christianity, Princeton University, 1923-29; Goucher College, 1925-28; professor of Biblical literature, Goucher, since 1928; Northfield Conferences, 1917-26; mission conferences in China in 1924; summer preacher, Westminster Chapel, London, 1922-40; Sprunt lecturer, Union Theological Seminary, Richmond, 1916; University preacher, Princeton, Yale, University of Virginia and other important institutions. He was moderator of the General Assembly of the Presbyterian Church in U.S., 1928.

His books include The Religion of Power, The Consuming Fire, The Spirit of Protestantism, Stars, Atoms, and God, A Man of Property, A Design for Living.

Dr. Kirk's discussion of the relation between the worker and the work to be done in the physical and spiritual world will be helpful to many. As men work and pray and live they find new paths with God. This sermon represents Dr. Kirk as he has preached in the Franklin Street pulpit for forty-eight years.

Sermon Fifty=one

TEXT: Some indeed preach Christ even of envy and strife; and some also of good will: the one preach contention, not sincerely, intending to annoy me as I lie in prison, but the other of love of me, knowing that I am set for the defence of the gospel. What then? Notwithstanding, everyway, whether in pretence, or in truth Christ is preached; and I rejoice over that; yes, and I will rejoice.
PHILIPPIANS 1:15-18

IF WE wish to do anything in the world that is worth-while, and be happy while doing it, we must be content to ask only the right to do our work well, and gain our reward from the approval of God and a good conscience. He who endeavors to sell his service to others in exchange for approval is likely to be disappointed. Any good work is worth doing for its own sake, without any external reward attached to it. So the wise disciple will endeavor to enlarge his motive for service, and bring mind and spirit closer to the will of Christ, until obedience becomes the ruling passion of his life.

Such a man will in the course of years develop a character of noble quality; and in spite of indifference or envy of others will command an abiding influence. That is very precious in itself, for after all the highest gain of such a purpose will be victory over self; to learn not only to be ignored by those he serves, but to lose himself in the wonder and glory of the work he is doing. He will learn that his work is part of a greater whole, and that its durability results from union with the plan of God. This beyond controversy is the only foundation of happiness in this world. To keep alive this great purpose in the soul is the sure safeguard to all forms of anxiety, bitterness and disappointment, and directly leads to the Pauline position of being content in all conditions of life.

The power to forget self in the importance of the work one is doing is an ideal. Now ideals by themselves are not hard to come by. But to embody them in practice is another matter. On the one hand, we may view them remotely in their pure and abstract form, like mountains seen in the distant haze; yet such visions seen afar while arousing admiration, rarely inspire us to come closer to them. On the other hand, when we closely approach ideals, they are usually embedded in difficult and often repulsive association, so that we draw back from them. It is only when we see a great pattern ideal expressed in a life vitally exercising its authority under conditions that frequently appear improbable, that we are drawn to it, and that is what we gain from this fine sentence from Paul's letter to the Philippians. I do not think Paul has ever written anything better than this, about the state of mind that comes from complete surrender to Christ. In this his most beautiful letter, he speaks without reserve of his private affairs. He is in a Roman prison, under the shadow of death. He has many friends and some like the Philippians have sent him their greetings. His zeal for the gospel has even impressed his Roman guards and penetrated the recesses of Nero's palace; for there were saints in Caesar's household even in those days. But all round him were enemies who spoke evil of him, putting false interpretations on his character, motives, and especially on his teaching. They called him heretic, apostate and other ugly names. They would not be sorry to see him executed by the Romans, and to have finally done with him. Yet these people after their fashion were also preaching the gospel of Christ. How easy it would have been for Paul to denounce them, and return evil for evil. There in his dark prison he had leisure to brood and bitterly to resent their attitude. Plainly their zeal was prompted for the most part to add to his afflictions. Comparing their attitude with that of his friends afforded a background on which their evil intentions appeared in a darker phase. This was a very realistic temptation and most difficult to meet after the manner of a saint. We can do our work when people love and understand us, whose loyalty is beyond questioning. But among people who deliberately pervert our motives, twist our words into false meanings, and pursue us with slanderous gossip— it is always difficult to avoid bitter feelings. And if we are weak enough we can simply abandon our work and let the world go its evil way. A man who has never faced this temptation has yet to realize the costliness of following Christ. This is the cross that the mature Christian has to bear—and bear it through a lifelong devotion, even when he realizes that it is making no change at all in those for whom he is working. It is here that much of the bitterness and strife in religious controversy arises; and to normal-minded people it creates such a wholesome repugnance for such types, as to make them wish to get as far from them as possible. What Paul faced in Rome is precisely the thing that alienates many high-minded people from the Church today. To get away from such people and blot them and all their works out of mind is a natural desire, but it is here that Paul's attitude appears in the highest possible way. Of course he did not like this, yet he knew that he was sharing in the sufferings of his Divine Master. He intended to follow Christ all the way and expressed his determination in words that deserve to be remembered: "Notwithstanding, everyway, whether in pretence, or in truth Christ is preached; and I rejoice over that; yes, and I will rejoice."

Let us now think of these things. Every advocate of Christ must determine whether he is to serve for the sake of approval, or because he believes the work is sufficient unto itself. Not one of us but can remember how often we have been forgotten or neglected. Sometimes too we have been deliberately misunderstood and it is not difficult to find reasons for disliking certain people, and even cultivate the vain wish of Jeremiah who wanted a lodging place in the wilderness for wayfaring men, that as he put it he might leave his people because they were a bundle of rascals. The longing for human intercourse without responsibility is a common desire among all who have been disappointed in the people whom they serve. But this was never our Lord's way. Had he done so there never would have been a crucifixion. Had Paul acted on this impulse there never would have been any Pauline letters; in fact there never would have been a Church or a gospel or any of the blessings that surround our life today. Among the chances and changes of this life we see both influences at work, but our perception of the evil must never tempt us to ignore the good. To love Christ with high-hearted determination, to place his will first is to go a long way toward self-forgetfulness, and thus to live in harmony with one of the great laws of the kingdom. That law, to state it bluntly, is that in the long reaches of history the work is always more important than the worker; or to put it otherwise, to do our work well in the world is more important than that we should be appreciated by the world. To reach this conclusion is never easy, but once to have attained it is to have gained the victory over the world. There are many examples of this in the Bible. There is the moving simplicity of the story of the passing of Aaron, the first high priest who is taken by God's commandment by Moses, into the mountain and stripped of his priestly robes and left there to die. Eleazar assumes the office and he and Moses return to the tribes. This and nothing more. The workman passes, but the work goes on. This teaches one of the most impressive lessons of spiritual history that with God there are no indispensable men. God taught this impressive but bitter truth to Elijah when He put Elisha in his place. With impressive simplicity John the Baptist accepted this law when he said of Jesus, "He must increase, I must decrease." The principle is embodied in the phrase "some shall sow and others shall reap." If we have any success much of it is due to the work of those who went before us. Only a fool will boast of being a self-made man. To accept this formidable fact will enable us to believe that the work we do according to our ability and opportunity is never done in vain, for each service is part of a great whole that slowly but surely is forming amid the welter of change around us. Why do we draw lessons of significance from the sayings and deeds of men who lived and died thousands of years ago, but for the fact that their work and influence abide in the Divine fabric, to which we also belong? Moreover, out of this involvement in a great past we gain a sense of future glory, for it is evident that the work we are doing cannot be finished in our lifetime. So far as we are concerned we must pass, leaving it to others to carry on. Yet from this conviction God's children have ever drawn their finest inspiration; they do it because they reach their maturity where they, too, begin to care more for the permanence of their work than they do for their earthly comfort. This appears in the great prayer in Psalm 90: "Let thy work appear unto thy servants, and thy glory upon their children. And let the beauty of the Lord our God be upon us; and establish thou the work of our hands upon us; yea, the work of our hands establish thou it." Consider the encouragement Jeremiah drew from the conviction that although his life was difficult and lonely, the work he was doing was going to last, for God had given him a future and a hope. Remember Paul's conclusion in the great resurrection chapter in I Corinthians: "Therefore, my beloved brethren, be ye steadfast, unmoveable, always abounding in the work of the Lord, forasmuch as ye know that your labour is not in vain in the Lord." And out of the heart of the Book of Revelation comes this comforting voice: "Write, Blessed are the dead which die in the Lord, from henceforth, yea saith the Spirit, that they may rest from their labours, for their works do follow with them."

Thus in all the high judgments of those who follow on to know the Lord, the words of Lord Bacon express their deepest conviction: "Be the workmen what they may be, let us speak of the work, that is; the true greatness of kingdoms and estates, and the means thereof."

This tremendous truth underlies the entire Bible. It is a conviction that is reached only in spiritual maturity, but when fully accepted becomes the final and sustaining conviction of the religious life. We are not allowed to ask how safe, or comfortable or prominent we are going to be; but can we by toil, and suffering, and self-denial spread the gospel of God throughout the world. That is our mission and our vocation. The differences that men stress are of no consequence with God. Let not your apparent obscurity deter you from discerning the unique significance of the individual soul. The differences that men make are of no importance, for does not Paul in a certain place speak of the brother for whom Christ died? And this man was one of the obscure class called weak, or of little account. Each life is a possible medium for Divine communication. The rush light and the electric torch differ only in degree, but both in their order give essential light. And perhaps the greatest influence a man can have on others is one of which he is never aware. How well indeed does George Eliot teach this in *Middlemarch*: "The growing good of the world is partly dependent on unhistoric acts; and that things are not so ill with you and me as they might have been, is half owing to the number who lived faithfully a hidden life, and rest in unvisited tombs."

History teaches no lesson more thoroughly than that no man by himself alone ever began a great movement; for all round him were multitudes of obscure folk who took up the light and carried it into the future. As a modern historian has well put it, "The fabric of a vision that worketh great marvels is the experience of common men." That is taught in Isaiah 32 in which the function of the leader is to teach the stammering tongue to speak plainly, and the deaf ear to hear distinctly. Luther never could have begun the Reformation, nor Washington founded the American Republic, had there not been multitudes of common folk who dimly wanted what they more clearly perceived. Sometimes amid darkness depressed multitudes feel in some mysterious way that a finer something has come into the world, a something that has a voice, which like the sweet tones of the Angelus descends like the gentle rain from heaven upon the toilers, and causes them to pause in their work and to bow their heads and think of God and eternity. So amid the dark confusions of our present time, there is something sweet, clean and life-giving: the Spirit of God is pouring out upon the weary hearts the redeeming mercy of Christ, and contact with the world's need is made through men who are willing to be overlooked or even forgotten, who ask only the right to do their work well. Let us then think worthily of the work we do, and learn how by devotion to Christ, to find our peace in his approval. Let him become the beginning and the end of all our striving, and through our life, no matter how placed, will surely be given light to those of us who sit in darkness. This is our bitter-sweet vocation. This is the way Jesus walked on earth, and we must follow in his steps. And if in times of great responsibility we realize we must fulfill these obligations without those happy human relations we most desire, we always remember that we have access to our Divine Lord and Master, and can say to ourselves:

> Yea, thro' life, death, thro' sorrow and thro' sinning,
> He shall suffice me, for He hath sufficed:
> Christ is the end, for Christ was the beginning;
> Christ the beginning, for the end is Christ!

WORSHIP

Invitation to Worship

REVEREND HAROLD COOKE PHILLIPS, D.D., L.H.D.
Minister, The First Baptist Church, Cleveland, Ohio

Dr. Phillips is one of the outstanding Baptist ministers of the country, a forceful, thoughtful, and deeply spiritual preacher. He was born in Westmoreland, Jamaica, British West Indies in 1892, came to the United States in 1912 and was naturalized in 1922.

He attended Denison University and Columbia University and took his divinity work at Union Theological Seminary (B.D., 1922), New York City. He was ordained in the Baptist ministry in 1922 and was pastor of First Baptist Church, Mount Vernon, New York, 1922-28. Since 1928 he has been minister of First Baptist Church, Cleveland, where his work has been recognized with the honorary D.D. by Wesleyan University and the L.H.D. by Denison University.

He is the author of Life That is Life Indeed, Seeing the Invisible, Sails and Anchors, Life's Unanswered Questions, *and contributes to various religious journals.*

He is a trustee of Denison University and is active in community work. This sermon sounds a call for a return to worship in our Protestant churches where ritual and worship can supplément and complement preaching.

[311]

Sermon Fifty=two

TEXT: O come, let us worship and bow down: let us kneel before the Lord our Maker.   PSALM 95:6

OUR subject today is "Invitation to Worship." It is indeed an old invitation, as old as man's quest for God. The Psalmist voiced it long ago in words of reverent beauty. "O come, let us worship and bow down: let us kneel before the Lord our maker." And there has never been an age nor a country in which the Christian God is known but people have accepted that invitation.

The question is sometimes asked, "Why don't people go to church?" But as someone has said, there is a more significant question: "Why do they go?" On the Sabbath there are worshipers in every church in Christendom. In some churches many, in others few, but in all some. Why? Because the invitation to worship appeals to something deep in the human soul, and universal.

Of course, as we know, this invitation falls on many deaf ears. The majority of the people in this city and in this nation never accept it at all. But that fact tells us nothing about worship, though it tells us a great deal about ourselves.

It has been said that whereas Roman Catholics have a church, Protestants have a pulpit. Roman Catholics put the emphasis on worship, Protestants on preaching. There is some truth in that observation. It is, however, a salutary fact that many of our Protestant leaders are now coming to see that preaching itself is a part of worship, and worship the unique contribution of the church. Listen to a few testimonies to this truth.

Here is Professor A. Campbell Garnett: "If religion is to be revived as a power to instill into the community a sense of brotherhood, of social solidarity and of Christian idealism, it cannot be done without measures that will call the multitude back into the organized worship of the churches." Dr. F. R. Barry has this to say: "When we made every qualification, it remains true that the influence of the church depends upon the quality of its worship, which is . . . its most vital contribution to the Christianization of the social order . . ." Or here are the words of the late Archbishop of Canterbury, William Temple. "This world," said he, "can be saved from political chaos and collapse by one thing only, and that is worship." These are not the opinions of the unbalanced or uninformed, but the sober judgment of thoughtful men.

Let us then see what is involved in this invitation to worship. To what is one called when he accepts this invitation? There are as I see the matter three truths in this word of the Psalmist which, while they do not exhaust the

[312]

meaning of worship, certainly comprise three essential aspects of the worship experience.

For one thing, invitation to worship is invitation to fellowship. The pronouns the Psalmist uses are all first person plural. "Come let *us* worship . . . let *us* kneel before the Lord *our* Maker." One of the striking facts about this religion of ours is that it is at one and the same time individualistic and collectivistic. The Christian is first of all an individual. "Adam, where art thou?" "Simon Peter . . . I have prayed for thee." "Matthew, follow me." "Zacchaeus . . . today I must abide at thy house." Jesus individualized. As you read the New Testament individuals just walk out at you from its pages.

Yet along with this there is the emphasis on the group and the need of belonging to it and sharing in its common life. "Where two or three are gathered in my name, there am I in the midst of them," said the Master, who speaks of his followers as a "flock." "They were all with one accord in one place," says Luke. "Not forsaking the assembling of ourselves together," writes the author of Hebrews. And St. Paul writes: "That ye . . . may be able to comprehend with all saints what is in the breadth, and length, and depth, and heighth; and to know the love of Christ . . ." as much as to say that the individual cannot comprehend the divine love alone but only in fellowship "with all the saints."

I like to come into this church at times when no one is here, sit in a pew, meditate and pray. "When thou prayest, enter into thy closet, and when thou hast shut thy door, pray to thy Father which is in secret. . . ." Such moments of solitude in religion are essential. Yet I confess that on a Sunday morning, in the warmth of Christian fellowship, something happens to me that does not occur when I am alone. "One loving spirit sets another on fire." You may have a bundle of sticks but if you want to start a fire you will not try to light just one stick. You must bring them together. Even so it is through the assembling of ourselves together that worship becomes contagious and its warmth diffused.

It is here that one runs headlong into a snag, so to speak. Someone was asked what church he attended. He replied that he did not go to any church regularly but he thought the Baptist church was the one he stayed away from the most. One fears that unfortunately Baptists have no monopoly on these "stay-awayers." Two-thirds of our Protestant church members are not in church today. They are stay-awayers, cut off from the uplifting, enriching, challenging experiences of Christian fellowship in worship. We sometimes refer to the Church of God as being "a mighty army." We sing, "Like a mighty army moves the Church of God." Some army this, with two-thirds of its fighting force at ease. Really, when one realizes that the work of the Protestant church in the world today is being done by one-third of our Protestant Christians, it is amazing how much is being done. It stirs one to think of the religious upsurge—revival is not too strong a word—that would occur if our "at ease" soldiers would come to attention, fall in line.

Soldiers of Christ arise
And put your armor on.

Invitation to worship then is, first of all, an invitation to fall in line, an invitation to Christian fellowship. You have sometimes seen the statement printed on tickets or on checks, "Not good if detached." That could be printed on every Christian—"Not good if detached," detached from the fellowship of the Church which is the body of Christ. "As the branch cannot bear fruit of itself, except it abide in the vine; no more can ye, except ye abide in me." And to abide in Christ yet isolate one's self from the Church which is his body is a feat too difficult for most of us. In fact, it is well-nigh impossible.

But now, in the second place, invitation to worship is not only invitation to fellowship, it is also invitation to creative fellowship, to participation. "Let us worship and bow down; let us kneel." To "bow down" and "kneel" indicates that the true worshiper is not just a spectator or onlooker but a participant. The Roman Catholics have a happy phrase, "to assist at mass," "descriptive of the function and attitude of the congregation in attendance at the worship service." Protestants, too, ought to assist.

It was in 1661 that some Puritan divines entered into quite a discussion with certain Anglican bishops upon this very matter of congregational participation. The Puritans were opposed to participation by the congregation, the Anglicans were for it. The Puritans thought that worship was a matter wholly in the hands of the clergyman and that for the laity to take part in worship was to encroach on the rights of the clergyman. Therefore the Puritans were opposed to such items in the service as responses and litanies. Clarence Day in his little book *God and My Father* says something about his father's attitude to worship which makes it clear that his father belonged to the Puritan tradition. He writes, "When my father went to church and sat in his pew he felt he was doing enough. Any further spiritual work ought to be done by the clergy." One fears Mr. Day has many disciples in Protestantism. At least, however, the Puritans did think it was proper for the congregation to say "Amen." We seem to be outdoing the Puritans here, for even the "Amen" is said so weakly that you need a hearing aid to pick it up. The Psalmist said, "Let the redeemed of the Lord say so." But the redeemed of the Lord seem to be very quiet. I notice that the redeemed of the Lord can be very vocal when it comes to other aspects of church life and activity, but on this question of worship the redeemed participate with marked restraint.

Sometime ago I attended a religious service. I arrived a little late. There were no ushers so I opened the door leading from the narthex to the sanctuary and stepped in. It took me a little time to realize that the minister was offering a prayer. You never would have guessed it by observing the congregation. A good half of them were sitting upright, looking about the room, as though the minister were talking to them instead of talking to the Lord on their behalf. Fine participation that!

[314]

When we meet a lady what do we do? We tip our hats. When the national anthem is sung what do we do? We stand up. When we pledge allegiance to the flag what do we do? We bring our hands up to salute. When the minister says, "Let us pray," what do we do? Many of our people do nothing —just stay "as you were." Does that mean that our congregation has less reverence for Almighty God than it has for the flag? Not necessarily. It means rather that many of our people when they come to church to worship God, come as spectators rather than as participants. They come to see what is going on rather than to help create, give direction and enrichment to what is going on.

It is right here that one discovers the big difference between an audience and a worshiping congregation. You go to hear a concert or lecture and all you have to do is to sit back and listen to what is going on—you are in the passive voice. You have no responsibility at all except to say "I liked it" or "I did not like it." That attitude is as far removed from a worshiping congregation as day from night. The mood of the true worshiper is not passive. He does not come in the passive but in the active voice. He comes not just to get but to give, not to observe but to participate; not just to see what is going on but to help through his sympathetic, reverent and prayerful spirit, to contribute to what is going on. The fellowship to which he belongs is a creative fellowship.

Whenever a church really does something for God it is *the church* that does it, not just the ministers. And it is the worshiping church that does it, not those who are out on the edges. It is the worshiping church that becomes the witnessing church; those who truly participate in its worship within the walls participate in its work which goes outside, "unto the uttermost part of the earth."

In the third place, invitation to worship is not only invitation to fellowship and to creative fellowship; it is also invitation to transforming fellowship, to the adoration of God. "Let us kneel *before the Lord* our maker." God comes into the picture—the God through fellowship with whom life is changed.

Every once in a while I meet someone who says, "Oh, yes, you are the minister of the First Baptist Church. Some Sunday I am coming up to hear what you have to say." That always leaves me cold. More than that, it leaves me chilly! Let us hope the minister has something to say; if not he ought not to be saying it. But you see when you come to church just to hear what the minister has to say, the whole transaction is kept on the human level. It is a matter between two human beings—you and the minister.

Now to be sure one is not saying that such an experience is valueless. We are only saying that it is not worship. Worship establishes a relationship on a plane that transcends the human. "Let us kneel before the Lord our maker." "For he is our God; and we are the people of his pasture, and the sheep of his hand." Worship is worthship, giving of his value to God, is "the acknowledgment of transcendence." To worship is to remember that

[315]

Whether we be young or old,
Our destiny, our being's heart and home,
Is with Infinity, and only there.

One of the great preachers of Scotland was the Rev. Charles Sylvester Horne. His volume of Yale Lectures on Preaching, *The Romance of Preaching*, is still one of the very finest in that notable list. He used to enjoy telling his class of the noble thoughts that would come to him in his garden. These thoughts of his so inspired his students that they were anxious to see the garden where he enjoyed his meditations. One day two of his boys came and he took them to his garden. They were terribly disappointed when they saw it. Imagine their anstonishment when they saw nothing but a narrow strip of earth surrounded by high walls. "Why, doctor," said one of the boys, "surely this is not the garden where all your inspiring thoughts come!" "Oh, yes," he replied. "But it is so small," the student protested. "Yes," replied the professor, pointing to the sky, "but look how high it is!"

It is that dimension modern life lacks. Our garden is wide, very wide. In a real sense the frontiers have disappeared—even the iron curtain may be pierced by our broadcasts. It is a wide world we inhabit, but a flat world. The crust has fallen into batter. Our world lacks altitude. Life moves on the human level, it is horizontal. It is a matter between you and your minister, you and your neighbor, between employer and employee, between the United States and Russia. It lacks altitude—sky.

Now it is precisely this quality which the world needs so desperately and which our secularized age cannot possibly supply that the Christian Church offers through worship. It essays through worship to lift the human spirit to a higher plane, to give perspective and balance, to restore the soul through fellowship with God. The Church does not do this as well as it should. Many churches are mechanically or technically ill equipped to do it. But the Church aims to do it, and it is the only institution that makes the attempt.

For how can man be lifted above himself save as he is in contact with that which transcends him? It is here we confront a great paradox. "Let us . . . bow down: let us kneel before the Lord our maker." We gain altitude when we bow down. We are lifted up when we humble ourselves before God. We find our true self when we lose ourself, get out of ourself, forget and move beyond ourself. And that is what worship does for us.

Nothing else does it just that way. How else can man be really elevated, lifted up, save as he humbles himself before that which transcends him. Sometimes we try to lift ourselves up by pride, the pride of race, possession, position or power. But that is not elevation, that is inflation. And just as an inflated dollar goes down in value, so does an inflated man. And the bigger he blows himself up the less value he has. The whole process reminds one of nothing so much as a child blowing up a toy balloon. The bigger it gets the hollower it gets, and the hollower it gets the bigger it gets—bigger and hollower. At last, you know what happens—nature takes care of it!

The people of Shinar tried this method of elevation, through pride. They set out to build a tower to reach heaven. They were going to lift themselves by their boot straps, to rival God, to be as great as God. You know the end—confusion of tongues. They are the littlest people of the Old Testament. Man is never so puny as when he struts.

We do not get altitude by pulling ourselves up or blowing ourselves up, but by bowing down before that which transcends us. "Lead me to the rock that is higher than I."

"O come, let us worship and bow down: let us kneel before the Lord our maker." An old invitation, but this grim and tortured world makes it more important than ever. For it is a call to fellowship, creative fellowship, transforming fellowship—the fellowship of faith out of which comes not death but life, the fellowship that has its being in God. Worship can help us to find the lost God. The lost God, did I say? No. The lost self. For when man loses God it is not God who is lost. Man is. One wonders whether in this troubled world there is any more basic or important task than that of trying to bring man to God and so to his true self and rightful destiny.

INDEX

[324]